JOURNAL FOR THE STUDY OF THE NEW TESTAMENT
SUPPLEMENT SERIES
155

Sheffield Academic Press

Stewardship and Almsgiving in Luke's Theology

Kyoung-Jin Kim

Journal for the Study of the New Testament
Supplement Series 155

Published by Sheffield Academic Press Ltd
Mansion House
19 Kingfield Road
Sheffield S11 9AS
England

Printed on acid-free paper in Great Britain
by Bookcraft Ltd
Midsomer Norton, Bath

British Library Cataloguing in Publication Data

A catalogue record for this book is available
from the British Library

ISBN 1-85075-834-4

CONTENTS

PREFACE

In order for me to be where I am now, many people have been involved in the completion and publication of this book that I have worked on for more than five years in Scotland in one way or another. First of all, I should thank the Lord our heavenly Father for his unfailing love which has enabled me to go through the long, difficult and lonely way to reach the goal.

Stewardship and Almsgiving in Luke's Theology is a slightly revised version of my 1993 Glasgow PhD dissertation. Thus it is my pleasant duty to thank in print those without whose help my stay in Glasgow would have been either impossible or fruitless.

I will never forget the love and help I have been given from my mentor, Dr John M.G. Barclay of the Faculty of Divinity at the University of Glasgow, without whom I believe this work might not have been brought into the world. To him I owe an immense debt of gratitude for his patient guidance, penetrating comments and helpful criticisms with an exemplary degree of dedication and interest. He suggested numerous fruitful lines of enquiry and saved me from many errors I could have made.

I should also express my gratitude to Dr David L. Mealand of the Department of New Testament at the University of Edinburgh for his helpful counsel and incisive comments for my study during the period when Dr Barclay was away for his sabbatical leave (September 1989– August 1990). My deep gratitude should also be given to Professor John K. Riches, head of the Department of Biblical Studies at the University of Glasgow, and his family for their consistent help and love for my work and my family. I owe deep gratitude to Professor Stanley Porter, Executive Editor of the *JSNT* Supplement Series, for reading and commenting upon the manuscript of this book. And also I should thank Revd Dr David Graham at Glasgow Bible College for his helpful assistance in polishing the final manuscript of this book.

From my point of view, to study abroad for five-and-a-half years cannot be fulfilled without others' financial help. The Torch Centre for Evangelism and Mission based in Seoul, S. Korea, supported the monthly living expenses of my family from October 1989 until April 1993, Tyndale House offered me a research grant, and the Faculty of Divinity of the University of Glasgow allowed me the William Barclay Memorial Scholarship—all of which were of great financial assistance to continue my research. I am also grateful to Revd Hyun-Shin Cho, a missionary in Namibia and Revd Sae-Won Shin, my pastor in Seoul, S. Korea, for their financial help and prayers for my thesis. I would like to thank Dr Jong-Hyun Chang, Founder of Christian Theological University who kindly invited me to teach New Testament Theology at the University.

Finally, special thanks go to my family: my wife, Shin-Ja, and my three lovely daughters, Heyon, Jeyon (born in Scotland) and Chanmey. Without their daily patience, encouragement and prayers, this work could never have been completed.

Kyoung-Jin Kim
January 1998
Christian Theological University
Seoul, S. Korea

ABBREVIATIONS

AB	Anchor Bible
BAGD	Walter Bauer, William F. Arndt, F. William Gingrich and Frederick W. Danker, *A Greek–English Lexicon of the New Testament and Other Early Christian Literature* (Chicago: University of Chicago Press, 2nd edn, 1958)
Bib	*Biblica*
BNTC	Black's New Testament Commentaries
BWANT	Beiträge zur Wissenschaft vom Alten und Neuen Testament
CBQ	*Catholic Biblical Quarterly*
CQR	*Church Quarterly Review*
EKKNT	Evangelisch-Katholischer Kommentar zum Neuen Testament
EncJud	*Encyclopaedia Judaica*
ExpTim	*Expository Times*
HTKNT	Herders theologischer Kommentar zum Neuen Testament
HTR	*Harvard Theological Review*
IBS	*Irish Biblical Studies*
ICC	International Critical Commentary
JBL	*Journal of Biblical Literature*
JSNT	*Journal for the Study of the New Testament*
JSNTSup	*Journal for the Study of the New Testament*, Supplement Series
JTS	*Journal of Theological Studies*
MNTC	Moffatt NT Commentary
NB	*New Blackfriars*
NCB	New Century Bible
NICNT	New International Commentary on the New Testament
NIGTC	The New International Greek Testament Commentary
NLCNT	*The New London Commentary on the New Testament*
NovT	*Novum Testamentum*
NovTSup	*Novum Testamentum*, Supplements
NTS	*New Testament Studies*
RB	*Revue biblique*
RelSRev	*Religious Studies Review*
RevQ	*Revue de Qumran*
SE	*Studia Evangelica I, II, III* (= TU 73 [1959], 87 [1964], 88 [1964], etc.)
Sem	*Semitica*
SJT	*Scottish Journal of Theology*
SNTSMS	Society for New Testament Studies Monograph Series

SNTU	Studien zum Neuen Testament und seiner Umwelt
Str–B	[Hermann L. Strack and] Paul Billerbeck, *Kommentar zum Neuen Testament aus Talmud und Midrasch* (7 vols.; Munich: Beck, 1922–61)
TDNT	Gerhard Kittel and Gerhard Friedrich (eds.), *Theological Dictionary of the New Testament* (trans. Geoffrey W. Bromiley; 10 vols.; Grand Rapids: Eerdmans, 1964–)
THKNT	Theologischer Handkommentar zum Neuen Testament
TNTC	Tyndale New Testament Commentaries
TPINTC	Trinity Press International New Testament Commentaries
TynBul	*Tyndale Bulletin*
TZ	*Theologische Zeitschrift*
ZNW	*Zeitschrift für die neutestamentliche Wissenschaft*

Chapter 1

INTRODUCTION

This book begins by questioning Luke's idea of the relationship between wealth and discipleship. There have been several attempts among Lukan scholars in the last three decades to define and solve this problem, but it appears that an answer sufficient to solve the problems related to this theme has not been offered. This failure motivates me to investigate this theme in Lukan theology afresh with a view to obtaining a satisfactory answer to the problem.

In this chapter, first of all, I will review several major works related to our theme, which will help us recognize where we stand in dealing with this theme of Lukan studies, what has been developed and what will have to be further developed. Secondly, after identifying the areas that need to be developed in Lukan studies, the proposal of this book will be presented. Thirdly, I will discuss the methods which will be employed in proceeding with this study, and introduce the limit with which this study will be faced in handling our material in Luke–Acts.

1. *Survey of Previous Studies*

During the last three decades the attention of those who were engaged in the study of Luke–Acts has been devoted to the theme of wealth, or the poor and the rich, in a rather disproportionate way.[1] Thus before

---

1. Although this subject was once picked up and dealt with early in the twentieth century, it is the arrival of redaction criticism that has made it blossom in the full sense.

For the list of the works that have been done early in this century, see D.L. Mealand, *Poverty and Expectation in the Gospels* (London: SPCK, 1980), pp. 103-104; J.R. Donahue, 'Two Decades of Research on the Rich and the Poor in Luke–Acts', in D.A. Knight and P.J. Paris (eds.), *Justice and the Holy* (Atlanta: Scholars Press, 1989), p. 130. Cf. L.W. Countryman, *The Rich Christian in the Church of the Early Empire: Contradictions and Accommodations* (New York: Edwin Mellen Press, 1980), Introduction, pp. 1-45.

I proceed to a full discussion of this subject,[2] it would be very helpful
to survey what has been explored in the realm of the wealth theme in
relation to discipleship in the context of Lukan theology.

a. *H.-J. Degenhardt:* Lukas Evangelist der Armen *(1965)*[3]
Degenhardt appears to be a pioneer in applying redaction criticism
seriously to the interpretation of the wealth material in Luke–Acts,
and he paves the way for subsequent exploration of the theme of wealth
in terms of discipleship, which seems to be his major contribution in
this area. Degenhardt's investigation in his book proceeds from his
interest in an apparent contradiction between the material that exhibits
the demand of total renunciation of wealth on the one hand and that
which shows the right use of possessions on the other hand.

The thesis falls into three sections. In the first section, Degenhardt
introduces Luke's conception of 'Heilsgeschichte' advocated by Conzelmann[4] and takes it as a fundamental ground of his whole work. Based
on this, he proceeds to describe how the poor were understood in Old

For a general survey of the works concerning the theme of wealth and poverty in
Luke–Acts from 1950 to 1983, see F. Bovon, *Luke the Theologian: Thirty-Three
Years of Research (1950–1983)* (Alison Park, PA: Pickwick Publications, 1987),
pp. 390-400.

2.   Donahue affords us a recent, though brief, bibliography on this theme, and
also has epitomized summaries of the major works that have been done up to 1987
('Two Decades', pp. 130-31).

Apart from those works introduced in his book which I will review in more detail
in what follows, there are several more works related to our theme we will look at
whenever needs occur; R.J. Karris, 'Poor and Rich: The Lukan *Sitz im Leben*', in
C.H. Talbert (ed.), *Perspectives on Luke–Acts* (Edinburgh: T. & T. Clark, 1978),
pp. 112-25; Mealand, *Poverty*; J.A. Fitzmyer, *The Gospel according to Luke* (2
vols.; AB; New York: Doubleday, 1981), Introduction, pp. 247-51, and *idem*, *Luke
the Theologian* (London: Geoffrey Chapman, 1989), pp. 117-45; T.E. Schmidt, *Hostility to Wealth in the Synoptic Gospels* (JSNTSup, 15; Sheffield: JSOT Press,
1987); H. Moxnes, *The Economy of the Kingdom: Social Conflict and Economic
Relations in Luke's Gospel* (Philadelphia: Fortress Press, 1988); B.E. Beck, *Christian
Character in the Gospel of Luke* (London: SPCK, 1989); D.M. Sweetland, *Our
Journey with Jesus: Discipleship according to Luke–Acts* (Collegeville: The Litur-
gical Book, 1990); D.J. Ireland, *Stewardship and the Kingdom of God: An
Historical, Exegetical, and Contextual Study of the Parable of the Unjust Steward in
Luke 16:1-13* (Leiden: E.J. Brill, 1992).

3.   H.-J. Degenhardt, *Lukas Evangelist der Armen* (Stuttgart: Katholisches
Bibelwerk, 1965).

4.   H. Conzelmann, *The Theology of St Luke* (London: Faber & Faber, 1961).

Testament times, and to present the Jewish idea of good works and caring for poor fellow Jews, not poor foreigners, in their times. After this historical sketch, he lays a foundation for his whole thesis by introducing the μαθηταί conception in Luke–Acts. Here relying on Luke's unique expression in 6.17, 12.1 and 20.45, he intends to distinguish μαθηταί from λαός and then almost universally restricts the application of the wealth material to the μαθηταί.[5]

In the second section, 'Besitz und Besitzverzicht nach dem Lukasevangelium', Degenhardt deals with almost all the wealth material in Luke's Gospel in terms of discipleship. Here he intends to distinguish Jesus' conception of wealth from Luke's application of it to his community, which he presupposes consists of Gentile Christians only.[6] With respect to the former, Degenhardt takes the position that Luke regards Jesus' original conception of wealth as related to spiritual salvation, that is, Jesus considered wealth as a major obstacle to gaining spiritual salvation.[7] With respect to the latter, he argues that Luke tries to apply Jesus' basic attitude of wealth to members of his community, especially church leaders, without losing the original essence of Jesus' ethical teaching. This distinction which Degenhardt makes through his thorough examination of Gospel tradition is of significance, and we may surmise that Luke inherits the idea of the relation between wealth and spiritual salvation, which is expressed in the incidents of the rich ruler and Zacchaeus, from tradition, perhaps even from the historical Jesus.

In the third section, 'Besitz und Besitzverzicht nach der Apostelgeschichte', Degenhardt intends to describe the attitude of the Early Church towards wealth and the renunciation of it, which is presented mainly in terms of the summary narratives in Acts, and to compare it with that of the Qumran community. In dealing with the attitude of the Early Church, he insists that since Christianity originated in Judaism, many religious customs of the Christian community, surely including almsgiving and high respect for charity, are taken over from Judaism, but the difference is focused on the motivation of the two:

---

5.   It should be taken into account, however, that Degenhardt does not apply all of Jesus' and John the Baptist's ethical admonitions solely to the μαθητής but his heavy emphasis on the μαθητής appears frequently throughout his book.

6.   Degenhardt, *Lukas*, p. 221.

7.   Degenhardt, *Lukas*, p. 210.

> Die Urgemeinde hat ihre Wohltätigkeit nach Inhalt und Praxis der jüdischen
> angeglichen, wenn die Begründung der Liebestätigkeit auch unterschiedlich
> ist. Die christliche Bruderliebe wurde von Christus her begründet.[8]

In explaining the summary narratives in Acts, an attractive idea of his
is that here Luke tries to mix Jewish notions of almsgiving with the
Graeco-Roman notion of κοινωνία in order that his readers, the Gentile Christians, may not feel awkward about a Christian way of almsgiving which is totally unknown to them.[9]

Having sketched his argument in outline, we would state that in
general his whole argument is based on his sharp distinction between
μαθητής and λαός or ὄχλος,[10] from which he contends that the group
of Jesus' disciples were a limited number of followers, among which
the apostles are included as the inner core:

> Aus all dem ergibt sich, daß Lukas in seinem Evangelium μαθητής
> ausnahmslos für einen engeren Kreis der Anhänger Jesu verwendet; die
> Gesamtheit derer, die Jesu Wort hören, ihm in irgendeiner Weise
> nahestehen und zu ihm halten, wird mit λαός und unbestimmter ὄχλος
> bezeichnet . . . Lukas sieht die Zwölf—wohl ihm Blick auf die Kirche
> seiner Zeit—als inneren Kern einer größern Schar von μαθηταί (Lk. 6,
> 13 und 6, 17).[11]

Thus in line with this foundation, taking heed of the fact that while in
Luke dispossession was required of all the disciples, in Acts not all
members of the Christian Community at Jerusalem who are called
μαθηταί were asked to renounce their wealth, Degenhardt develops
the notion of two tiers of discipleship, that is, literal renunciation of
wealth is demanded only of the church leaders contemporaneous with
Luke, including missionaries or itinerant preachers, whereas the laity
are free from this strict requirement but can forgo their material
possessions on a voluntary basis.[12]

8.   'The Early Church followed its benevolence according to the contents and
practice of Judaism, even though the grounds of loving acts are different. The Christian love for neighbourhood was established by Jesus.' Degenhardt, *Lukas*, p. 184.
9.   Degenhardt, *Lukas*, pp. 182-83.
10.   Degenhardt, *Lukas*, pp. 27-33.
11.   'From all this it results that Luke applied μαθητής without exception to a close
circle of the followers of Jesus; the whole crowd who heard Jesus' preaching and
were in close relationship with him in whatever ways were called as λαός and uncertain ὄχλος. . . Luke sees the Twelve—in light of the church of his time—as an inner
core of a greater flock of μαθηταί (Lk. 6.13, 17).' Degenhardt, *Lukas*, pp. 31, 33.
12.   Degenhardt, *Lukas*, p. 166, says, 'Hinzu kommt, daß die Jüngerschaft Jesu

Here we can notice inconsistency in his argument. First, against his effort to describe the group of the disciples as a small circle, Lk. 6.17 (ὄχλος πολὺς μαθητῶν αὐτοῦ; cf. v. 13; 5.30) and Lk. 19.37 (ἄπαν τὸ πλῆθος τῶν μαθητῶν) clearly show that they are not a small group, and Degenhardt does not dwell upon them enough to reconcile these apparent contradictions. Secondly, although Jesus commanded those who would follow him to renounce all they possessed, there are quite a few accounts in Luke's Gospel in which a number of followers of Jesus did not forsake all their wealth, but Jesus appears to have accepted them as they were, not reproaching them for not taking his demands as strictly as the itinerant disciples.[13] In sum, his rather undue dependence on the usage of μαθητής to build up his whole thesis seems to have made his argument vulnerable.

b. *L.T. Johnson:* The Literary Function of Possessions in Luke–Acts *(1977)*[14]

Johnson starts his thesis with two questions concerning Acts 4.32-35: 'Why are there two passages describing the community of goods in Luke–Acts, and only two? Why do they occur where they do?'[15] After this questioning proposal, he makes his own formula in answer to these questions, that is, 'prophecy and the fulfilment of the prophecy',[16] and tries to prove it by dealing with almost all the narratives and passages in Luke–Acts related to material possessions in one way or another.

In determining an underlining principle of his thesis Johnson regards the general category of Luke's writings as a story, and contends that as a story Luke–Acts has main characters and a plot.[17] Thus we should

---

als wandernde kleine Gruppe, die ehelos lebte und ohne Beruf, Familie und Besitz sich ganz Jesus angeschlossen hatte, eine ganz andere Lebensform gewählt hatte als die, in der die Glieder der Urgemeinde ihr Leben führten. Insofern lassen sich beide Gruppen nicht ohne weiteres in Beziehung setzen. Auch konnte die Urgemeinde als ganze nicht die Praxis des Jüngerkreises zum Vorbild nehmen.'

13. Among this group of people, some followed Jesus literally such as Levi (Lk. 5.27-29) and the Galilaean women (Lk. 8.1-3), whereas others (Martha and Mary [Lk. 10.38-42], Zacchaeus [Lk. 19.1-10] and Joseph of Arimathea [23.50-54]) did not. We will discuss this feature at length in Chapter 4.

14. L.T. Johnson, *The Literary Function of Possessions in Luke–Acts* (Missoula, MT: Scholars Press, 1977).

15. L.T. Johnson, *Literary Function*, p. 9.

16. L.T. Johnson, *Literary Function*, p. 16. Cf. pp. 15-21.

17. L.T. Johnson, *Literary Function*, pp. 21-22.

take heed of the author's portrayal of the characters and the descriptions of their actions, because they are 'the force which moves the plot to a satisfactory conclusion'.[18] As the main characters in his writings, Johnson argues, Luke chose Jesus and the Apostles who played the role of the prophet, and the people's attitude towards them is revealed by way of acceptance and rejection. Johnson claims that this reaction by the people towards the prophets which is consistently observed in Luke–Acts, constitutes a literary pattern to be noticed. At this point, relating this pattern to the motif of possessions, Johnson holds that 'Luke uses possessions to express the dynamic of acceptance and rejection, and the language of possessions expresses the interior disposition of the one who responds either positively or negatively'.[19] In keeping with this point, he insists that in Luke–Acts material possessions function either as a sign of alienation when people reject the prophets, or as a sign of conversion when they accept them.[20] From this assertion it is made manifest that:

> he [Luke] employs the language about possessions to express symbolically: a) the identity of God's People; b) acceptance and rejection in relation to God's People; c) authority over God's People; d) the transmission of authority within God's People.[21]

Although Johnson does not argue that the literary pattern he describes here is the only significant one in Luke's writings, yet his claim that 'the larger part of Luke's language about possessions finds an intelligible and convincing literary role'[22] makes us feel that the literary pattern is not to be dismissed as just a theory.

Our concern in Johnson's thesis is again with his treatment of the theme of the poor and the rich. His argument on this subject is that possession is used as a literary motif, strengthening the literary pattern of the Prophet and the People he proposed at the outset of his thesis: 'the thematic statements on the rich and the poor form a parallel to the pattern of the prophet and the people'.[23] From this schematic statement he draws a proposition suitable for his purpose: 'this poverty is not an

---

18. L.T. Johnson, *Literary Function*, p. 22.
19. L.T. Johnson, *Literary Function*, p. 144.
20. L.T. Johnson, *Literary Function*, p. 148.
21. L.T. Johnson, *Literary Function*, p. 126.
22. L.T. Johnson, *Literary Function*, p. 221.
23. L.T. Johnson, *Literary Function*, p. 138. Cf. p. 131.

economic designation, but a designation of spiritual status'.[24] Thus we are invited to discuss this point to see whether it is appropriate or not.

We should not fail to notice that when Luke quoted Isa. 61.1 in Lk. 4.18, he left out 'he has sent me to bind up the brokenhearted'. The reason for this seems to me that for Luke this phrase does not fit into his purpose, because it illustrates a spiritual status rather than a literal and economic status.[25] If Luke really wanted to stress the spiritual implications in Lk. 4.18, as Johnson insists, this omission made by Luke would have seriously undermined his intention. Thus we are reluctant to accept Johnson's proposal derived from these passages. In addition to this, it is apparent that a contrast of Luke's version of the Sermon on the Plain (6.20-23) with its parallel in Matthew also indicates Luke's particular interest in the physical and literal implications of the terms such as πτωχός and πλούσιος, since τῷ πνεύματι and τὴν δικαιοσύνην in Mt. 5.3, 6 do not appear in Luke.[26]

We are also invited to question the validity of Johnson's unilateral categorization of the poor as outcasts.[27] He argues that the poor who accept the Prophet but are rejected by men are to be identified as outcasts, while the rich who reject the Prophet but enjoy acceptance and power are to be identified as leaders of the people of Israel. There is a plausibility in this formula, but we ought not to neglect some cases that run against his contention. First, Joseph of Arimathea in Lk. 23.50-51 was a member of the Sanhedrin and rich enough to possess his own tomb. So according to Johnson's theory, he is to be regarded as the rich in a metaphorical sense, who must reject the Prophet because he was a leader of the people. Unfortunately, however, Joseph accepted the Prophet by laying Jesus' corpse in his own tomb. Secondly, the Galilaean women in Lk. 8.1-3 also belong to this category. If we are to follow Johnson's formula they should also have rejected the Prophet, because like Joanna who was the wife of Chuza, Herod's steward, and belonged to the class of the leaders and other women, they were also rich enough to support the Prophet and his followers out of their means. But the fact is that they not only accepted the Prophet and the Apostles

24. L.T. Johnson, *Literary Function*, p. 139.

25. P.F. Esler, *Community and Gospel in Luke–Acts* (Cambridge: Cambridge University Press, 1987), pp. 180-81.

26. C.F. Evans, *Saint Luke* (TPINTC; London: SCM Press, 1990), p. 270; J.A. Fitzmyer, *Gospel*, p. 532.

27. L.T. Johnson, *Literary Function*, p. 139.

but also helped them with their possessions. In this context, what we should take notice of is that the point of this story is not sharing goods which Johnson wants to stress but a practice of almsgiving towards the penniless wandering preachers. The case of a centurion in Lk. 7.2-10 is also to be included in this category. Thirdly, we can also mention Jairus, a ruler of the synagogue, in Lk. 8.41-48, because he was clearly one of the leaders of the people and as such he was possibly affluent. Johnson should make Jairus reject the Prophet for these reasons for the sake of his formula, but it is evident that Jairus accepted Jesus. Accordingly, there are serious doubts concerning his argument. Finally, there appears to be self-contradiction in Johnson's argument. Regarding the parable of the Rich Man and Lazarus he states that 'his [the Rich Man's] wealth had made him insensitive to the demands of the Law and the Prophets that he give alms to the poor'.[28] Here the term 'the poor' is clearly used by Johnson in a literal meaning indicating those who are economically so destitute as to need others' financial help to survive. So this is a sign that Johnson plunges himself into self-contradiction in his use of the terms πτωχός and πλούσιος in his thesis.

In the final analysis, we would conclude that Johnson's careful observations on Luke's use of language of possessions in terms of the prophetic mode is worth being recognized. However, as we have noticed, the literary pattern he tries to prove is one which does not emerge from the text itself as he argues,[29] but from his forcible way of dealing with the material on possessions in Luke–Acts.

c. *W.E. Pilgrim:* Good News to the Poor *(1981)*[30]

Pilgrim's interest in the Lukan studies is in a puzzling problem regarding the matter of wealth, that is, the apparent discrepancy within the Bible itself between one strand of material that supports the total renunciation of possessions and the other material that supports the idea of wealth as a gift of God.[31]

In tackling this problem, in order to understand the Lukan presentation of the theme of possessions, in the first part Pilgrim explores the background to the teaching of the Lukan Jesus regarding poverty and

---

28. L.T. Johnson, *Literary Function*, p. 142.

29. L.T. Johnson, *Literary Function*, p. 121.

30. W.E. Pilgrim, *Good News to the Poor: Wealth and Poverty in Luke–Acts* (Minneapolis: Augsburg, 1981).

31. Pilgrim, *Good News*, p. 11.

wealth by surveying the passages in the Old Testament and intertestamental literature which deal with this theme, and reviewing the political and social atmosphere at the time of Jesus with the people with
whom Jesus was closely associated during his earthly ministry, such as
tax-collectors, sinners, prostitutes, beggars and the *anawim*.

The conclusion of this exploration is that the poor in Luke's writings
are not to be conceived spiritually but in a social and economic sense,
and the good news to them means 'physical, social and economic libera-
tion', but without losing sight of the spiritual dimension.[32] In the second
main part, Pilgrim directly deals with the material on possessions in
Luke–Acts, sorting the diverse traditions roughly into three categories:
the call to total surrender of possessions, the dangers of wealth and,
thirdly, the right use of possessions. And then he is confronted with
the Acts material linked to the theme with the assumption that 'the
Lukan attitude toward wealth and poverty expressed in the gospel finds
its fullest confirmation in Luke's description of the life of the early
church'.[33]

One of the noted merits of Pilgrim's thesis is his endeavour to link
the theme of wealth to that of discipleship: faithful discipleship means
readiness to use material possessions on behalf of the poor. In his words,
'possessions are to be placed radically in the service of Christian discipleship'.[34] Thus in Pilgrim's view, Luke's intention in the material on
possessions is to exhort the rich Christians in his community to emulate
the paradigm of Zacchaeus who gave away one half of all he possessed
to the poor. But here Pilgrim asserts that it is not to be taken as a literal
or exact role, but in the spirit of his generous behaviour. Hence, it is
clear that Pilgrim uses the case of Zacchaeus as a spotlight which focuses the whole essence of Luke's teaching on possessions. But this idea
of Zacchaeus cannot be accepted without question, because Zacchaeus
merely stated his promise to give alms to the poor and the text itself
does not reveal the fulfilment of his promise, although Jesus' announcement of Zacchaeus's salvation after his hearing of Zacchaeus's promise
might be regarded as an implicit indication of it. The point I want to
make here is that by neglecting other significant accounts in Luke which
also exhibit faithful discipleship in terms of the use of wealth, such
as the episodes of the Galilaean women (8.1-3), of Martha and Mary

32. Pilgrim, *Good News*, pp. 82-84.
33. Pilgrim, *Good News*, p. 147.
34. Pilgrim, *Good News*, p. 146.

(10.38-42) and of Joseph of Arimathea (23.50-54), Pilgrim puts an excessive weight on this single incident, in making the account of Zacchaeus the paramount paradigm of faithful discipleship, which can hardly be counted as a certain piece of evidence by itself.

Secondly, Pilgrim's idea on total renunciation is also to be questioned. Basically following Schottroff and Stegemann's view on this subject,[35] he argues that for Luke the demand to leave everything and the call to poverty should be considered as one restricted to 'earthly discipleship in Jesus' time',[36] that is, to the Twelve. Behind this argument lies his own view of the disciples which consists of two levels: one is a limited circle of the Twelve, and the other is a wider circle of disciples. With this division of the disciples, Pilgrim goes on to insist that the call for total surrender was applied exclusively to the Twelve, while the wider circle of disciples were exempt from this strict command of Jesus. How then can we understand Jesus' own injunction of total renunciation of wealth to the crowds in Lk. 14.33? In relation to this point, we can notice that Pilgrim is inconsistent in determining the range of the disciples because in one place he identifies the Seventy with the limited group of the Twelve,[37] but in other places, with a wider circle of disciples.[38] Thus on the whole, his idea of the two levels of disciples does not appear to be sufficient to be safely established; so in consequence his exclusive application of the call of total renunciation of wealth to the Twelve is also called into question.[39]

Thirdly, his treatment of the case of the Rich Ruler is called into question. Pilgrim contends that the Rich Ruler failed to sell all he

35. L. Schottroff and W. Stegemann, *Jesus and the Hope of the Poor* (New York: Orbis Books, 1986). This book was originally published in German in 1978, and, as Pilgrim himself admits in his book, it seems that the general skeleton of his thesis emulated that of Schottroff and Stegemann.

For instance, his application of a total surrender of possessions only to the disciples (the Twelve), his particular emphasis on the case of Zacchaeus as a paradigm that the rich Christians in his community are exhorted to emulate, not literally but in spirit, and his claim that Luke's teaching on wealth and poverty is addressed primarily to the rich, and the example of the first disciples, served as a critique of the rich Christians—all these are derived in the main from Schottroff and Stegemann.

36. Pilgrim, *Good News*, p. 101.

37. Pilgrim, *Good News*, pp. 94, 97.

38. Pilgrim, *Good News*, p. 90.

39. We will be able to answer this question later when we are led to discuss the Lukan discipleship in Chapter 4.

possessed because the call to total renunciation was only required of the Twelve, and, accordingly, it is revealed that the Rich Ruler was not called into full-time discipleship like the Twelve.[40] How does Pilgrim know that? What are his criteria for judging?

Fourthly, in relation to this topic of total surrender, very interestingly Pilgrim asserts that Levi joined the limited circle of the Twelve because he forsook everything to follow Jesus. But he is wrong in making this point, because the immediate context (Lk. 5.29) shows that after Levi left πάντα, he held a banquet for Jesus and his disciples; how can these two facts be reconciled? If it is true that Levi left all behind, where did the money for the banquet of not a small size and the house in which it was held come from? Thus, careful consideration of the context (Lk. 5.27-30) and the crucial factor that Levi was not a member of the Twelve in Luke's view (Lk. 6.14), which Pilgrim assumes without any justification, enable us to doubt his case.

Apart from these major problems, there are also minor points to be exposed as demerits. First, it appears that Pilgrim's reconstruction of the historical background of the practice of Jesus and his followers as regards possessions is not appropriate for Pilgrim's effort to explore Luke's theology on poverty and wealth; Luke's own context might be very different from that of the historical Jesus. Secondly, there occurs a problem in Pilgrim's sweeping categorization of the diverse groups of Jesus' time; his concept of the poor in Luke–Acts is usually defined in a social and economic sense, and with this basic concept he also tries to identify them with outcasts (tax-collectors) and sinners.[41] Then, if we are to follow his argument, Zacchaeus, the chief tax-collector, and the sinful woman in Lk. 7.36-50 who was apparently rich enough to waste the expensive oil should have been poor. But were they? Thirdly, Pilgrim is incoherent in employing the term 'disciples'. In general, by the 'disciples' he means the Twelve and insists that they are socially and economically poor. This feature is certainly seen in his dealing with the disciples in the Beatitudes.[42] But when he comes to deal with Lk. 12.33 where the disciples are exhorted to sell all for almsgiving, conveniently he regards the disciples here as a wider circle of disciples.[43] Thus it is apparent that Pilgrim does not have a definite

40. Pilgrim, *Good News*, pp. 89-90.
41. Pilgrim, *Good News*, p. 80.
42. Pilgrim, *Good News*, pp. 74-77.
43. Pilgrim, *Good News*, p. 94.

rule for deciding such matters. Besides, it is also wrong for Pilgrim to treat Lk. 12.33 as a call to total surrender of wealth, because when this verse in Luke is compared with the Matthaean parallel (6.20; cf. 19.21), it is clear that the motif of almsgiving is the predominant feature of the verse.

d. *D.P. Seccombe:* Possessions and the Poor in Luke–Acts *(1982)*[44]
The beginning of Seccombe's thesis launches off with the acknowledgment of two apparently contradictory aspects in Luke–Acts:

> [For] on the one hand there is much of the material which appears to glorify poverty, condemn the rich, and demand the renunciation of all possessions, but on the other the well-to-do are shown receiving favour from Jesus, and in Acts the Christian movement is portrayed making its way among socially and economically advantaged people.[45]

In order to solve this problem, the first task he deals with is to define πτωχοί in the New Testament and עֲנָוִים in the Old Testament, especially in the Psalms, Isaiah and the intertestamental literature, and as a result he comes to conclude that πτωχοί in Luke–Acts are not the pious, nor a particular social group, nor those who have voluntarily abandoned wealth, but an appellation applied to Israel as a whole nation in need of God's salvation.[46] This is the foundational argument, on which he develops his whole thesis. In keeping with this presupposition, Seccombe contends, 'There is nothing socio-economic or socio-religious about Luke's use of "poor" terminology in the passages we have considered... The poor are Israel and the answer to their poverty is the messianic Kingdom.'[47]

With regard to dispossession, examining three accounts, such as Jesus' commands to those who would follow him (Lk. 14.25-35), the incidents of the Rich Ruler (Lk. 18.18-30) and of Zacchaeus (Lk. 19.1-10), Seccombe insists that these passages illustrate 'what discipleship meant in an extreme situation', that is, when discipleship has no limits,[48] so that true disciples of Jesus must be prepared to forsake everything

44. D.P. Seccombe, *Possessions and the Poor in Luke–Acts* (SNTU, 6; Linz: Fuchs, 1982).

45. Seccombe, *Possessions*, p. 12.

46. Seccombe, *Possessions*, pp. 21-43.

47. Seccombe, *Possessions*, p. 95. This contention of Seccombe is to be refuted by Esler who applies socio-redaction criticism to Luke–Acts.

48. Seccombe, *Possessions*, p. 133.

when such an extreme situation arises. Here we notice that the kernel of his argument regarding dispossession is that what matters is not 'the general demand of renunciation of possessions', but 'a paradigm of the limitless character of discipleship'. So Seccombe tends to deny that these passages show 'the Christian's ongoing *use* of possessions'.[49]

One problem in Seccombe's argument on renunciation of wealth is his situational approach to this subject, which focuses on Jesus' journey to Jerusalem, the end of which is his death. It seems to me that although he does not assume persecution as the *Sitz im Leben* of these accounts, it does appear that the situation which Jesus faced is so extreme that it can be thought of as a kind of persecution.[50] Two problems arise in relation to this point. First, it is not clear whether Seccombe is attempting to explore Luke's theology or that of the historical Jesus. Secondly, as I will examine in Chapter 2, there is a difficulty in defining the *Sitz im Leben* of Luke's Gospel as one of persecution.

Above all, the most serious objection one would have to Seccombe's thesis is the ambivalence of terminology regarding πτωχόι and πλούσιοι, because there is no consistency in his interpretation of such terms; in one place they are used with spiritual connotations,[51] while in other places (Chapters 3 and 4 of his book) they are employed to signify literal poverty or wealth.

e. *L. Schottroff and W. Stegemann:* Jesus and the Hope of the Poor *(1986)*
Schottroff and Stegemann launch their thesis with a realization that the First-World churches and biblical scholarship tend to interpret the Bible spiritually, in particular in relation to the matter of wealth and poverty. So they state that it is 'unjust to deprive the poor of their gospel by interpreting it in such a way that it becomes our promise, a promise to the wealthy'.[52]

There are three parts to the thesis, but my concern is with the third one which deals with the theme of the poor and the rich in Luke's Gospel: 'the following of Christ as solidarity between rich, respected

49. Seccombe, *Possessions*, p. 134. Cf. p. 132.
50. Seccombe, *Possessions*, p. 93. Cf. p. 107.
51. That is, the poor are Israel in need of salvation, the rich are 'non-Israel who refuse to identify with the despised Son of man in the light of 6.22-23' (Seccombe, *Possessions*, pp. 90-91; cf. pp. 24-43, 66, 87-92).
52. Schottroff and Stegemann, *Hope*, p. v.

Christians and poor, despised Christians'. One of the main points of the thesis which concerns us is that for Luke a complete renunciation of possessions was demanded exclusively of the disciples, and constitutes an essential requirement of discipleship. In other words, the disciples forsook all they possessed voluntarily to respond to Jesus' command to follow him, which is 'a phenomenon of the past' that cannot be reiterated in Luke's time. Along with this voluntary poverty exercised by the disciples, the simple mode of life of the disciples that was comparable to that of the Cynic and Stoic philosophers functions as a critique of the rich Christians in Luke's community.[53]

This idea of the voluntary poverty of the disciples is based on the sharp distinction made between the disciples and the crowd in the Sermon on the Plain (Lk. 6.20–7.1); with regard to v. 12a, 'But I say to you that hear', Schottroff and Stegemann argue that the first part (vv. 20-26) is intended for the disciples only because they became poor after leaving πάντα to follow Jesus, while the second part (vv. 27–7.1) is addressed to the crowd who are 'the community of disciples, i.e., the church'.[54] Schottroff and Stegemann insist that this distinction occurs again in Luke 12; vv. 13-21 are addressed explicitly to the crowd, while vv. 1b-12 are addressed to the disciples.

A main objection to this contention is that in a few respects their distinction between the disciples and the crowd is not valid: first, in the same context (Lk. 6) Jesus chose the Twelve Apostles from the disciples, who are seen as a great crowd in v. 17, and this greatness of number of the disciples is confirmed in Lk. 19.37 (6.17, ὄχλος πολὺς μαθητῶν αὐτοῦ; 19.37, ἄπαν τὸ πλῆθος τῶν μαθητῶν). In consequence, secondly, when we allow for the fact that such technical terms as ἀπόστολοι and μαθηταί are employed in the same context, it becomes apparent that what matters here for Luke is not the distinction between the disciples and the crowd but the distinction between the Apostles and the disciples. Thirdly, if we are to accept their case, how can we understand that the more radical nature of Jesus' commands, for example, v. 29, is applied to the ordinary disciples, not the especially chosen disciples. Taking these three objections into account, therefore, it would be unreasonable for us to restrict the disciples in Lk. 6.20-26 to a limited circle of followers of Jesus, for whom the term

---

53. Schottroff and Stegemann, *Hope*, pp. 80-86.
54. Schottroff and Stegemann, *Hope*, p. 71.

ἀπόστολοι is specially reserved by Luke.[55] Thus it seems to me that Schottroff and Stegemann's distinction between the disciples and the crowd can hardly be justified, and since this becomes the foundation of their argument, we may say that their thesis is built upon sand.

Schottroff and Stegemann's idea of almsgiving is a challenging motif in relation to our study, so it needs to be discussed in detail. Their position on almsgiving is that Luke did not 'offer an ethic of undifferentiated "almsgiving"', but had 'a far more comprehensive idea of "almsgiving"'.[56] From this foundational statement on almsgiving, they claim that in Luke's view almsgiving refers to charity directed to non-Christians, and since alms is charity intended for destitute persons, there were no destitute persons in Luke's community.

Against this notion of almsgiving advocated by Schottroff and Stegemann, we must point out a few problems inherent in their argument:

(1) They appear inconsistent in applying the method articulated by themselves at the outset of the thesis; initially they are determined to interpret the Bible in a literal sense, but while interpreting the parable of the Great Banquet they are inclined to interpret it metaphorically, since they regard the four individual groups who appear in Lk. 14.13, 21 as 'eschatological substitutes for those originally invited to the banquet in the heavenly *basileia*'.[57]

(2) Why are they silent about Lazarus, ὁ πτωχός, who appears in Lk. 16.20, 22? The fact that the poor man is introduced with a concrete name, Lazarus, whereas the rich man is not, is not just accidental, regardless of whether it is a parable or not. Thus, it seems plausible to suppose that the reason why Luke refers especially to the name of the beggar here is because people comparable to Lazarus were present in his community.

(3) In Lk. 4.18 and 7.21, Jesus' mission is shown as preaching the good news to the poor. If the poor were not in Luke's community at all, why did Luke assert that the poor are primary recipients of the

---

55. For more information about the apostles in Luke, see G. Schneider, 'Die zwölf Apostel als "Zeugen": Wesen, Ursprung und Funktion einer lukanischen Konzeption', in *Lukas, Theologie der Heilsgeschichte* (Könnigstein: Peter Hanstein, 1985), pp. 61-85; K. Haacker, 'Verwendung und Vermeidung des Apostelbegriffs im Lukanischen Werk', *NovT* 30 (1988), pp. 9-38.

56. Schottroff and Stegemann, *Hope*, p. 109.

57. Schottroff and Stegemann, *Hope*, p. 110.

good news brought about by Jesus, and why did Luke contain more material where πτωχός appears than in Mark and Matthew?

(4) Taking note of Luke's omission of Mk 14.6, 'you always have the poor with you', they hold that Luke 'must omit this observation precisely because there are no poor in his community'.[58] But it might be argued to the contrary; since Luke is said to exhort the rich Christians to use wealth on behalf of the poor, it would be a minus factor for Luke's case that the sinful women did not use the expensive oil for the benefit of the poor. Possibly, thus, Luke wanted to leave out the phrase in question for the sake of the continuity of his position towards the right use of possessions, but not because there were no poor in his community, as Schottroff and Stegemann insist.

(5) Their assertion that in Acts πτωχός does not occur and is replaced by ἐνδεής (Acts 4.34) appears also to lead to the wrong conclusions. We know that in Acts ἐλεημοσύνη occurs more frequently than in the Gospel,[59] and this would be indicative of the fact that there were in fact recipients of almsgiving in Luke's community, but definitely not the idea that the poor did not exist in the community. Besides, as far as the absence of the term πτωχός in Acts is concerned, we might say that since the Early Church in Jerusalem practised Jesus' exhortation to almsgiving faithfully, the extreme poverty which πτωχός signifies would have been eradicated so that πτωχός is replaced by ἐνδεής.

In the final analysis, Schottroff and Stegemann's argument regarding the disciples' attitude towards wealth also does not seem to provide appropriate answers to a significant problem we are currently dealing with in Luke's Gospel: how can we understand the apparent discrepancy that Jesus who commanded the would-be disciples to renounce all they possessed, for example at 14.33, appears not to reproach his followers who did not forsake their possessions but accepts them as they were (8.1-3; 10.38-42; 19.1-10; 23.50-56)?

f. *P.F. Esler:* Community and Gospel in Luke–Acts *(1987)*
The work of Esler can be considered to be a fruitful result of the social-scientific approach to the study of Luke–Acts, which he himself labels 'socio-redaction criticism'. Esler holds the view that Luke's community was composed of both Jews and Gentiles in the midst of a Hellenistic

58. Schottroff and Stegemann, *Hope*, p. 111.
59. Lk. 11.41; 12.33, twice; Acts 3.2, 3, 10; 9.36; 10.2, 4, 31; 24.17, eight times.

city,[60] and from this mixed community as such, he infers that there was a conflict between the two groups within the community and critical pressure from outside of the community. In this context, by making good use of the sociological concept of 'legitimation', and assuming that Luke's theology is grounded in social and political reality,[61] Esler argues that Luke's primary target is the need of his own community for 'legitimation' for their new faith:

> Luke's two volumes may be described as an exercise in the legitimation of a sectarian movement, as a sophisticated attempt to explain and justify Christianity to the members of his community at a time when they were exposed to social and political pressures which were making their allegiance waver.[62]

The thesis is explored in terms of table fellowship, the law, the Temple, poor and rich, and relationships with Rome.

First, the pressure from outside of the community is linked to 'the axis of their religious affiliation', which results from the mixed composition of the members of the community. A typical problem related to it was 'table fellowship'. Facing this problem, Luke intended to solve it in rewriting the Early Church history,[63] contrary to the real history, and reinterpretating existing traditions, that is, by making Peter and James who were still regarded as the great authority at Luke's time recognize table fellowship, and by making the Jerusalem Council (Acts 15) approve it again. To legitimate table fellowship which prevailed in his community,[64] Luke also attempted to afford his readers another great assurance which was drawn from the activity and attitude of Jesus their Lord towards the law and the Temple. With respect to the law and the Temple, Esler makes the point that dealing with the law and the Temple was indispensable in legitimating table fellowship, because as a part of Judaism it was intermingled with them. Expounding the attitude of Jesus towards the law and the Temple, Luke intended

60. Esler, *Community*, p. 31.

61. Esler, *Community*, pp. 1-2.

62. Esler, *Community*, p. 222.

63. Esler, *Community*, pp. 97, 106. Against this idea that 'Luke falsified the history in order to achieve his objects', see I.H. Marshall's review of his book in *JTS* 39 (1988), pp. 564-66 (566).

64. At this point, Esler refutes Dunn's argument that Jews did not eat with Gentiles at this period (pp. 76-77; 83-84). Cf. J.D.G. Dunn, 'The Incident at Antioch (Gal. 2.11-18)', *JSNT* 18 (1983), pp. 3-75.

to legitimate the belief of the community in suggesting that it was the Christians who followed Jesus who were truly loyal to the law and the Mosaic tradition, and it was the Jews who rejected Jesus who actually contravened them.[65]

Secondly, the problem from within the community is related to the 'socio-economic axis', which Esler argues derived from the class conflict between the rich and the poor. Esler's position towards the composition of Luke's community, that is, a mixture of the rich and the poor, is to be noted,[66] because Theissen and Meeks who apply the same sociological method to the Pauline studies argue that the Pauline communities consisted by and large of the middle class but lacked the extreme lower classes of society.[67] In this context, Esler's investigation of the socio-economic standing of the rich and the poor in the Roman East in the first century CE is so rewarding as to help us properly appreciate how miserable and desperate the poor in Luke's time were and how arrogant and egocentric the rich were.

Since this topic is related directly to our study, we will dwell upon Esler's argument on this matter a bit further. What really arrests our attention in Esler's thesis is his treatment of the theme of the poor and the rich in terms of a socio-economic perspective, which he claims has never been seriously applied to Lukan studies. It is true that his research is to be acknowledged as a fresh enterprise which serves to enrich our understanding of the socio-economic setting of Luke's community which was immersed in the first century Hellenistic culture.

Nonetheless, there are two points we can make against his argument. First, Esler is not fair in dealing with the material in Acts, since he does not discuss a few accounts of significance which speak of the right use of wealth by rich Christians or a church, such as the incidents of Tabitha (Acts 9.36-43), Cornelius (Acts 10.1-48), the Antioch church (Acts 11.27-39) and Jesus' command cited by Paul in Acts 20.35, and his treatment of the summary passages is also not sufficient to make any significant point. It is reasonable to infer that as a second part of Luke's writing, Acts is supposed to have a continuity of the theme Luke intended to highlight in the Gospel. But poor treatment of the Acts

---

65. Esler, *Community*, p. 129.

66. Esler, *Community*, pp. 183-87.

67. We will return to this point again later when we deal with the *Sitz im Leben* of Luke–Acts, pp. 36-44.

material by Esler makes us doubt the validity of his argument in general. It appears that this unbalanced treatment of Acts is due to wrong labelling of his subject; Esler does not seem to pay due attention to a practical method which the rich members in Luke's community had to help the poor, whom Luke was concerned about. That is almsgiving.[68] This motif of almsgiving is clearly seen in those passages referred to above, so that they can be regarded as evidence that Luke wanted to continue to stress this motif in the second volume of his writings.

Secondly, it is evident that Esler does not deal properly with the matter of total renunciation of wealth in the Gospel, a point that Luke is obviously seen to accentuate more than Mark and Matthew do in their Gospels.[69] Esler tries to answer this question by relating it to the incident of Ananias and Sapphira in Acts 5.1-11 that he regards as a case of failure in the Early Church at Jerusalem, which might have occurred not infrequently in Luke's community:

> One suspects, however, that Luke's picture of early Christianity, apart from the story of Ananias and Sapphira, was an idealization serving to remind his contemporaries of how far they had fallen short of the ideal. Otherwise, it is difficult to explain his concern to sharpen material in his sources or add new sayings and passages which stress the need for almsgiving and the renunciation of possessions.[70]

Then, we may ask a question of Esler. Is this material relating to total renunciation of wealth employed by Luke just to show his readers how far they had fallen short of the ideal? What would be the reaction of the rich disciples in Luke's community when they were confronted with this apparently harsh command of Jesus? Esler seems to avoid facing this problem, and in this context it is not surprising to observe that he never alludes to discipleship in relation to the theme of wealth and poverty. In a word, Esler appears not to have explored in sufficient depth

---

68. Note the distinction Luke makes in such passages as Lk. 12.33 (Mt. 6.20; cf. 19.21) and Lk. 11.41 (Mt. 23.26), which clearly exhibit Luke's particular concern with almsgiving. In addition to these, this motif of almsgiving can also be detected in Lk. 3.10; 6.30, 35, 38; 10.33-35; 14.13, 21; 18.22; 19.8.

Esler does allude to the motif of almsgiving, but just in passing (pp. 195-96), so that he appears to fail to make a point of it. So it seems fair to state that he is still far from recognizing Luke's especial interest in this motif.

69. We should be advised to take a note of Luke's insertion of πάντα in the following passages: Lk. 5.11/Mk 1.18, 20; Lk. 5.28/Mk 2.14; Lk. 14.33; Lk. 18.22/Mk 10.21; Lk. 6.30/Mt. 5.42.

70. Esler, *Community*, p. 196.

the matter of total renunciation that the Lukan Jesus demanded of his disciples.

Finally, generally speaking, his conclusion to the theme of the rich and the poor in Luke–Acts appears correct; out of 'unusual compassion for the poorest members of his community and of society generally',[71] Luke exhorted the rich Christians in his community to distribute money and meals for the poor. This point made by Luke was radical insofar as it 'challenges the deeply held beliefs in his Hellenistic milieu, where the ruling elite not only treated the lower orders unjustly and with contempt, but congratulated themselves on doing so'.[72] But it is unfortunate that Esler does not touch on the radical nature of Jesus' command to forsake πάντα, directed towards those who would follow Jesus as his disciples. Later we will suggest a solution to this puzzling problem in Lukan study which Esler is not able to answer. Incidentally, Esler's careful attention to historical, economic and social factors in the first century Hellenistic culture is very useful, and I have made extensive use of this insight in Chapters 1 and 8 of this book.

2. Proposal

As we have seen thus far, a number of investigations have been carried out in the realm of the theme of wealth and poverty in Luke–Acts in various manners. Thus it might seem that scholarship on Luke's theology of wealth and poverty is already overcrowded. However, the above discussion has shown that there is still some uncertainty over major issues in this area of Luke's theology:

(1)   Does Luke have in mind two types of disciples?

(2)   Is a total surrender of possessions required of all or just the Twelve? And what might Luke mean by such a total surrender?

(3)   In discussing the relationship of wealth and discipleship, is the 'discipleship' metaphor sufficient, or are there other terms/metaphors to help us understand Luke?

71. Esler, *Community*, p. 199.
72. Esler, *Community*, p. 199.

(4)   Does Luke have any specific emphasis on the practical consid-
        erations of how wealth is to be employed?

Recently after reviewing several major works done in the field of
the theme of the rich and the poor in Luke–Acts in the last two decades,
Donahue also recognizes the uncertainty over these issues in Luke's
theology.

> While there is almost universal agreement on the importance of posses-
> sions, there is no consensus on major issues of interpretation, nor any
> consistent perspective within Luke–Acts. While the Gospel stresses com-
> plete dispossession as a condition of discipleship, it and, more strongly,
> Acts praise those who use (rather than abandon) their resources to aid the
> disciples. Dispossession of goods, common possession, and almsgiving
> are all praised.[73]

Thus, motivated by this uncertainty and encouraged by Donahue's
challenge, I want to tackle this problem again with a fresh look focusing on the relationship between wealth and discipleship in Luke's theology, because it appears to me that discipleship is not a sufficient motif
for us to reckon with the matter of wealth and poverty in Luke–Acts.
Hence arises a need to look at another paradigm that can serve to solve
this problem. In this context, it would seem that one theme which has
not yet been properly explored in Lukan study is that of 'stewardship'.
This theme appears mainly in such important places as Lk. 12.42-48,
16.1-13 and 19.11-27, that is, the so-called stewardship parables, and
can be noticed in the places where Luke intended to apply this motif in
a practical way to the material relating to the theme of wealth and poverty in Luke–Acts.[74]

In order to explore this theme of stewardship properly, the procedure I shall take to conduct the investigation is as follows:

(1)   The *Sitz im Leben* of Luke–Acts is to be examined, so that we
        may gain a proper understanding about the situational back-
        ground of Luke's community (Chapter 1).

(2)   Since Mark was used as a major source for Luke, Mark's view
        of discipleship and his conception of the disciples are to be
        compared with those of Luke so as to highlight the different
        conceptions of discipleship and the disciples (Chapters 2, 3).

73. Donahue, 'Two Decades', p. 135.
74. For the wide range of this material in Luke–Acts, see Chapters 6 and 7.

(3)   Having the result of the previous chapters in view, I shall investigate a conspicuous motif which prescribes the relationship between God and Christians in Luke, that is, the theme of slavery (Chapter 4).

(4)   I shall examine three stewardship parables in order to extract major ideas that constitute Luke's notion of stewardship (Chapter 5).

(5)   Based on stewardship, I shall examine a number of accounts in Luke–Acts illustrating the theme of wealth and poverty in order to appreciate the practical requirements of almsgiving as the proper stewardship of wealth, and some aspects of wrong stewardship of wealth as well (Chapters 6, 7).

(6)   Finally, in order to clarify the social context of Luke's community, I shall look at benefaction systems that prevailed in Graeco-Roman society around the first century CE, and then compare Luke's notion of almsgiving with other forms of benefaction in his time (Chapter 8).

3. *Methods and Limit of the Study*

The main tool with which I shall pursue this study is redaction criticism. This method is useful in that we can highlight differences and similarities amongst the Synoptic Gospels, in order to point out distinctive ideas of Luke on the themes of wealth and discipleship. However, contrary to the common assumption held by many scholars who presuppose the two-source hypothesis, that is Mark and 'Q', I feel uneasy in accepting the 'Q' document as one of the main sources Luke may have used when he wrote his Gospel, since whether it existed or not and where the boundary of the document should be determined are still in dispute, remaining as one of the unproved hypotheses in scholarly argument in the area of Synoptic study.[75] Thus it is appropriate for us to

75. This two-source hypothesis has come under continuing and vigorous challenge. For instance, B.C. Butler, *The Originality of St Matthew* (Cambridge: Cambridge University Press, 1951); A. Farrer, 'On Dispensing with Q', in *Studies in the Gospels: Essays in Memory of R.H. Lightfoot* (Oxford: Basil Blackwell, 1957), pp. 55-88; N. Turner, 'The Minor Verbal Agreements of Mt. and Lk. against

deal with Mark as one of Luke's main sources, for Mark is in our hands as an indisputably complete form of a Gospel. Apart from Mark and 'Q' as Luke's possible sources, scholars have talked of 'L' which is regarded as material that may have been available to Luke only, for instance, a large portion of the Birth Narrative and the Travel Narrative. This 'L' is important, but also not reconstructible as an independent body of material which one can compare with Luke.[76] Apart from Mark as a main source material of Luke's Gospel, I shall consult Matthew from time to time in order to compare parallels and to highlight similarities and dissimilarities between them. But in this case, I would think that the two Gospels were composed and written independently by their authors reflecting their own situational background, so that there would be no trace of one's dependence upon the other.

Along with redaction criticism as a major tool, literary or narrative criticism which has been seriously applied in the New Testament studies recently will also be employed in various places, because it helps us grasp an idea of how the author develops his theme as he writes the Gospel as a story, so we can appreciate the flow and structure of prominent themes that appear in the Gospels.[77]

Mk', *SE*, I, pp. 223-34; W. Farmer, *The Synoptic Problem* (New York: Macmillan, 1964); M.D. Goulder, 'A House Built on Sand', in A.E. Harvey (ed.), *Alternative Approaches to New Testament Study* (London: SPCK, 1985), pp. 1-24; Goulder, *Luke: A New Paradigm* (JSNTSup, 20; 2 vols.; Sheffield: JSOT Press, 1989), I, pp. 27-71; and D.A. Carson, D.J. Moo and L. Morris, *An Introduction to the New Testament* (Grand Rapids: Zondervan, 1992), pp. 26-38.

76. Cf. B.H. Streeter, *The Four Gospels: A Study of Origins* (London: Macmillan, 1953), pp. 199-272; V. Taylor, *Behind the Third Gospel* (Oxford: Clarendon Press, 1926); L. Gaston, *No Stone on Another: Studies in the Significance of the Fall of Jerusalem in the Synoptic Gospels* (NovTSup, 23; Leiden: E.J. Brill, 1970), pp. 244-56; J.M. Creed, *The Gospel according to St Luke* (London: Macmillan, 1950), pp. lvi-lxxv; B.S. Easton, *The Gospel according to St Luke* (Edinburgh: T. & T. Clark, 1926), pp. xiii-xxx; W. Grundmann, *Das Evangelium nach Lukas* (THKNT, 3; Berlin: Evangelische Verlagsanstalt, 1974), pp. 7-17; and E.E. Ellis, *The Gospel of Luke* (The Century Bible; London: Nelson, 1966), pp. 27-30.

77. Talbert and Tannehill appear to be leading scholars who have taken serious steps to apply literary criticism to Lukan study. They have written the following distinctive commentaries to which I shall frequently refer as I proceed with this study: C.H. Talbert, *Reading Luke: A Literary and Theological Commentary on the Third Gospel* (New York: Crossroad, 1982); R.C. Tannehill, *The Narrative Unity of Luke–Acts* (2 vols.; Philadelphia: Fortress Press, 1986).

Finally, since my purpose here is not an exhaustive analysis of every aspect of Luke's theology as a whole but rather the discernment of the motif of almsgiving based on stewardship of wealth, my treatment of the material in Luke–Acts will be selective.

4. *The* Sitz im Leben *of Luke–Acts*

In order to understand Luke's theology of wealth better, a knowledge of the *Sitz im Leben* of Luke–Acts as a basis of this study would be helpful. To explore the Lukan *Sitz im Leben*, two major elements need to be considered together: the audience at which Luke primarily aimed his two-volume work, and the social setting in which he wrote it. So in what follows we will consider these elements in turn.

a. *The Audience of Luke–Acts*
Who is Luke's intended audience? Here 'audience' clearly does not mean the specific addressees to whom Jesus gave teaching and instruction in his earthly ministry, but Luke's contemporary fellow Christians for whom he designed his work. It would be helpful for us to identify the audience of Luke's work in order that we may have a better understanding of the *Sitz im Leben* of Luke–Acts.

In order to identify the audience of Luke–Acts which constituted Luke's community, we first need to take the prologue into account, because Luke's two volumes are formally dedicated to a man called Theophilus.[78] We know from comparison with other books in the New Testament that it is unique for Luke to have written a prologue at the beginning of his work. We may appreciate that Luke would just have followed contemporary literary custom, dedicating his work to this patron under whose financial support and protective care he would have been able to write these two volumes. Then, was Theophilus just nothing more than a patron or was he also a representative recipient of Luke's work? To answer this question, first of all, it may be helpful to discuss whether Theophilus was a real figure or just a suppositional one.

---

78. It is quite interesting and can be seen to be a valid translation where the third Gospel in the version of the New English Bible starts with a formal literary dedication: THE AUTHOR TO THEOPHILUS. Cf. R.E.O. White, *Luke's Case for Christianity* (London: The Bible Reading Fellowship, 1987), p. 20.

b. *Theophilus: Real or Fictitious?*
Some have supposed that Theophilus was a name which was artificially
coined to represent any 'lover of God', or 'anyone loved by God', and
could be understood in a symbolic way as a discreet pseudonym for
'the average Christian', or 'the typical convert'.[79] However, if we take
Theophilus as just an artificially coined name, discarding any historical authenticity, three doubts arise.

First, the title that Luke accords to Theophilus, κράτιστε (κράτιστος), seems too artificial for use in relation to an imaginary figure.
Κράτιστος is used four times in Luke–Acts,[80] so we might expect consistency from the author's employment of the same word in his books.
In a formal and official letter (Acts 23.26), it means '(to) His Excellency (the Governor Felix)'; in personal address (Acts 24.3), it occurs
as 'most Excellent Felix'; and in Acts 26.25 as 'most Excellent Festus'.[81]
These usages of the epithet in Acts show us apparently that in Luke–
Acts κράτιστος is used as a title attached to real persons who held
official positions in the Roman government of equestrian or higher
rank.[82] Accordingly, in view of Luke's usage of this term, it seems unlikely that κράτιστος can be interpreted merely as 'dear' here in the
Gospel, as Schweizer argues.[83] If we are allowed to take κράτιστος as
a title of a Roman official, then it seems natural to regard Theophilus
as a real person, either one who also held high office in the Roman government,[84] or, more generally, one who was 'socially respected and
probably well off, or highly placed in the society to which Luke had
access'.[85]

Secondly, the conventional practice of dedicating treatises to the
nobility in the Graeco-Roman society of Luke's time is to be taken into
consideration.[86] This practice of dedication was prevalent in antiquity,

79. Cf. White, *Luke's Case*, pp. 20-24; F.F. Bruce, *The Book of the Acts*
(NLCNT; London: Marshall, Morgan & Scott, 1972), p. 31.

80. Lk. 1.3; Acts 23.26; 24.3; 26.25.

81. In all three places, the NEB translates 'Your Excellency', as also in Lk. 1.3.

82. Bruce, *Acts*, p. 31; White, *Luke's Case*, p. 21.

83. E. Schweizer, *The Good News according to Luke* (London: SPCK, 1984),
pp. 12-13. Contra Schweizer, see Evans, *Saint Luke*, p. 134.

84. White, *Luke's Case*, p. 21.

85. Fitzmyer, *Gospel*, p. 300.

86. W. Schmithals, *Das Evangelium nach Lukas* (Zürich: Theologischer Verlag,
1980), p. 17: 'Die Widmung eines Buches an einen Freund oder Gönner war damals
weit verbreitet'. See also D. Guthrie, *New Testament Introduction* (Leicester: IVP,

and closely linked with the correlative practice of patronage by which the publication and dissemination of a book was possible:

> Lukas dem angesehenen Christen Theophilus sein Werk widmete, damit dieser, antikem Brauch entsprechend, für dessen Verbreitung sorge.[87]

In keeping with this custom, we may infer from Luke's dedication of his books to Theophilus that Theophilus would have been the sort of patron who would have provided Luke with financial support in order that Luke may write his books, and in response to such benevolence, Luke would have dedicated his works to Theophilus. In consequence it does not appear unreasonable that Theophilus should be a real figure.

Thirdly, another point that must be considered in this discussion of the dedication is that the preface of Luke's Gospel is written not in ordinary Greek but 'in excellent Greek with a most carefully wrought sentence structure',[88] which can be clearly distinguished from what follows.[89] What in fact made Luke write the preface in such a different way? Attempts have been made to answer this question, among which one that seems probable is that Luke used excellent Greek with well-organized sentence structure in order to make it correspond to the status of his patron who would have been educated and cultured in the milieu of the Graeco-Roman world. This notion would confirm our assumption that Theophilus was a government official in the Roman Empire, or a person of similar social standing, not to mention that he was a real figure.[90]

1978), p. 95; G.B. Caird, *The Gospel of St Luke* (The Pelican Gospel Commentaries; London: A. & C. Black, 1968), pp. 14, 44; N. Geldenhuys, *The Gospel of Luke* (NICNT; Grand Rapids: Eerdmans, 1977), p. 54; L. Morris, *The Gospel according to St Luke* (TNTC, 3; Leicester: IVP, 1986), p. 66; Fitzmyer, *Gospel*, 299; Creed, *Gospel*, p. 5.

87. 'Luke dedicated his work to the respectable Christian Theophilus, in order that he might have taken care of its dissemination according to the ancient custom.' Schmithals, *Lukas*, p. 17.

88. I.H. Marshall, *Commentary on Luke* (NIGTC; Exeter: Paternoster Press, 1989), p. 39. Cf. Fitzmyer, *Gospel*, pp. 287-89; Morris, *Gospel*, p. 65; Schweizer, *Luke*, p. 10; Caird, *Luke*, p. 43.

89. Geldenhuys, *Gospel*, pp. 54-55, says, 'Where in the rest of his Gospel he does not continue in this style but in the Hebraising style of the Greek translation of the Old Testament, in Greek which reflects Aramaic idiom, or in the daily colloquial style of that time, he does not do so through his inability to write classical Greek'.

90. Recently L. Alexander produced an intriguing article, 'Luke's Preface in the Context of Greek Preface-Writing', *NovT* 28 (1986), pp. 48-74; see also *The Preface*

To conclude, we may state that the title, κράτιστος, a form of dedication and the artful Greek sentence in the prologue suggest that Luke's two volumes were designed to be presented to a real person, possibly a government official, which might entail that he was endowed with the education and culture of contemporary Hellenistic society.[91]

c. *Theophilus: Christian or Not?*

The next problem with which we deal is whether or not Theophilus was a Christian, or what kind of relationship he had with Christians, such as would have caused Luke to dedicate his work to him. It would seem that whether Theophilus was already a Christian or not partly depends on the meaning of κατηχήθης in Lk. 1.4, so we need to investigate this particular word in Luke's Gospel. It may mean 'to report, inform', or 'to instruct'.[92] But there are a range of different opinions about the

to Luke's Gospel (SNTSMS, 78; Cambridge: Cambridge University Press, 1993), which challenged directly the traditional way in appreciating the prologue of Luke–Acts, which has been adopted as a common assumption.

First, as compared with other classical Greek literature, Luke's preface 'is not actually very successful rhetoric' (p. 50), which leads to denial of its literary excellence. Secondly, the formula of Luke's preface, 'a label with address', does not have any parallel in classical Greek literature, but in 'scientific literature', or 'technical prose' in antiquity (p. 60). Thirdly, from the two findings it is derived that Luke may have belonged to the 'middlebrow class' (p. 60), which would be congruous with the general picture of the congregations of the Pauline communities. In summing up, her contention can be summarized as follows: 'the scientific tradition provides the matrix within which we can explore both the social and the literary aspects of Luke's work, both the man himself and the nature of his writings' (p. 70).

Indeed, this discovery would 'broaden our definition of literature, that is, widen the canon of contemporary literature with which the New Testament writings can properly be compared' (p. 61). However, in relation to the subject here, my impression is that her stress appears to be directed mainly to the uniqueness of the formula of the preface, but not the literary skill which seems to remain in its own right (Evans, *Saint Luke*, p. 122; F.Ó. Fearghail, *The Introduction to Luke–Acts: A Study of the Role of Lk. 1.1-4.11 in the Composition of Luke's Two-Volume Work* [Rome: Pontificio Istituto Biblico, 1991], pp. 10-11). Even if her contention is to be followed, I may still state that Luke made his best endeavours to honour his dedicatee, 'drawing on the only style he knows which is at all appropriate to the occasion' (p. 65), as she says.

91. I.H. Marshall, *Commentary*, p. 39; Schweizer, *Luke*, p. 10; Caird, *Luke*, p. 43.

92. F. Bovon, *Das Evangelium nach Lukas (Lk. 1.1-9.50)* (EKKNT, 3.1; Zürich: Benzinger Verlag, 1989), p. 41. Originally it means 'to sound in ears', and then 'to teach by word of mouth', but sometimes also (in the passive) 'to be informed through

interpretation of it, so that we are invited to discuss them.[93]

Generally speaking, this word, κατηχήθης, can be rendered in two ways. First, the passive of κατηχέω can imply 'to be instructed', which is based on the fact that the word is so often used of the instruction of Christian converts or inquirers (Acts 18.25; 1 Cor. 14.19), therefore it seems possible that it refers to Christian instruction which Theophilus has already received.[94] In this case, we can say that Theophilus was already a Christian, but his knowledge concerning Jesus and his Gospel was too incomplete and not sufficiently based on firm ground, which would have caused Luke to address his writing to him, so that he might learn the truth with full certainty (ἀσφάλεια).[95]

Secondly, it can denote 'to be informed', which is based on the meaning of Acts 21.21, 24, where Luke uses the word twice in the sense of 'to receive an unfavourable (or hostile, wrong) report'. In this case, Theophilus may still have been an outsider, but interested in Christianity.[96] In either case, κατηχήθης indicates that certain things are lacking in Theophilus's knowledge of the Gospel story, so it would seem

rumours' (Acts 21.21, 24; cf. 18.25; Rom. 2.18; 1 Cor. 14.19; Gal. 6.6; Geldenhuys, *Gospel*, p. 57).

93. Cf. F. Mussner, 'καθεξῆς im Lukasprolog', in E.E. Ellis and E. Grässer (eds.), *Jesus und Paulus: Festschrift für W.G. Kümmel* (Göttingen: Vandenhoeck & Ruprecht, 1975), pp. 253-55; M. Vögel, 'Exegetische Erwägungen zum Verständnis des Begriffs καθεξῆς im lukanischen Prolog', *NTS* 20 (1973–74), pp. 289-99; G. Schneider, 'Zur Bedeutung von καθεξῆς im lukanischen Doppelwerk' (1977), in *Lukas, Theologie der Heilsgeschichte* (Könnigstein: Peter Hanstein, 1985); R.J. Dillon, 'Previewing Luke's Project from his Prologue (Luke 1.1-4)', *CBQ* 43 (1981), pp. 219-23; and R.J. Karris, *Luke: Artist and Theologian* (New York: Paulist Press, 1985), pp. 8-10.

94. Creed, *Gospel*, p. 5; Fearghail, *Luke–Acts*, p. 113. Cf. H. Schürmann, *Das Lukasevangelium* (HTKNT, 3; Erster Teil; Freiburg: Herder, 1969), p. 15.

95. Geldenhuys, *Gospel*, p. 54; I.H. Marshall, *Commentary*, p. 43; Schweizer, *Luke*, p. 13. Guthrie, *Introduction*, p. 96, and Fitzmyer, *Gospel*, p. 300, render this word as 'catechetical instruction', while Schmithals, *Lukas*, p. 17, asserts that 'Er schreibt für solche, die im christlichen Glauben unterricht sind (v. 4); Christen sind seine Leser'.

96. W. Manson, *The Gospel of Luke* (MNTC; London: Hodder & Stoughton, 1930), p. 3; R. Maddox, *The Purpose of Luke–Acts* (Göttingen: Vandenhoeck & Ruprecht, 1982), p. 12; W.E. Bundy, *Jesus and the First Three Gospels* (Cambridge, MA: Harvard University Press, 1955), p. 4; Morris, *Gospel*, p. 67; Caird, *Luke*, p. 44. Cf. Geldenhuys, *Gospel*, p. 54. In line with this, Beyer holds that Theophilus had learned about Jesus by hearsay (H.W. Beyer, κατηχέω, *TDNT*, III, pp. 638-40).

that Luke desired to supplement what was lacking on the part of Theophilus.

It would be insufficient to discuss only κατηχήθης when we are gathering information about Theophilus. We need to discuss other words in the prologue which might be related to κατηχήθης, or Theophilus himself directly or indirectly. In this context, the first word that attracts our attention is the word λόγοι in Lk. 1.4, because in this context λόγοι might be rendered as referring to 'the various pieces of instruction which Theophilus has already received',[97] so related to πράγματα of v. 1, by which Luke means the life, death and resurrection of Jesus.[98] Along with this word, ἐπιγινώσκω is also of crucial importance in appreciating v. 4. According to its lexical meaning, ἐπιγινώσκω means 'to recognize' or 'to perceive', which is chosen sometimes to mean to confirm knowledge already received.[99] Consequently what Theophilus is meant to recognize or perceive is the assurance or certainty (ἀσφάλεια) of the instruction or information he has already received.[100] Therefore if we consider these words, ἐπιγινώσκω and λόγοι along with κατηχήθης, it would be likely at least in this context that the term refers to Christian instruction Theophilus had already received, although κατηχήθης itself may be used in a neutral sense. To sum up, when Luke wrote and dedicated his work to Theophilus, Theophilus was probably already a Christian who had received formal Christian instruction in certain ways, and was very interested in it. Hence, Luke dedicated his two volumes to him in order to supplement his insufficient knowledge about Jesus and his Gospel.

d. *The Cultural Background of Luke's Community*
Up to now on the grounds of Theophilus's title, κράτιστε, which can refer to Roman officials (Acts 23.26; 24.3; 26.25), we may assume that Theophilus was a Gentile. However, when we are reminded that Luke presupposes a knowledge of the Old Testament and Jewish history (1.7;

---

97. I.H. Marshall, *Commentary*, p. 44. Cf. Schweizer, *Luke*, p. 13.

98. Bovon, *Lukas*, p. 35; Fitzmyer, *Gospel*, p. 292.

99. Bovon, *Lukas*, p. 40: 'Ἐπιγινώσκω hat hier die Bedeutung "genau erkennen", nachdem die Aufmerksamkeit auf (ἐπί) die Person oder die Sache gelenkt worden ist, meint also eine bewußte und erarbeitete Einsicht, nicht vollständiges Wissen'. Cf. Geldenhuys, *Gospel*, p. 57.

100. Maddox, *Purpose*, p. 13.

4.38; 8.9-10; 9.28-36), and that what Jesus means by the self-designation 'the Son of Man', or by 'the Kingdom of God' is never explained in the Gospel,[101] we cannot rule out the possibility that the intended audience of Luke's work included Jewish Christians. Apparently this argument seems contrary to the above conclusion if the Gentile Theophilus is representative of the intended audience of Luke–Acts. Owing to these elements, Esler insists that Luke's community was

> A mixture of Jew and Gentile, in which each group is significant . . . with the qualification that most of the Gentiles in Luke's community had not converted to Christianity from idolatry, but had previously been associated with Jewish synagogues.[102]

But when we encounter the universalist theme in Luke–Acts, noted as significant by the vast majority of scholars and indicating that in essence Luke–Acts was designed for Gentile missions,[103] this compromising solution to our problem cannot be regarded as an ultimate answer.

In view of this understanding of two differing elements in Luke's writing, that is, the atmosphere of the Old Testament and Judaism on one side, and universalism on the other, we may come to the conclusion that Theophilus was originally a Gentile, but heard about the Christian faith and received various pieces of Christian information and instruction, so that finally he might have come to be aware of these things that were originally Jewish concepts. In other words, it would seem plausible that since the Gentile Christian audience for whom Luke wrote his work had already obtained Christian instruction which would have included a wide range of knowledge of the Old Testament and Jewish history, Luke would have presupposed that his readers had some knowledge of basic motifs which would be essential for a clearer understanding of Christian themes, such as the Kingdom of God, the Son of Man, and the history of Israel based on the Old Testament.

---

101. Maddox, *Purpose*, pp. 14-15.

102. Esler, *Community*, p. 31. Cf. Maddox, *Purpose*, p. 15.

103. There is ample evidence to support a Gentile destination of Luke's two-volume work; major evidence of Luke's universalism is to be found in Lk. 2.14, 32; 3.4-6; 4.25-27; 9.54; 10.33; 17.16; 24.47. For more details of Luke's interest in Gentile Christians, see Fitzmyer, *Gospel*, p. 58; Morris, *Gospel*, pp. 36-37; Guthrie, *Introduction*, p. 90; and R.H. Gundry, *A Survey of the New Testament* (Grand Rapids: Zondervan, 1981), pp. 92-93.

e. *Theophilus: A Representative of Luke's Audience?*
After having examined the question of the reality of Theophilus, we could conclude that Theophilus was a patron, but no more than that. In other words, Theophilus would have provided Luke his client with money and personal care to enable Luke to write Luke–Acts, but would have had nothing to do with the work itself.

But if we look carefully into the content of the Gospel in particular, we cannot fail to notice a very significant feature unique to Luke that there is a large quantity of material in the Gospel which on most occasions is related either to the problem of wealth or to the right or wrong use of material possessions one way or another.[104] If Theophilus was a real figure, then he must have been very rich, his title being properly allowed for. Hence, it seems likely that as a rich man, he would have been interested in these issues being addressed in Luke's Gospel, and that might be connected with the original intention of Luke in writing his work and dedicating it to the rich patron. Therefore, on the grounds of this result, we can build our hypothesis that when dedicating his work to Theophilus, at the same time Luke would have included in his intended audience any others of similar social standing to Theophilus.[105] This would imply that Theophilus stands for Luke's intended readers who might also have been rich and educated or cultured Gentiles and who knew something about the Christian faith.[106]

f. *Summary and Conclusion*
The examination of the preface of Luke's Gospel with a focus on the identity of Theophilus has revealed that Theophilus was not only a patron of Luke by whom the publication and dissemination of Luke's work was made possible, but also a recipient of Luke's information, and as such he could also represent the intended audience whom Luke would have had in view when writing his two volumes.

This conclusion concerning Theophilus is singled out because it seems relevant to exploring the general Lukan *Sitz im Leben*. That is to say,

104. See Chapters 6 and 7 for this subject.
105. D.C. Allison, 'Was there a "Lukan Community"?', *IBS* 10 (1988), pp. 62-70 (70); cf. p. 66.
106. With regard to the representativeness of Theophilus, G. Schneider (*Das Evangelium nach Lukas* [2 vols.; Würzburg: Echter Verlag, 1977], I, p. 42), states that 'Theophilus, aller Wahrscheinlichkeit nach eine historische Persönlichkeit, steht stellvertretend für die Christen der betreffenden Zeit'.

by means of the above conclusion regarding Theophilus, the *Sitz im Leben* of Luke–Acts can be explored in such a way that follows the hypothesis that Theophilus represents Luke's intended audience in Luke–Acts. This would suggest that the contemporary community of Luke for which the two volumes were written probably included those who were rich and educated Gentiles, who possessed some knowledge of the basic conceptions of the Christian gospel which are rooted in the Old Testament, and who were also genuinely interested in having a historical account of the origin of Christianity. To conclude, we might suggest that the readers envisaged by Luke in his writing of Luke–Acts were 'mainly Gentile Christians in a Gentile setting, and Theophilus was one of them'.[107]

5. *The Social Setting of Luke's Community*

Thus far we have tried to discover the Lukan *Sitz im Leben* mainly focusing on some information gathered about Theophilus, developing the hypothesis that Theophilus was not just Luke's patron, but also a recipient of Luke's writings, and as such he may be regarded as a representative of the intended audience to whom Luke delivered his two volumes.

Before pursuing further evidence which might support this hypothesis concerning Luke's community,[108] it might be helpful at this stage

107. Fitzmyer, *Gospel*, p. 59.

108. Allison puts the effort at identification of the Lukan community into question form in his article, 'Was there a "Lukan Community"?'. Describing Luke as a peripatetic who accompanied Paul, the wandering missionary, Allison argues that there can be no so-called Lukan Community, because Luke along with Paul did not belong to any specific community in a geographical sense, but had 'the church universal' in view (p. 63). In accordance with this stance, he goes on to contend with confidence that there is no evidence that there were specific problems in Luke's community, otherwise it 'would have manifested itself in some obvious fashion' (p. 67).

As a response to this challenge, we may ask the question, 'how can he explain the theme of poor and rich in Luke's Gospel which is made manifest as a distinctive feature as Luke is compared with the other Evangelists, particularly Mark, and can be consistently observed throughout the Gospel?' Rather, when we are honest and face the sheer mass of material on poor and rich in Luke–Acts, we cannot resist the idea that there was a problem related to the rich and poor in Luke's community, which, contrary to Allison's argument, was clearly manifested 'in an obvious fashion'. Therefore, it does not seem to be easy to lend credence to Allison's challenge to the notion of a Lukan community.

to deal with some details concerning other early Christian urban communities which may be comparable to Luke's. In particular, it may be fruitful for comparison with the *Sitz im Leben* of Luke's community to note the investigation of the Pauline communities that Meeks and Theissen have made by means of sociological analysis.

a. *The Social Setting of the Pauline Communities*
Theissen and Meeks are engaged in applying a sociological method to analyse social stratification of the Pauline congregation (Theissen)[109] and Hellenistic primitive Christianity (Meeks) in order to refute a prevailing theory, that is, that the Early Church is composed of the lower classes or proletariat, and Christianity has been a movement of the lowest classes.[110] Protagonists who champion this conservative theory use 1 Cor. 1.26-29 as their evidence, but in using the same passage, Theissen presents a different explanation, that is, that there were some in the Corinthian congregation who were wise, powerful and well born, and although they were a minority in numbers, yet they were 'a dominant minority' in the communities.[111]

To prove their cases, Theissen and Meeks attempt to interpret the socio-economical status of all the figures who appear in the Pauline Epistles, mainly in those to the Corinthians and Romans, as far as the biblical material permits. As a result, Theissen singles out some wealthy members of the communities, such as Erastus, Gaius, Lydia, Priscilla and Aquilla, Titus Justus, Crispus, Phoebe, Sosthenes, Stephanas, and Chloe's people, and Meeks adds to them Barnabas, Mark (Acts 12.12), Philemon and Apollos, too. The criteria employed to analyse such figures are also noteworthy. Theissen presents as criteria for elevated social status, 'statements about holding office, about "houses", about

109. The case of G. Theissen (*The Social Setting of Pauline Christianity* [Philadelphia: Fortress Press, 1982]) is confined to the Corinthian Church, although the result of his analysis could be applicable to other churches in the Roman Empire of that age.

110. As one source of this common view, Meeks refers to Celsus's statement which appears in *Contra Celsum* written by Origen (3.44): 'Celsus. . . alleged that the church deliberately excluded people because the religion was attractive only to "the foolish, dishonourable and stupid, and only slaves, women, and little children"' (W.A. Meeks, *The First Urban Christians* [New Haven: Yale University Press, 1983], p. 51).

111. Theissen, *Social Setting*, pp. 70-73; cf. Meeks, *Urban Christians*, pp. 51-53.

assistance rendered to the congregation, and about travel',[112] which it seems to me work quite effectively in this type of analysis. In the case of Meeks, being cautious 'in applying to ancient society a theory that has been empirically generated from observations about a modern society',[113] he chooses some major figures from 65 individuals who would be of help in analysing the Pauline communities. After having analysed their socio-economic status, Meeks comes to the conclusion that the Pauline communities consisted of people of the middle class of that time:

> The extreme top and bottom of the Greco-Roman social scale are missing from the picture. It is hardly surprising that we meet no landed aristocrats, no senators, *equites*, nor (unless Erastus might qualify) decurions. But there is also no specific evidence of people who are destitute—such as the hired menials and dependent handworkers; the poorest of the poor, peasants, agricultural slaves, and hired agricultural day laborers, are absent because of the urban setting of the Pauline groups.[114]

Theissen's conclusion is similar to that of Meeks: 'In conclusion it can be said that Hellenistic primitive Christianity was neither a proletarian movement among the lower classes nor an affair of the upper classes'.[115]

In addition to this, it is well worth noting that the urban environment of Pauline Christianity described by Meeks[116] contributes much to our appreciation of the socio-economic setting of the Pauline communities. In particular, that he connects Roman imperialism, Hellenism and urbanization together is fairly instructive for our understanding of the areas where Paul travelled to and fro in order to advance the gospel of Jesus.[117] And that the major places in the Roman East where Paul worked are cities is also significant, and explains the relation between Paul's mission and his contemporary situation.

b. *Is Luke's Community the Same as Paul's?*
My question raised in relation to the conclusions derived from the application of the sociological analyses of the Pauline congregations made

---

112. Theissen, *Social Setting*, p. 73.
113. Meeks, *Urban Christians*, p. 55.
114. Meeks, *Urban Christians*, p. 73.
115. Theissen, *Social Setting*, p. 106.
116. Meeks, *Urban Christians*, pp. 9-50.
117. Meeks, *Urban Christians*, p. 13.

by Theissen and Meeks, is whether it has to do with the background of Luke's community with which my research is concerned.

Before providing a proper answer to this question, it would be requisite for us to compare some aspects of Luke with Mark in order to find particular aspects in Luke relevant to discovering the *Sitz im Leben* of Luke's community. It is noteworthy, for instance, that Luke uses πόλις four times more than Mark does, and describes on the whole the earthly ministry of Jesus centring around πόλεις.[118] Based on this aspect, we may suggest at least that Luke is more concerned with πόλις than χώρα, which offers us some grounds favourable to our hypothesis that Luke–Acts was written under the circumstances of an urban setting.[119]

In keeping with this feature, we may reckon with another feature which Luke's community seems to have shared in common with the Pauline communities. That is, there are a certain number of wealthy people in Luke's congregation as there are in Paul's. As evidence that they were present in Luke's community, first of all, Luke's literary artifice can be mentioned, which is to be found in the Prologue (Lk. 1.1-4), and the narrative of the sea voyage and shipwreck in Acts 27. Since 'the literary education offered by the Hellenistic cities was largely inaccessible to the lower orders',[120] it would be possible to surmise that 'its author came from the upper segment of Greco-Roman society'.[121] But he clearly wrote to be understood and appreciated and we may thus surmise that there were also other members with the same background as Luke in his community. This would indicate that Luke wrote the two volumes in and for an urban Christian community which might be a city of the Roman Empire where Hellenistic culture was strong.[122]

Secondly, when we consider figures who appear in Luke–Acts, such as Levi who appears to be rich enough to hold a banquet for Jesus and his disciples (Lk. 5.27-29), Joanna, the wife of Herod's steward Chuza

118. Mark, 9 times; Luke, 39 times in the Gospel; Lk. 4.29, 31, 43; 5.12; 7.11, 12, 37, etc.
119. H.J. Cadbury, *The Style and Literary Method of Luke* (Cambridge, MA: Harvard University Press, 1920), pp. 245-49.
120. A.H.M. Jones, *The Greek City from Alexander to Justinian* (Oxford: Clarendon Press, 1940), p. 285.
121. Esler, *Community*, p. 186.
122. Cf. Cadbury, *Style*, pp. 245-49; Esler, *Community*, p. 30; Marshall, *Commentary*, p. 33.

(Lk. 8.3), Joseph of Arimathea (Lk. 23.50), Zacchaeus (Lk. 19.1-10), the Ethiopian Eunuch (Acts 8.26-39), Manaen, a member of the court of Herod the Tetrarch (Acts 13.1), Sergius Paulus, the proconsul of Cyprus (Acts 13.7), Greek women and men of noble birth from Beroea (Acts 17.12) and the Ephesian Asiarchs, who are described as Paul's friends (Acts 19.31), it can be said that Luke's focus on such figures probably indicates the sort of milieu with which some in Luke's community could identify.

In addition, that wealthy Christians were present in Luke's community is confirmed by the material in the Gospel which Jesus uses as warnings and exhortations towards the rich as to how to use possessions in a Christian way. This material includes the parables of the Good Samaritan (10.30-37), the Rich Fool (12.13-21), the Unjust Steward (16.1-13), the Rich Man and Lazarus (16. 19-31), the Great Banquet (14.16-24), and the incident of Zacchaeus (19.1-10), all of which occur in Luke's special material, and finally, the incident of the Rich Ruler (18.18-30). The commands to give alms (12.33; 11.41) and to share food and clothing (3.10-11) with those who have none are also to be taken as tokens of the presence of wealthy members in Luke's community. Among these passages, it would be helpful to note especially the parable of the Great Banquet and the account of the Rich Ruler. Firstly, in the parable of the Great Banquet and Jesus' sayings attached to it (14.1, 12-24), we notice that Jesus' command to the rich Pharisee who invited him to a meal is to be taken as an indication of the presence of rich people in Luke's community, who can afford to invite other people, social equals of affluence, who will do the same thing to them in return (v. 12).[123] Secondly, in the incident of the Rich Ruler, it is to be noticed that as compared with Mark (10.22) and Matthew (19.22), Luke's treatment of the Rich Ruler is different, because he did not depart from the scene as he did in Mark and Matthew. This change by Luke enables us to suppose that there would have been problems that the rich members may have caused in Luke's community.[124]

123. Cf. Karris, 'Poor and Rich', pp. 120-21.
124. Cf. Esler, *Community*, p. 185; Karris, 'Poor and Rich', p. 123. It appears that influenced by other Synoptists' accounts, I.H. Marshall, *Commentary*, p. 683, assumes that the Rich Ruler went away from the scene. This results from lack of attention to the text. In fact he remains present to hear Jesus' instruction.

Having established that Luke's community was situated in an urban setting, so that it was very similar to those of Paul, we may ask a question in relation to this fact: 'Is it probable that the settings are so similar that the result of sociological analysis drawn from the Pauline communities can apply without any modification to the situation of Luke's community?' In order to afford an appropriate answer to this question, it should be borne in mind that although in Luke there is plenty of material about (οἱ) πλούσιοι which appears in relation to exhortations to almsgiving and warnings about the wrong use of wealth,[125] there is also ample material about (οἱ) πτωχοί in relation to injunctions of almsgiving.[126] What is to be noticed particularly in this context is that the poor who appear in Luke's Gospel are not the ordinary poor, but the crippled, the blind, lepers, who are not able to provide for themselves at all, so that without others' donations they would have been left to die of hunger.[127] It is apparent that such a helpless, destitute group of people do not appear in the Pauline epistles, leading Meeks to conclude that the lower stratum of society is missing. If the οἱ πτωχοί had not been in the community and the numbers had been so small that they might have been negligible, how can it be explained that there occur so often exhortations to almsgiving on behalf of the poor in the Gospel, which makes it so distinctive among the Gospels that it is called 'the Gospel for the poor'? Accordingly, it would be wrong to neglect this element in analysing the social stratification of Luke's community in terms of a sociological approach. Thus to be short, it is probable that poor and destitute people comparable to Lazarus (16.20) were present in Luke's community.

125. Lk. 6.24-25; 12.16-17; 16.19-20; 18.23-24; 19.2-3; 21.1-2.
126. Lk. 14.13, 21; 16.20, 22; 18.22; 19.8; 21.3. In some passages such as 4.18; 6.20; 7.22, οἱ πτωχοί are referred to, although exhortations relevant to almsgiving are not mentioned. And Lk. 12.33; 11.41 can also be singled out as tokens of the presence of the οἱ πτωχοί in the community.
127. Lk. 7.22; 14.13, 21; 16.20-22. In addition to these accounts, Esler, *Community*, pp. 186-87, points out three more cases which would indicate the presence of the poor in Luke's community; (1) the Lord's prayer (11.1-4) where the disciples are commanded to pray for daily bread (καθ' ἡμέραν); (2) the parable of the Lost Drachma (15.8-10)—the woman who appears in this parable is seen to have as her total wealth just ten drachmae that are equal to 'the income from ten days' labour'; (3) the Birth Narrative where Jesus' earthly parents appear to have been poor so as to afford 'the offering of the poor when his mother was purified in the Temple' (2.24).

Therefore, it is certain that there is a point of difference between Luke's community and the Pauline communities, and as a result it would be unreasonable that we should adopt indiscriminately the results of the sociological analysis of the Pauline communities made by Theissen and Meeks, and apply them without hesitation to analyse Luke's community. To put it another way, when we take into account the presence of both classes, that is, the poor and the rich in Luke's community, it would not be unreasonable to suppose that unlike the Pauline communities where, according to Theissen and Meeks, the extreme lower stratum of society is absent, Luke's community can be characterized as a society in which the wealthy and the destitute are mixed up.[128] In other words, although the extreme top of the contemporary social scale may be missing, it is probable that the extreme lower stratum of society is present in Luke's community.[129]

This conclusion on the Lukan *Sitz im Leben* appears fairly similar to that of Karris, so a need to compare these two opinions on the *Sitz im Leben* of Luke–Acts is desirable.

Karris's effort to discover the Lukan *Sitz im Leben* through the eyes of the theme of poor and rich yields valuable results in this regard. His view on the issue emphasizes 'the general Greco-Roman cultural background',[130] which is drawn initially from Acts 2.41-47 and 4.31-35, and confirmed one after another as the passages in the Gospel chosen for the theme are reviewed. I would accept in principle the view of Karris, but at the same time there is one element which makes me reluctant to accept it as a whole. That is the element of persecution in Luke's community, for which he enumerates as evidence 4.18, 6.20-23, 7.22 and 14.25-33. In response to this argument, I suppose that

128. Karris, 'Poor and Rich', p. 124.
129. Esler (*Community*, pp. 183-84) also attempts to compare Luke's community with that of Corinth, referring to the work of G. Theissen, but this attempt appears to be unreasonable, for he overlooks Theissen's point (*Social Setting*, p. 106) that there was no lower stratum of the society present in the Corinthian Church, which refutes Esler's position. Cf. Meeks, *Urban Christians*, p. 73. The theme of the poor and rich in Acts will be examined at length in Chapter 7.
130. Karris, 'Poor and Rich', p. 117. J. Dupont (*Les Béatitudes* [3 vols.; Paris: J. Gabalda, 1973]) and W. Schmithals (*Lukas*) also advocate the idea of persecution as an element in the *Sitz im Leben* of Luke's Gospel. Cf. Seccombe, *Possessions*, pp. 14-16; Karris, 'Poor and Rich', p. 115.

two factors are to be reckoned with; one is the interpretation of καθ᾽ ἡμέραν,[131] and the other is Jesus' exhortations to almsgiving themselves.

First, among the five occurrences of καθ᾽ ἡμέραν in Luke's Gospel, our primary concern is with Lk. 9.23, because Luke's insertion of καθ᾽ ἡμέραν in this verse[132] seems to indicate that the cross which can be identified with persecution does not need to be taken in a literal sense.[133] If Luke's community had been faced with imminent persecution, it would be very awkward for Luke to have inserted καθ᾽ ἡμέραν here, because it would seriously damage the force of the threat of the cross. In addition to this, Lk. 11.3 and 16.19 along with the seven occurrences in Acts would be thought of as allusions to the ongoing stage of the current situation rather than an anticipation of persecution to come in the near future. Secondly, it would be odd to suppose that people who are wealthy are asked to give alms, when they are confronted with persecution which could lead to a total loss of their own material possessions.[134]

Thus, because of these two reasons singled out above, I am not inclined to adopt the view of Karris on the Lukan *Sitz im Leben* as a whole, but content to accept it after deducting the element of persecution from it.

c. *Possible Differentiating Factors*

An objection may be raised against this conclusion about the social stratification of Luke's community: 'How can the constituency of both communities which may have shared similar urban settings in the Roman East be so different?' To put it another way, if we follow the general theory that Antioch in Syria is the possible setting of Luke's community,[135] the question may be put like this: 'Is the environmental

131. Lk. 9.23; 11.3; 16.19; 19.47; 22.53. Cf. Acts 2.46, 47; 3.2; 16.5; 17.11, 17 (κατὰ πᾶσαν ἡμέραν); 19.9.

132. This phrase is absent in its counterparts in Mark (8.34) and Matthew (10.38).

133. Cf. Beck, *Character*, p. 100; Evans, *Saint Luke*, p. 409; J.L. Houlden, *Ethics and the New Testament* (London: Mowbray, 1987), p. 57.

134. Cf. Heb. 10.32-39; Karris, 'Poor and Rich', p. 121.

135. Ellis, *Luke*, p. 54; Schweizer, *Luke*, p. 6. Cf. A.M. McNeille, *An Introduction to the Study of the New Testament* (Oxford: Clarendon Press, 1927), p. 39. The anti-Marcionite Prologue which is found in Eusebius (*Hist. Eccl.* 3.4) and Jerome (*De Vir. Illus.* 7) also identifies Luke as a native or resident of Antioch,

situation of Syrian Antioch different from that of the Pauline communities?'

Since Paul never mentions Syrian Antioch in his Epistles except in
Galatians, and after being sent forth from the Antioch church, the
major area of his ministry covers Galatia, Asia, Macedonia and Achaia,
and there remains a possibility that the situation of Syrian Antioch is
fairly different from that of the area where Paul travelled and worked.
To substantiate this possibility, we may point out a famine factor, a
prominent feature in antiquity which affected very greatly the socio-
economic situation of ancient societies, particularly that of the poor.[136]
Palestine is said to have suffered from frequent famines in the first
century CE, and afterwards (compare Acts 11.28).[137] So it is unlikely
that Syria situated just north of Palestine would not have been affected
by the same famines that occurred in Palestine.[138]

Alongside this historical aspect, we find that Luke has a particular
interest in famine, as can be seen from his use of λιμός.[139] These
references to λιμός by Luke may not be a direct indication to explain
the background of Luke's community as a whole, but that λιμός occurs
five times in his work cannot be simply regarded as incidental. Thus,
Luke's usage of λιμός and the historical setting of Luke's community

Syria. In this context, appealing to the Codex Bezae, a witness to the Western Text,
Geldenhuys, *Gospel*, p. 21, argues that 'Luke was possibly a native of Antioch'.

It is also interesting to notice that Luke manages to mention Antioch 13 times and
describes the church there very vividly (Acts 11.19-27; 13.1-2) (W. Manson, *Luke*,
p. xxix; White, *Luke's Case*, p. 11). For recent attempts to localize the place of
writing of Luke's works, see W.G. Kümmel, *Introduction to the New Testament*
(London: SCM Press, 1972), p. 151; Fitzmyer, *Gospel*, p. 57; W. Marxsen,
Introduction to the New Testament (Oxford: Basil Blackwell, 1968), p. 161.

136. More information on this feature will be discussed in Chapter 8.

137. Famines in Palestine would certainly affect concerned members of con-
tiguous countries, as Josephus makes clear in relation to the 47/48 CE famine in
Judaea (*Ant.* 20.51-53).

138. In this context, it should be noticed that Luke's community was *not per-
manently* under famine so much as continually vulnerable to fluctuations in agricul-
tural conditions and thus more aware of the threat of famine than some of Paul's
churches may have been. Then my corollary would be that Luke's community might
have been under famine when Luke wrote his two-volume work.

139. λιμός occurs five times in Luke–Acts; three times in Luke (4.25—the story
of the widow of Zarephath [cf. Esler, *Community*, p. 182]; 15.14, 17—the parable
of the Prodigal Son), and twice in Acts (7.11; 11.28), while only once each in Mark
and Matthew.

being taken together, our suggestion would be that Luke–Acts was written under the particular circumstances of famine which might have seriously affected the district to which Luke's community belonged. If we adopt this hypothesis, then it seems probable that the problem referred to above, that is, the outstanding difference between Luke's community and the Pauline communities, is resolved.

To conclude what I have discussed thus far, I should suggest that being faced with a natural disaster, such as a famine or bad harvest, which might have struck Luke's society at the time when he lived and wrote, with increased numbers of οἱ πτωχοί in that society,[140] Luke intended to write his works so as, among other reasons, to afford his congregation, particularly wealthy Christians, appropriate ethical teachings on how to deal with wealth and to behave themselves as Christians.

140. Theissen, *Social Setting*, p. 118.

Chapter 2

MARK'S VIEW OF DISCIPLESHIP

As the result of my presuppositions mentioned in the introduction as to the tools and methods used in pursuing the present study, before proceeding with Luke's idea of stewardship, it is relevant to take into account Mark's idea of discipleship and then to compare it with that of Luke in order to shed light on Luke's views on stewardship.

Thus my work in this chapter is based on the assumption that Mark is one of Luke's main sources in writing his Gospel,[1] so that it would be proper procedure to look into Mark's treatment of the discipleship motif in his Gospel, and after that we may be able to compare Luke's view of discipleship with that of Mark. By so doing, we can hope to appreciate what features are Luke's unique contribution to the theme of discipleship, which would eventually help us to grasp the main theme of this study, that is, Luke's idea of stewardship.

Prior to proceeding immediately with a study of the Markan material, however, it seems necessary to take into account the *Sitz im Leben* of Mark's Gospel since it appears essential to appreciate properly Mark's view on discipleship owing to its close connection with it.

1. *The* Sitz im Leben *of Mark's Gospel*

In order to find out the *Sitz im Leben* of Mark's Gospel, it is necessary to know where and when it was written. Many suggestions have been made to determine the place where Mark's Gospel was written and the time when it was done. Here, in order to avoid involvement in this matter beyond what is necessary for the present study, I feel it is sufficient to follow general assumptions on this matter held by most

---

1. The reason why only Mark is treated here as a major source of Luke's Gospel has been given in Chapter 1 (see pp. 34-36).

scholars in this field. This common opinion has, as we shall see, good supporting evidence.

a. *The Place of Writing*

With regard to the place where Mark wrote his Gospel, a dominant theory held by the majority of scholars in this field prefers Rome to Antioch[2] and Galilee.[3] To prove this theory, though dominant, two sorts of evidence require to be considered: external and internal evidence.

As for the external evidence that we can rely on in this case, first of all, we can point to the fragmentary anti-Marcionite prologue,[4] and secondly, to Clement of Alexandria's statement on Mark the Evangelist quoted by Eusebius,[5] both of which suggest Italy as the place for

2.   Antioch as the place of writing is favoured by Allen who suggested that Mark's Gospel was first composed in Aramaic at Jerusalem and later translated into Greek at Antioch, where John Mark joined St Paul's missionary journey, c. 44–47 CE (W.C. Allen, *The Gospel according to St Mark* [London: Macmillan, 1915], pp. 5-6; cf. R.P. Martin, *Mark: Evangelist and Theologian* [Exeter: Paternoster Press, 1972], p. 62). However, M. Hengel, *Studies in the Gospel of Mark* (London: SCM Press, 1985), criticizes this theory by arguing that it is drawn from 'the complete ignorance of the situation in Judaea between 66 and 69' (p. 28), concerning which he provides enormous evidence while explaining Mk 13 in the light of the historical situation of that time (pp. 21-28). The other point on which Hengel relies to refute the theory is the Syro-phoenician woman who comes to Jesus in the region of Tyre, Mk 7.24-30. He insists that 'if the Gospel came from Syria, Συροφοινίκισσα, which in that case would be geographically vague, would seem nonsensical' (p. 29).

3.   Galilee is advocated by W. Marxsen (*Mark the Evangelist* [London: SCM Press, 1969]), p. 66, who argues that Mark wrote his Gospel to persuade the Christians to leave Jerusalem and go to Pella in Galilee where they would meet their Lord. The difficulty this theory faces is in explaining why Mark translates Aramaic phrases (5.41; 7.34; 15.22, 34) and explains Jewish customs (7.3, 4, 11, 19).

4.   '. . . Mark [. . .] who is called 'stump-fingered', because he had rather small fingers in comparison with the stature of his body. He was the interpreter of Peter. After the death of Peter himself he wrote down this same gospel in the region of Italy' (cited from V. Taylor, *The Gospel according to St Mark* [London: Macmillan, 1952], p. 3). Other important patristic texts referring to the relationship between Mark and Peter and the authorship of the Second Gospel are collected and presented by Taylor, *Mark*, pp. 1-8.

5.   'When Peter had preached the word publicly in Rome and announced the gospel by the Spirit, those present, of whom there were many, besought Mark, since for a long time he had followed him and remembered what had been said, to record his

and in which Mark wrote his Gospel. And if it is possible to assume, with the majority of scholars, that Peter was martyred at Rome during the Neronian persecution, it may be likely that Mark, Peter's ἑρμη- νευτης according to Papias,[6] wrote down his Gospel responding to the Church's request to preserve what Peter had proclaimed concerning the words and deeds of Jesus as her Lord.[7]

With regard to the internal evidence which indicates Rome as the place of writing, there is much to be pointed out.

1. *Evidence Indicating a Non-Palestinian Setting.* First, Mark is seen to have a preference for Latinized words, which he makes use of not infrequently in writing his Gospel. The following are some examples of this: (a) in relation to the army, Mark uses λεγιών (*legio*; 5.9, 15), πραιτώριον (*praetorium*; 15.16), and κεντυρίων (*centurio*; 15.39, 44); (b) concerning the courts, he employs Greek transliterations of σπεκουλάτωρ (*speculator*; 6.27), φραγελλόω (*flagellare*; 15.15); (c) as for commerce, δηνάριον (*denarius*; 12.15) and κοδράντης (*quadrans*; 12.42) are employed. Here, μόδιος (*modius*; 4.21), ξέστης (*sextarius*; 7.4)[8] and κῆνσος (*census*; 12.14) are to be noticed as well. Among these terms, two in particular attract our attention, that is, *quadrans* and *praetorium*, which Mark adds in explanation of common Greek expressions for the interest of his Gentile Christians, because

---

words. Mark did this and communicated the gospel to those who made request of him' (*Hist. Eccl.* 6.14.6-7).

6.   Eusebius, *Hist. Eccl.* 3.39.15; Cf. Irenaeus (c. 175 CE), *Adv. Haer.* 3.1.2, 'And after the death of these (Peter and Paul), Mark, the disciple and interpreter of Peter, also transmitted to us in writing the things preached by Peter'.

7.   This does not mean that the death of Peter was the sole 'precipitating cause' of the writing of the Gospel. It might have been a major cause, but should not be regarded as decisive. Possibly the delay of the παρουσία would also have been a precipitating cause. Cf. E. Best, *Mark: The Gospel as Story* (Edinburgh: T. & T. Clark, 1988), p. 28.

8.   ξέστης is said to be a corruption of the Latin *sextarius* which appears in rabbinic literature as a loanword and implies liquid capacity, roughly one pint or half a litre. From this original meaning it comes to mean simply *pitcher, jug* without reference to the amount contained (BAGD, p. 550); cf. C.E.B. Cranfield, *The Gospel according to Saint Mark* (Cambridge: Cambridge University Press, 1963), p. 234; Taylor, *Mark*, p. 336.

the *quadrans* in particular is known not to have been in circulation in the Roman East at that time.[9]

Secondly, there are also to be noted in Mark a few Latin expressions which lie behind the Greek:[10] 14.65, *verberibus eum acceperunt*;[11] 15.15, *satisfacere*;[12] 15.19, *genua ponere*.

Thirdly, that Mark regularly translates into Greek the Aramaic words and phrases possibly transmitted from his sources may also demonstrate the Gospel's orientation to non-Palestinian readers (3.17; 5.41; 7.11, 34; 14.36; 15.22, 34).[13]

Fourthly, Mark appears to use the Roman method of reckoning time which consists of four watches of the night instead of the Jewish reckoning which consists of three watches of the night (6.48; 13.35).[14]

Fifthly, it is highly significant that Mark explains Jewish customs and practices that he might have thought were difficult for his Gentile readers to understand due to their cultural unfamiliarity (7.3-4; 14.12; 15.42).

Sixthly, it is noteworthy that Mark assumes Roman marriage law (10.12) that may reflect the legal situation prevalent in Rome and elsewhere in the Roman West.[15]

---

9. W.M. Ramsey, 'On Mark iii 42', *ExpTim* 10 (1898–99), pp. 232, 336.

10. A.E.J. Rawlinson, *The Gospel according to St Mark* (Westminster Commentary; London: Methuen, 1960), p. xxxiii; H. Anderson, *The Gospel of Mark* (NCB; London: Oliphants, 1976), p. 27; Martin, *Evangelist*, p. 64.

11. Cranfield, *Mark*, p. 446.

12. Taylor, *Mark*, pp. 583-84; Cranfield, *Mark*, p. 452.

13. Against this position, i.e. to depend on Latinisms and Aramaic formulae in the Gospel for determining the place of writing as Rome, it may be argued that these translated Latinisms and translations of Aramaic expressions could show only a bilingual community with slight preference for Latin or a western community somewhere in the Roman Empire. However, the similar accumulation of Latinisms in *The Shepherd of Hermas*, c. 170–210, written in Rome, is probably significant. Thus, Hengel, having this point in mind, makes the point that 'these (numerous Latinisms) cannot simply be dismissed with a reference to the language of the Roman administration in Palestine' (*Studies*, p. 29).

14. The Roman watches are morning, the third hour, the sixth, and evening (F.C. Grant, *The Gospels: Their Origin and their Growth* [London: Faber & Faber, 1957], p. 114).

15. According to Jewish law, it is not permitted for a wife to divorce, so v. 12 has been explained as an 'adaptation of Jesus' statement to the legal situation which prevailed in Rome and elsewhere in the Empire' (W.L. Lane, *The Gospel of Mark* [NICNT; Grand Rapids: Eerdmans, 1978], p. 358). Cf. Taylor, *Mark*, p. 420; Martin,

2. *Evidence Indicating Rome*. First, Mark's mention of Alexander and Rufus (15.21) is also noteworthy because Rufus in fact appears in Rom. 16.13 as the name of one of the church members at Rome. Thus it is probable that here Mark inserts the name, Rufus, along with his brother's name, which are not shown in Matthew's and Luke's version of this story, for they might have been well known to the members of the Roman church.[16]

Secondly, 1 Pet. 5.13 is also of significance. In this passage, we may be able to see a certain link between the Christian church in Rome and Mark the author of the Second Gospel. It is generally recognized that 1 Peter is designed for encouraging and strengthening the Christians in Asia Minor facing the hardships of persecution,[17] and 'Babylon' here seems to be used as a sort of code word for Rome.[18] Therefore, the relation between Mark and the church in Rome in this passage

Evangelist, p. 65; F.J. Matera, *What Are They Saying about Mark?* (New York: Paulist Press, 1987), p. 15.

16. Taylor, *Mark*, p. 588; Martin, *Evangelist*, p. 64; Lane, *Mark*, p. 563.

17. C. Bigg, *Commentary of St Peter and St Jude* (ICC; Edinburgh: T. & T. Clark, 1969), pp. 24-33; F.W. Beare, *The First Epistle of Peter* (Oxford: Basil Blackwell, 1947), pp. 6-8; J.N.D. Kelly, *A Commentary on the Epistles of Peter and Jude* (BNTC; London: A. & C. Black, 1969), pp. 5-11; C.E.B. Cranfield, *I and II Peter and Jude* (Torch Bible Commentary; London: SCM, 1960), pp. 17-18; E. Best, *1 Peter* (NCB; London: Oliphants, 1971), pp. 13-14. The persecution motif is mentioned on four occasions in 1 Peter such as in 1.6; 3.13-17; 4.12-19; 5.9.

18. The majority of commentators identify ἡ ἐν Βαβυλῶνι συνεκλεκτή with the church in Rome, interpreting this phrase metaphorically: Beare, *Epistle*, p. 183; Cranfield, *Peter and Jude*, p. 139; Best, *1 Peter*, pp. 178-79; Lane, *Mark*, p. 15.

But it is worthwhile reviewing this explication. (1) ἡ. . . συνεκλεκτή could be Peter's wife, but if this is the case it would be awkward to introduce her in this context, as 'she would hardly have been so well-known over so wide an area that such a vague reference would identify her' (Best, *1 Peter*, p. 177). (2) In favour of Babylon as a cryptic reference to Rome, Kelly, *Commentary*, pp. 218-19, enumerates a variety of material showing this phenomenon in contemporary and later Judaism, and also the Christian Church itself; 2 Bar. 11.1-2; 67.7; 2 Esd. 3.1-2, 28; *Sib. Or.* 5.143, 157-58; the rabbinic literature (Str-B, III, p. 816); Rev. 14.8; 16.19-18.24.

In relation to this point, Bigg, *Commentary*, p. 197, puts a note that 'ℵ after Βαβυλῶνι adds ἐκκλεσία: the Vulgate has "ecclesia quae est in Babylone", and the same addition is found in the Peshito, in the Armenian, in Theophylact, and Oecumenius'.

appears to lend some weight to our preference for Rome as the place of writing the Second Gospel.[19]

To sum up what we have discussed thus far, when we accumulate the external and internal evidence that has been enumerated so far, it appears that Rome is a more appropriate place than Antioch or Galilee, and that Mark wrote his Gospel for the benefit of the Gentile Christians at Rome.[20]

b. *The Time of Writing*
It has been generally held that Mark's Gospel was written during 64–70 CE, after the Neronian persecution caused by the disastrous fire in Rome in July, 64 CE, but before the destruction of the Jerusalem Temple in 70 CE.[21] In determining the date when Mark's Gospel was written, as the external evidence, the anti-Marcionite Prologue to the Gospel, Papias's and Irenaeus's statements which are cited above are valuable in this case, too. That is to say, Mark, as Peter's interpreter, was committed to writing his Gospel after the death of Peter who is assumed to have been killed during the Neronian persecution. Thus it might be understood that the Gospel was recorded from 64 CE onwards

19. Relying on 'a strong tradition going back to Papias' (Eusebius, *Hist. Eccl.* 3.19.15), scholars in this area agree that Mark here is Peter's interpreter who wrote the earliest Gospel: 'His is thus a suitable name to appear in a work emanating from a Petrine school' (Best, *1 Peter*, p. 179). Cf. H.B. Swete, *The Gospel according to St Mark* (London: Macmillan, 1902), pp. xx-xxi; Taylor, *Mark*, pp. 30-31; Kelly, *Mark*, p. 220; A.R.C. Leaney, *The Letters of Peter and Jude* (Cambridge Bible Commentary; Cambridge: Cambridge University Press, 1967), pp. 72-73; Lane, *Mark*, p. 21.

20. Rawlinson, *Gospel*, p. xxx; D.E. Nineham, *Saint Mark* (The Pelican Gospel Commentaries; London: A. & C. Black, 1963), pp. 42-43; Hengel, *Studies*, pp. 28-30; R.E. Brown and J.P. Meier, *Antioch and Rome* (London: Geoffrey Chapman, 1983), p. 197; Best, *Story*, p. 35; C.D. Marshall, *Faith as a Theme in Mark's Narrative* (Cambridge: Cambridge University Press, 1989), p. 6; Matera, *What Are They*, p. 15.

21. In timing the writing of the Gospel, there is also another well-known argument maintained by S.G.F. Brandon (*Jesus and the Zealots* [Manchester: Manchester University Press, 1967]), pp. 221-82, which points to 71–72 CE, after the Flavian triumph in 71 CE over insurgent Judaea. The main cause by which Brandon wants to fix the time at that period is his allegation that Mark's Gospel has an apologetic purpose, written to vindicate incipient Christianity to the Roman authorities in order to get favour from them. For details of the counter-argument, see Martin, *Evangelist*, pp. 75-78 and Best, *Story*, pp. 31-34.

but before 70 CE because of Mark's prophetic description of the destruction of the Temple (13.14).

In relation to the interpretation of 13.14, Hengel, *Studies*, argues that this verse along with Mk 13.2 is not to be regarded as a description of a certain fulfilled historical event. The basis of his argument is that first, as external evidence, apart from the fortresses of Herodian and Massada, other cities in Judaea, possibly including Jerusalem, did not face sudden occupation and destruction (p. 16), and secondly, as internal evidence, he pinpoints ἑστηκότα (13.14), the masculine perfect participle, saying that it 'points more to the beginning of a permanent state of affairs associated with a specific person' (p. 18), who, according to Hengel's argument, is the Antichrist portrayed as τὸ βδέλυγμα τῆς ἐρημώσεως (13.14) by Mark in the text. From this reasoning Hengel eventually comes to the conclusion that 'The decisive verse Mark 13.14 therefore also has nothing to do with the siege or capture of the temple by Titus in 70' (p. 18). Therefore, in Hengel's view, 13.14-20 does not reflect 'any authentic historical situation', but rather 'reproduces earlier pictures of apocalyptic terror of the kind that had been in circulation since the Maccabean revolt, expressing the experiences of the people of the land under foreign invasion' (p. 17). In consequence, Hengel does not accept the view that 13.14 has taken place (p. 20).

On the grounds of this argument Hengel rejects the view that the Gospel was written after 70 CE. Rather, relying on external material, such as the works of Tacitus, Suetonius, and Eusebius, as well as *Sibylline Oracle* 4, and Revelation, Hengel makes a case that the Gospel was probably written in 69 CE: 'It presumably came into being in the politically turbulent time after the murder of Nero and Galba and before the renewal of the Jewish war under Titus, i.e. say between the winter of 68/69 and the winter of 69/70' (p. 28).

In order to claim this exact time for the writing of the Gospel, he argues that, even though the disastrous fire at Rome in 64 CE entailed harsh persecution of Christians in Rome, it was not considered a large incident when the huge territory of the Roman Empire at that time is allowed for. So up to 68 CE, he asserts, the whole world of the Roman Empire enjoyed a relatively peaceful time, which was changed dramatically after Nero's suicide in 68 CE. That is, after 68 CE, a series of incidents, such as earthquakes, famines, and big fires, were reported to have happened throughout the Roman Empire (p. 23).

Also after Nero's death, a rumour spread in the Roman Empire, according to the ancient historians, that Nero was about to return in order to rule over 'the kingdom of Jerusalem',[22] which, Hengel argues, had a considerable impact on Christians. Thus making use of this historical evidence and seeking biblical support from 2 Thess. 2.3-5, Rev. 12.6, and Jn 11.48, Hengel builds up his contention that τὸ βδέλυγμα τῆς ἐρημώσεως was a Nero redivivus, the Antichrist (p. 28), who would stand at 'the place which is not his due' (ὅπου οὐ δεῖ; 13.14) in the near future. But he insists that the Gospel was written before 70 CE, owing to the lack of specific reference to the destruction of the Temple in the Markan text.[23]

c. *The Social Context of Mark's Gospel*
To support this view on the date of writing, it would be helpful to take into account the social context of Mark's Gospel. This may be called internal evidence, intertwined with the external evidence by its nature, which is focused on the persecution motif in Mark's Gospel. If this motif is to be found frequently, it would enable us to infer the social milieu of Mark's community as one of persecution.

In this connection, first we have to look at the proportion that the Passion Narrative occupies in the Gospel, which distinguishes it from that of Luke and Matthew. Mark's Passion Narrative begins at 8.27[24]

22. Suetonius, *Nero.* 40.2; *Vesp.* 4.5; Josephus, *War* 6.312; Tacitus, *Hist.* 5.13.2.

23. With respect to the destruction of the Temple at 13.2, Hengel, *Studies,* asserts that it is in line with a long prehistory of tradition, saying that 'In one way or another the destruction (of the Temple) was an expression of divine judgement' (p. 15). And also referring to 14.58 in which those who accused Jesus of planning to destroy the temple are depicted as false witnesses, and to the conspicuous difference between Mk 13.2 and its parallel in Lk. 19.41-44, he does not accept the idea that 'Mark 13.2 is only conceivable as a *vaticinium ex eventu*' (p. 14).

24. There is a question as to where the Passion Narrative begins in Mark's Gospel. Strictly speaking, it appears to begin at 14.1 after Jesus enters Jerusalem. But what is to be noted in Mark's Gospel is that from 8.27 where the first prediction of Jesus about his passion and death is recorded, the suffering and death of Jesus, of which predictions are repeated three times, becomes a predominant theme in Mark's idea of discipleship (Cf. Best, *Story,* pp. 66, 44; M.D. Hooker, *The Gospel according to St Mark* (BNTC; London: A. & C. Black, 1991), p. 88; M. Kähler, *The So-called Historical Jesus and the Historical Biblical Christ* (Philadelphia: Fortress Press, 1970), p. 80.

Thus what I want to hold in this connection is to include Jesus' predictions of his

and continues until the end, comprising nearly nine chapters, which occupies approximately 56 per cent of the material in Mark's Gospel,[25] while the Passion Narrative in Matthew starts off with Mt. 16.12 and continues till the end, comprising nearly nine chapters too, but in fact it occupies roughly 46 per cent of the whole material in Matthew. The case of Luke's Gospel is somewhat different. Although his Passion Narrative begins at 9.18, we should deduct eight chapters, since Luke comprises the long Travel Narrative which in general is absent in Mark and Matthew; then the Passion Narrative itself comprises just eight chapters, which occupies roughly 33 per cent of the material in Luke. What emerges from this comparison is that proportionately more room is allocated to the Passion Narrative by Mark than by the other Evangelists.

Secondly, several references related to this motif[26] can be pointed out. Particularly significant is 10.30 which can be seen to attest the immediate relevance of the persecution motif in Mark's Gospel. His addition, μετὰ διωγμῶν, absent in both Luke and Matthew, is a clear token to indicate the *Sitz im Leben* of Mark's Gospel which was threatened with inexorable persecution.[27]

Thirdly, attention should be paid to 4.17, which indicates that Christians may fall away from their faith because of persecution and tribulation (θλῖψις and διωγμός).[28]

Fourthly, 13.9-13 speaks of the fate that Christians would suffer in persecution because of Jesus.[29]

suffering and death in the boundary of the Passion Narrative, for it does not seem reasonable to isolate the predictions from their fulfilment later in the Gospel. Consequently, here by the term 'Passion Narrative' we mean to take a broad view, and as for the material describing the events of Jesus' ministry during his last week at Jerusalem (11.1–16.8), we may call this the 'Jerusalem Narrative'.

25. Kähler, *Historical Jesus*, argues somewhat 'provocatively' that 'one could call the Gospels passion narratives with extended introductions' (p. 80). Gundry, *Survey*, p. 77, also states that Mark's Gospel can be called 'a passion account with a prologue'.

26. Mk 8.31, 34-38; 9.31; 10.30, 33, 45; 13.9-13. Cf. Taylor, *Mark*, pp. 31-32; Martin, *Evangelist*, pp. 65-66; Hengel, *Studies*, pp. 23, 134.

27. T. Baumeister, *Die Anfänge der Theologie des Martyriums* (Münster: Aschendorff, 1980), p. 89; Hengel, *Studies*, p. 134; Best, *Story*, p. 53.

28. Baumeister, *Die Anfänge*, p. 89; Hengel, *Studies*, p. 134; Best, *Story*, p. 53.

29. Taking heed to the fact that ἕνεκεν ἐμοῦ in 13.9 occurs again as in 8.35 and 10.29, Baumeister, *Anfänge*, p. 87, regards it as Mark's own addition related to the persecution motif. And particularly 13.12, he argues, clearly exposes 'eine

Fifthly, other passages relating to the persecution motif, although they have almost exact parallels in Matthew, and some in Luke, may help us, in comparison, to determine the life setting of the Markan community.

In the case of Luke, first of all, it is quite clear that Luke appears to be tendentious in toning down the persecution motif in Mark. For instance, (1) Luke leaves out θλῖψις and διωγμός in Lk. 8.13 from the Markan text (Mk 4.17).[30] (2) In Lk. 9.23, by adding καθ' ἡμέραν into the saying taken from Mark (Mk 8.34), Luke is seen to allegorize the significance of bearing one's cross which to Mark and his readers seems to have been a literal reality.[31] (3) In reference to the signs of the Great Tribulation, such as Mk 13.9-13/Lk. 21.12-19, what is different between the two Synoptists is Luke's unique insertion of v. 18, 'But not a hair of your head will perish', which appears a positive assurance of Jesus toning down the threat of horrible torment in the future.[32] (4) In line with this element, in the words Jesus uttered, Luke omits the last words of Jesus on the cross, Ελωι Ελωι λεμὰ σαβαχθανι, preserved in Mark (15.34). This final sentence uttered by Jesus would have meant so much to Mark's community because it was also exposed to harsh persecution. Thus this omission by Luke seems in line with his insertion of Lk. 21.18. In summing up this comparison in relation to the persecution motif, we may suggest that Luke's community may not have been confronted with such harsh persecution as that which threatened Mark's community.

Secondly, in the case of Matthew's Gospel, what emerges from comparison between Mark and Matthew in view of the persecution motif is their apparent similarity. Except for Mt. 19.29 (Mk 10.30),

Verfolgungssituation' (p. 88). Cf. Best, *Story*, p. 53; Hengel, *Studies*, p. 23; Anderson, *Mark*, pp. 294-95.

30. Some scholars are inclined to argue that πειρασμός in Luke is more or less similar to θλῖψις and διωγμός in Mark (I.H. Marshall, *Commentary*, p. 326; B.H.P. Thompson, *The Gospel according to Luke* [New Clarendon Bible; Oxford: Clarendon Press, 1979], p. 135; A. Plummer, *St Luke* [ICC; Edinburgh: T. & T. Clark, 1922], p. 221), but it is also not to be dismissed that πειρασμός in Luke is a more general expression than θλῖψις and διωγμός in Mark (Evans, *Saint Luke*, p. 375; Ellis, *Luke*, p. 129).

31. Cf. Evans, *Saint Luke*, p. 409; I.H. Marshall, *Commentary*, pp. 373-74.

32. Creed, *Gospel*, p. 256. Plummer's suggestion, *Luke*, p. 480, that this verse ought to be understood spiritually rather than literally is also supported by I.H. Marshall (*Commentary*, p. 769).

all other passages saturated with the persecution motif in Mark are present in Matthew, although the contexts in which some of the passages are placed are not always similar.[33] Although this difference is not to be dismissed with ease, at the same time it ought not to be dwelled on too much. On the whole, it may be safe to state that though the degree that each community would have been involved in persecution may have been slightly different, yet each community would have been confronted with persecution one way or another.[34] Therefore, the fact that the persecution motif is also prevalent in Matthew should not be claimed against the view that the Markan community was faced with severe persecution. In a word, it should not be regarded as conflicting but as compatible evidence.

d. *Summary and Conclusion*

From what we have discussed thus far, we can arrive at the conclusion that the community for which Mark wrote the Gospel of Jesus Christ was probably in the circumstances of, or fearing in anticipation, severe persecution, suffering, even martyrdom, such as their Teacher Jesus himself suffered;[35] this is probably best located in Rome, after the Neronian persecution and before the destruction of the Temple at Jerusalem, approximately from 65–69 CE. Thus, we may suggest that one of the purposes which Mark bore in mind in writing his Gospel was to console and strengthen Christians in his community trapped in

33. For instance, Matthew puts a famous persecution passage in Mk 13.9, a part of the apocalyptic signs which would happen in the final days, into the context of mission instructions of Jesus addressed to his disciples (Mt. 10.17-18). This difference between them may suggest that in Mark's community all members as a whole would have been confronted with persecution, but in Matthew's community persecution would have been confined to a part of the membership, particularly the wandering preachers.

34. It is generally acknowledged that Matthew's community was under considerable pressure from the synagogue. For the details of the persecution motif in Matthew's Gospel, see Baumeister, *Anfänge*, pp. 90-107.

35. After the persecution of Nero onwards for quite a long time, persecution of Christians by the Roman authorities became 'a matter of course'. It would be probable that when Mark wrote his Gospel, the Christians in Rome who had just escaped the harsh persecution by Nero were still fearing persecution of all kinds exercised by the Roman state. See Hengel, *Studies*, pp. 23-24.

the critical situation of dangerous persecution, and also, at the same time, to warn the would-be apostates in this critical moment.[36]

In this connection, it appears that to achieve this goal of pastoral care, Mark made use of the theme of discipleship, which is highlighted distinctively in the vocabulary and structure of the Gospel. Thus it would be appropriate at this stage to explore this theme in detail.

2. *Methods and Procedure*

a. *Methods*

In identifying the theme of discipleship in Mark, one may have to take into consideration various sorts of methods, because it is the earliest Gospel, without extant sources with which we can compare it.[37] So we know that redaction criticism has been applied to Mark only after it had been applied to both Luke and Matthew. One of the main reasons for this late approach of redaction criticism to Mark is the difficulty of identifying pre-Markan material which could be a source used by Mark; how can one be confident which material should belong to tradition or to Mark's redaction, and what are our criteria in threshing wheat from chaff among the material preserved in Mark?[38]

Although many have carried out studies detecting the theme of discipleship in Mark employing their own criteria of redaction criticism, and have yielded some valuable fruit in this area so far, however, because of the methodological problem posed above, their findings

36. In this sense, Mark's Gospel is characterized as 'pastoral' by some scholars in this area (Best, *Story*, pp. 51, 93; M.D. Hooker, *The Message of Mark* [London: Epworth, 1983], p. 21; Lane, *Mark*, p. 15).

37. Instead of a monopoly of redaction criticism on the study of the Second Gospel, C.C. Black (*The Disciples according to Mark* [JSNTSup, 27; Sheffield: JSOT Press, 1989]), pp. 241-48, suggests that other methodological tools, such as historical criticism, tradition criticism, literary criticism, and reader–response criticism, as well as redaction criticism, should be employed for better understanding of the Gospel. Cf. Matera, *What Are They*, pp. 1-3; C.D. Marshall, *Faith*, p. 14.

38. J.D. Kingsbury ('The Gospel of Mark in Current Research', *RelSRev* 5 [1979]), pp. 101-107 (104), puts his critical assessment of Markan redaction criticism as follows: 'The debate over the alleged creativity of Mark as a redactor is largely the result of the inability of scholars to reach a consensus on the vexing problem of separating tradition from redaction'. For redaction criticism's inability to deal with 'the literary and theological integrity of Mark's Gospel', C.D. Marshall, *Faith*, pp. 8-14, notes that literary criticism has emerged as its promising alternative, particularly in America. Cf. C.C. Black, *Disciples*, Introduction, pp. 17-22.

may have to be carefully reconsidered in the light of criticisms made against the redaction-critical explorations of the theme of discipleship in Mark's Gospel. For this reason, we may not be able to take for granted the yield that the forerunners in this field left behind in applying redaction criticism to Mark.

Instead of redaction criticism, recently many are disposed to develop literary or narrative criticism as an appropriate method for evaluating the Markan theme of discipleship. Thus we know some valuable results are in our hands, and still more are coming.[39] However, this is not to say that narrative or literary criticism has replaced redaction criticism completely. It cannot be judged too simply like this, because these newborn criticisms themselves are not to be labelled as mature enough to cope adequately with every problem raised in the study of Mark's Gospel. It means that they cannot provide answers to all questions posed in the study of the Gospels, and Mark's Gospel in particular.

In this state of affairs, there is no definite solution as to the methods that can be rightly and with confidence employed in the study of the Gospel: compromise seems to be the best solution. That is, in delving into Mark's theology, one should be impartial in choosing appropriate tools to deal with the questions in mind. Thus my position on the methodology is that I would share with redaction criticism an interest in the original historical context of Mark's Gospel, but remain sceptical of the attempts of redaction criticism to distinguish between Markan and pre-Markan material.

Accordingly, in what follows we will be engaged in the discovery of the Markan theme of discipleship making use of the fruits yielded from both redaction criticism and narrative criticism, with allowance for their drawbacks, too. A most important feature common to both criticisms is the text itself. Although redaction criticism seeks to delve into pre-Markan material as well, nonetheless it starts from, and returns to, the final form of the text. So it would be an appropriate procedure for us to put emphasis on the text itself, no matter what methods are being employed.

b. *Procedure*

Recently the theme of discipleship has been explored heavily by quite a few scholars in this area, highlighting its role as a major theological motif preserved in the Second Gospel. Thus such scholars in this field

39. C.D. Marshall, *Faith*, p. 14.

as Best, Schweizer and Stock tend to interpret the Gospel with consistency in the light of the discipleship motif, and apart from these scholars, a number of other scholars, such as Meye, Weeden, Tyson, Tannehill, Melbourne, Hawkin, Keck and Black also express their particular interest in the disciples in Mark, mainly attempting to explain the reason why Mark portrays them in a poorer light.[40] Accordingly, the theme of discipleship has now become an important subject in the theology of Mark arresting interpreters' particular attention.

While keeping this broad discussion in view, what I want to pursue in dealing with this subject is the connection between the discipleship motif and the predominant persecution motif. It would be awkward to assert that one of the important theological motifs in the Gospel does not reflect properly the historical and social setting of the community to which it was devoted. Thus it will be necessary to bear in mind the outcome of our observation on the *Sitz im Leben* of Mark's Gospel in exploring the discipleship motif in the Second Gospel.

40. Among them J. Tyson ('The Blindness of the Disciples', *JBL* 80 [1961], pp. 261-68) and T.J. Weeden ('The Heresy that necessitated Mark's Gospel', *ZNW* 59 [1969], pp. 145-58; *Mark—Traditions in Conflict* [Philadelphia: Fortress Press, 1971]) are well known for arguing that Mark's Gospel is a polemical writing against the historical disciples.

First, Tyson's position is that Mark's portrayal of the disciples must be seen as a literary device in the service of a polemic against a conservative Jewish-Christian group in Palestine, i.e. the family of Jesus and the disciples, which placed no positive meaning on Jesus' death, held to the long-established Jewish practices, and rejected the necessity of the Gentile mission. Therefore Tyson insisted that one of the reasons Mark wrote his Gospel was to attack the position of the reactionary group and its leaders who were represented by the disciples in the Gospel.

Secondly, assuming Mark as a creative theologian and using redaction criticism proficiently, Weeden, *Conflict*, intends to explicate this feature of the negative image of the disciples by way of another sort of polemic against the twelve disciples who represent a heretical group in Mark's community that threatened its faith. Thus in order to attack his opponents, Mark, according to Weeden, attacks the twelve disciples in every way possible, for which the negative picture of the disciples is utilized.

One vital flaw that is to be exposed is that both scholars do not take seriously into account the *Sitz im Leben* of Mark's Gospel. In such a critical situation as the persecution with which the readers of the Gospel were confronted, what is the use of attacking the disciples who might have been consoling and encouraging the community as its leaders? In this connection, therefore, it seems to me that there is less room for advocating Mark as a polemicist than as a pastor.

As pointed out above, the discipleship motif in Mark is regarded commonly as being related to one of the most notable features in the Gospel, that is, the blindness of the disciples. As Stanton remarks,[41] if we look at the Gospel, we cannot fail to notice that in Mark the disciples are portrayed in a bad light, and it becomes much clearer as we compare Mark with the other Gospels. Thus it would be appropriate to build on this basis our argument which is to identify Mark's idea of discipleship.

Consequently, first of all, we will have to look into the text focusing on what is written by Mark with respect to the disciples and discipleship, and secondly, we will have to deal with one puzzling problem in Mark, that is, the negative image of the disciples. But at the same time, it would also be relevant to look at how favourably the disciples are treated by Jesus in Mark, for it may reinforce the effect that Mark desires to create by depicting the disciples negatively.

3. *Features of Markan Discipleship: Following Jesus' Way*

By and large the Gospel may be divided into three sections. The first and the second sections are clearly divided by the event of Caesarea Philippi (8.27-30) and the third section mainly deals with the final events of Jesus' life in Jerusalem (11.1–16.8).

The first section (1.1–8.21) begins with a thrice-repeated general description of Jesus' activity (1.14-15; 1.32-34; 1.39), followed by the call (3.13-19) or sending of his disciples (6.7-13). The entire first section of the Gospel exhibits the blindness of the Pharisees and scribes (2.6-7, 16, 24; 3.1-6, 22-30), of Jesus' fellow citizens (6.1-6), and even of his own disciples (4.40-41; 6.52; 7.17-18; 8.14-21). The second section of the Gospel (8.22–10.52) begins and ends with the healing of blind men whose eyes are opened by the miraculous acts of Jesus (8.22-26; 10.46-52). What makes this section prominent is the predictions of Jesus on his forthcoming passion and death and his teaching on discipleship in particular. So in Mark most of the explicit teaching of Jesus is given in this part, after Peter's confession at Caesarea Philippi, and that teaching is devoted especially to discipleship.[42] The third section

---

41. G.N. Stanton, *The Gospels and Jesus* (Oxford: Oxford University Press, 1989), p. 46.

42. For this reason, E. Schweizer (*Jesus* [London: SCM Press, 1971], p. 131), notes that 'This whole second period is dominated by the notion of discipleship'.

is composed of the Jerusalem Narrative and the Easter story (11.1–16.8), but the Jerusalem Narrative which focuses on Jesus' suffering and death appears rather more predominant. One of the most interesting features of Mark's Gospel is found in the end of the Gospel; it ends at the young man's commands to the women to go and tell Jesus' disciples that Jesus is going to Galilee before them, and their unexpected trembling and astonishment (16.7-8). Therefore, from the beginning to the end Mark's Gospel as a whole may be depicted as the Gospel of discipleship.[43]

a. *Discipleship Foreshadowed: A Stage of Preparation*
As mentioned above, the most essential teaching about discipleship appears in the central section of the Gospel, but this section is by nature not to be separated from the rest of the Gospel. Thus even in the first section of the Gospel we are able to notice the notion of discipleship. But what is to be noticed here is that the earliest notion of discipleship does not so much function in its own right as forebode major teaching which will appear later on, particularly in the central section.

The first incident that belongs to this category is Jesus' calling of the first disciples and Levi, the tax collector. That Jesus' calling of the first disciples, Peter, Andrew, James, and John (1.16-20) is singled out as his first activity that opens his public ministry appears to have considerable weight in its own right when we view this incident in the perspective of the whole structure of the Gospel narrative. The calling of the disciples appears to be the first priority of Jesus' ministry, and this in turn reminds us of Mark's particular interest in the disciples and discipleship. In 2.13-14, Jesus also calls Levi, the tax collector, to follow him, and responding to Jesus' call, Levi immediately follows him forsaking his secular, profitable job. What emerges as an element of discipleship from these two scenes of calling of disciples is that he who wants to follow Jesus should break with old ties, such as relationships to family and material possessions, for he is invited to enter into a new relationship with Jesus as his Teacher.[44]

This motif of 'breaking away' appears again in the purposes of Jesus' appointment of the Twelve (3.14-15), in particular in 3.14: ἵνα

---

43. Matera, *What Are They*, p. 38.

44. E. Schweizer, *Lordship and Discipleship* (London: SCM Press, 1986), pp. 13, 20; G. Bornkamm, *Jesus of Nazareth* (London: Hodder & Stoughton, 1984), p. 146.

ὦσιν μετ' αὐτοῦ. The fact that this is a unique expression exclusive to Mark, and absent in its counterparts in Luke and Matthew reminds us that this phrase conveys Mark's particular concern on this point. A lesson this feature can bring about in respect of discipleship would be that followers of Jesus are supposed to be with him, namely, to be found beside him in any circumstance and situation. Therefore, being with Jesus implies in fact a new relationship entailing the severance of any other ties. In sum, in these incidents, that is, the calling of the disciples and choosing of the Twelve, we may come to see that these stories reveal a stage of preparation that he who wants to follow Jesus has to make, that is, to break with other ties and relationships in order to enter into a new relationship with Jesus. This motif appears again later on in the central section as one of the major elements of discipleship: 10.28-30[45] and 10.21-22.

To Mark this motif of breaking off old ties for participating in a new relationship would have been significant for his community, because it would be possible that in such circumstances as persecution Christians fail to be followers of Jesus because they cling very much to the old ties of their relationship to their family (compare 10.9-13; 13.12) and material possessions (compare 10.17-22). And also by the unique expression, ἵνα ὦσιν μετ' αὐτοῦ, Mark appears to appeal to the members of his community that whatever their circumstance turns out to be, that is, whether or not it deteriorates so that they may be going to face suffering and death because of their Christian faith, they must be with him and not abandon or forsake him.

b. *Following Jesus' Way*
It is generally acknowledged in respect of discipleship that the central section of Mark, 8.22–10.52, is carefully constructed for it.[46] This section depicts mainly a journey of Jesus and his disciples towards Jerusalem and the cross, which is bracketed by two incidents of the healing of the blind men. This section falls roughly into three parts,

45. Taking heed of the tenses of ἀφήκαμεν (aorist) and ἠκολουθήκαμεν (perfect) used in Peter's confession (10.28), Schweizer, *Lordship*, p. 15, remarks that 'This also demonstrates that the latter (following which is continuing) is the decisive act to which the severance of ties is merely meant to be a preliminary'.

46. Baumeister, *Anfänge*, p. 81; E. Best, *Disciples and Discipleship* (Edinburgh: T. & T. Clark, 1986), p. 2; Lane, *Mark*, p. 292; A. Stock, *Call to Discipleship* (Wilmington: Michael Glazier, 1982), p. 140; Matera, *What Are They*, p. 47.

each of which begins with a prediction by Jesus of his suffering, death, and resurrection, which is followed by teaching on the nature of discipleship.[47] Thus it can be said that in each part discipleship is set in the light of the cross and resurrection.[48] Therefore it appears that proper understanding of discipleship is to proceed from an understanding of the cross and resurrection.

It is generally acknowledged that the central section of Mark's Gospel begins with the incident of the opening of the eyes of a blind man (8.22-26). Here Mark's preservation of this story arrests our attention, for Luke and Matthew do not include it in their Gospels at all. Along with this feature, many scholars notice that Mark's arrangement of material in this section is purposeful, because this incident is immediately followed in the context by the incident of Peter's confession of Jesus as Christ at Caesarea Philippi and the first prediction of Jesus about the necessity of his passion and death (8.27-31).[49] This arrangement of the material appears to show an element of discipleship Mark would have had in mind, that is, the physical blindness of the blind man appears to be matched metaphorically by the spiritual blindness of the disciples.[50]

To put it in detail, from Peter's confession we find that he acknowledges only the Messianic nature of Jesus as Christ, but fails to recognize his destiny as the Suffering Son of Man (8.32), that is, Jesus must go to his glory by way of a cross. So his confession is to be only half

47. Mk 8.27-9.29; 9.30-10.31; 10.32-52.

48. Baumeister, *Anfänge*, p. 81; Rawlinson, *Gospel*, p. xvii.

49. On the basis of his presupposition that 'Der Verfasser des Markusevangeliums dürfte der erste gewesen sein, der die Traditionen über das Wirken Jesus mit der Passionsgeschichte verbunden hat', Baumeister, *Anfänge*, p. 81, argues that 'Mk nimmt die Passionsthema in seine Zeichnung der Tätigkeit Jesu vor Beginn der eigentlichen Leidensgeschichte auf und beschreibt den Weg Jesus als einen Weg zum Leiden'. From this contention, he characterizes Mark's Gospel as centred on the theology of the cross, stating, 'Das Kreuz nimmt einen zentralen Platz in der Theologie des Mk ein' (p. 81). Meanwhile, δεῖ in Mk 8.31 shows the divine necessity of Jesus' passion and death.

50. Anderson, *Mark*, p. 204, argues that this gradual cure of the blind man is 'a symbolic parallelism with Jesus' gradual opening of the disciples' eyes to the truth about himself'. Cf. E. Best, *Following Jesus* (JSNTSup, 4; Sheffield: JSOT Press, 1981), p. 201. Baumeister, *Anfänge*, also notes that 'Die markanische Christologie bestimmt das Verständnis der Jüngernachfolge (p. 81) . . . Das Motiv des Jüngerunverständnisse ist ebenso wie das Geheimhaltungsthema ein kennzeichnender Zug der markanischen Theologie' (pp. 82-83).

of the truth, like the first stage of Jesus' healing of the blind man (8.23-24). This incomprehension of Peter regarding Jesus' mission which appears as a form of rebuke (8.32-33) may indicate the disciples' unwillingness to admit Jesus' way of mission and their reluctance to follow the way Jesus goes before them. From this situation, Jesus delivers his view of discipleship referring to the conditions required of his follower (8.34-38): to deny himself, to take up his own cross, and to lose his life for the sake of Jesus and the gospel. Therefore, by these words of Jesus the nature of discipleship is defined: being a true disciple of Jesus would possibly entail suffering and death, as Jesus does suffer and die.[51] But this element of discipleship is extremely strange and hard for those who want to follow Jesus to accept, as Peter's half-sight confession illustrates. We can surmise that these conditions are put by the author of the Gospel against the background of a suffering community under harsh persecution—when the Christian readers in the Roman church listen to, and hear of, these passages, it would not be unnatural for them to take these words as a literal reality.[52] In

51. Rawlinson, *Gospel*, p. xvii; Nineham, *Mark*, p. 33; Anderson, *Mark*, p. 55; W.H. Kelber, *The Kingdom of Mark: A New Place and a New Time* (Philadelphia: Westminster Press, 1977), p. 6; Baumeister, *Anfänge*, p. 83; Best, *Following*, p. 13; Stock, *Call*, p. 141.

52. Best takes a different view on the interpretation of the cross in these passages; he does not want to view the cross as a literal reality, but as an allegorical way, saying that 'in the persecutions under Nero crucifixion had not been the usual means of death; 9.1 implies that Mark expects that some Christians will still be alive when Jesus returns' (*Story*, p. 86). Regarding this argument, first, although it was not the only means of execution that Nero imposed on Christians, yet crucifixion was certainly a means of execution, so Best himself admits that 'the cross was a terrifying means of execution and many of Mark's readers must have seen crucifixion' (p. 86).

This point can be confirmed by Tacitus who records that Christians at Rome suffered and were killed in many different ways being scapegoats of Nero for the conflagration of Rome, 64 CE, one of which was crucifixion: 'Dressed in wild animals' skins, they were torn to pieces by dogs, or crucified, or made into torches to be ignited after dark as substitutes for daylight' (*Ann.* 15.44).

It is clear that Luke allegorizes the meaning of the cross by inserting καθ᾽ ἡμέραν (Lk. 9.23), so Luke's version of this passage displays exactly what Best intends to say, 'The call to the cross does not then necessarily entail a literal crucifixion but always involves a continual dying which the disciple must take to himself' (p. 86). However, Matthew does not insert καθ᾽ ἡμέραν (Mt. 10.38), although it is written later than Mark, like Luke. From this it could be inferred that Matthew was just more conservative with his material, or perhaps that Matthew's community was also confronted with persecution as Mark's community was. Secondly, to quote Mk 9.1

other words, it would appear that Mark advises his fellow Christians that if they desire to be true disciples, they should be ready to deny themselves, willing to take up their own crosses, and unafraid of being killed on behalf of Jesus and the gospel. In sum, the meaning and definition of discipleship emphasized here is that Jesus calls his disciples to the realization that suffering and death are not only his own destiny but also theirs.

In the second part (9.31–10.31), the blindness of the disciples seems to be more aggravated than in the first part, not only because of 9.34, but also because of the contents of the second section as a whole: a dispute as to who is the greatest among the disciples (9.33-37), an attempt to limit membership among the followers of Jesus whom the disciples recognize as such (9.38-41), the prohibition of children from coming to Jesus (10.13-16). These three faults of the disciples are flatly rebuked by Jesus, so from this picture it may be gleaned that as the Gospel narrative goes on the spiritual blindness of the disciples is getting worse rather than getting better. Since they do not understand properly who Jesus is and what he is doing, they appear unable to appreciate how to behave as disciples of Jesus among themselves and in relation to others.

In this context, narrating the incident of the Rich Young Man who receives Jesus' call to follow but declines because of his strong attachment to wealth, Mark seems to accentuate his version of discipleship that being a true disciple is always a matter of total commitment. In the ensuing scene, therefore, there arises a conversation between Jesus and

---

in this connection does not appear to produce convincing evidence. It may be improbable that all members of the Markan community were martyred under Nero's persecution; but it is possible that some might have escaped. Meanwhile, some interpret this verse as indicating the powerful experience of the Holy Spirit on the Day of Pentecost recorded in Acts 2.1-4.

With respect to this point, Baumeister, *Anfänge*, p. 84, asserts in favour of a literal meaning of the cross:

> Die Forderung, das Kreuz auf sich zu nehmen, bezieht sich hier, in unmittelbarer Nachbarschaft zur Leidensansage in 8,31, auf den Tod Jesu am Kreuz, auf den die nachösterliche Gemeinde zurückblickt. Der Jünger trägt nun nicht das Kreuz Jesu, sondern sein eigenes, d. h. er muß bereit sein, in der Nachfolge des leidenden Jesus das ihm etwa drohende Geschick eines gewaltsamen Todes in seiner eigenen Situation auf sich zu nehmen. Von dieser Aufforderung her zeigt sich, daß man den vorausgehenden Imperativ nicht in dem spiritualisierten Sinn einer asketischen Selbstverleugnung auffassen kann.

Peter on behalf of the rest of the disciples, which is concerned about the total commitment of the disciples and its reward (10.23-31). What appears to be stressed here is that those who wish to be followers of Jesus should be prepared to lose everything of their own, including material possessions and family relationships for the sake of Jesus and the gospel; this seems to correspond to 8.35 where the conditions of discipleship are defined for the first time.[53] Consequently, it would seem that in these passages, which are distinguished from the parallels in Luke and Matthew because of μετὰ διωγμῶν (10.30), the disciples are seen to be invited to recognize the fact that the way to discipleship is to be through persecution, and by implication, for Mark's community too.

In the third part (10.32-52), it is to be noticed that against Jesus' repeated efforts to teach, the blindness of the disciples reaches its peak. When they come near to Jerusalem, the disciples are now afraid of following Jesus apparently because of Jesus' third prediction of his death that is supposed to take place at Jerusalem. This indicates that they are still not prepared to accept the way Jesus fulfils his mission, not to mention admitting it as the way they should take too. Thus it is not surprising that in the ensuing scene, James and John ask of Jesus things they are not allowed to request (10.35-37), and it causes a row among the disciples (10.41). This picture also exhibits clearly their misunderstanding and incomprehension, so Jesus once again teaches the disciples how they should behave as his followers (10.42-44).[54]

53. An indication of this motif of total commitment that requires forsaking old relationships has already been shown in Jesus' calling of the first disciples and his appointment of the Twelve in the first section of the Gospel. It is striking that Mark emphasizes this point, despite earlier depicting Peter and Andrew as entering their own house (1.29). Does this suggest that the commission of the disciples in 6.7-11 established a new and more radical phase of discipleship?

54. This scene shows that James and John along with the rest of the disciples still seek to share the glory of Jesus rather than the suffering fate of their Teacher. It is generally known that cup and baptism here can be understood as metaphors for passion and suffering (14.36), according to the Old Testament (Ps. 11.6; Isa. 51.17). Cf. A.M. Hunter, *The Gospel according to Saint Mark* (London: SCM Press, 1959), pp. 105-106. In this context, taking notice of the fact that there are in fact no exact parallels in the Old Testament and Matthew leaves out the reference to τὸ βάπτισμα in his version (Mt. 20.23), Nineham, *Mark*, p. 284, suggests that 'The idea would be that, in the conditions of St Mark's day, to accept baptism and become a partaker of the eucharistic cup is to take a step which might well lead to martyrdom; let would-be converts count the cost!'

Immediately after this final scene of the threefold prediction, Mark records the incident of Bartimaeus. This arrangement also seems by no means accidental: the cure of the physical blindness of Bartimaeus appears to be well placed by Mark to make a good contrast with the rather consistent blindness of the disciples as regards Jesus' mission and teaching. While Bartimaeus, cured from physical blindness by Jesus, follows Jesus on the way (ἐν τῇ ὁδῷ; 10.52), the disciples are still in darkness being afraid to follow their Teacher (10.32).

To conclude, what is revealed is that by intertwining the threefold prediction with the discipleship discourses and putting them into the narration of the journey to Jerusalem, Mark interweaves the life of Jesus with that of the disciples.[55] As a result, we come to note a significant feature of the Markan theme of discipleship that the way of Jesus is the way of the disciples.

c. *Example of Discipleship*
From this situation the third section of the Gospel (11.1–16.8) commences taking up the discipleship motif that waits for its full illumination in the way Jesus goes on his own. Although some explicit teaching on different subjects is given in this section, it is the behaviour of Jesus itself that appears to be thrown into bold relief being a living lesson to his disciples. That is, since, after strenuous efforts made by Jesus to awaken his disciples to the appreciation of discipleship, nobody, particularly his disciples, understands what the nature of Jesus' mission on earth implies and what discipleship is meant to be, a final resort that seems to be left in Jesus' hands is to set a living example before the blind eyes and the deaf ears. Thus with his death and resurrection, Jesus would call his disciples again, in spite of their failure, to discipleship and encounter them in a way that would enable them to see the meaning of his mission and of discipleship.[56] In conclusion, by going his own way and being completely obedient to God, Jesus leaves behind a model of discipleship that all of those who want to follow Him should take for their own way to discipleship.[57]

---

55. 'Durch die Verbindung der Jüngerbelehrung 8,34-9,1 mit der Ankündigung vom Leiden und Auferstehen des Menschensohnes (8,31-33) macht er deutlich, daß das Leiden der Jüngen Konsequenz der Passion und Teilnahme am Geschick Jesu ist' (Baumeister, *Anfänge*, p. 90).

56. E. Schweizer, *The Good News according to Mark* (London: SPCK, 1977), p. 373.

57. 'The example of Jesus is the pattern for the disciple and yet the disciple cannot

d. *Conclusion*

To conclude, we have seen that the theme of discipleship continues to flow through the whole Gospel dispersing various elements of discipleship which Mark thinks to be important to his readers in the Roman church. What appears to be of significance in this discussion is that in Mark's Gospel the way and destiny of Jesus should also be the way and destiny of the disciples;[58] so discipleship is to follow after Jesus by sharing his destiny and mission which should entail taking up one's own cross, self-denial, the rending of old ties of family and occupation, and forsaking of certain wealth and property in a literal sense.[59]

---

really be like Jesus' (Best, *Disciples*, p. 13). To clarify the meaning of the second half of this sentence, we had better compare the relationship of Jesus and his disciples with that of rabbis and their disciples and also with that of Greek philosophers and their pupils. (1) The disciples of Jesus are passively called by Jesus, while disciples of rabbis and of Greek philosophers take the initiative to call their teachers asking them to accept them as disciples or pupils. (2) During the course of their education, if disciples of rabbis or pupils of Greek philosophers wish to, they can change their teachers and go to other teachers, but once they become disciples, the disciples of Jesus should always remain his alone. (3) Eventually disciples of rabbis are themselves supposed to become rabbis, and pupils of philosophers are expected to become philosophers after their education, whereas the disciples of Christ can never expect to become Christ but always to follow him (M. Hengel, *The Charismatic Leader and his Followers* [Edinburgh: T. & T. Clark, 1981], pp. 50-57; Best, *Story*, pp. 85-86).

58. After an effort to explicate the call of the disciples in the Synoptic Gospels in the light of the Old Testament pattern of the call, such as the call of Elisha by Elijah, and to differentiate the concept of 'following' in the Synoptic Gospels from that of the prophetic-charismatic movements in first-century Palestine and of the Hellenistic world (Hengel, *Charismatic Leader*, pp. 16-37), Hengel defines the meaning of 'following' by stating that it means 'in the first place unconditionally *sharing of the master's destiny*, which does not stop even at deprivation and suffering in the train of the master, and is possible only on the basis of complete trust on the part of the person who 'follows'; he has placed his destiny and his future in his master's hands' (p. 72). Cf. F. Hahn, 'Pre-Easter Discipleship', in F. Hahn, A. Strobel and E. Schweizer (eds.), *The Beginnings of the Church in the New Testament* (Edinburgh: The Saint Andrew Press, 1967), pp. 9-39.

59. J. Blinzler ('Jesus and his Disciples', in H.J. Schultz [ed.], *Jesus in his Time* [London: SPCK, 1971], pp. 88-90), summarizes succinctly the meaning of following Jesus as involving 'a radical renunciation of almost everything which is commonly thought of as making life worth living', such as previous occupation, families, personal possessions, marriage (Mt. 19.11-12), and being prepared to share the lot of the teacher, that is, suffering, homelessness, persecution and even death. Cf. Schweizer, *Lordship*, p. 20.

But the disciples turn out to fail to understand this aspect of discipleship, which becomes a stumbling block for the historical disciples, so that they are depicted in the Gospel in a negative light.

This finding is firmly buttressed when we are reminded of the fact that the Markan community to which the Gospel was devoted was under severe persecution and affliction by the Roman authorities. Thus it is probable that the members of Mark's community would have been encouraged and consoled when they came to know that Jesus their Lord was also confronted with the same suffering and death, but overcame by way of resurrection which is the solid ground of the ultimate hope of all disciples.

4. *Mark's Description of the Disciples*

After we reach this conclusion on the Markan theme of discipleship, it would be helpful for us to examine Mark's description of the disciples, addressing the question, 'How and why does Mark portray the disciples in a negative light?' For the sake of procedure, first of all, it would be better for us to discuss Jesus' special favour to the disciples.

a. *Jesus' Preferential Treatment of the Disciples*
When we look through Mark's Gospel as a whole, we cannot fail to recognize the fact that there are a range of passages showing that the disciples receive particular teaching and instruction in private from Jesus their Teacher when they happen to be alone with him, and that the disciples thus enjoy special favour from Jesus.

1. *Jesus' Personal and Private Instructions*[60]

(a)   4.10: 'And when he was alone [κατὰ μόνας], those who were about him with the twelve asked him concerning the parables.'

---

60. Taking note of this feature in Mark, A.W. Mosley ('Jesus' Audiences in the Gospels of St Mark and St Luke', *NTS* 10 [1963–64]), pp. 139-49, argues that 'Mark had a strong reason for distinguishing teaching given to the crowds from private teaching given to the disciples' (p. 140). The reason he suggests is that Mark probably intended to retain some of the explanations of Jesus' teaching which are different from Jesus' teaching itself in the pre-Markan tradition (p. 145), so Mark makes the disciples ask for the explanations from Jesus privately, which Mosley regards as Mark's literary device.

(b)   4.34b: 'he did not speak to them without a parable, but privately [κατ' ἰδίαν] to his own disciples he explained everything'.

(c)   7.17: 'And when he had entered the house, and left the people, his disciples asked him about the parable.'

(d)   9.28: 'And when he had entered the house, his disciples asked him privately [κατ' ἰδίαν], "why could we not cast it out?"'

(e)   10.10: 'And in the house the disciples asked him again about this matter.'

(f)13.3: 'And as he sat on the Mount of Olives opposite the temple, Peter and James and John and Andrew asked him privately [κατ' ἰδίαν].'[61]

2. *Jesus' Special Favour to the Disciples*

(a)   6.31: 'And he said to them, "Come away by yourselves [κατ' ἰδίαν] to a lonely place, and rest a while". For many were coming and going, and they had no leisure even to eat. And they went away in the boat to a lonely place by themselves [κατ' ἰδίαν].'

(b)   9.40: 'For he that is not against us is for us.'[62]

(c)   5.35-47; 13.3; 14.33-42: Among the twelve disciples three or four disciples (13.3; Andrew) are selected by Jesus to have the benefit of more intimate fellowship with their Teacher.[63]

61. Cf. Best, *Following*, p. 159.

62. This is another saying in the Gospel that belongs to this category. In its parallel, Luke changes ἡμῶν into ὑμῶν (Lk. 9.50), which would indicate that in Mark Jesus wants to identify himself with his disciples, but in Luke he seems to intend to keep his distance from them (Creed, *Gospel*, p. 139). This remark, therefore, can be thought of as a sign of Jesus' preferential attitude towards the disciples (Matthew has no parallel to this saying).

63. On this ground of intimate fellowship related to revelation of secrets, the three disciples can often be regarded by Mark as 'a representative inner circle' of the body of the disciples (Anderson, *Mark*, p. 224; cf. Taylor, *Mark*, p. 294).

From these passages we are able to see clearly how favourably the disciples are treated by Jesus who explains everything in private that his disciples are unable to understand properly. The private nature of Jesus' teaching to his disciples, manifested by such phrases as κατ᾽ ἰδίαν, κατὰ μόνας, εἰς τὴν οἰκίαν (10.10), ὅτε εἰσῆλθον εἰς οἶκον (7.17), and εἰσελθόντος αὐτοῦ εἰς οἶκον (9.28), seems to demonstrate Jesus' personal concern for his disciples.

b. *The Negative Image of the Disciples*
1. *Negative Aspects*. Despite such personal and private instruction from Jesus which occurs frequently to awake his disciples to their lack of understanding and faith, the disciples in Mark do not appear to appreciate Jesus' teaching and to have faith in God, but to be preoccupied with their self-interest. Thus they appear to be depicted more frequently by Mark in a poorer light than by Luke and Matthew and, as far as the degree of the negative delineation is concerned, Mark's portrait is stronger than that of the other Evangelists.

We may categorize the material related to the negative image of the disciples in Mark into five divisions:

(a)   Lack of faith: 4.40; 9.19.

(b)   Lack of understanding: 4.13; 6.51-52; 7.18-19; 8.17-18, 21; 9.32; 10.38.[64]

(c)   Lack of discretion: 8.32-33; 10.13-16.[65]

64. It could be asserted that the passages referring to Jesus' private instruction and special favour to the disciples are to be seen as a positive image of the disciples. In fact, however, the very fact that the disciples ask Jesus to explain his parables and teaching may well indicate their inability to understand; among six passages mentioned above in relation to Jesus' private instruction, almost all passages, except 4.34, show that because of their incomprehension the disciples ask explanations of Jesus (4.10; 7.17; 9.28; 10.10; 13.3).

And it will be revealed, as we explore this theme further, that if we take into account Mark's attitude towards the disciples as a whole which appears rather consistently negative in the Gospel, it seems likely that Jesus' private instruction, signalling his special favour, is devised by the author to throw into relief the negative image of the disciples.

65. Jesus showed to his disciples his acceptance of children already in 9.33-37. But in 10.13-16, the disciples still appear to try to prevent them from coming to Jesus, which demonstrates well their indiscretion. It should be noticed that in its parallel

(d)   Fear: 4.41; 6.50; 9.32; 10.32.[66]

(e)   Self-concern: 9.33-37; 10.35-45.

In addition to these typical cases revealing general features of the disciples' weakness and inability, there are some other indications in this regard which are to be noticed through comparison of the incidents related to this motif among the three Synoptic Gospels:

(a) When Jesus predicts their betrayal, particularly Peter's three-fold denial of him, Peter, along with all the other disciples, says to Jesus vehemently (ἐκπερισσῶς), 'If I must die with you, I will not deny you' (14.31). Here ἐκπερισσῶς[67] omitted by Luke (Lk. 22.33) and Matthew (Mt. 26.33) alike, seems to add weight to Mark's bad portrait of the disciples, because despite this vehement affirmation, Peter denied Jesus three times and all the other disciples also deserted their Teacher.

(b) With regard to Peter's repentance, we find an interesting point of difference among the Synoptists' descriptions. That is, Luke and Matthew in this context insert πικρῶς (Mt. 26.75/Lk. 22.62); in doing so they appear to attempt to rescue Peter from Mark's bad portrait.[68] However, in Mark it is not easy to find a sign of Mark's relenting

account in Matthew and Luke, ἠγανάκτησεν is left out. It would be likely that Mark here seeks to accentuate the indiscretion of the disciples, for Jesus' indignation takes 'the form of rebuke' (Taylor, *Mark*, p. 423; cf. Cranfield, *Mark*, p. 323; Lane, *Mark*, p. 360; Anderson, *Mark*, p. 245).

66. Fear expressed by the disciples appears related to incomprehension (9.32; 10.32) and lack of faith (4.41; 6.50), so it can be included in this context. However, φοβέομαι, which in Mark occurs frequently in the contexts of miracle stories, such as 5.15, 33, 36; 16.8, does not always indicate lack of faith, but sometimes religious awe.

67. Since this word is found neither in classical Greek nor in the LXX, but only here in Mark throughout the New Testament, Taylor, *Mark*, p. 550, claims that it is 'a Markan coinage rendering the original Aramaic'. Cf. Cranfield, *Mark*, pp. 429-30.

68. Evans, *Saint Luke*, p. 828, says, 'In that case Luke's story will have ended, not with Peter's bitter tears of remorse, but with Jesus' gaze evoking Peter's recollection; and so with the suggestion that Jesus, by his presence, look and omniscient word, embraced the situation, and preserved Peter from the consequences of his faithlessness (vv. 31-34), as he had preserved the rest from their incomprehension and violence (vv. 35-51)'.

gesture towards the prime disciple (14.72).[69]

(c) Along with Peter, James and John (Andrew once) in Mark's Gospel also appear to enjoy Jesus' special fondness among the twelve disciples: 5.35-47 (resuscitation), 9.2-8 (transfiguration), 14.33-42 (Gethsemane),[70] 13.3 (signs of last days; Andrew included). In the parallel to 5.35-47, Matthew does not insert Peter, John and James particularly, leaving Jesus to enter into the house alone (Mt. 9.25). In the incident of Jesus' final prayer in the Garden of Gethsemane, Jesus is accompanied by the three disciples in Mark (14.33), while in Luke there is no mention of them at all (Lk. 22.39-40) and in Matthew, instead of direct names, the 'two sons of Zebedee' is used (Mt. 26.37), so these narratives might show Luke and Matthew's reluctance to reveal their names in connection with their failure. From this comparison, we may be able to recognize that although in Mark, Peter, James and John (Andrew) appear to be treated favourably by Jesus, nonetheless, in spite of this partial affection, Peter denied Jesus three times with curse and oath, and James and John requested of Jesus something wholly inappropriate, not knowing what they were really asking (10.38). In relation to the latter incident, it is noteworthy that Luke leaves it out and Matthew had the mother of the sons of Zebedee plead with Jesus on behalf of her sons, James and John (Mt. 20.20). By doing so, Luke and Matthew seem to strive to shift any blame from them,[71] while, by contrast, in Mark, James and John are left with blame imposed on them. Here is another example of the bad image of the disciples presented by Mark.

(d) *The Disciples' Dereliction of Jesus*: If we rely upon the result of the above discussion, then it would be a natural corollary that the disciples' inability to understand and to believe appears to lead to their

---

69. It would not be sensible to suggest that there are no positive portraits of Peter in Mark. For instance, 16.7 might be a token among them. What I want to state is that Mark's general tendency towards the disciples is negative rather than positive.

70. Lane, *Mark*, pp. 515-16, seems to provide a reasonable answer why the three disciples were selected to be with Jesus privately in his critical time at Gethsemane: 'The failure to understand what it means to share Jesus' destiny and to be identified with his sufferings, rather than privileged status, appears to be the occasion for the isolation of the three from the others. Their glib self-confidence exposes them to grave peril of failure in the struggle they confront, and for that reason they are commanded to be vigilant.'

71. Anderson, *Mark*, p. 254.

dereliction of their Teacher, when the time comes for Jesus to be delivered to the hands of the elders and the chief priests and the scribes
(14.50). There seem to be two particular points that can be mentioned
in this regard.

First, it may be worth taking into consideration that only Mark
records an incident immediately after the scene of the disciples' dereliction of Jesus, that a young man who followed Jesus when he was
arrested by the soldiers fled away naked leaving behind his linen cloth,
as he was also about to be seized (14.51-52). The uniqueness of this
event has caught the commentators' attention, and it has been held that
the young man's flight, naked of any cloth on his body, encapsulates
symbolically the disciples' utter abandonment of their Teacher Jesus.[72]

72. What is interesting here is that the νεανίσκος followed with Jesus after all
the disciples fled away (Taylor, *Mark*, p. 561, notes that συνηκολούθει in this verse
suggests 'an action continued after the disciples had fled'), and also that just as Jesus
was arrested, so he was arrested, though temporarily. Pointing out this feature, J.P.
Heil ('Mark 14.1-52: Narrative Structure and Reader–Response', *Bib* 71 [1990], pp.
305-32 [329]), argues that 'This young man, then, stands as a possible candidate to
fulfil the role of an ideal disciple'. Unfortunately, however, at last he also fled away.
Thus H. Fleddermann ('The Plight of a Naked Young Man [Mk 14.51-52]', *CBQ*
41 [1979], pp. 412-18 [417]), states that 'He (νεανίσκος τις) is a fleeing disciple.
The pericope is a dramatization and concretization of the universal flight of the
disciples', which is by Mark put in sharp contrast with Jesus' acceptance of his
passion and death. Therefore, Fleddermann argues eventually that 'he is a symbol of
those who oppose God's will in the passion' (p. 417; cf. Heil, 'Reader–Response',
p. 330).
    Recently, however, J.M. Ross ('The Young Man who Fled Naked', *IBS* 13
[1991], pp. 170-74) refutes this idea saying that 'The difficulty about this is that
Mark had already made clear that every one of Jesus' followers had abandoned him
and fled; it does not heighten the tragedy to add what happened to a minor character
in the drama . . . if it were merely an illustration of the desertion of Jesus it would
have been more appropriately introduced by γαρ than by και' (p. 172). A crucial
weakness in his argument is, however, his isolation of this story from the Markan
context as a whole, and it is to be noticed particularly in this context that και (14.50,
51, 53) connects this story with its previous account of the flight of the disciples and
also with the account of Jesus' passion and death (14.53–15.37). We know from
Mark's use of vocabulary that και is one of his favourite words, employed 'instead
of the use of participles or subordinate clause' (Taylor, *Mark*, p. 48; cf. Rawlinson,
Gospel, pp. xxxi-xxxii), which could have different implications in accordance with
individual contexts (C.F.D. Moule, *An Idiom Book of New Testament Greek*
[Cambridge: Cambridge University Press, 1953], p. 165). Cf. Fitzmyer, *Theologian*,
p. 127; R.C. Tannehill, 'The Disciples in Mark: the Function of a Narrative Role', in

Secondly, another point of significance is that in Matthew although the disciples are also described as deserting Jesus, they are explicitly restored at the end of the story: the disciples went to Galilee as Jesus instructed them before he was crucified, met him there, and received a new mission to be carried out after Jesus' ascension.[73] However, Mark's Gospel ends with the women's fear, astonishment, and their failure to speak (16.8),[74] from which it might be imagined that they would not have been able to convey to the disciples the command announced by the young man at the tomb that Jesus was risen from the dead, and his reminder of Jesus' prediction that he would go to Galilee before them (16.6-7). Thus from this last scene of Mark's Gospel, one could draw no assurance that there would be a chance for the disciples to be restored after their betrayal of Jesus. Consequently, the dereliction of Jesus by the disciples in the Gospel narrative appears to be a climactic culmination of Mark's negative description of the disciples as failures.

To sum up what I have discussed so far, it has been shown that the disciples in Mark do not have appropriate understanding, faith and discretion to comply with Jesus' meticulous teaching and instruction which run almost from the beginning to the end of the Gospel. Therefore it would not be an exaggeration to state that Jesus' efforts to enable his disciples to perceive what his teaching and instruction really meant, and what discipleship is to be, seem not to be effective.

W. Telford (ed.), *The Interpretation of Mark* (London: SPCK, 1985), p. 151; Lane, *Mark*, pp. 527-28; Stock, *Call*, pp. 188-89.

73. Mt. 28.16-20. Luke does not say they forsook Jesus their Lord.

74. It is generally acknowledged that 16.8 is the original end of the Gospel, for the oldest manuscripts, such as ℵ, B, k, sy[sin], and the testimony of Eusebius and Hieronymus, do not contain the report of the Resurrection and Ascension (16.9-20), and 'the divergent character of the text in respect to the other Gospels' appears in the report (Kümmel, *Introduction,* p. 71). Thus it is said to be a literary device of Mark to highlight the negative image which he puts on the disciples. Cf. Matera, *What Are They*, p. 51.

In favour of the short ending of the Gospel, Stock, *Call*, pp. 50-53, provides his finding from comparison of Mark's Gospel with a Hellenistic drama that 'the epilogue of Mark's Gospel has several characteristics in common with the conventional finale of a Hellenistic drama' (p. 53).

2. *Possible Modifying Features*. It would be unbalanced to argue that there is only a negative picture of the disciples in Mark. On the contrary, there are certainly also some positive descriptions of the disciples in Mark, for examples of which we can point to 1.16-20; 2.13-14; 3.13-19; 6.7-13. (1) The first disciples, and Levi later, follow Jesus immediately as they receive a call from him to follow, leaving behind their families and property and quitting their jobs.[75] (2) The twelve disciples are chosen by Jesus to be with him and to carry out the same mission that their Teacher did by himself (3.13-19). (3) Later on they are seen to accomplish successfully the mission entrusted by Jesus (6.7-13). (4) Jesus' prediction in 14.28 and the young man's announcement in 16.7 might possibly suggest that the relationship between Jesus and his disciples, that is, of discipleship, is not to end with Jesus' death, but to continue afterwards.[76] In consequence, we notice here that even though Jesus knows that all his disciples will fall away, deserting and betraying him,[77] he does not lose his faith in them at all. This shows that there is something still left in the disciples on which Jesus can count, and this aspect we can regard as a piece of positive portrayal of the disciples.[78]

Taking heed of the fact that in the first six chapters of the Gospel, such as 1.16-20; 2.13-14; 3.13-19; 6.7-13, the disciples are depicted in a better light, Tannehill makes the point that hinging on the turning

75. Mk 1.16-20; 2.13-14; 10.28.

76. B.L. Melbourne (*Slow to Understand: The Disciples in Synoptic Perspective* [Lanham, MD: University Press of America, 1988]) expounds this passage as follows: 'This doubtlessly suggests that Mark, like Matthew, did not regard their flight as the end of their discipleship. There would be a reunion in Galilee. He sought a continuous relationship with them' (p. 48).

77. Mk 14.7, 18, 30.

78. In this context, what should be noticed is that the expected reunion in Galilee predicted by Jesus at 14.28 and announced by the angel at 16.6-7 does not in fact take place in Mark's Gospel (in fact this aspect of the Gospel has been discussed heavily in order to find an appropriate meaning from it; see Kümmel, *Introduction*, p. 71). However, it is also not difficult to believe that just as Jesus' threefold prediction was fulfilled as he prophesied, so this prediction will be.

Regarding this matter, Best argues that the physical sense that the fulfilment of 14.28 and 16.7 would bring was not important to Mark's community, because 'the fact of the appearance of the risen Jesus would have been known to his community' (*Following*, p. 199; *Disciples*, p. 14); what mattered to them is the 'spiritual sight' that sees Jesus is ever with them and they with Jesus (p. 201).

point, that is, the third boat scene (8.14-21), Mark's portrait of the disciples changes from positive to negative.[79]

However, the matter does not seem as simple and clear-cut as he argues. Even in the first six chapters, references have been made to the disciples' blindness to what Jesus' teaching signifies: (1) In 3.19 Mark adds a negative assessment about Judas Iscariot into the original tradition. (2) 4.13 indicates the disciples' lack of understanding. (3) In 4.30-41 the disciples express their fear and unbelief when they are confronted with a great storm of wind during their voyage by ship. (4) And also in 4.17 a hint is dropped which will be related to the disciples' dereliction of Jesus that is supposed to happen later in the Gospel. (5) In 6.37 we note also the disciples' lack of belief in Jesus who performs so many miracles in front of them, when they are charged by Jesus to feed the crowd. This point of the disciples' unbelief related to Jesus' miracles appears again in 6.52, which in turn gives us the author's interpretation of the event of Jesus' feeding the crowd in 6.35-44, adding again to the negative image of the disciples.

Summing up what we have discussed above, Tannehill's assertion that Mark's portrayal of the disciples changes initially from a positive picture to a negative one later seems hardly to be justified. Although there are some bright aspects in Mark's portrait of the disciples in the first six chapters, they appear to be well offset by the negative references pointing out the blindness, fear and lack of understanding on the part of the disciples which are also found in those chapters.

3. *Conclusion: The Balance of the Matter.* After having discussed both aspects of Mark's depiction of the disciples, positive and negative, we come to conclude this matter: although it is true that the Gospel contains some positive images of the disciples, particularly in the earlier chapters, they are well offset by the negative images that occur more frequently and explicitly throughout the Gospel. In other words, it can be said that Mark describes the disciples occasionally and implicitly in a favourable light, but frequently and explicitly in a poor light. Therefore, if we take into account the Gospel as a whole, it would appear eventually that the negative portrait of the disciples, in which the

---

79. As for this turning point, Tannehill, 'Function', p. 147, puts it as follows: 'A clear shift in the disciples' role has taken place. From a position with Jesus as his followers, the disciples have moved to a position which associates them with Jesus' enemies and the outsiders of 4.11-12.'

author's particular interest possibly lies, is thrown into bold relief in the Gospel.

c. *Mark's Purpose in the Negative Portrayal of the Disciples*
With this final result drawn from Mark's depiction of the disciples, we may glean a rather strong impression that Mark's attitude towards the disciples is negatively jaundiced. Now it is time to think about the author's intention to finish his story like that, and also to describe the disciples in a poorer light. It seems to me that there are two motives that underlie this negative description of the disciples by Mark.

First, it may be designed to warn Christian brothers and sisters in Mark's community confronted with harsh affliction and suffering not to follow the failures of the historical disciples, because even though they followed Jesus literally in his lifetime as the disciples chosen personally by himself, enjoying his favour to a great extent, the disciples made serious mistakes when faced with similar circumstances in Jesus' lifetime. Denial, betrayal and dereliction following incomprehension, unbelief, indiscretion, fear and self-concern are characterized as the disciples' notorious failures as followers of Jesus in his ministry on earth. Hence it appears that by portraying the disciples in a negative light, Mark seeks to show a model of failed discipleship[80] as a warning that must be heeded by his readers who were in a similar situation of severe persecution that might lead them to deny and betray Jesus

---

80. In this regard, Best, *Following*, p. 12, argues that of two possible approaches to talk about discipleship, such as good discipleship and bad discipleship, Mark chose to instruct through bad discipleship, i.e. the failures of the disciples. For the reason why Mark chose this method, Best suggests four points: '(i) Jesus himself is the "hero" of the story. (ii) The tradition as it was known to his readers already contained stories of the failure of disciples; these failures could not then be eliminated. (iii) The New Testament shows generally that success in discipleship depends not on the degree of robust faith or courage which the disciple can generate within himself but on his willingness to accept help from God. (iv) Many of Mark's readers may have already failed through public or private persecution or through other causes.'

Meanwhile, M.A. Beavis (*Mark's Audience: The Literary and Social Setting of Mark 4.11-12* [JSNTSup, 33; Sheffield: JSOT Press, 1989]), p. 182, construes the negative view on the disciples at the paraenetic level, making use of 'the device of covert allusion' that Greek and Latin rhetoricians employed in their writings in order to avoid direct offence to their audience or readers. According to this theory, the disciples in Mark are 'a foil for true discipleship' because their failure and faults serve to enable the audience not to follow in their tracks on their way to true discipleship.

Christ. There would surely have been apostates and defectors in Mark's community due to the severe afflictions and persecutions of that time.[81]

Secondly, however, it may not be Mark's intention to write a Gospel only for a warning against apostasy in a time of persecution. It may be likely that Mark is also eager to introduce to the congregation of his community as an alternative to failed discipleship a model of successful discipleship in order to encourage their weakened faith and low morale which might have resulted from persecution.[82] Thus, as well as the failed disciples, Mark appears to introduce two figures to show what a true disciple is like: Bartimaeus, the blind man, and Jesus, their Teacher.

Bartimaeus follows Jesus on the road immediately without hesitation when he gained his sight, having been cured by Jesus. This picture of Bartimaeus is well contrasted with that of the disciples who till the end of the Gospel are seen not to be cured from their spiritual blindness that eventually leads to their desertion of Jesus, although they had not infrequently received the benefit of special favour from Jesus, as Bartimaeus had. In other words, the openness of Bartimaeus's eyes in a physical sense appears to be used by the author so as to contrast it with the blindness of the disciples in a spiritual sense, for it would mean in a figurative sense that all incomprehension, unbelief, fear, indiscretion and self-concern are overcome. Thus it may be that Bartimaeus is shown by Mark as a symbol of a true disciple whose eyes are open so that he may be able to follow Jesus.

Having said this, we would still not be sure that Bartimaeus could be regarded rightly as an ultimate model of a true disciple whom the Christians in Mark's community should feel obliged to imitate, for he just appears once in the Gospel as a passing character like Levi who also followed Jesus leaving his secular business (2.14), never playing a role as important as that of the disciples in the Gospel story. Thus it is probable that Bartimaeus's appearance is devised by the author to make

81. See the above note. Best seeks to explain the disciples' failure as part of Mark's pastoral effort to instruct the Church rather than as a polemic against the disciples: 'His [Mark's] primary objective was pastoral: to build up his readers as Christians and show them what true discipleship is' (*Following*, p. 12). Cf. W. Dicharry, *Human Authors of the New Testament. I. Mark, Matthew and Luke* (Slough: St Paul Publications, 1990), p. 44.

82. For this reason Mark seems to advise them to endure till the end (13.13).

a good contrast between Bartimaeus and the disciples in view of following after Jesus. In this context, we may claim that Bartimaeus functions as a figure to anticipate a true model of a disciple, that is, Jesus himself.[83]

Therefore it can be asserted that a true disciple from Mark's point of view is Jesus himself, who, by undergoing all the persecution and suffering that he was supposed to face, left an exemplary track on which the disciples should follow.[84]

5. Conclusion

Above I have first discussed Mark's view of discipleship, and then dealt with his description of the disciples. From the initial discussion, I have drawn a conclusion that Mark's idea of discipleship is following Jesus: breaking with old ties of family relationships, occupation, and material possessions, and sharing his lot—suffering and death. But this motif of following Jesus by way of the cross is so difficult for the disciples to accept that it becomes a stumbling-block to them. For this reason, in the Gospel they are depicted frequently in a negative light. This is the second topic of my discussion.

It may be that Mark wants his readers, the Christians of the Roman church, to follow Jesus faithfully as his disciples under the hardship of persecution, not forsaking or betraying Him. That is what Mark thinks a disciple ought to do in such a critical time. At the same time, however, to make his intention more effective, Mark seeks to delineate the disciples in a negative light, by preserving original tradition or adding his comments. By doing so, Mark seems to intend to show his readers the examples of failed discipleship, so that they might shun this way. Instead, he introduces the way they should follow, in which Jesus went before them, as the rule of true discipleship.

83. Bearing this notion in mind, Best, *Disciples*, p. 3, makes a remark that 'the rule of discipleship is: Jesus. As Jesus was, so the disciples must be'.

84. Best, *Following*, p. 92, states, 'For Mark the goal might be more adequately described as Jesus himself rather than the cross or even the cross and the resurrection. Jesus is not however a fixed or static goal to whom travellers are always drawing nearer but a dynamic goal who is continually moving ahead of them'.

Chapter 3

LUKE'S VIEW OF DISCIPLESHIP

As generally acknowledged, Luke relies on Mark's Gospel as one of his major sources in writing his Gospel. Hence it is noted that Luke depends on a range of material in Mark in relation to the discipleship theme. For instance, we can enumerate the threefold prophecy of Jesus' passion which plays an important role in developing the discipleship theme in Mark, the calling of the first disciples and of Levi, the tax collector, and the sending out of the twelve disciples for evangelism. Although Luke utilizes a lot of material related to discipleship in Mark, and there are many similarities between the two Evangelists' descriptions of the disciples and their views of discipleship, yet Luke does not simply copy the way that Mark presents his view of discipleship. Rather, by adding, changing and omitting some material in Mark according to his own theological purposes, Luke appears to develop his own view of discipleship.

My procedure in this chapter will be as follows. First of all, keeping in mind the result drawn from the previous chapter on Markan discipleship, I will shed light on how Luke describes the disciples in his Gospel in comparison with Mark. Here I will discuss Luke's positive portrait of the disciples compared with Mark's rather negative portrait of them. Secondly, I will look at Luke's less sectarian and extremist portrait of the disciples in contrast to Mark, allowing for the *Sitz im Leben* of each Gospel. Thirdly, I will consider two types of disciples that emerge from Luke's depiction of the disciples, that is, the itinerant type of disciples and that of sedentary disciples.

1. *More Positive Portrait of the Disciples*

One of the prominent discrepancies between Mark and Luke in relation to the theme of discipleship is their descriptions of the disciples. As we have already seen in the previous chapter, the disciples are not seen favourably in Mark, but negatively and somewhat disgracefully: they are described as ignorant of who Jesus is and what Jesus teaches (Mk 6.52; 7.18; 8.21, 32-33; 9.19, 32; 10.32), greedy to pursue their secular ambitions (Mk 10.35-45), and cowardly in abandoning Jesus their Teacher at his arrest and trial (Mk 14.50).

Among these negative descriptions of Mark, Luke appears to take over only a couple of verses with some modification that are recorded in the passion predictions from Mark, that is, Mk 9.32/Lk. 9.45; Mk 10.32/Lk. 18.34,[1] leaving out the rest of them. Above all, these omissions by Luke clearly show that Luke does not want to describe the disciples unfavourably. Bearing in mind this basic attitude of Luke in what follows, let us examine in detail some examples of Luke's more favourable description of the disciples, which becomes a good contrast to Mark's rather negative portrait of the disciples.

a. *Dereliction of Jesus*

Among the passages Luke omits, there is one particularly important verse. It is the omission of Mk 14.50, that is, the disciples' dereliction of their Master. By omitting this verse, Luke is seen to try to show that the disciples did not abandon and forsake Jesus their Master utterly. Rather there is one passage in which we can suppose that the disciples were actually in the place where Jesus was crucified: πάντες οἱ γνωστοὶ αὐτῷ in 23.49 expresses this idea. Here γνωστοί denotes initially 'known', so the meaning of the phrase is literally 'all those known to Jesus'. It means that they were already known by Jesus, so it would not be unreasonable to assume that it includes some disciples, even the apostles.[2] And also in relation to this motif of dereliction, Luke omits Jesus' quotation of Zech. 13.7: 'I will strike the shepherd, and the sheep will be scattered' that is rendered in Mk 14.27. And in the scene of betrayal, by omitting Peter's cursing (ἀναθεματίζειν) and swearing (ὀμνύναι) in Mk 14.71, Luke also weakens the degree of Peter's betrayal initially portrayed in Mark.[3] Instead of this, Luke records that

---

1. These two verses are related to the famous threefold prophecy of Jesus' passion. Since these are a part of deep-rooted tradition about Jesus, and so possibly known widely even among the members of his community, it seems to have been very difficult for Luke to eliminate these verses altogether.

2. Fitzmyer, *Gospel*, p. 1520; Plummer, *Luke*, p. 540; Evans, *Saint Luke*, p. 879.

3. Grundmann, *Lukas*, p. 417.

Jesus prayed for Peter that he might not fail, and commanded him to strengthen his brothers once he has turned again (22.32).[4] Therefore, in doing so, Luke is seen to rescue the disciples from the negative image given by Mark. Luke even seems to partially mitigate Judas's betrayal, noting that his betrayal had to be done because of divine necessity and to fulfil an Old Testament prophecy.[5] As a result of these observations, we may conclude that in Luke the disciples did not forsake Jesus as completely as in Mark, and this clearly indicates that Luke's portrayal of the disciples is more positive.[6]

b. *Some Other Positive Features*
In addition to the examples discussed thus far, there are a few points which can also be shown as an indication of Luke's endeavour to minimize the disciples' failure in order to improve their reputation so badly rendered by Mark:

(1) Luke omits some passages in Mark referring to dullness of the disciples, for example, 7.18; 8.21; 9.19, where they are seen not to understand what Jesus taught and meant. This omission may be deemed as Luke's defence of the disciples.

4.   S. Brown (*Apostasy and Perseverance in the Theology of Luke* [Rome: Pontifical Biblical Institute, 1969]), pp. 69-71, makes the point that Peter did not deny Jesus' Messiahship but only his acquaintance with Jesus at 22.54-62.

5.   Note δεῖ in Acts 1.16 and a prophecy fulfilled at Acts 1.20 (cf. Ps. 41.9). Cf. E. Haenchen, *The Acts of the Apostles: A Commentary* (Oxford: Basil Blackwell, 1971), p. 159. See L.T. Johnson, *Literary Function*, pp. 15-16, 177.

6.   Giles may be right to state that the disciples in Luke make only one mistake: not to recognize the fact that Jesus must suffer and die before he enters glory (K.N. Giles, 'The Church in the Gospel of Luke', *SJT* 34 [1981], pp. 121-46 [132-33]). But he appears to make a mistake in combining discipleship with the theme of suffering which is not quite appropriate in Luke's Gospel. Regarding the theme of suffering, he argues that 'Jesus' own suffering explains the suffering demanded of the Christian community' (p. 132), resorting to F. Schütz (*Der leidende Christus: Die angefochtene Gemeinde und das Christuskerygma der lukanischen Schriften* [BWANT, 89; Stuttgart: Kohlhammer, 1969]) and H. Flender (*St Luke: Theologian of Redemptive History* [London: SCM Press, 1967]) for support.

However, if the Christian community is to be Luke's, we may have to ask him if the theme of suffering in Luke is so prominent that it can be so closely combined with the theme of discipleship? We cannot be sure about this question, because the *Sitz im Leben* of Luke's Gospel and a large number of ethical teachings of Jesus recorded in Luke lead us to doubt whether the theme of suffering and persecution is as prominent as Giles suggests.

(2) In relation to the threefold passion prediction, Luke seems to take over the first prediction faithfully from Mark (Mk 8.31/Lk. 9.22), but in the case of the second and third predictions he makes some changes to suit his own idea of the disciples. The disciples in Mark are reported not to understand what Jesus really meant and also to be afraid to ask about it (Mk 9.32), while the disciples in Luke seem to be excused for their misunderstanding because of Luke's assertion that what Jesus meant was hidden from them (ἦν ... παρακεκαλυμμένον ἀπ' αὐτῶν; Lk. 9.45). So this concealment is rendered by Luke as divine order.[7] This occurs again in the third prediction (Mk 10.32/Lk. 18.31-34); while the disciples in Mark are depicted as astonished and afraid (ἐθαμβοῦντο, ἐφοβοῦντο; Mk 10.32)[8] about the journey to Jerusalem related to Jesus' passion, in Luke they are once again pardoned for their incomprehension about the prediction because it was hidden from them (ἦν κεκρυμμένον ἀπ' αὐτῶν; Lk. 18.34).[9] Thus in Luke one may take it for granted that the disciples cannot grasp what Jesus meant concerning his passion and suffering, because to grasp it is beyond human reasoning.

(3) A significant change made by Luke to Mark's account of the scene of the disciples' failure at the Garden of Gethsemane should be considered as a strong clue to Luke's more positive conception of the disciples. In Mark the three disciples, Peter, James, and John did not pay heed to Jesus' request to watch and pray with him, and fell asleep. In Luke all the disciples, not just the three, did the same. But there are two remarkable differences between the two accounts: one is Luke's insertion of ἀπὸ τῆς λύπης in 22.45, and the other is that the Lukan Jesus did not scold the disciples for their sleep, while Mark depicts Jesus as having rebuked them (Lk. 22.46/Mk 14.37). With these differences Luke appears once again to excuse the disciples from their faults.[10]

---

7.   Most commentators take note of this point; Plummer, *Luke*, p. 256; I.H. Marshall, *Commentary*, p. 394; Thompson, *Luke*, p. 156; Bovon, *Lukas*, p. 51.

8.   Both verbs are rendered in the imperfect tense, which might mean that the disciples' amazement and fear did not happen just once but continued for some while. It would be apparent that their reaction shown here is related to the forthcoming suffering and death Jesus predicted (cf. J. Gnilka, *Das Evangelium nach Markus* [EKKNT, 2; Zürich: Benzinger Verlag, 1989], p. 96; Hooker, *Gospel*, p. 245).

9.   Morris, *Gospel*, p. 270; Schweizer, *Luke*, p. 163; Ellis, *Luke*, p. 219.

10.   '... in mentioning this cause of their slumber Lk. once more "spares the Twelve"' (Plummer, *Luke*, p. 511). Cf. Creed, *Gospel*, p. 273; I.H. Marshall, *Commentary*, p. 833; Schweizer, *Luke*, p. 344.

(4) *Peter's Confession* (Mk 8.27-30/Lk. 9.18-20). It is noteworthy that in the episode of Peter's confession of Jesus as Christ, Luke leaves out Jesus' rebuke to Peter, ἤρξατο ἐπιτιμᾶν αὐτῷ, which is preserved in Mark (Mk 8.32). This element also adds some weight to our argument that Luke describes disciples in a better light.[11]

These four cases of Luke's excuses for the disciples may be significant in determining Luke's more positive position towards the disciples.[12] Taking note of these omissions and changes by Luke of Mark's accounts, Giles helpfully concludes as follows:[13]

> The negative estimate of the disciples may be Markan redactional emphasis and in correcting this picture Luke may be returning to an earlier position, but the systematic way in which he presents the disciples positively does suggest that a deliberate motive is also to be detected. Luke understands that if his readers are to identify with the disciples and see in them a model of what the Church should be like in prosperity and adversity, then their strengths and not their weaknesses must be highlighted.

c. *Summary and Conclusion*

This favourable description of the disciples noticed in Luke seems to be related to his view of discipleship in his whole writings. To put it simply, the disciples in Luke's eyes appear to function as positive models for the members of his own community who should thus consider Jesus' teaching in his Gospel as directed towards themselves as

11. Contra Melbourne, *Slow to Understand*, p. 47.

12. In this context, we should take into consideration the different view on this matter which is advocated by Melbourne in his interpretation of discipleship in the Synoptic Gospels. The key point of his argument is that the unfavourable and negative images of the disciples are not unique to Mark, rather they 'must be seen as features of all three Gospels' (*Slow to Understand*, p. 88). This may be true insofar as we are able to insist that the negative picture of the disciples might have been kept in the layer of the tradition that would have been employed as sources for all the Synoptic Gospels. Nevertheless, even if we are to acknowledge this point, yet it would be incorrect to regard as the same all the Synoptists' views on the disciples, because the degree that the disciples are in fact delineated in a negative or positive light in each Gospel varies according to each Evangelist's theological purposes. Unfortunately it seems to me that this point is neglected by Melbourne. Apart from this point, as a fundamental question, his suspicion regarding Markan priority appears to contribute to weakening his argument. In the final analysis, as I conclude this matter, I would state that just as Mark's portrait of the disciples turned out more negative in the previous chapter, so that of Luke appears relatively more positive in comparison with Mark.

13. Giles, 'Church', p. 132.

his followers. So there is a strong need and a good reason on the part of Luke to describe the disciples favourably, not letting them forsake their Master, because the disciples are the prototype of all Christians of later generations, such as Luke's contemporary Christians. In doing so, Luke appears to be able to admonish his community not to forsake Jesus' teaching on their way to salvation, and to hold firmly what they learn from the Gospel of Jesus and the history of their Church.

This concluding remark concerning Luke's description of the disciples may appear to be little different from that of Mark's. It may be that the goal of both evangelists is similar, but the way they reach it seems to be opposite. In the case of Mark, as discussed earlier, the description of the disciples plays the role of a cautionary tale. That is, by depicting the disciples to have denied and forsaken their Teacher and to have been slow to understand what Jesus taught and prophesied, Mark seems to want to admonish his audience that they should not follow the way the disciples did in the past, being alert lest they be trapped in the same mistakes as their predecessors.

On the other hand, by describing the disciples not to have forsaken their Master so absolutely, but to have been with him until his execution, Luke appears to want to encourage his audience that they should follow the way the disciples did who were with him till the last days of his life on earth, making of them a positive rather than a negative example.

2. Less Sectarian Descriptions of the Disciples

Now let us explore another feature of significance in Luke, which is concerned with the general atmosphere of Luke's Gospel. Since this feature in Luke is also in contrast to that in Mark, it would be helpful to compare these features in both Gospels.

It seems to me that the first thing to be done in dealing with this task is to take into account the *Sitz im Leben* of Mark's Gospel, for it may be determinative in identifying the general situation of Mark's community. As we have already drawn a conclusion on this subject, we may apply it directly to our task here: Mark's community turned out to be under the ever-present threat of persecution and suffering, expecting the imminent end of the world within its generation, so that it might be properly tagged as an apocalyptic community.[14] It appears that such

14. Mk 8.38; 9.1; 10.29-31; 13.3-37. For detail of the discussion of the apocalyptic

an adverse circumstance prescribes Mark's unique view of discipleship, namely, to follow faithfully the way of the cross which Jesus followed to the end, in order to help the members of his community to
cope with such a hardship. Thus it may seem appropriate to call Markan
discipleship a discipleship of crisis.

Another crucial element in this regard is to be found in the Gospel:
the private nature of Jesus' teaching in Mark's Gospel. In Mark the
disciples are specially chosen for hearing and receiving lessons from
Jesus in private on many occasions.[15] By their nature, the private, not
public, lessons cannot include a large audience, so an impression is
given of a limited number of followers of Jesus. In relation to this, it
is also to be noticed that Mark appears reluctant to depict an ὄχλος as
recipients of Jesus' teaching and preaching, while normally he makes
μαθηταί to be the chief audience.[16]

In this context, Mk 4.10-12 (Lk. 8.9-10) needs to be discussed. Here
Mark clearly draws a line of distinction between the band of the disciples and those outside (Mk 4.11), which makes the circle of the disciples appear rather closed and Jesus' teaching limited to a small coterie
of followers.[17] Conversely Luke presents a different view on this point
with changes he made. First, by leaving out ὅτε ἐγένετο κατὰ μόνας
and οἱ περὶ αὐτὸν σὺν τοῖς δώδεκα (Mk 4.10/Lk. 8.9), Luke appears
to eliminate the private and sectarian nature of Jesus' teaching noted in
Mark's version of this story.[18] Secondly, by altering ἐκείνοις δὲ τοῖς
ἔξω (Mk 4.11) into τοῖς δὲ λοιποῖς (Lk. 8.10), Luke seems to blur
the distinction between the circle of the disciples and those outside,

character of Mark, see Hengel, *Studies*, pp. 14-28.

15. Mk 4.10-20, 33-35; 7.17-23; 8.27-33; 9.9-13, 28-29; 10.10-12; 12.43-44.
Cf. Mosley, 'Jesus' Audiences', pp. 139-45.

16. Mark uses ὄχλος 32 times in his Gospel, but except on three occasions,
3.31-35, 7.14, and 8.34, it is just used as a designation of general followers around
Jesus who come and go from time to time, but not as an audience for Jesus' teaching.

17. Cf. Beavis, *Mark's Audience*, pp. 72-78. At this point, Nineham's quotation
from A. Loisy (*Les évangiles synoptiques I et II* [Ceffonds: Chez l'auteur, 1907–
1908], p. 138) is notable: 'The parables are not intended to effect a selection among
the hearers—the selection is thought of as already made; Jesus confines his explanation of the parable entirely to disciples and nothing gives ground for thinking that
others could have obtained the same favour.'

18. Cf. Mosley, 'Jesus' Audiences', p. 146: 'Lk. does not state (like Mk) that the
question was put to Jesus in private, and this omission weakens the impression of an
esoteric communication.' Cf. Creed, *Gospel*, p. 115.

which Mark highlights.[19] In relation to this aspect, it is also to be noticed that Luke omits a number of passages in Mark which show that μαθηταί are recipients of private lessons from Jesus.[20]

What these omissions and alterations made by Luke suggest is that the boundary of the group of the disciples that Luke has in mind is larger than that which Mark has, and in line with this, Jesus' teaching and instruction in Luke is intended not as esoteric nor sectarian for a small circle of the committed disciples but as open and public to a wider circle of followers. This characterization of Lukan discipleship appears to tally with, first of all, the less beleaguered character of Luke's community which we have already drawn from the *Sitz im Leben* of Luke's Gospel. But if we want to carry it on, it seems necessary to get further evidence in order to be able to claim that Luke has in view a wider circle of the disciples in comparison with Mark. Thus in this sense, it may be worthwhile looking at how the disciples are regarded by Luke in terms of the size of the boundary.

To find out the boundary of the disciples Luke has in mind, it is worth, first, looking at the mission of the Seventy at 10.1-16. Although the ἑβδομήκοντα or ἑβδομήκοντα δύο[21] are not called disciples in the

---

19. Beck, *Character*, p. 93: 'He [Luke] preserves from Mark 4.10ff. the distinction . . . but softens it by substituting for Mark's "those who were about him with the twelve . . . those outside" words which mark the distinction less sharply, "his disciples . . . the others", suggesting boundaries which can be more easily crossed (8.9-10)'. Creed, *Gospel*, p. 115, also noted that 'τοῖς λοιποῖς is weaker than ἐκείνοις τοῖς ἔξω'.

In line with this, I.H. Marshall, *Commentary*, p. 322, suggests that Luke's use of τοῖς λοιποῖς 'may reflect church usage' because λοιπός is frequently used for designating non-disciples and non-believers (cf. Acts 5.13; 1 Thess. 4.13; 5.6; etc.). Cf. Schweizer, *Luke*, p. 145.

20. Mk 4.33-34; 7.17-23; 9.11-12, 28; 10.10-11. Taking heed of this prominent feature in Luke, Giles, 'Church', p. 128, remarks that 'for him [Luke] the teaching of Jesus is always public', and Tannehill, *Narrative Unity*, I, p. 207, also states that 'Luke's Gospel shows no interest in esoteric teaching'. Cf. Mosley, 'Jesus' Audiences', p. 143.

21. The exact number of those sent out is textually uncertain. As far as our theme is concerned, however, it does not matter. That at least 70 people are sent out for mission with the Gospel of Jesus is good enough for our purpose. For detailed discussion on this subject, see Evans, *Saint Luke*, pp. 444-45; I.H. Marshall, *Commentary*, pp. 414-15; B.M. Metzger, *A Textual Commentary on the Greek New Testament* (London: United Bible Societies, 1971), pp. 150-51.

given text, there are some indications which would support their identification as disciples:

(1)   ἑτέρους used here calls to mind the former mission of the Twelve Apostles (9.1, 10)[22], and so it can lead to a supposition that the mission of the Seventy or Seventy-two in 10.1-17 is the second one. In this sense, ἑτέρους is seen to link two missions.

(2)   In terms of the context (10.1-24) which seems to be closely integrated, we note that the ἑβδομήκοντα are called μαθηταί in 10.23.

(3)   Even if we may admit that the mission in 10.1 is recorded as an independent incident different from that in 9.1-9, it is significant that its contents (Jesus' injunctions) are not much different from those to the disciples in 9.1-9.[23]

(4)   ἀνέδειξεν (10.1) may also not be insignificant here, because it is known to have the technical sense of appointment to an office in LXX and Hellenistic literature.[24]

(5)   As Schweizer points out, the conclusion of Jesus' instructions (10.16[25]) shows they are addressed to none other than the disciples.

(6)   In this connection, finally, what is noteworthy is that in the last discourse of Jesus to the Apostles in 22.35-38, we find reference to the mission of his disciples in the early days of

22. Plummer, *Luke*, p. 271.

23. Jesus' instructions are largely divided into two categories, i.e. prohibitions and commands, which are shared in common in both mission incidents. Although specific items, such as βαλλάντιον and ὑπόδημα are different, the motifs of these commands are not completely different. In a sense, the case of the Seventy seems to be more rigorous than the Twelve, because they are not allowed to have even ὑποδήματα. It causes us to raise the question: If the Seventy were not μαθηταί, how could more rigorous prohibitions be given to them?

24. Polybius, *Hist.* 4.48.3; 4.51.3; Diodorus Siculus, *Bib. Hist.* 1.66.1; 13.98.1; Josephus, *Ant.* 14.280; 20.277; 2 Macc. 9.23, 25; 1 Esd. 8.23.

25. Schweizer, *Luke*, pp. 176-77. Cf. Mt. 10.40; Jn 12.48; 13.20; 1 Thess. 4.8.

his ministry: Jesus mentions βαλλάντιον, πήρα, and ὑπόδημ-
ατα that are found in 10.4, not in 9.3.[26] This indicates that
among the Seventy are included the Twelve Apostles, and
thus it would not be unreasonable to call them μαθηταί.[27]

Secondly, there is another difference to be noticed between Luke
and Mark which would be in favour of the above observation. Unlike
Mark's Gospel, it is significant that ὄχλος and λαός are often seen to
receive Jesus' teachings along with μαθηταί in Luke's Gospel.[28] Thus
in the sense that they are also recipients of Jesus' teaching and preaching, they can be claimed to be disciples in the broad sense of the word.
In this context, it is worth noting two passages which support this identification in Luke: 6.17, ὄχλος πολὺς μαθητῶν αὐτοῦ and 19.37, ἅπαν
τὸ πλῆθος τῶν μαθητῶν. What is interesting in these two verses is that
μαθηταί is related either to ὄχλος or to πλῆθος. In Luke, it is known
that ὄχλος and πλῆθος are respective designations of a large number
of people. What is clear from these two passages is that the disciples
are not in the least a limited number of followers of Jesus from Luke's
point of view.[29]

26. L.T. Johnson, *Literary Function*, p. 163; Karris, 'Poor and Rich', pp. 118-
19.

27. Cf. I.H. Marshall, *Commentary*, p. 824; Plummer, *Luke*, p. 505.

28. ὄχλος are given a number of teachings by Jesus and John the Baptist: (1) In
3.10-11, they are admonished by John the Baptist to share clothes and food with those
who do not have them. (2) In 8.4-8, the Parable of the Sower is addressed to them.
(3) In 9.23-27, they are commanded by Jesus to take their own crosses and to follow
Him, being prepared to lose their lives. (4) In 11.29-36, calls to repentance (29-32)
and for wholehearted openness to Jesus (33-36) are given to the crowd. (5) In 14.25-
35, they are called to discipleship, which only Luke among the synoptists preserves.
The Λαός are seen to hear the Parable of the Vineyard and Tenants in 20.9-18.

In addition to these separate hearings of ὄχλος and λαός, there are cases where
ὄχλος or λαός are shown to hear Jesus' teachings along with μαθηταί: (1) The
Sermon on the Plain is given both to μαθηταί (6.20) and λαός (7.1). (2) Various
teachings of Jesus in Lk. 12 are addressed both to μαθηταί (12.1, 22) and ὄχλος
(12.13, 54). Among these teachings, however, the Parable of the Faithful Steward
(12.42-48) seems to be intended for μαθηταί only, because of ἄρα in Jesus' answer
(12.42) to Peter's question as to whom Jesus addresses the parables (12.41).

Taking heed of Luke's special interest in λαός, J. Kodell ('Luke's Use of *Laos*,
"People", especially in the Jerusalem Narrative (Lk. 19.28-24.53)', *CBQ* 31
[1969]), pp. 327-43, makes a point that the λαός are friendly to Jesus and his
teaching, which is prominent particularly in the Jerusalem Narrative (19.28-24.53).

29. Beck, *Character*, p. 94; Giles, 'Church', pp. 125-28.

Taking these points together, our observation leads us to the conclusion that in Luke's view μαθηταί are not an enclosed circle of followers, but extend to a large number of general followers of Jesus who are eager to hear His teaching, actually following after Jesus, such as ἀπόστολοι, or remaining at their homes, and therefore, as a matter of fact, it can be said that in Luke's Gospel discipleship is open to a wide public (9.23-27; 14.25-35). Therefore, we can now see clearly that the boundary of the disciples in Luke is quite different from that of Mark.

Now let us examine the case of Acts in relation to this feature. In discussing Luke's description of the disciples in Acts, the first thing that ought to be noticed is that μαθηταί in Acts is employed to designate Christian individuals (9.36; μαθήτρια, 9.10) or congregations in the Early Church, being distinguished obviously from ἀπόστολοι (2.41; 6.2, 7; 9.1, 10, 26, 28; 11.29). Along with this, πλῆθος, ὄχλος and ἀδελφοί are also used to designate Christian believers in the early Christian community.[30] In addition to these, two passages ought to be singled out for our particular consideration: (1) Acts 6.2 where τὸ πλῆθος τῶν μαθητῶν incorporates πλῆθος with μαθηταί, which has a parallel in Lk. 19.37. (2) Acts 11.26 in which ὄχλος is put side by side with μαθηταί, which reminds us of Lk. 6.17. These points may be regarded as Luke's deliberate touch to maintain his idea on the disciples throughout his two books.

This picture of the disciples in Acts confirms that of the Gospel, and allows us to claim that depicting as μαθηταί the whole congregation of the Early Church in Acts, and making these to accord with the large number of followers around Jesus in his earthly ministry, Luke intends to show the members of his community that they are also, by the nature of the case, disciples of Jesus, possessing the same status that the disciples of Jesus had in the past.[31] To conclude what I have discussed

30. πλῆθος, 4.32; 5.14; 6.5. ὄχλος, 1.15; 11.24, 26. ἀδελφοί, 9.30; 11.1.

31. Cf. C.H. Talbert, 'Discipleship in Luke–Acts', in F.F. Segovia (ed.), *Discipleship in the New Testament* (Philadelphia: Fortress Press, 1985), pp. 71-73. This point is also made by Schnackenburg when he summarizes the two planes of the idea of discipleship as follows: 'The demands which Jesus addressed during earthly life [*sic*] to his followers in the narrower sense, that is to say, the disciples who were called by him into personal association with him and to collaborate in his preaching, were transferred in the community after the Resurrection to all Christ's faithful, when there was no longer any discipleship in the former special sense' (R. Schnackenburg, *The Moral Teaching of the New Testament* [London: Burns & Oates, 1982], p. 48, cf. pp. 50-51).

concerning the boundary of the group of the disciples in Luke–Acts, I might state that in contrast to Mark, the disciples in Luke's writings are neither a small number of followers nor an enclosed circle, but rather a wider circle of followers.

3. *Two Types of Discipleship*

In the Synoptic Gospels there are a number of occasions on which Jesus in fact admonishes his disciples to renounce what they have as their own, such as family relationships and possessions, so that they might be able to follow him. Luke appears to stress this element more emphatically, for he records more exhortations of Jesus in this regard than other fellow Evangelists.[32] But it is clear that all his followers did not respond to this call of Jesus literally: some are seen to have acted upon it as austerely as the disciples in Mark, while others are not. Thus here in Luke's Gospel we can find two different types of disciples among those who followed Jesus on his earthly path. To differentiate these two apparently differing types of disciples who appear in Luke, for the sake of convenience, we will use the terms which Beck uses in his book: the itinerant and sedentary.[33] Now let us explore further this element of Lukan discipleship.

a. *Itinerant Disciples*
With respect to the itinerant type of disciples in Luke, a few disciples are seen to have responded to Jesus' call, literally renouncing family relationships and wealth once and for all in order to follow after Jesus in his earthly ministry:

32. For instance, 14.33 is unique to Luke, and 9.57-62 is not found in Mark. In addition, 12.33 and 11.41 appear to contain Luke's own modification to make them suit his theological purpose.

33. Beck, *Character*, p. 95. Although Beck employs these terms for two different types of disciples in Luke, in fact he does not appear to explore this point enough; he refers to Martha and Mary and the cured demoniac at Gerasa, but omits the cases of the Galilaean women and Zacchaeus, not to mention that of Levi. G. Lohfink (*Jesus and Community* [London: SCM Press, 1985]), pp. 31-35, is also interested in this motif, but his ultimate concern is with the fact that the community of the disciples, which, he argues, is 'a firmly fixed group', is the *symbolic* representative of Israel.

(1) The first disciples, that is, Peter, John, and James, followed Jesus, leaving πάντα behind,[34] when Jesus called them to be fishers of men (5.11), and this renunciation by the disciples is later confirmed by Peter's confession at 18.28 where he professed that 'we followed you having left what we have (τὰ ἴδια)'.[35] And also it would not be absurd to suppose that the Twelve Apostles in Luke 9 and the Seventy in Luke 10 whom we have counted as disciples in the above also forsook their private means and property during their mission to proclaim the Kingdom of God, Jesus' commands to them being taken into account (9.3; 10.4).[36] These three episodes illustrate the case of the itinerant disciples: some of the disciples, responding rigorously, renounced in a literal sense everything of their own to follow Jesus.

(2) It is of great significance to observe that Jesus set a living example in this respect for those who wanted to follow him literally. In order to enter into the service of God, that is, to proclaim the Kingdom of God, Jesus left everything of his own, such as his house, mother, brothers, and sisters,[37] and became a penniless wanderer who had nowhere to

34. Luke's use of πάντα instead of the nets and father that Mark depicts the first disciples to have left appears to accentuate 'the totality of the call' (Pilgrim, *Good News*, p. 87), which in turn makes their renunciation absolute. Bovon, *Lukas*, p. 235, names this absoluteness of renunciation as 'lukanischen Radikalismus', gathering up the threads of passages, such as 5.11; 9.62; 12.33; 14.16, 33. Meanwhile, Evans, *Saint Luke*, p. 292, calls this renunciation of the disciples 'a generalization of the cost of discipleship', and Morris, *Gospel*, p. 114, also states that by renouncing all, 'they became disciples in the fullest sense'. Cf. Thompson, *Luke*, p. 98; Schmidt, *Hostility*, p. 140.

35. Luke replaces πάντα in Mk 10.28 with τὰ ἴδια. Noticing the fact that τὰ ἴδια is found only here in the Gospel and Acts 4.32 which reveals the communal aspect of sharing everything, the practice observed in the Early Church, Evans, *Saint Luke*, pp. 653-54, argues that '*ta idia* here is intended to summarize *house* (in the sense of property), *wife. . . children* considered as possessions'. Cf. Thompson, *Luke*, p. 228. Karris, 'Poor and Rich', p. 123, also takes note of Luke's use of this word, but suggests a different view: 'Luke 18.28 refers back to 5.11 (5.28) and ahead to Acts 4.32 and shows one of Luke's major answers to the problems of possessions: voluntary sharing of *ta idia* for the sake of the poor in the community.' Meanwhile, in line with this, relying on usages of ἴδιος in Luke's writings, such as Lk. 6.41, 44; 10.34; Acts 1.7, 19, 25; 3.12; 4.23, 32; 13.36; 20.28; 21.6; 24.23, 24; 25.19; 28.30, Schmidt, *Hostility*, p. 158, tends to interpret it as 'ownership'.

36. It is not clear whether the Seventy followed Jesus with the apostles throughout his journey.

37. Cf. Mk 6.3.

lay even his head (8.19-21; 9.58; cf. 2.41-51).[38] Thus in view of 6.40, 'A disciple is not above his teacher, but every one when he is fully taught will be like his teacher', it may not be surprising to see that Jesus demanded of those who wanted to follow him the same renunciation that he had already made.[39]

b. *Sedentary Disciples*
As mentioned earlier, among those who received a demand from Jesus to renounce all they had to be his disciples, in Luke some are seen not to have responded as rigorously as the former category of the disciples, still living at home, with their family and work. But even if their response was not as rigorous as that of the itinerant disciples, it is clear that they did respond to Jesus' demand in some other way. Let us examine some examples:

(1) Apparently the case of Levi, since it does not show a clear-cut picture, may suit this classification. A puzzling problem is that although he renounced πάντα to follow Jesus when receiving Jesus' call, in the scene that immediately follows he is seen to have held a great feast for Jesus and his disciples in his house (5.29-30).[40] So we cannot be sure

38. Schweizer, *Luke*, p. 286 (cf. p. 287), makes this point as follows: 'Jesus leads the way in practising a childlike life that renounces self-assurance and is focused entirely on God. Thus Jesus also makes this life possible for others'. Cf. Geldenhuys, *Gospel*, p. 296; Pilgrim, *Good News*, p. 97.

39. Cf. Ellis, *Commentary*, pp. 130, 151; Pilgrim, *Good News*, p. 97.

40. It is evident from Luke's view that Levi in 5.27-29 is not a member of the Twelve Apostles according to Luke's version of the list of the Apostles (6.13-16). However, there is a possibility that since the pattern of his call initiated by Jesus is the same as that of the first disciples who later become Apostles (5.1-11), Levi could have been a member of the Apostles, but appeared as a different name in the list (Pilgrim, *Good News*, p. 89; cf. Schottroff and Stegemann, *Hope*, pp. 71, 81; Sweetland, *Journey*, p. 26). The following are features of the pattern we can detect in common in both episodes of the callings: (1) In both cases the first disciples and Levi were approached by Jesus while they were in the midst of working for their daily living (5.2/5.27). (2) Jesus took initiatives to call them to be his followers (5.10/5.27). (3) As soon as they heard Jesus' calling, they immediately left everything and followed him (5.11/5.28).

Besides these common features, when we take into account the fact that among the Twelve Apostles only the three, i.e. Peter, John, and James (apart from Judas for his particular role), appear prominent, while the rest of them remain veiled, though Apostles, that Levi's call is described in detail appears in such contrast that Levi could have been a member of the select group. But at the same time, Luke's change of the

what his leaving of πάντα exactly means.[41] In this picture, however, our primary interest lies in the fact that Levi used his wealth and property, for example, his house, to entertain Jesus and his disciples. Levi used his goods to hold a feast for a wandering Preacher and his disciples who were known to have become voluntarily poor and dependent upon the hospitality of other people.[42]

(2) Luke records a unique pericope which shows brilliantly how the needs of the wandering Preacher and his disciples were met during their mission journey.[43] At 8.1-3 the Galilaean women, such as Mary Magdalene, Joanna, the wife of Chuza, and Susanna, are said to have followed Jesus with the Twelve and also to have supported their Master and his apostles out of their means. This is hardly in keeping with the custom prevalent at that time, particularly for such a teacher of the law as Jesus.[44] What is revealed in this story is, however, that although they

Markan text (Mk 3.17/Lk. 6.14) should be noticed, that is, his omission of 'the son of Alphaeus'. It is probable that Luke omits this phrase not to confuse James in the list of the Apostles (Evans, *Saint Luke*, p. 305; cf. Ellis, *Luke*, p. 107). Therefore, as far as the Lukan text goes, it is rather certain that he was not included in the select group.

41. Noticing that when leaving πάντα Levi was not at his house, which appears not to be included in the πάντα, Plummer, *Luke*, p. 160, remarks that 'πάντα refers to his whole mode of life, his business as a τελώνης'. Cf. J.A. Bengel, *Gnomon of the New Testament* (5 vols.; Edinburgh: T. & T. Clark, 1866), II, p. 61. I.H. Marshall, *Commentary*, p. 219, also takes Levi's action less literally.

42. Jesus' injunctions on the disciples' mission travel remind us of the fact that they were prohibited to carry money or a purse (9.3; 10.4), so that they were in reality πτωχοί.

43. Morris, *Gospel*, p. 151; Caird, *Luke*, p. 115.

With regard to the variant reading in Lk. 8.3, αὐτοῖς or αὐτῷ, see Metzger, *Textual Commentary*, p. 144, where he strongly supports the plural and considers the singular a possible christological correction.

44. On this point, B. Witherington (*Women in the Ministry of Jesus* [Cambridge: Cambridge University Press, 1984], p. 117), comments: 'For a Jewish woman to leave home and travel with a rabbi was not only unheard of, it was scandalous.' Cf. Schweizer, *Luke*, p. 142; Evans, *Saint Luke*, p. 366. But Ernst's suggestion in this respect may explain Jesus' behaviour: 'Jesus setzt sich über derartige tiefsitzende Vorurteile unbekümmert hinweg (Lk. 7,36-50; 10,38-42; Mk 14,3-9; Joh 11,1-6.17-27.28-33a.39f.); er macht aus seiner Haltung kein Programm, aber es werden "Anstöße" gegeben, die weiterwirken und trotz gelegentlicher konservativer Tendenzen in der späteren Verkündigung (vgl.1 Kor 11,7-16; 14,34ff.; Kol 3,18; Eph. 5,22; 1 Tim. 2,10-15) neue Orientierungsdaten gesetzt haben' (J. Ernst, *Das Evangelium nach Lukas* [Regensburg: Friedrich Pustet Regensburg, 1976], p. 262). Bengel

followed Jesus personally (compare 23.49, 54; 24.10), they did still possess private possessions at their disposal: they did not forsake possessions as completely as the itinerant disciples, while travelling with them.[45] Instead of this, they made use of material possessions of their own[46] for the benefit of Jesus and his disciples who left πάντα to preach the Kingdom of God. This enabled the wandering group to concentrate on their mission without being distracted by having to support themselves.[47]

(3) In Luke Jesus and his disciples are seen to have been invited more frequently to lunch or dinner by other people who were attracted by his teaching, when compared with Mark and Matthew (Lk. 7.36-50; 11.37-41; 14.1-24). So it is not surprising to see that this element of hospitality occupies room in Jesus' mission commands to his disciples sent out for preaching the gospel (9.3-5; 10.4-11).[48] Martha and Mary are among those who showed hospitality to Jesus and his disciples by receiving them into their house and entertaining

---

(*Gnomon*, II, p. 78), Grundmann (*Lukas*, p. 174), and Witherington (*Women*, p. 118) also mention this implication. Cf. Morris, *Gospel*, p. 150.

Besides, although these women from Galilee in Luke's report appear again at Jesus' crucifixion and burial, they do not appear with the band of Jesus' group during their journey. So it seems unclear whether they accompanied Jesus and his disciples all the time till the end of his ministry (cf. F.W. Danker, *Jesus and the New Age* [St Louis: Clayton Publishing House, 1974], p. 101). However, it seems probable that, as Schweizer and Evans suggest, Luke adds this story in advance, looking forward to 'the services provided by women in the communities with which he was familiar' (Schweizer, *Luke*, p. 142). Nonetheless, it is unlikely that Luke created this story out of nothing. Cf. Witherington, *Women*, p. 117; I.H. Marshall, *Commentary*, p. 317.

45. Cf. B. Gordon, *The Economic Problem in Biblical and Patristic Thought* (Leiden: E.J. Brill, 1989), p. 69.

46. Probably the scale of their expenses would have been large, the whole band of the wandering followers around Jesus being duly calculated; this would indicate that 'they were persons of substance' (Plummer, *Luke*, p. 216).

47. Gordon's opinion that 'the call to thoroughgoing disinvestment and economic dependence applied to men only, and merely for the period of "the Lord's year of favour" . . . ' (*Economic Problem*, p. 70) appears improbable, since although the Galilaean women did not abandon their capital at all, it is certain that they renounced the ownership of their capital for the benefit of other people. So in this sense it is not wrong to state that the Galilaean women went through the 'thorough-going disinvestment' in a different way as compared with that of the itinerant disciples.

48. Schweizer, *Luke*, p. 152, notes that in Palestine 'hospitality is an accepted social norm'. Cf. Caird, *Luke*, p. 116.

them.[49] Here too our primary attention is focused on the fact that their provision for Jesus and his disciples, which tallies with the picture we have seen at 8.1-3, also reminds us of the proper use of possessions and property which they exercised to serve their Master to whom they belonged.

The other point which we can take heed of here is Luke's portrait of Mary sitting at the Lord's feet (παρακαθέζομαι; v. 39), which can be regarded as 'a technical formula meaning "to be a disciple of"' (compare Acts 22.3; Lk. 8.35).[50] Thus it would be imagined from this picture of Mary that Luke introduces Mary as a model of the sedentary disciple, who lived according to the Lord's teaching, although she did not leave home or family nor abandon her wealth like the itinerant disciples.[51]

(4) The incident of Zacchaeus can be dealt with similarly to that of Martha and Mary. One thing that should not be missed here is that Jesus took the initiative to let Zacchaeus serve him (19.5). At any rate it appears evident that on that day Zacchaeus received the wandering

49. Admitting on the one hand that 'the picture of Martha as mistress of a house inviting men to come in is almost inconceivable in Palestine', Schweizer, *Luke*, p. 142, on the other hand, also recognizes that 'Jesus did not develop a program, but he initiated changes that were to have far greater effects' (pp. 142-43). Cf. Witherington, *Women*, pp. 100-103.

50. Witherington, *Women*, p. 101; Ellis, *Luke*, p. 161. In view of 8.35, 39, as Beck notes (*Character*, p. 95), the cured demoniac of Gerasa can also be thought of as a sedentary disciple of Jesus.

51. Even if Martha got a sort of reproach from Jesus for her minding many things (vv. 41, 42), it is to be acknowledged that it is Martha as the hostess who received Jesus and his group. In this sense, we may suggest that while Mary is introduced as a disciple eager to hear words of Jesus, Martha can be portrayed as a disciple willing to put into practice the teaching of Jesus concerning Christian love by providing for such a wandering Preacher and his disciples. This might be in keeping with Jesus' teaching at 8.21, 'My mother and my brothers are those who hear the word of God and do it', and Lk. 11.28, 'Blessed rather are those who hear the word of God and keep it!' (this verse is exclusive to Luke).

In this context, Grundmann's appreciation of this story as linked with the previous parable, i.e. the Parable of the Good Samaritan, appears to be worth noting: both stories place emphasis on the love of one's neighbour which must be expressed in accordance with the love of God (*Lukas*, p. 225). Danker, *Jesus*, pp. 133-34, also takes notice of this point, but appears to apply it inappropriately: 'Thus Luke's association of the story of Mary and Martha with that of the Good Samaritan illustrates well his (Luke's) grasp of the challenge of Jesus' address to legalistic dehumanization.' Is there anything related to 'legalistic dehumanization' in this story?

preacher and his companions into his house and entertained them. It is just in line with the case of Martha and Mary that Zacchaeus used his house and private means in the service of Jesus and his disciples. Another weighty element to be noticed in this story is Zacchaeus's promise to give half of his possessions to the poor and to reinstate fourfold if he had swindled other people. Even if his promise did not imply total renunciation,[52] yet it would be a considerable loss on his part laid down in the interests of the poor. This benevolence of Zacchaeus is acknowledged distinctively by Jesus who declared that 'Today salvation has come to this house, since he is also a son of Abraham' (19.9). From this picture we learn that in Luke's mind it would be acceptable for the rich not to sell πάντα, because 'Zacchaeus' response is also a legitimate one', and 'the response which Peter and the apostles (18.28-30) gave to Jesus' invitation is not the only one possible'.[53]

(5) Joseph of Arimathea should also be mentioned in this discussion (23.50-54). Luke describes him as having waited for the Kingdom of God which Jesus preached in his ministry, although he was a member of the council, the *Sanhedrin*. So it does not surprise us that he asked Pilate to hand over the body of Jesus, and wrapped it in an expensive linen shroud and buried it in a tomb cut in rock which had not been used previously.[54] It is worth noticing that Joseph disposed of part of his private means and property, for example, the linen shroud and a chamber of the tomb for Jesus willingly. This behaviour of Joseph shows us another valuable case where wealth was used in the service of the master to whom he belonged.

(6) Having discussed these actual episodes regarding the sedentary followers, we can pursue this point further by appraising the fact that Jesus' requirement to relinquish possessions and family relationships in order to be his disciples is not addressed exclusively to the itinerant disciples or such a selected group as the apostles, but to all followers of Jesus. It is clear from the texts that 14.26, 33 are addressed to the crowd and 5.27 and 18.22, to potential general followers, such as Levi and the Rich Ruler. And in the subsequent passages, 18.23-24, while in Mark the disciples are seen as the addressees of Jesus' teaching on the

52. Cf. Gordon, *Economic Problem*, p. 66.
53. Karris, 'Poor and Rich', p. 123.
54. From Luke's picture of Joseph, it is known that he was also a man of substance, because ordinary people were not able to afford to obtain such a tomb cut out of rock for their private use (Evans, *Saint Luke*, p. 882; Morris, *Gospel*, p. 331).

danger of riches, in Luke it is addressed to just οἱ ἀκούσαντες (18.26), definitely not the disciples as Mark records. So by omitting the reference to the disciples, Luke appears to articulate in this account that 'the comments of Jesus are to be considered as directed to non-disciples, attempting to stir them up to realize the danger of riches'.[55] 9.57-62 is also to be regarded as addressed to general followers, because it appears to be linked to the following passages, 10.1-16, in which the Seventy disciples are sent out to preach the Kingdom of God.

(7) A common point we can observe from these incidents is that although they did not follow Jesus literally, Luke records that Jesus appears to have accepted them as they were, not reproaching them for not taking his demand as literally as the itinerant disciples.[56] This aspect may lead us to claim that these followers who did not literally abandon their goods are also to be counted as the disciples of Jesus, because they put into practice Jesus' demand of renunciation of material possessions and family relationships[57] in a different way that Jesus recognized:[58] they used material possessions to serve their Master and his disciples who became voluntarily poor for the sake of God and his Kingdom, and to help the poor. In this sense, we may be able to state that the sedentary disciples also followed Jesus' requisition of renunciation giving up the *ownership* of their material possessions, while the itinerant disciples worked out his call to renunciation literally.[59]

55. I.H. Marshall, *Commentary*, p. 686.

56. Cf. Bornkamm, *Jesus*, p. 147.

57. In Luke there are quite a few accounts referring to family relationships, but less than those of possessions; 8.19-21; 11.28; 12.49-53; 14.26; 18.29-30. In the matter of family relationships it is to be noticed that unlike the injunctions about wealth, Jesus in Luke does not appear consistent in demanding his disciples to sever family relationships, but rather to advise them to give priority to the spiritual level of the new relationship in God rather than to the physical level of the old relationship. Plummer, *Luke*, p. 225, appears to explain this point quite appropriately while commenting on 8.21: 'Christ's reply is not a denial of the claims of family ties, nor does it necessarily imply any censure on His Mother and brethren. It asserts that there are far stronger and higher claims. Family ties at the best are temporal; spiritual ties are eternal.' Cf. Morris, *Gospel*, p. 154. Bearing this point in mind, Fitzmyer, *Gospel*, p. 723, describes Jesus' mother and his brothers as 'model or prime examples of disciples'.

58. 'Nowhere in this respect is an exclusive line drawn between them (the followers remaining at their home) and the disciples' (Bornkamm, *Jesus*, p. 147). Cf. Blinzler, 'Jesus', p. 93.

59. Cf. Gordon, *Economic Problem*, p. 64.

(8) Now it is time to think of the motive Luke might have borne in mind in letting Jesus accept the sedentary disciples, while preserving more rigorous commands of Jesus on renunciation of possessions than Mark and Matthew, for example, Lk. 9.61-2; 14.33.[60] These seemingly contradictory aspects seem to be related to the *Sitz im Leben* of Luke's Gospel. When we are reminded of Luke's emphasis on the ongoing situation of Christian living, which is supported by Luke's insertion of καθ' ἡμέραν in Lk. 9.23 (compare Mk 8.34), which appears indicative of 'the day-to-day implications of discipleship',[61] and the notion of the delay of the *parousia* to be found in Luke, it helps us appreciate how Luke can take a literal demand of Jesus in Mark in a metaphorical sense: renunciation of wealth[62] need not mean literally giving it all

60. Gordon, *Economic Problem*, pp. 64-76, also takes notice of the two differing layers of discipleship related to the economic problem, although his appreciation of it is not quite identical to that we have seen above. Luke's portrait of the disciples who abandoned their capital reveals, he argues, his 'anti-capital and pro-dependence propensities' (p. 65), but at the same time his description of the well-to-do figures in Luke–Acts, such as Zacchaeus, Martha and Mary, the Galilaean women, Lydia, shows the opposite side of the same coin. He concludes his treatment of the tension in Luke's thought as follows:

> The conclusion is that Luke failed to resolve the tension he experienced concerning discipleship and the economic problem. Personal predisposition suggested that the true disciple was concerned with that problem only in its short-run distributive aspect. Issues of production and forward-planning should be left to the Father. However, Luke's reflection on some of the sayings and actions of Jesus, on the empirical realities of the early Church, and on the role of women in the plan of salvation prevented him from writing Christian economic behaviour simply in his own image (p. 70).

It appears to me that the cause of Gordon's trouble with Luke's thought of discipleship and the economic problem is not to recognize properly the two different types of discipleship of Lukan discipleship and the two different implications of renunciation, e.g. literal and metaphorical renunciation, which I have discussed above. And in relation to the tension he brings to light, I also feel uneasy with the way that he distinguishes 'Luke's own image' from 'his reflections', which was mentioned just above. What is his criterion to do this? Finally, it seems improbable to judge Luke as having 'anti-capital and the pro-dependence propensities', which I find is too strong an expression of Luke's views.

61. Beck, *Character*, p. 100. So the notion of the cross is to be differently appreciated in Luke. In short, the cross in Luke's view does not necessarily imply a literal reality of suffering and death, but a metaphorical sense, that is, readiness to face hardships. This idea has support from Luke's version of the Lord's Prayer where disciples are asked to pray for bread καθ' ἡμέραν in Lk. 11.3 (cf. Mt. 6.11; σήμερον).

62. In favour of this element, Karris, 'Poor and Rich', p. 121, does not interpret

away. Put briefly, our conclusion would be that Luke is not preoccupied with total renunciation of possessions in a literal sense because
it would not have meant anything in his community, but with the right
use of wealth because his community seems to have faced problems
with the poor, or problems that the rich may have caused because of
their wealth.[63]

(9) What can we say then about the case of the itinerant disciples? It
seems that this case belongs to the tradition that was fashioned about
Jesus and his disciples from the beginning of Jesus' earthly ministry;
Jesus was seen to be with a band of followers who accompanied him on
his earthly path, the apostles he appointed in particular being a major
part of it.[64] Thus it seems probable that Luke does not have much room
to manoeuvre in dealing with this case.

(10) I shall sum up and conclude. In Luke there are quite a few followers of Jesus whom we can classify into the category of the sedentary disciples: Levi (5.27-29), the Galilaean women (8.1-3), Martha
and Mary (10.38-42), Zacchaeus (19.1-10), and Joseph of Arimathea
(23.50-54). Interestingly the number of incidents of this category exceeds that of the itinerant disciples, and except for the cases of Levi and
Joseph, the other three cases referred to here are exclusive to Luke
among the Synoptists. These two features with the results drawn from
my discussion would indicate that Luke's concern lies as much in the
sedentary as in the itinerant, and that, as pointed out earlier, Luke is
more preoccupied with the right use of possessions than with literal
renunciation of them.

Having noticed this point, we can state that Luke seems to keep and
even emphasize the radical notions of total renunciation of goods, but
understands that as the renunciation of the *ownership* of goods, which
some exercised by giving them all away and others by using them in

---

14.33 literally but somewhat metaphorically: 'Its verbs show that the proper translation should go: all disciples must be *ready* to renounce their possessions'. Cf. I.H.
Marshall, *Commentary*, p. 594.

63. Cf. H. Wansbrough, 'St Luke and Christian Ideals in an Affluent Society',
TNB 49 (1968), pp. 582-87 (587).

64. Bornkamm, *Jesus*, p. 150, states that the appointment of the twelve disciples
is not created by the post-Easter Church, but goes back to the historical Jesus. For
more information about the apostles in Luke, see Schneider, 'Die zwölf Apostel',
pp. 61-85; cf. Blinzler, 'Jesus', p. 93.

the service of the poor and the Master to whom they belonged. Thus in the next chapter I will explore the theme of the master–servant relation in Luke's Gospel.

Chapter 4

THE MASTER–SLAVE MOTIF IN LUKE'S GOSPEL

After having discussed Luke's concept of discipleship related to possessions in the previous chapter, I cannot help wondering if the idea of
discipleship is after all appropriate to embrace fully his re-oriented
concept of wealth. When we look at Luke–Acts carefully with this
suspicion, then possibly we cannot fail to notice another predominant
motif which would define the Christian relationship to God/Jesus in
Luke–Acts, instead of the teacher–pupil relation which constitutes discipleship. Thus in this chapter I will look at the material in Luke–Acts
relating to this motif, and see how Luke developed it as one of the
conspicuous features of his writings.

1. Analysis of the Use of Terms

In order to investigate Luke's particular interest in the master–slave
motif, it would be helpful first to investigate Luke's use of terms to
describe masters, slaves, and related concepts. In dealing with this task,
it would be appropriate to divide the terms into four categories: the first
is the terms Luke alone employs, the second is the terms Luke shares
with Matthew, the third is the terms Mark and Matthew also employ
in their Gospels, and the last is the terms not explicitly confined to the
master–slave motif.

a. Terms Used Only by Luke
To stress his focus on the relation between masters and slaves Luke
appears to utilize a variety of terms available to him. It is particularly
striking that most of the terms used by him do not appear in the other
Gospels.

1.   *The Designation of Jesus or God*
     • ἐπιστάτης: Lk. 5.5; 8.24, 45; 9.33, 49; 19.13 (seven times).
     • δεσπότης: Lk. 2.29 (Acts 4.24).[1]

2.   *The Designation of Servants*
     • οἰκέτης: Lk. 16.13 (Acts 10.7).
     • οἰκονόμος: Lk. 12.42; 16.1, 3, 8 (four times).
     • δούλη: Lk. 1.38, 48 (twice), (Acts 2.18).

3.   *Other Terms Alluding to the Master–Slave Motif*
     • οἰκονομία: Lk. 16.2, 3, 4 (three times).
     • οἰκονομέω: Lk. 16.2.
     • διακονία: Lk. 10.40 (Acts 1.17, 25; 6.1, 4; 11.29; 12.25; 20.24; 21.19 [eight times]).
     • περιζώννυμι: Lk. 12.35, 37; 17.8 (Acts 12.8).
     • κυριεύω: Lk. 22.25.
     • ὑπηρετέω: (Acts 13.36; 20.34; 24.23).

b.   *Terms Luke Shares with Matthew*
     • οἰκοδεσπότης: Lk. 12.39; 13.25; 14.21; 22.11 (four times)/ Mt. 10.25; 13.27, 52 (three times).
     • δουλεύω: Lk. 15.29; 16.13 (twice)/Mt. 6.24 (twice).
     • παῖς (servant): Lk. 1.54, 69; 7.7; 12.45; 15.26 (five times)[2]/ Mt. 8.6, 8, 13; 12.18; 14.2 (five times).[3]
     • ἐπίτροπος: Lk. 8.3/Mt. 20.8.

1.   Since my concern in this chapter is mainly the master–slave motif in Luke's Gospel in contrast with the other dominant motifs found in Mark and Matthew's Gospels, the case of Acts is introduced as secondary in terms of value.
2.   With the meaning 'child' παῖς is used four times (Lk. 2.43; 8.51, 54; 9.42). In Acts it is employed once to mean a servant (4.25) and four times for a youth (3.13; 4.27, 30; 20.12). It is generally acknowledged that in ancient Greece and Rome slaves were called 'child' (παῖς, *puer*) and addressed as children, because they were seen as similar to children (T.E.J. Wiedemann, *Slavery* [Oxford: Clarendon Press, 1987], p. 25). M.I. Finley (*The Ancient Economy* [Berkeley: University of California Press, 1973], p. 96), is of the opinion that this was 'another dehumanizing device' prevalent at the time.
3.   In Matthew there are three occasions where παῖς is used with the meaning of child (2.16; 17.18; 21.15).

c. *Terms Shared with Mark and Matthew*

• κύριος:	Jesus[4]	Parable	God	Total
Luke	42	25	38	105
Mark	6	2	7	15
Matthew	31	29	21	81

- δοῦλος: Luke, 27 times;[5] Matthew, 30 times;[6] Mk 10.44; 12.2, 4; 13.34; 14.47 (five times).[7]
- διακονέω: Lk. 4.39; 8.3; 10.40; 12.37; 7.8; 22.26, 27 (twice) (eight times)[8]/Mk 1.13, 31; 10.45; 15.41 (four times).

d. *Terms Not Explicitly Confined to the Motif*

- ἡγέομαι: Lk. 22.26 (Acts 7.10; 14.12; 15.22; 26.2).
- ἡγεμονία: Lk. 3.1.
- ἡγεμονεύω: Lk. 2.2; 3.1 (twice).
- λειτουργέω: (Acts 13.2).
- λειτουργία: Lk. 1.23.
- λατρεύω: Lk. 1.74; 2.37; 4.8 (three times)[9]; Mt. 4.10.
- ἡγεμών: Lk. 20.20; 21.12 (twice)/Mk 13.9.
- ἄρχων: Lk. 8.41; 11.15; 12.58; 14.1; 18.18; 23.13, 35;

---

4. In this analysis *Jesus* and *God* mean that κύριος is used to designate Jesus or God, *Parable* means that it is used in the parables, mainly designating a master in those stories. For details of the references, see G.D. Kilpatrick, 'ΚΥΡΙΟΣ in the Gospels', in J.K. Elliott (ed.), *The Principles and Practice of N.T. Textual Criticism: Collected Essays of G.D. Kilpatrick* (Leuven: Leuven University Press, 1990), pp. 213-22 (207-22).

5. Lk. 2.29; 7.2, 3, 8, 10; 12.37, 38, 43, 45, 46, 47; 14.17, 21 (twice), 22, 23; 15.22; 17.7, 9, 10; 19.13, 15, 17, 22; 20.10, 11; 20.50. 21 times out of 27 it is used in the parables; in the other cases, such as Lk. 2.29; 7.2, 3, 8, 10; 22.50, it is used for a real character.

6. Mt. 8.9; 10.24, 25; 13.27, 28; 18.23, 26, 27, 28, 32; 20.27; 21.34, 35, 36; 22.3, 4, 6, 8, 10; 24.45, 46, 48, 50; 25.14, 19, 21, 23, 26, 30; 26.51. Among these 30 occurrences, it is used 25 times in the parables, two times for a real character (8.9; 26.51), and three times in Jesus' teaching (10.24, 25; 20.27).

7. In Mark's case, among five occurrences, it is used three times in the parables (12.2, 4; 13.34), once in Jesus' teaching (10.44), and once for a real character (14.47).

8. Acts 6.2; 19.22. Among the terms connected with the motif, there is only one word which is present in Mark and Matthew but absent in Luke, that is, διάκονος (Mt. 20.26; 22.13; 23.11/Mk 9.35; 10.43).

9. Acts 7.7, 42; 24.14; 26.7; 27.23 (five times).

24.20 (8 times);[10] Mk 3.22.
* ὑπηρέτης: Lk. 1.2; 4.20[11]/Mk 14.54, 65.

After enumerating the terms in Luke explicitly or implicitly related to the master–slave motif, I now draw attention to a few key words which play an important role in this regard: κύριος, ἐπιστάτης and δοῦλος.

First, it is remarkable to note that although Luke employs διδά-σκαλος 17 times (12 times by Mark and 10 times by Matthew[12]), it is used mostly by those who are non-disciples, while ἐπιστάτης is employed only by his disciples to designate Jesus.[13] In this context, it is also to be noticed that on two occasions Luke alters Jesus' designations in Mark from διδάσκαλος to ἐπιστάτης (Mk 4.38/Lk. 8.24; Mk 9.38/Lk. 9.49).[14]

Secondly, with respect to δοῦλος, Luke's employment of the term far exceeds that of Mark (Luke, 27 times; Mark, 5 times), and so it can be regarded as an important token of Luke's concern about the master–slave motif in his Gospel.[15]

Thirdly, among those terms referred to above, what interests us most is κύριος. The initial meaning of this word in the Hellenistic period is

10. Acts 3.17; 4.5, 8, 26; 7.27, 35 (twice); 13.27; 14.5; 16.19; 23.5 (eleven times).

11. Acts 5.22, 26; 13.5; 26.16.

12. But in the case of μαθητής, Mark's 46 uses of the term exceeds by far Luke's 37 occurrences. On the motif of the teacher–pupil relationship in Mark's Gospel, see the next section.

13. Cf. B.B. Warfield, *The Lord of Glory* (Grand Rapids: Baker Book House, 1976), pp. 99-100; G. Vos, *The Self-Disclosure of Jesus* (Phillipsburg: Presbyterian and Reformed Publishing, 1978), p. 135. In Mark the disciples, the Pharisees and others all use διάσκαλος in addressing Jesus, and only one occasion is recorded in Mark when κύριος is employed by the Syro-Phoenician woman (Mk 7.28). Matthew uses both terms. Cf. F. Hahn, *The Titles of Jesus in Christology* (London: Lutterworth, 1969), pp. 73-80.

14. In addition, Luke also changes ῥαββί and ῥαββουνί in Mk 9.5 and 10.51 into κύριος (Lk. 9.33; 18.41).

15. The term itself is used more frequently by Matthew (30 times) than by Luke (27 times), but when we put together the other terms referring to slave in Luke, such as οἰκέτης (once), οἰκονόμος (four times) and δούλη (twice), which are not found in Matthew but only in Luke, we may be confident to state that Luke is very consistent in showing his interest in the master–slave motif in his work.

the owner of slaves and property, who has the right and power to control them.[16] This secular notion of the term can still be found throughout the New Testament.[17] Later this word applied to gods in the oriental-Hellenistic religions, and this phenomenon might have influenced the designations of God in the Old Testament, so in the LXX κύριος replaces יהוה and אדון becoming 'the standard Biblical name for God'.[18] It is therefore of great significance to see that among the 42 occurrences of κύριος Luke as narrator calls Jesus κύριος 15 times,[19] while Mark and Matthew as narrator never call Jesus κύριος in their Gospels.[20] After reviewing the uses of the term made by the Synoptic Evangelists, Vos[21] also makes the point that 'the Evangelists observe great restraint from injecting the title *Kyrios* into their own discourse within the Gospels, although they might have done so with entire propriety'.[22] This general tendency observed in Mark and Matthew throws Luke's case into bold relief, because only Luke as narrator refers to Jesus as κύριος among the Synoptic Evangelists.[23] This finding shows us that Luke has a particular interest in κύριος, and it is a natural corollary that this feature is linked to the master–slave motif in Luke's Gospel.

16. W. Förster and G. Quell, 'κύριος', *TDNT*, III, pp. 1041-46.

17. Mk 12.9; Mt. 15.27; Lk. 19.33; Acts 25.26; Eph. 6.5, 9; Col. 3.22; 4.1; 1 Pet. 3.6.

18. Hahn, *Christology*, pp. 68-73. Cf. O. Cullmann, *The Christology of the New Testament* (London: SCM Press, 1973), pp. 195-99; C.F.D. Moule, *The Origin of Christology* (Cambridge: Cambridge University Press, 1980), pp. 35-46. However, Förster and Quell, 'κύριος', p. 1046, hold to the view that 'The first example of κύριος used of deity is to be found in the LXX', arguing that κύριος in the environment of Hellenism is used primarily in a political or legal sense but not in a religious sense. Bousset and Bultmann take a different view by asserting the Hellenistic character of the title. Cf. Hahn, *Christology*, p. 68.

19. Lk. 7.13, 19; 10.1, 39, 41; 11.39; 12.42; 13.15; 17.5, 6; 18.6; 19.8; 22.61 (twice); 24.3.

20. Kilpatrick, 'ΚΥΡΙΟΣ', pp. 211, 214. Cf. I.H. Marshall, *The Origins of New Testament Christology* (Leicester: IVP, 1985), pp. 99-100.

21. Vos, *Self-Disclosure*, pp. 118-40.

22. Vos, *Self-Disclosure*, p. 127.

23. This feature unique to Luke can be explained by saying that 'Luke retrojects the title *kyrios* into the first phase of Jesus' earthly existence', which must have been current in his contemporary community (Fitzmyer, *Gospel*, p. 203). Cf. Warfield, *Lord*, pp. 103-104.

To conclude from the study of the terms in relation to the master–slave motif in Luke, it is clear that Luke among the Synoptic Evangelists tends to employ many more terms related to the motif than the other Evangelists, and even where he uses the same terms, in general he tends to employ them more frequently than Mark and Matthew: κύριος, οἰκοδεσπότης, δουλεύω and διακονέω are particularly clear examples. Therefore, even from this statistical observation it appears that Luke has a particular interest in the master–slave motif as compared with the other Evangelists.

2. *Prominent Motifs in the Other Gospels*

Now that we have seen this feature in Luke highlighted by his use of terminology, it would be helpful to look into corresponding features which can be detected in the other Gospels.

a. *The Teacher–Pupil Motif in Mark*
In the previous chapter we have noticed that Mark has a special interest in discipleship, so it would not be surprising that Mark shows the same interest in the teacher–pupil motif, because a μαθητής is a learner in the proper sense of the word.

(1) References to διδάσκω in Mark number 17, among which 15 apply to Jesus; Luke uses the term 17 times too, but among them 14 apply to Jesus; and Matthew employs the term 14 times of which 9 apply to Jesus.

(2) Mark mentions διδάσκαλος 12 times, all of which apply to Jesus, while Luke employs it 17 times (12 times for Jesus), and Matthew, 10 times (8 times for Jesus).

(3) In the case of μαθητής, Mark refers to it 46 times, whereas Luke refers to it just 37 times, and Matthew, 73 times. Presumably, on the grounds of Matthew's rather frequent use of μαθητής, we could claim that he is also interested in the teacher–pupil motif, along with the motif of father–son relation which will be discussed in the next section.

(4) Mark employs διδαχή five times (1.22, 27; 4.2; 11.18; 12.38), while Luke uses it just once in his Gospel (4.32), and Matthew, three times.

(5) In addition to these, it is noteworthy that ῥαββί (Mk 9.5; 11.21; 14.45) and ῥαββουνί (Mk 10.51), designations applied to Jesus, are only used by Mark.

(6) In all these cases, what we should bear in mind is the fact that compared with Luke and Matthew, in view of the volume of material each Gospel retains, Mark is the smallest, surpassed far and away by Luke and Matthew.[24] Therefore, in spite of his small volume of material, that Mark utilizes more terms regarding the teacher–pupil relation and refers to them more frequently than Luke and Matthew may be significant evidence to demonstrate his concentration on the teacher–pupil motif.[25]

b. *The Father–Son Motif in Matthew*

It is noteworthy that Matthew uses the terms linked to the father–son motif, such as πατήρ and υἱός, much more frequently than Mark and Luke.[26] A more remarkable thing to be observed while reading Matthew's Gospel is that in most cases the terms are employed in the material where Jesus addresses moral teaching to his hearers, such as the Sermon on the Mount (Mt. 5.1-7.29). Meanwhile, in Luke and Mark

---

24. Here it is worth taking note of the density of the Synoptic Gospels: Matthew contains 1070 verses from 28 chapters, Luke 1150 verses from 24 chapters, while Mark has 666 verses from 16 chapters presupposing the short end of the Gospel. So the proportional rate is that Mark is 58 per cent as compared with Luke, and 62 per cent in comparison with Matthew. This figure shows that Mark's use of these terms in relation to the teacher–pupil motif should be regarded as significant because its density is much higher than that of the other Gospels:

	Mark	Luke	Matthew
διδάσκω	17 (15)*	17 (14)	14 (9)
διδάσκαλος	12 (12)	17 (12)	10 (8)
μαθητής	46	37	73
διδαχή	5	1	3
ῥαββουνί	1	0	0
ῥαββί	3	0	0

* The numbers in brackets signify their applications to Jesus.

25. This characteristic motif observed in Mark appears in keeping with the atmosphere of Mark's Gospel as a whole. Since the Markan community is regarded as one which was facing impending severe persecutions, it would be plausible that if one wants to be a true disciple of Jesus, he should follow Jesus to the end in spite of death, acting upon the example and teaching of his Teacher. Thus, as a result, it might be understandable that emphasis is laid on the teacher–pupil motif in the second Gospel.

26. πατήρ, 63 times in Matthew; 19 times in Mark; 55 times in Luke; υἱός, 90 times in Matthew; 34 times in Mark; 77 times in Luke.

the terms are usually used in the descriptive narratives and actual incidents, but not very often in the material of Jesus' teaching and instruction.

Accordingly, while Mark mentions ὁ πατήρ ὑμῶν just once in Mk 11.25 and Luke refers to it only three times (Lk. 6.36; 12.30, 32), Matthew refers to it 19 times.[27] In the case of Jesus' mention of God as his father, ὁ πατήρ μου, Mark does not mention it at all, and Luke, only three times (10.22; 22.29; 24.49), whereas Matthew refers to it 16 times.[28] It is also meaningful to note that in most cases πατήρ is not used in Matthew without genitive pronouns (ὑμῶν or μου), which leads us to suppose that Matthew wants to show that God should be acknowledged in this intimately personal relationship to his people.

That these terms, such as ὁ πατήρ and ὁ πατήρ μου, are mentioned in Jesus' addresses to his hearers may be indicative of Matthew's interest in showing his readers that Christians are the children of God and that God is their father. It is also of significance that Matthew places even Jesus himself under this relationship—he who in fact teaches people that same relationship between God and his people. Consequently, these features in Matthew suggest that he was much keener to highlight the father–son motif than Mark or Luke.[29]

To sum up: what is drawn from the observation of Luke's use of the terms related to the master–slave motif and the contrast among the three Gospels in the light of certain prominent motifs is that Luke seems more preoccupied with the master–slave motif, whereas Mark is more concerned with the teacher–pupil motif and Matthew, the father–son motif, alongside that of teacher–pupil.[30] But, as usual, it is

27. Mt. 5.16, 45, 48; 6.1, 4 , 6 (twice), 8, 9, 14, 15, 18 (twice) 26, 32; 7.11; 10.20, 29.

28. Mt. 7.21; 10.32, 33; 11.27; 12.50; 16.13; 18.10, 19, 35; 20.23; 25.34; 26.29, 39, 42, 53.

29. This particular motif in Matthew seems to tally with the character of Matthew's Gospel; since the Matthean community disclosed in the first Gospel has been thought of as consisting of mainly Jewish Christians, it would seem that Matthew wants to portray the relation between God and believers in terms of the traditional Old Testament concept of the relation between God and His people, Israel, that is, the father–son relationship.

30. D. Guthrie, *New Testament Theology* (Leicester: IVP, 1981), pp. 292-93, also takes heed of this point, acknowledging the significance of Luke's use of κύριος in relation to the master–disciple relationship which he regards as strong in the Synoptic Gospels.

a matter of degree rather than an absolute contrast in this regard.

3. *Material Related to the Master–Slave Motif*

As the terms related to the master–slave motif have been examined, it would now be appropriate to look into the material which expresses the master–slave motif in Luke's Gospel, comparing Luke's material with that of Mark and Matthew, which might reveal Luke's particular concerns and interests.

In what follows, therefore, I will discuss the master–slave motif in detail, attempting to appreciate Luke's theology on this particular theme. For the sake of convenience, I divide the material into two categories: one is Luke's special material, and the other is that which overlaps with Mark and Matthew.

a. *Material Unique to Luke*
It is to be noticed that in relation to the master–slave motif Luke has considerable material unique to him which Mark and Matthew do not have: the Parable of the Unjust Steward (Lk. 16.1-13), the Parable of the Unworthy Servant (Lk. 17.5-10), the Parable of the Fig Tree (Lk. 13.6-9), the Birth Narrative (1.26-56; 2.22-40), and the Parable of the Prodigal Son (15.11-32). Hence these pericopae need to be explored to some extent to detect Luke's interest in the motif.

1. *The Parable of the Unjust Steward (16.1-13).* Since I will deal with this parable elsewhere,[31] here I want to point out simply the significance of this parable in relation to the master–slave motif, which is a lesson that the Lukan Jesus wants to address to his readers. In this parable Jesus exhorts his hearers to use possessions on behalf of the poor neighbours in the way that the steward of this parable reduces the debt in order to help his poor neighbours who are in great debt to his master. So the steward in this parable is in fact described as a paragon whom Christians may have to follow (16.8-9). Accordingly, this parable appears to be typical material that illustrates very clearly Luke's idea of stewardship with the motif of the master–slave relation for a background. That this parable is special material unique to Luke adds extra weight to this significance.

31. See Chapter 5.3.

2. *The Parable of the Unworthy Servant (17.5-10)*. Responding to the Apostles' request to increase their faith, Jesus tells them this parable as a part of his answer to their request. In fact, however, this parable does not seem to have anything to do with the Apostles' request.[32]

One thing which interests us in the analysis of this parable is the fact that although apparently the apostles appear to be addressees of this parable, when we are reminded that they were not rich enough to own slaves as they left their houses and possessions,[33] this parable may be particularly intended for the rich Christians in Luke's community[34] rather than the apostles who left behind their homes and material possessions literally to take part in the itinerant ministry of Jesus.[35] This reminds us of Luke's concern about the rich Christians in his contemporary Christian community.

But this is not a pivotal point in this parable. What matters here is not the attitude of the master but that of the servant.[36] That is to say, what is to be pointed out here is that however faithfully a slave may

32. Although some scholars want to contend, relying on the motif of forgiveness of sin in Lk. 17.1-4 and that of faith to forgive others (vv. 5-6) (Ellis, *Luke*, p. 207), that there is a continuity between this parable and its precedent, yet this contention seems to be a 'forced and unsatisfactory' attempt (Plummer, *Luke*, p. 401), because apparently there is no possible link that could connect one with another; vv. 5-6 deal with the power of faith that can make a miracle, while vv. 7-10 deal with the duty of a Christian as a servant. Jesus' saying in Lk. 17.6 is placed in different settings in Mark (11.23) and Matthew (17.19, 20), and there is no obvious connection between 17.1-4, 5-6 and 7-10. Thus most scholars regard this parable as separate from the preceding sayings (Cf. Evans, *Saint Luke*, p. 621, Creed, *Gospel*, pp. 214-15, and Plummer, *Luke*, pp. 398, 401).

33. Lk. 5.11; 18.28.

34. 'The words almost necessarily imply that they were addressed to a mixed audience of well-to-do persons' (Plummer, *Luke*, p. 401). It is also to be noted that some followers of Jesus, such as the sedentary disciples, might have been able to own slaves (Lk. 5.27-29; 19.1-10; 23.50; Ellis, *Luke*, p. 208).

35. Counting on Jesus' answer to the apostles in the text, some scholars argue that this saying of Jesus is addressed to the church leaders or missionaries of Luke's time (Evans, *Saint Luke*, p. 622). To the contrary, Schweizer, *Luke*, p. 264, presents an opposite view on this saying that 'there is no allegorical reference to missionaries and community leaders'.

36. In this sense it can be said that this parable wears a double face, since it appears to expose not primarily an attitude of the master towards the servant, but in fact rather an attitude of the servant towards his master. Cf. Evans, *Saint Luke*, p. 622. Plummer makes a remark as regards this parable that 'It is the ordinary duties of the Christian life that are meant' (*Luke*, p. 401).

carry out his duty and obligation, he is not supposed to claim anything from his master on that ground.[37] To take it a step further, if we can paraphrase this point of the parable, it can be said that the master is God, and the slave is a Christian believer.[38] In this sense, although Christians ought to be faithful to the tasks given to them, yet that does not enable them to claim any reward from their Master because it is a basic attitude required of any servant of God. The key point of this argument extracted from this parable bolsters well Luke's notion of stewardship, for an important attitude required of a servant is faithfulness to his given tasks and assignments.

Further evidence for this may be found in other passages in Luke's Gospel, such as Lk. 19.17, 19; 12.37-38, and 12.42-44, where slaves who are faithful in their work are generously rewarded with praise, and, in contrast, Lk. 12.45-48, 16.2, and 19.22-24, where slaves who are not faithful in their work are severely reprimanded. Consequently, this parable is of significance in that it deals with a matter of faithfulness on the basis of the master–slave motif which is an essential aspect of stewardship in Luke's conception.

3. *The Birth Narrative (1.5-80; 2.22-40).* This part of the Birth Narrative, exclusive to Luke among the four Gospels, describes vividly what Mary experienced before and after she gave birth to the baby Jesus. What draws our attention in this Birth Narrative which is known to be influenced particularly by the LXX[39] is that Mary calls herself

---

37. ἀχρεῖοι (Lk. 17.10) signifies initially 'unprofitable' as in Mt. 25.30. Creed appears to show an appropriate reason why this word is employed here by Luke: 'The emphasis must not fall on the quality of the service rendered, but on the circumstance that those who have done all are, at the end, servants and no more' (*Gospel*, p. 216). Cf. Plummer, *Luke*, p. 402; Evans, *Saint Luke*, p. 622.

38. Cf. Creed, *Gospel*, p. 216.

39. R.E. Brown, 'Luke's Method in the Annunciation Narrative of Chapter One', in C.H. Talbert (ed.), *Perspectives on Luke–Acts* (Edinburgh: T. & T. Clark, 1978), pp. 126-38 (128); D.L. Barr and J.L. Wentling, 'The Conventions of Classical Biography and the Genre of Luke–Acts: A Preliminary Study', in C.H. Talbert (ed.), *Luke–Acts: New Perspectives from the Society of Biblical Literature Seminar* (New York: Crossroad, 1984), pp. 63-88 (72); Guthrie, *Theology*, p. 292.

Fitzmyer, *Gospel*, pp. 343-55, 418-43, enumerates a number of similarities between Luke and the LXX in this area of the Birth Narrative, but denies that 'the Christian use of *kyrios* for Jesus in the absolute as "Lord" or "the Lord" comes from this Septuagintal or Palestinian usage' (pp. 200-204).

ἡ δούλη κυρίου (1.38),[40] while κύριος is referred to 17 times.[41] This frequency of the term is indicative of Luke's indebtedness to the LXX where κύριος is the regular title for God.[42] In line with this element, another concern of ours is the fact that Simeon who has been waiting to see τὸν Χριστὸν κυρίου (2.26) according to the promise proffered to him, designates himself as δοῦλος (2.29) after he sees the baby Jesus, while addressing God as δέσποτα (v. 29). In addition to this, it is also remarkable to note that, apart from δεσπότης, κύριος is employed seven times from 2.22 to 2.40,[43] and that Israel in the Magnificat (1.54) and King David in Zechariah's song (1.69) are designated as παῖς (servant).[44]

To sum up from this observation, what is clear is that as well as the constant repetition of the title κύριος, people who play major roles in the Birth Narrative are designated as δοῦλος or παῖς.[45] In this context, it might be worthwhile to take into account that although Luke could refer to θυγάτηρ or θυγάτριον instead of δούλη, and τέκνον, νήπιος and παιδίον instead of δοῦλος and παῖς, yet he tends to designate Mary as δούλη, Simeon as δοῦλος, and Israel and David as παῖς.

Thus, Luke displays his intention to delineate the relation between God and Christian believers as the master–slave relation from the outset of the Gospel. This is good evidence for the significance of the master–slave metaphor in Luke, because it is found at the beginning of the Gospel and in Luke's *Sondergut*.

4. *The Parable of the Fig Tree (13.6-9)*[46]. It might be right to interpret this parable in the light of an exhortation to repentance depending

---

40. Cf. 1.48, τῆς δούλης αὐτοῦ; Acts 2.18.

41. Lk. 1.6, 9, 11, 15, 16, 17, 25, 28, 32, 38, 43, 45, 46, 58, 66, 68, 76.

42. Förster and Quell, 'κύριος', pp. 1039-95.

43. Lk. 2.22, 23 (twice), 24, 26, 38, 39.

44. In Zechariah's song κύριος is referred to twice (1.68, 76).

45. In some cases, παῖς is used to mean a child, but here it implies a slave or a servant.

46. With respect to this parable there is nothing in common between Luke's parable and the actual incident in Mark (11.12-13) and Matthew (21.18-19) in which the fig tree is referred to, except the mere mention of the fig tree. Thus it can be claimed that this parable is also peculiar to Luke (Creed, *Gospel*, p. 181; Schweizer, *Luke*, p. 220).

To the contrary, interestingly, Goulder, *Paradigm*, II, pp. 561-62, argues that in this parable Luke combines the actual incident in Mk 11.15-18 and the Parable of the

upon the link, δέ (13.6), between this parable and its precedent.[47] However, it is worth noticing again the setting of the parable in the relationship between master and slave which is unfolded in the conversation between the κύριος (v. 8) and his ἀμπελουργός (v. 7).

Although it is not primary, however, the relation between the owner and his gardener draws our attention in view of stewardship as well. Here the ἀμπελουργός appears to be in charge of the whole vineyard which belongs to the master (κύριος, v. 8), and to be responsible for the well-being of all trees in the vineyard. Since he does not get any fruit from the fig tree for three years, the master wants to cut it down immediately. Apparently it might be the servant's fault that the fig tree has not borne fruit for three years. However the conversation between the master and his servant does not display any fault on the part of the slave, so that we may infer from this that the servant is not blamed for the unproductivity of the fig tree, in other words, the problem lies in the tree itself. Thus the servant pleads with his master for the fig tree to be saved, with the promise that he would do his best to get him fruit, that is, 'to dig about it and put on manure' (v. 8). This must be a piece of good advice to the owner,[48] so that it is evident that the faithfulness of the slave is thrown into relief in this parable. To put it another way, the servant is seen to make every endeavour to make his master's assets and property profitable, which is a definite qualification demanded of the servant. Thus here in this brief parable we are able to ascertain some important features of the Lukan stewardship already discovered in the previous parable. That this parable is peculiar to Luke may add extra weight to our case here.

5. *The Parable of the Prodigal Son (15.11-32)*. As regards the master–slave motif in this parable, apart from its main theme, our attention is

Vineyard in Mk 12.1-11 along with Mt. 3.8 where the fate of an unfruitful tree is introduced in order to 'rewrite the incident as a parable'. Against this assertion, Plummer, *Luke*, pp. 339-40, makes clear that 'It is arbitrary to assert that the withering of the barren tree in Mt. xxi. and Mk. xi. is a transformation of this parable into a fact, or that the supposed fact has here been wisely turned into a parable'.

47. Plummer, *Luke*, p. 340; Evans, *Saint Luke*, p. 548; Schweizer, *Luke*, pp. 219-20; Schmithals, *Lukas*, p. 151.

48. Morris, *Gospel*, p. 222, notes that 'The vinedresser counsels patience. Perhaps treatment of the soil and the application of manure for a further year will bring results. It will give the tree one last chance to produce. But the vinedresser recognizes facts'.

focused on the terms employed to designate a servant, such as δοῦλος (v. 22) and παῖς (v. 26). This would indicate the world Luke takes for granted, for it would be natural that the rich owned lots of slaves under their command in Luke's contemporary society. While the master–slave relationship is not the focus of the parable, Luke's setting shows his familiarity with the institution of slavery which he takes for granted as a 'natural' feature of his social context.

6. *Other Minor Stories with this Motif in the Background.* (1) In the story of the mission of the Seventy at Lk. 10.1-16, we can note that to preach the kingdom of God in advance of his journey to the towns and places, Jesus who is referred to as κύριος here (v. 1) sent out (ἀπέστειλεν) his disciples as a Master dispatches his servants. (2) In the incident of Martha and Mary at Lk. 10.38-42, it is to be noticed that Martha, calling Jesus κύριε (v. 40), appears to regard Jesus as a Master 'who ought to distribute the work of the slaves properly'.[49] (3) The story of Zacchaeus also interests us in this regard, not only because both Luke as narrator and Zacchaeus in the account refer to Jesus as κύριος (v. 8), but also because Zacchaeus's behaviour before Jesus reminds us of the attitude the servant should take before his master: 'a good slave, or imperial subject, is supposed to move before he is asked'.[50]

b. *Material which Overlaps with Mark and Matthew*
1. *The Calling of the First Disciples (5.1-11).* It is remarkable that Luke's version of Jesus' calling of the first disciples is patently differ-ent from those in Mark and Matthew (Mk 1.16-20; Mt. 4.18-22). It is not our concern here to discuss the origin of the difference, but simply to note its effects.

Heed should be taken here of the attitude of Simon Peter towards Jesus who performs a miracle under the eyes of Peter, his brother and partners. After seeing the miraculous catch of fishes Peter, kneeling down to Jesus, calls him κύριε (v. 8), but even before that, in v. 5, Peter called Jesus ἐπιστάτα.[51] This bearing and this designation of

49. F.W. Danker, *Luke* (Proclamation Commentaries; Philadelphia: Fortress Press, 1983), p. 42.

50. Danker, *Luke*, p. 42.

51. 'Lk. alone uses ἐπιστάτης (viii. 24, 45, ix. 33, 49, xvii. 13), and always in addresses to Christ. He never uses Ῥαββεί, which is common in the other Gospels,

Peter towards Jesus might be significant because they lay bare clearly the master–slave relation between Jesus as a master and Peter as his servant. Therefore we may assert ultimately that at the programmatic call of the archetypical Christian Luke attempts to bring this feature to light, making his own version of the calling of the first disciple(s) obviously different from its counterparts in Mark and Matthew.

2. *The Parable of the Watchful Servant (12.35-40).* Mark has a parable (13.35-37) that can be thought of as being related to Luke's parable but it has a different setting from that of Luke.[52] Meanwhile, there is no compatible counterpart in Matthew with this parable of Luke, yet Mt. 25.1-13 can be presented as having some affinity to it.

In this parable what attracts our attention is that although in Mark the parable is written with the master–slave relation for a background,[53] yet it is too short to get stressed; on the contrary, however, Luke's parable is detailed and extended enough to reveal his concern for the master–slave relation motif. With respect to the motif, vv. 35 and 36 display a primary attitude required of a servant, namely, the readiness for serving his master, which is later applied to every Christian believer at the concluding remark of Jesus (v. 40). Also περιζ-ώννυμι, exclusive to Luke, which occurs in vv. 35, 37 and also in 17.8, is noticeable here for its close association in this Gospel with readiness of the slave to serve. The other point of importance to be noticed here is the master's recompensing behaviour, that is, his humble service for his slaves who turn out to be faithful to their master in being ready for him at any time. This exceptional act of the master to his slaves in this

esp. in Jn, but would not be so intelligible to Gentiles. The two words are not synonymous, ἐπιστάτης implying authority of any kind, and not merely that of a teacher. Here it is used of one who has a right to give orders' (Plummer, *Luke*, p. 143). Cf. Creed, *Gospel*, p. 74. This word is also argued by Glombitza to be used here in order to 'distinguish Jesus from a "teacher" (διάσκαλος) of a theological school' (Ellis, *Luke*, p. 103).

52. In Luke the master is gone to attend a wedding banquet, while in Mark he is gone just for a journey.

53. τοῖς δούλοις, v. 34; ὁ κύριος τῆς οἰκίας, v. 35. It appears that watchfulness is the main theme in Mark's version of the story, γρηγορέω (vv. 34, 35) being used three times. This seems appropriate because this short parable is placed in the chapter of the 'little apocalypse' of the Gospel.

parable, which Luke alone records (using διακονεῖν as well),[54] appears
in conflict with the view of 17.7-10 and 22.24-27 where Jesus is
shown like a servant who is ready for service. However, it is to be
understood that the exceptional behaviour of the master in this parable
anticipates that of Jesus serving his disciples there, supporting Luke's
unique idea of the master–slave motif.[55] Therefore, we may state that
this parable of Luke is distinctively based on the master–slave relationship.[56]

3. *The Parable of the Wise and Faithful Steward (12.42-48)*. It is true
that this parable, in view of the contents, is connected with the preceding parable, yet it appears unreasonable to regard the two parables as
a single unit. A chief reason for this is the different characters who
appear in both parables: while in the preceding parable, the servant is
just an ordinary one, the servant in the current parable is a steward
who is assigned to be in charge of all property and belongings of his
master, including other slaves. Thus the steward in this parable is supposed to be not only watchful being ready for service but also faithful
in carrying out his assignment as a steward. So unless these two parables are to be dealt with separately we would not be able to appreciate
their primary import.

This parable of Luke has its counterpart in Matthew. However, they
differ in detail in unfolding their stories, although the import both
Evangelists intend to convey may be the same, namely, the watchfulness
of a servant. The character in Luke's parable is a steward being in
charge of all property and belongings of his master, including other
slaves,[57] whereas the character in Matthew's parable is just one of the
ordinary servants which is seen in v. 49, συνδούλους αὐτοῦ.

The difference in the terms used here to designate the servants, that
is, οἰκονόμος (Luke) and δοῦλος (Matthew), is also not to be neglected.
It may be that in expressing his main idea Luke could have succeeded

54. C.H. Dodd, *The Parables of the Kingdom* (New York: Charles Scribner's
Sons, 1961), p. 127.

55. Cf. Dodd, *Parables*, p. 127; J. Jeremias, *The Parables of Jesus* (London:
SCM Press, 1963), pp. 53, 95; Evans, *Saint Luke*, p. 534. Concerning the import of
this paradoxical behaviour of the master in this parable, see the later discussion of
Lk. 22.24-27.

56. Cf. Vos, *Self-Disclosure*, p. 126.

57. Here θεραπεία implies 'household' or 'body of servants' (Creed, *Gospel*,
p. 177).

in conveying the main import of the parable sufficiently, even if he did not use the term, οἰκονόμος, simply employing δοῦλος as Matthew does and thus not introducing the concept of stewardship at all. However, that he makes use of οἰκονόμος and the notion of stewardship related to it may be indicative of his particular interest in stewardship.[58]

4. *The Parable of Ten Minas (19.11-27)*. Although this parable in Luke takes a similar form to that of the Talents in Matthew, its composition appears awkward, unlike Matthew's parable, because two dissimilar stories are put together into one story.[59] No matter what the structure may be, however, it is important that both parables concur with each other as far as the master–slave motif is concerned.

On the ground that a major character here in this parable is ἄνθρωπός τις εὐγενής who goes to a distant country to accede to the throne and returns, it could be asserted that the dominant underlying motif is not the master–slave but the king–subject relation as we have seen in Mt. 22.1-14. But when we are reminded that this nobleman orders his private servants as a master before he becomes a king, and οἱ πολῖται[60] are referred to as a separate category from οἱ δοῦλοι in the context, it is clear that the master–slave relationship is, once again, a dominant metaphor.

5. *The Parable of the Tenants of the Vineyard (20.9-18)*. This parable is common to all three Synoptists (Mk 12.1-12; Mt. 21.33-46). It develops with the relation between the owner of a vineyard (ὁ κύριος τοῦ ἀμπελῶνος, vv. 13, 15) and his hired tenants (οἱ γεωργοί, vv. 10, 11, 14, 16) as main characters. But servants also appear (vv. 10, 11), even though they are simply playing the role of extra characters. Thus at least we may state bearing this in mind that this parable is also written against the social background of slave ownership that Luke takes for granted.

6. *Jesus who Serves (22.24-27)*. Here Luke seems quite free to make his own version of the story because its parallels in Mk 10.42-45 and

58. Full discussion of this parable is found in Chapter 5.2.
59. See Chapter 5.4.
60. These may be understood as the king's subjects as the NIV puts it (I.H. Marshall, *Commentary*, p. 705). πολίτης is exclusive to Luke, and occurs twice more in his writings (15.15; Acts 21.39).

Mt. 20.25-28 are very similar to each other. One point that draws our attention in this material is that in Mark and Matthew, Jesus still refers to himself in the third person in the past, ὁ υἱὸς τοῦ ἀνθρώπου . . . ἦλθε (Mk 10.45/Mt. 20.28), which is impersonal, whereas in Luke he employs the first person in the present, ἐγώ . . . εἰμι (Lk. 22.27), to designate himself 'in the form of a personal statement by Jesus of himself as exemplar'.[61] We may ask here why Luke makes Jesus refer to himself ὡς ὁ διακονῶν at this stage where material related to the master–slave motif comes to an end: why does Luke attempt here to depict Jesus as a slave who should be portrayed as a master, at the climax of the master–slave material, despite his persistence in defining the relation between the Lord and Christians as that of master to slave?

We may answer this question by saying that Luke intends to portray Jesus as a model of a slave which he has tried to show to his readers. To develop this point a bit further, after referring to many lessons concerning the attitude a Christian as a slave ought to hold, enumerating as much material related to it as he can, finally here by describing as a slave, ὁ διακονῶν, Jesus who taught these lessons, Luke appears to succeed in presenting a concrete model that every Christian who comes to be his disciple should follow.[62] Therefore, Luke's lesson that Jesus, the Master, is present among us as a slave may summarize adequately what Luke tries to tell his readers by means of the master–slave motif in his Gospel.

4. *Summary and Conclusion*

Let me now sum up what I have discussed thus far: (1) by recording a number of passages focusing on the master–slave motif which exceed those in Mark and Matthew, (2) by selecting a variety of terms related to the master–slave motif, and (3) in the case of the same terms which the three Evangelists use in common, by employing them more frequently than the other Evangelists, Luke seems to endeavour to throw the master–slave motif into bold relief. The significance of this motif is that it reveals the position of a Christian as a servant with regard to his

---

61. Evans, *Saint Luke*, p. 797.

62. Evans paraphrases Lk. 22.24 in his own words, which I think reveal what Luke really wants to say in this passage, as 'I am in your company as the master who serves your needs, or "as your exemplar in serving the needs of men"' (*Saint Luke*, p. 798).

relationship to God or Jesus as the Lord.[63] This motif uniquely empha-sized by Luke seems in accordance with the general atmosphere of Luke's Gospel: since Luke's community is regarded as one in which the demeanour of a Christian in the context of daily life is stressed due to the delay of the *parousia*, it is reasonable that in that community the master–slave relation is highlighted so that a Christian as servant should live up to the Lord's instruction recognizing the sovereignty of the Lord in his daily life.

Now having discussed the master–slave metaphor so far in Luke I summarize my discussion as follows:

(1) Luke's terminology and the frequency of the appearance of slaves in his parables and narrative shows his familiarity with the presence of slaves in society—slavery is a social fact which is readily available as a metaphor for Christian living.

(2) Luke 1–2 show Luke's indebtedness to the LXX, where κύριος is the regular title for God. Luke is representative of the early Christian application of this title to Jesus and even refers to Jesus in the narrative frequently as ὁ κύριος.

These two factors combined make it natural that Luke should use the master–slave relationship as a metaphor for the Christian relationship to God/Jesus, as we have found both in archetypical cases (Mary, Peter, and the like) and in central parables which establish the nature of Christian obligation. From this new prevailing motif in the Gospel it is shown that Luke intended to define the proper relationship between God/Jesus and Christians as the master–slave relationship, rather than simply the teacher–pupil relationship.

Thus far we have discussed the Lukan idea of discipleship and, in relation to this, the master–slave motif in Luke's writings, and as a result discovered two prominent features of Luke's theology. On the one hand, in Luke's view, proper discipleship does not necessarily involve the adoption of literal poverty, but rather is related to the right use of possessions, forgoing the *ownership* of goods; on the other

---

63. Danker, *Luke*, pp. 41-43, also takes notice of this motif, though in passing, but connects it with the motif of benefaction in the Gospel: 'Luke's application of the term slave to a follower of Jesus is consistent with his view of God as the supreme Benefactor and of Jesus as the chief expression of his benefactions' (p. 41).

hand, Luke is seen to be preoccupied with the master–slave motif, presenting a Christian disciple as servant and God or Jesus as the Master. When these two characteristic features of Luke's work are combined, we may understand why Luke seems to have a particular interest in the steward figure, because a steward has resources at his disposal like the sedentary disciples, and also, as slave, is responsible to a higher authority for his use of the material possessions entrusted to him. So bearing this point in mind I shall explore Luke's view of the theme of stewardship in the next chapter.

Chapter 5

LUKE'S VIEW OF STEWARDSHIP

The aim of this section is to draw out Luke's basic ideas of steward-ship by discussing three accounts in Luke's Gospel, incidentally all the parables, which speak of his essential thoughts on stewardship. I could deal directly with the key points of Lukan stewardship, but it seems better to discuss the parables one after another, not only because each parable speaks for itself with regard to stewardship, but also because the context of each parable is to be taken into account.

1. *Stewards and their Household Functions*

In order to have an understanding of stewardship in Luke's perspec-tive, it is, first of all, important for us to know who and what a steward was and what his role and function were in Luke's Gospel and also in his contemporary society.

First, let us examine the functions which the stewards (οἰκονόμοι) in Luke's Gospel play in their duties and responsibilities. In Lk. 12.42-48, the parable of the prudent and faithful steward, the steward is seen to be in charge of the whole household (θεραπεία, v. 42), so that his function is like a superintendent who has full authority to take care of other servants of his master by distributing the food allowance at the proper time.[1] If he succeeds in this task, he will be given greater

---

1. The point that the steward is not one of the ordinary slaves but a chief slave in the house gets support from a comparison with Luke's counterpart in Matthew in regard to the description of the other slaves, i.e. παῖδες (παιδίσκαι) in Lk. 12.45 and σύνδουλοι in Mt. 24.49. Creed, *Gospel*, p. 177, claims that Luke on purpose 'alters this to conform with his substitution of οἰκονόμος for δοῦλος above'. Mean-time, Plummer, *Luke*, p. 332, identifies the οἰκονόμος here with the Roman *dispen-sator* or *vilicus* who is 'a superior slave left in charge of the household and estate'. Cf. Evans, *Saint Luke*, p. 536; T.W. Manson, *The Sayings of Jesus* (London: SCM Press, 1957), p. 291. The Vulgate renders *vilicus* here.

responsibilities as well as authority to take care of the master's property and possessions (ὑπάρχοντα, v. 44). In the parable of the unjust steward (Lk. 16.1-13), we find that the role of the steward appears to be that of a treasurer or an accountant who has a commissioned authority to transact financial dealings on behalf of his master with the debtors who owe a considerable amount of money to his master.[2] The ten servants in the parable of the ten minas (Lk. 19.12-27) appear to play the role of trader or banker;[3] they are allocated the same amount of money, one mina, and supposed to make profits with it for the interests of their master.

Having outlined the functions that the stewards in Luke's parables play in discharging their obligations, we can now look into what sort of roles stewards played in Luke's contemporary society.

Slavery existed throughout the history of antiquity from the ancient age of Greece onwards, and it seems that it reached its peak at the age of the Roman Empire. In ancient Greece and Rome, slaves were owned by both states and rich individuals,[4] so it is known that there were a variety of jobs and occupations allocated to the slaves according to their masters' concerns. The slaves owned by states were employed usually in the areas of administration and finance, such as accountants, treasurers, and policemen in the city of classical Athens, and so were called 'civil servants',[5] which may be the origin of the current system of our age. The slaves owned by wealthy individuals were also given various sorts of jobs in domestic affairs. The following are some examples of the domestic jobs allocated to household slaves in the Graeco-Roman world:

2.   The Vulgate has *vilicus* here, and Plummer, *Luke*, pp. 381-82, takes him as a *procurator* who is sometimes superintended by a *dispensator* and *vilicus*. Meanwhile, Evans, *Saint Luke*, p. 595, takes him as 'the factor of an estate or a financial agent'. Cf. H.J. Cadbury, 'Erastus of Corinth', *JBL* 50 (1931), pp. 42-58.

3.   Plummer, *Luke*, p. 439.

4.   Slaves owned by the emperors were also called 'public slaves' because they did imperial civil services as well (R.H. Barrow, *Slavery in the Roman Empire* [London: Methuen, 1928], p. 130). Cf. T.E.J. Wiedemann, *Slavery* (Oxford: Clarendon Press, 1987), pp. 43-44.

5.   T.E.J. Wiedemann, *Slavery*, pp. 41-43. Cf. J. Stambaugh and D. Balch, *The Social World of the First Christians* (London: SPCK, 1986), pp. 66-67. For more details about the public slaves, see Barrow, *Slavery*, pp. 130-50.

(1)   Male Slaves: *unctor* (masseur), *auri custos* (jewellery atten-
        dant), *balneatores* (bath attendants), *nuntii* and *renuntii cur-
        sores* (messengers), *muliones* (mule drivers), *pedisequus*, or
        διάκονος (attendant), *salutigeruli pueri* (pages), *agaso*
        (groom), *calator* (footman), *cellarius* (store-keeper), *paeda-
        gogus* or παιδαγωγός (chaperon of children), *coquus* (cook),
        insularius (porter and rent collector), *lecticarii* (litter-
        bearers), *horrearius* (warehouse man).

(2)   Female Slaves: *nutrix* (nurse), *obstetrix* (obstetrician), *cistel-
        latrix* (wardrobe keeper), *vestiplica* (clothes folder), *ianitrix*
        (doorkeeper), *tonstrix* (hairdresser), *pedisequa* (attendant),
        cantrix (singer).[6]

Apart from the matter of ownership, the domestic slaves on the whole
were also divided into two categories in the light of the place where
they worked, that is, the urban and rural slaves, and each sort of slave
had different jobs resulting from the surroundings in which they were
placed.[7] As for the rural slaves who were normally engaged in farming and shepherding, we know from Cato's *De Agricultura* that there
were various occupations allocated to the rural slaves, such as *bubulci*
(ploughmen), *subulcus* (swineherd), *opilio* (head shepherd), *asinarius*
(donkeyman), *salictarius* (osier manager), *pastores* (shepherds), *politor*
(cleaner), *capulator* (oil drawer), *leguli* and *strictores* (olive pickers),
custodes (overseers), *vilicus* and *vilica* (bailiff).

What attracts my attention most among these various kinds of privately owned slaves is the *vilicus* and *vilica*, because their role appears
to be similar to that of the οἰκονόμος I am currently dealing with.

6.   K.R. Bradley, *Slavery and the Rebellion in the Roman World, 140 BC–70 BC*
(London: Indiana Press, 1989), pp. 29-30; Barrow, *Slavery*, pp. 22-64; W.L.
Westermann, *The Slave Systems of Greek and Roman Antiquity* (Philadelphia: The
American Philosophical Society, 1955), p. 13. Bradley notes that this job specifi-
cation was established at the periods of the late Republic and early Empire. For more
details of household slaves, see T. Wiedemann, *Greek and Roman Slavery* (London:
Croom Helm, 1981), pp. 122-53; T.E.J. Wiedemann, *Slavery*, pp. 33, 38; R.P.
Saller, 'Slavery and the Roman Family', in M.I. Finley (ed.), *Classical Slavery*
(London: Frank Cass, 1987), pp. 65-87.
7.   For the discussion of the condition of domestic slaves, see J.M.G. Barclay,
'Paul, Philemon and the Dilemma of Christian Slave-Ownership', *NTS* 37 (1991),
pp. 161-86 (165-70).

According to *De Agricultura* written by Cato, a *vilicus* is said to be 'the most elevated slave worker on the farm' because of the character of his job which was to supervise 'the slave workers, both at work and in the material sphere'.[8] Plautus introduced in one of his comedies, *Casina*,[9] an example of a *vilicus*, Olympo:

> his sphere of command is a *praefectura* or *provincia*; he is able to appoint a deputy in his absence, to assign jobs on the farm, to supervise the hands' food and sleeping arrangements; and his threats to put Chalinus in the yoke or make him a water carrier serve to illustrate how any *vilicus* might maintain discipline.[10]

Columella who wrote a systematic treatise on agriculture in 12 books plus a thirteenth book on trees in the mid-first century CE, also left a valuable piece of work as regards the role and function of managers or stewards while giving advice about the selection of managers and labourers and their tasks.[11] The managers' roles referred to by Columella are very similar to those of the *vilicus* that we have discussed above in reviewing Cato's *De Agricultura* and Plautus's comedies. In addition, Xenophon (c. 425–355 BCE), an Athenian soldier, historian and writer on moral philosophy, also left some essays in this regard in his book, Οἰκονόμικος,[12] recognizing the importance of the οἰκονόμος (ἐπίτροπος) which Brockmeyer explains as follows:

> Als wichtige Person erschien lediglich der Verwalter ἐπίτροπος, weil ihm die Aufgabe des Stellvertreters des Herrn zukam, damit dieser für die politischen Aufgaben in der Stadt frei wurde. Die Heranziehung dieser privilegierten Sklaven stand für Xenophon ganz im Vordergrund.[13]

---

8. Bradley, *Rebellion*, p. 27; cf. Barrow, *Slavery*, pp. 75-76; Westermann, *Slave Systems*, pp. 68-69; Stambaugh and Balch, *Social World*, pp. 68-69. Cato (234–149 BCE), a censor of 184 BCE, acknowledged the importance of the manager in order to maintain and improve productivity of his farm, because usually it was difficult for an owner of the farm like Cato himself to visit his estate frequently due to his personal job in the city. Thus in his book, *De Agricultura*, which he wrote for his son, Cato the Elder prescribed a code of conduct which his manager must keep while taking care of his master's property and slaves (*De Agric.* 2.1-3; 5).

9. *Cas.* 52, 99, 103, 105, 109, 117-31, 255-59, 418.

10. Bradley, *Rebellion*, p. 28.

11. Columella, *De re rustica*, 1.8.1-20; 1.7.1-7. Cf. N. Brockmeyer, *Antike Sklaverei* (Darmstadt: Wissenschaftliche Buchgesellschaft, 1979), pp. 184-90.

12. Οἰκονόμικος, 9.11-13.

13. 'The steward appears as an important person, for the master makes him be his representative. In doing so, the master becomes free to carry out his political duty

Moreover, this function of the managers in Greek and Roman literature appears to correspond to that of בְּדְרִת in rabbinic literature, who is known as 'a kind of chief slave who superintended the household and even the whole property of his master'.[14]

Having examined various ancient writings with regard to the role and function of a manager or steward, we may draw the conclusion that although the terms employed to designate those figures[15] are different in comparison with οἰκονόμος in Luke's use, it is to be recognized that the role and function of the manager are almost the same as those of the οἰκονόμος in Luke's Gospel. Hence from this finding we may go on to argue that, being aware of this function of the manager from his personal experience in contemporary society, Luke appears to have attempted to employ the function of the manager to explain the demands of Christian stewardship for the benefit of his readers, the members of his church.

2. *The Parable of the Faithful and Wise Steward*
(12.41-48/Mt. 24.45-50)

The Parable of the Faithful and Wise Steward shows us for the first time in the Synoptic Gospels a motif related to a steward and lessons related to stewardship. Before entering into a detailed exegesis of the text, first of all it may be helpful to consider the context in which the parable is placed.

for the city. Thus, employing this privileged slave is very important for Xenophon.' Brockmeyer, *Sklaverei*, p. 125; cf. *Sklaverei*, pp. 124-27.

14. O. Michel, 'οἰκονόμικος', *TDNT*, V, p. 149.

15. Apart from *vilicus* and ἐπίτροποι, there occur other terms used for a steward figure who is said to have done supervisory work as a slave, such as *dispensator* and *a veste* (in charge of the slaves caring for clothing) and their function appears similar to that of *vilicus* and ἐπίτροποι (Saller, 'Slavery and the Roman Family', p. 78). It is known that οἰκονόμος itself was in fact used in the ancient literature, and employed with the same meaning as the other terms referred to above. Cf. J. Reumann, ' "Stewards of God"—Pre-Christian Religious Application of οἰκονόμος in Greek', *JBL* 72 (1958), pp. 339-49; *idem*, 'OIKONOMIA-Terms in Paul in Comparison with Lucan *Heilsgeschichte*', *NTS* 13 (1966), pp. 147-67. W. Tooley, 'Stewards of God', *SJT* 19 (1966), pp. 74-86; D. Webster, 'The Primary Stewardship', *ExpTim* 72 (1960–61), pp. 274-76; S. Belkin, 'The Problem of Paul's Background', *JBL* 54 (1935), pp. 41-60 (52-55); Michel, 'οἰκονόμος', pp. 149-50.

The common terms employed for the designation of an ordinary slave in the secular literature are δοῦλος and οἰκέτης. Cf. T.E.J. Wiedemann, *Slavery*, p. 13.

a. *Setting of the Parable*

When we look at the flow of Luke's thought in ch. 12 as a whole, it is possible to note that the passage from 12.13 to 12.48 constitutes one unit holding an unswerving theme, even though the parts are loosely joined. In detail, 12.13-15 deal with the matter of possessions related to inheritance; in response to which the Parable of the Rich Fool (12.16-21) is introduced as a warning against covetousness. In 12.22-32 Jesus teaches his disciples not to be anxious about material possessions of this world; vv. 33-34 could be described as a provisional conclusion thus far (12.12-32),[16] where we find that Luke's particular emphasis is laid on almsgiving, which is revealed clearly when these verses are compared with the Matthean counterpart (Mt. 6.19-21). In 12.35-40 there is an eschatological message in relation to the *parousia*,[17] under the condition of which the parable of the waiting servants (vv. 35-40) and the parable of the faithful and wise steward (vv. 41-46) appear as a guide as to how a disciple of Jesus has to manage possessions entrusted to his care during the critical moment. In this connection, Fitzmyer's analysis on how these collections of Jesus' sayings are related to each other appears appropriate:

> Watchfulness and faithfulness are not unrelated to the treasure in heaven and the meaning of life itself. Freedom from care, like that of ravens and the lilies, receives another dimension or perspective, when it is related to vigilance and fidelity in human life. Though the Lucan joining is prima facie literary, it is not without some rooting in human life itself, for detachment from material things of earthly existence (the treasures that are attacked by thieves and moths) is related to the expectation of human life (a treasure not yet within reach, a blessedness to be pronounced by the master of life).[18]

Finally, vv. 47-48 are presented as a final passage of conclusion drawn from 12.13 to 12.46.[19] Consequently, 12.13-46 can be regarded

---

16. Talbert, *Reading Luke*, p. 140, notes that 'the section on possessions is climaxed by 12:33-34, a specific injunction to almsgiving'.

17. Talbert, *Reading Luke*, p. 144.

18. Fitzmyer, *Gospel*, p. 984. Schmithals, *Lukas*, pp. 143, 147, also suggests a continuity from 12.13-48 by saying that 12.13-34 deal with the earthly possessions, and the three parables (12.35-48) stood already in 'Q' in association with Jesus' sayings on anxiety about, and storing up of, material possessions.

19. These two verses seem to be a conclusive remark on the immediate parable (vv. 42-46) because they elaborate further on the rewards that the good steward and the bad steward are supposed to receive according to their services. But if we take into

as a coherent section, and its unity is strengthened when we note that totally different stories are introduced before and after this section: that is, 12.1-12 is a word concerning witness and martyrs, and 12.49-53 concerns the signs of this age. Thus this parable of stewardship is closely bound up with Luke's concern with the proper use of possessions entrusted to the believers.

b. *The Steward Figure*

It would be useful, as the next step, to examine and compare the key words which Luke and Matthew use for designating the slave in this parable, namely, οἰκονόμος (Luke) and δοῦλος (Matthew). Notice ought to be taken of the fact that Luke employs οἰκονόμος, a concrete term which is peculiar to Luke, whereas Matthew uses δοῦλος which is used so commonly by all the Evangelists that it appears difficult for us to determine its specific type or function.[20] Along with this aspect it is also to be noticed that οἰκονόμος is used at the start of the section (v. 42) prior to the non-specific δοῦλος (v. 43), and that the servant's role and function that we note in this parable may be better disclosed by οἰκονόμος, a technical term,[21] than δοῦλος which has a more general and comprehensive meaning. Hence by this arrangement Luke seems to intend to show that οἰκονόμος employed in the first place prescribes the function of δοῦλος used in the following sentences.[22]

With regard to the stewardship motif that is the main issue in this chapter, we can take note of a few pivotal features of stewardship from

account Lk. 12.13-46 as a whole, where the theme of material possessions (vv. 13-24) is seen to be related to that of servantship (vv. 35-40) and stewardship (vv. 41-46), then it can be inferred that vv. 47-48 are presented as a conclusion of the whole section, for they bind together the two themes dealt with above.

20. On the ground that δοῦλος is employed more frequently in Luke's parable than οἰκονόμος, some assert that Luke's use of οἰκονόμος here does not reflect Luke's emphasis on οἰκονόμος (S.J. Kistemaker, *The Parables of Jesus* [Grand Rapids: Baker Book House, 1985], p. 126).

This suggestion, however, does not consider Luke's initial placement of οἰκονόμος before δοῦλος, nor afford us an appropriate answer to the question why Luke had οἰκονόμος here instead of δοῦλος in Matthew (cf. Dodd, *Parables*, p. 125).

21. As we have examined in the previous section, οἰκονόμος is a slave among the slaves, who is given authority over the whole household (θεραπεία, Lk. 12.42), and sometimes the whole property of his master (τὰ ὑπάρχοντα, Lk. 12.44) (Michel, 'οἰκονόμος', p. 150; cf. Kistemaker, *Parables*, p. 126).

22. 'The function of the slave is that of an οἰκονόμος' (Dodd, *Parables*, p. 125).

the text; the steward does not hold any possessions and property of his own, but just takes care of his master's belongings entrusted to his care provisionally (v. 42). This element of Luke's view of stewardship seems to be presented well in the form of a summary at vv. 47-48, particularly in v. 48b, which is peculiar to Luke with his unique expressions:[23] 'Everyone to whom much is given, of him will much be required; and of him to whom men commit much they will demand the more.' In these sentences two terms utilized by Luke in particular appear to demonstrate a significant element of Luke's idea of stewardship: ἐδόθη means 'has been given', and παρέθεντο means 'has been entrusted'. Thus the implication of these words in this regard is that what a steward owns does not belong to him, but is given or entrusted by someone else. So Ernst expresses this idea of stewardship as 'geliehene Autorität'.[24] Also from such words as ἐλθών (v. 43) and χρονίζει (v. 45), we may infer that the timescale which is allowed to a steward is not indefinite but limited. So we may refer to the period of special responsibility of the stewardship—obedience is harder but all the more important in the absence of the master.[25] Thus Luke overtly portrays a steward as a unique sort of servant who is temporarily given and entrusted with material possessions by a master, so that he should use them in accordance with his master's will (v. 47).

The second element of stewardship which is to be mentioned here is a steward's behavioural attitude in carrying out his duty as steward. Lk. 12.42, 43, and 45 may be regarded as the passages indicating the attitude of a steward, that is, how a steward has to discharge his responsibility and duty. First, Luke introduces the faithful and wise steward at vv. 42-43 who takes care of his master's property and goods well,[26] distributing the food to the master's servants at the proper time, which must be the will and order of the master.[27] As a result, the faithful and

23. Cf. Evans, *Saint Luke*, p. 538.

24. 'borrowed authority'. Ernst, *Lukas*, p. 410.

25. 'Sie (Verwalter) sollen aber auch bedenken, daß ihnen nur "geliehene Autorität" zukommt, die bemessen ist auf eine bestimmte Zeit, "bis der Herr kommt". Sie sind eingesetzt "auf Abruf"' (Ernst, *Lukas*, p. 410).

26. Weiser argues that the adjectives associated with the steward, e.g. πιστός and φρόνιμος, 'describes the kind of conduct the steward should practise, rather than the qualities necessary for his appointment' (cited from I.H. Marshall, *Commentary*, p. 541).

27. Evans, *Saint Luke*, p. 536: 'Behind this language may lie the figure of Joseph, the Jewish model of the wise one (*phronimos* = 'prudent'), who was set by Pharaoh

wise steward is praised by his master and offered an honour taking over the whole property and possessions of his master (v. 44). This appears a clear indication of a model of a good steward which Luke intends to introduce to the members of his community. Secondly, v. 45 refers to another kind of steward who neglects his duty as a steward and abuses his position by beating[28] his master's servants and eating and drinking until he gets drunk. He appears so wicked as to make use of the temporary delay of his master's return in indulging himself in licentious behaviour. This bad steward thinks that everything he has under his control is absolutely his own, so that he may dispose of it at his own will without considering the good of others. This malicious conduct of the steward eventually results in severe judgment (v. 46).[29] What is remarkable in the description of this judgment is that Luke depicts the evil steward who disposes of the capital of his master as like the ἄπιστοι rather than the ὑποκρίται of Matthew (24.51). Here Luke's use of ἄπιστοι would indicate that the unfaithful steward whose conduct is against his master's will can be treated as a non-believer, whereas the faithful steward is a model for believers.[30]

The motif of eschatology is also prominent in this parable as well as the previous one (12.35-40).[31] Then how can we relate this motif to

over his *household* (*therapeia*, v. 42; cf. Gen. 45[16]; 41[33,39f.]; Ps. 105[21]), and who dispenses supplies (Gen. 47[12-14], *sitometrein*, only here in the LXX).'

28. 'Τύπτω is the action of one who thinks that he can act as master and has a position of dominion' (I.H. Marshall, *Commentary*, p. 542).

29. Literally the master wants to cut him in half (διχοτομήσει). Whether this word ought to be interpreted literally (Plummer, *Luke*, pp. 332-33) or metaphorically (Evans, *Saint Luke*, p. 537) cannot be easily determined. At least it is a clear indication of the severity of the judgment the unfaithful steward has to face (Kistemaker, *Parables*, p. 125).

Meanwhile, J.A. Findlay (*Jesus and His Parables* [London: Epworth, 1951], p. 58), is of the opinion that this parable is founded on the story of Ahikar, because of the similarity between the two accounts. Cf. R.H. Charles, *Apocrypha and Pseudepigrapha* (Oxford: Clarendon Press, 1977), II, p. 715.

30. J. Drury (*The Parables in the Gospels* [London: SPCK, 1985], p. 119), draws attention to Luke's omission of κακός at v. 45, and makes the point that in this parable Luke does not deal with two different figures of steward, but one who can play his role in two different ways. Cf. Goulder, *Paradigm*, II, p. 550. Meanwhile, Danker, *Jesus*, p. 154, holds that vv. 45-46 depict the darker side of the Church's life contemporary to Luke.

31. Schweizer, *Luke*, p. 214. In Luke's Gospel there occur a number of parables which appear to be related to the motif of eschatology, or an imminent *parousia*,

that of stewardship? Despite v. 45, 'my master is delayed in coming', which is a piece of evidence to disclose the Lukan *Sitz im Leben*, what matters here is not the delay of the master so much as his unexpected return which may occur at any time (v. 46).[32] Thus this parable also offers the steward a warning not to abuse the temporary delay of his master and the position given to him to take care of his master's assets, because no one knows when the master will return. Consequently from this passage it is clear that a steward is supposed to be always watchful in carrying out his duty, for the crisis of an eschatological catastrophe will come as unexpectedly as the master of the house who returns late from the wedding feast (12.35-40, 46).[33] The typical model of this sort of event is the case of the unfaithful steward at v. 45 who loses or neglects such an awareness of the eschatological crisis.

In line with this motif of eschatology, one more element is to be added to the Lukan point of stewardship: the steward is supposed to account for his work eventually (vv. 43-48). In other words, he must be judged in the end by what he has done and how he has managed what has been given or entrusted to him. Thus according to his service during the allowed period, he will be praised or punished, 'denn der Herr fordert Rechenschaft über die Verwaltung des Anvertrauten'.[34]

c. *Church Leaders or Rich Christians?*
Many scholars tend to interpret this parable in one particular way, that is, that it is metaphorical as applying to the Apostles or the church leaders of Luke's time.[35] This argument is largely based on καταστήσει

such as the stories of Noah and Lot (17.26-32), the two women sleeping and the two grinding corn (17.34-37) and the Unjust Judge (18.1-8). Cf. Esler, *Community*, p. 63.

32. Esler, *Community*, p. 63, makes the point that although there are a number of parables in Luke which appear to be linked to an imminent *parousia*, 'None of these, however, refers to an End which will come soon; they refer rather to one which will come suddenly' (cf. 12.46).

33. Schweizer's contrast of vv. 42-46 with vv. 39-40 appears appropriate: 'In vv. 39-40, the coming of Jesus is viewed as a threatening catastrophe for which one must be prepared at all times . . . vv. 42-46, by contrast, show that the interim of waiting demands responsible action on behalf of others' (*Luke*, p. 214).

34. '. . . because the master demands an account for the management of what has been entrusted'. Grundmann, *Lukas*, p. 267.

35. Jeremias, *Parables*, pp. 50, 56-58; I.H. Marshall, *Commentary*, p. 540; Ellis, *Luke*, p. 180; L.T. Johnson, *Literary Function*, pp. 166-67; and Goulder,

at v. 42 and Peter's question to Jesus at v. 41: 'Lord, are you telling this parable for us or all?'[36] So this argument leads us to enquire into the implication of καταστήσει and who 'we' (ἡμεῖς) are in Peter's question.

First, let us examine Peter's question. Proponents of a 'church-leader' interpretation may want to say that ἡμεῖς points to the Apostles, then indirectly the church leaders of Luke's time. But what is to be considered first of all is the fact that Jesus does not directly answer Peter's query as to whom the parable is addressed,[37] and secondly that there is no reference to the Twelve, nor the Apostles in this context (Lk. 12.13-49).[38] Rather, when we consider that Jesus' teaching that starts from v. 22 afresh continues on till v. 53 without interruption, and that Luke uses λέγω ὑμεῖς four times,[39] which can be thought of as a catch-phrase to connect the parables with the previous teaching of Jesus, then it is probable that in view of the context ἡμεῖς indicates the disciples (vv. 1, 22).[40] Having reached this conclusion, some still tend to identify the disciples with the Apostles, bearing in mind the 'little

Paradigm, II, p. 549. Even if we were to admit this assumption, it would not exclude responsibilities such as 'the ministering of material possessions' (Seccombe, *Possessions*, p. 193).

36. Schmithals' statement can be presented as one which represents the ecclesiastical interpretation of this parable: 'Der Fortgang zeigt, daß Petrus mit "uns" die Gemeindeleiter, mit "alle" die Gemeindeglieder meint' (*Lukas*, p. 148). Cf. Fitzmyer, *Gospel*, p. 989; Ernst, *Lukas*, p. 409.

37. Seccombe, *Possessions*, p. 193, notes that Peter's inquiry 'is given an open-ended answer'.

38. Fitzmyer, *Gospel*, p. 989: 'Since the last time that we read of "the apostles" was in 9.10, it is scarcely likely that Peter's words refer to them as "us". . . . It has nothing to do with "the Twelve", who are not mentioned, and who by Luke's time are no more than a distant memory.' Cf. Bengel, *Gnomon*, II, pp. 112-13; T.W. Manson, *Sayings*, pp. 117-18.

39. Lk. 12.22, 27, 37, and 44. Apart from this particular clause, ὑμεῖς with various forms appears frequently (14 times) in Jesus' teaching to his disciples from v. 22 to v. 34: ὑμεῖς, vv. 24, 29, 36, 40 (four times); ὑμῶν, vv. 25, 30, 32, 33, 34 (twice), 35 (7 times); ὑμᾶς, v. 28; ὑμῖν, vv. 31, 32 (twice).

40. Fitzmyer, *Gospel*, p. 989, also takes note of this point: 'In the immediate Lucan context a distinction has been made between "the crowd(s)" (12.1, 13, 54) and the "disciples" (12.1, 22). Hence, Peter's "us" must refer to the disciples, and *pantas*, "all", to the crowd(s).' I.H. Marshall, *Commentary*, p. 540, also acknowledges that ἡμεῖς refers to the disciples in the Lukan context. But both fail to recognize the wide range of application of the term μαθητής in Luke's work.

flock' at v. 32. Regarding this matter, in the first place, what we should be reminded of is that (as we have discussed earlier in Chapter 3) in Luke's view the disciples are not a limited number of followers who are to be identified with the Twelve or the Apostles, but a large number of followers, which anticipates μαθητής in Acts, a general term used for all members of a Christian congregation in the Early Church. It is also to be noticed that this teaching of Jesus is announced in the presence of the multitudes (vv. 1, 13, 54). 'Therefore it seems best to interpret these words as intended for all who would follow him, that is, disciples in the broadest sense of the term.'[41] Thus it would be unwise to determine that this parable is addressed solely to the Apostles,[42] with the assumption that here Peter speaks out representing the Twelve Apostles.[43]

Secondly, focusing on the element of responsibility which results from καταστήσει, some make the point, by interpreting καταστήσει in the light of appointment to a post, that the steward figure points to 'those with responsibilities of leadership',[44] such as the immediate Apostles, the church leaders, or the community officials of Luke's time.[45] However, this idea is dependent on an allegorical interpretation of this particular detail in the parable.[46] It seems natural that καταστήσει should be used in this context because the steward is appointed by his master to take care of the whole household and his material

41. Pilgrim, *Good News*, p. 94.

42. Cf. Kistemaker, *Parables*, p. 127.

43. A formula similar to Peter's question is found at 18.28, whereas in 12.41 Peter blurts out a question, apparently representing the body of the Apostles: 'Lo, we have left our homes (τὰ ἴδια) and followed you.' But when we take into account the context of the verse (18.18-30), compared with its parallels in Mark and Matthew, we see that in Luke there is no reference to the Twelve nor even to the disciples, while the disciples appear twice respectively in Mark and Matthew's version of this story (Mk 10.23, 24/Mt. 19.23, 25). In other words, it appears that replacing οἱ μαθηταί with οἱ ἀκούσαντες (18.26), Luke intends to generalize the implication of this story (cf. vv. 29-30). Thus here again it seems difficult to determine whether Peter speaks up as a representative of the group of the Apostles or not.

44. I.H. Marshall, *Commentary*, p. 540.

45. Fitzmyer, *Gospel*, p. 989.

46. Schmithals, *Lukas*, p. 148, presents succinctly the essence of this interpretation: 'Lukas beobachtete, daß im folgenden Gleichnis zwischen dem Oberknecht (Lukas nennt ihn redaktionell "Haushalter") und den Unterknecht unterschieden wurde, und er allegorisiert dies Motiv im Blick auf die Gemeindesituation seiner Zeit.'

possessions, and there is no obvious reason why this term is to be construed allegorically. The other terms used in this parable which are related to material possessions one way or another, such as ὑπάρχοντα (v. 44), θεραπεία (v. 42), and σιτομέτριον (v. 42), are used in a natural, literal sense, without any clear allegorical significance.[47] Thus it would be odd that in the same context one word should be given a special allegorical meaning, while others are to be construed literally. Therefore, there is no strong reason to confine the interpretation of this parable to an allegory of church leadership.

In addition to this, there is still one thing which needs to be taken into consideration, that is, Luke's use of ἄπιστοι at v. 46. Luke employs this word to describe the judgment with which the unfaithful steward has to be confronted. Here a question arises against the 'church leader' interpretation: if the unfaithful steward is to be regarded as a spiritual leader, then is it appropriate to threaten him with condemnation as a non-believer when he merely fails to carry out his duty sincerely? In this context, some are of the opinion that ἄπιστοι does not imply unbelievers, trying to equate it with ὑποκριταί in Mt. 24.51.[48] Against this position, notice is to be taken of the fact that Luke employs ὀλιγόπιστοι in v. 28 for his disciples, where it is not used by means of utter condemnation, but by way of exhortation to encourage the disciples. To the contrary, it is obvious that ἄπιστοι in v. 46 is used to describe those utterly condemned. Therefore it would be reasonable to hold that ἄπιστοι here signifies unbelievers in the context of this parable.[49] If so, although he is to be blamed for his unfaithful attitude towards the given tasks, it is unduly extreme to judge an unfaithful leader as an unbeliever. In this case, Matthew's description, ὑποκριταί, may be more appropriate than Luke's. But what matters here is that Luke does not use ὑποκριταί but ἄπιστοι in this context. Therefore, there is a good

47. Cf. their use elsewhere in the New Testament: θεραπεία (v. 42), Lk. 9.11; Mt. 24.45; Rev. 22.2; σιτομέτριον (v. 42): only used here; ὑπάρχοντα (v. 44), Lk. 8.3; 11.21; 12.15, 33, 44; 14.33; 16.1; 19.8; Acts 4.32; 1 Cor. 13.3; Heb. 10.34.

48. Plummer, *Luke*, p. 333.

49. 'The Gk. word *apistos* can mean either "unfaithful" or "unbeliever". Its opposite, *pistos*, in the analogy of 12.42, is rightly translated "faithful" rather than "believing". But in 12.46, where the application of the analogy is to the fore, *apistos* is surely intended to have the meaning "unbeliever" as it does everywhere else in the New Testament' (D. Gooding, *According to Luke* [Leicester: IVP, 1988], p. 246). Cf. Evans, *Saint Luke*, p. 537; Bengel, *Gnomon*, II, p. 114; Kistemaker, *Parables*, p. 126.

reason we ought to consider that the steward in this parable does not point specifically to church leaders or the Apostles but to all disciples.

So, we can now ask who the steward stands for ultimately in Luke's eyes. The answer to this question is to be found in v. 48b: 'Everyone to whom much is given, of him will much be required; and of him to whom men commit much they will demand the more.' In principle, he could be anyone who claims to be a disciple of Jesus in view of v. 22. But in reality the steward figure who is seen here to be given much to take care of cannot be any follower of Jesus, but he who has much, or he to whom men commit much among the general disciples of Jesus. In this context it is probably right that 'much' (πολύ) in this verse refers to the ὑπάρχοντα in v. 44, from which we may be able to claim that he is a person of means and possessions. Adding to this feature, when we allow for vv. 42-45 where the steward is seen to have a responsibility to take care of his master's slaves,[50] we may suggest that in Luke's view since he appears to control property as well as people, the steward in this parable is one of the benefactors who in Luke's time distributed food and material possessions out of their means in the interests of the poor in their community.[51] In favour of this position, we can note that unlike the previous two sentences, for example, vv. 47-48a, we might expect—but do not in fact find—some such contrasting sentence as 'of him to whom a little is given, of him will a little be required'. Thus what is made manifest in this verse is that as far as the theme of material possessions is concerned, Luke's interest is specially in those who are given or entrusted much because their attitude and behaviour are the focus of the parable.

From this reasoning, we may now draw the conclusion that this parable is not designed for church leaders in relation to their spiritual

---

50. It is to be noticed that Luke does not use just δοῦλοι but specifically παῖδες and παιδίσκαι, which are different from σύνδουλοι in Matthew (24.49). From this and θεραπεία in v. 42 peculiar to Luke, we know that the steward 'has a large *familia* of slaves under him' (Plummer, *Luke*, p. 332). This means that, as pointed out above, οἰκνονόμος here is clearly differentiated from an ordinary δοῦλος because of his particular job as a manager of all the belongings of his master, including property as well as slaves.

So bearing in mind this peculiar point, Creed, *Gospel*, p. 177, states that 'Lk. is anxious to bring out his [the steward's] superiority in office to the other servants'. Cf. W.L. Knox, *The Sources of the Synoptic Gospels* (Cambridge: Cambridge University Press, 1957), p. 70.

51. This feature will be discussed at length in Chapter 8.

responsibilities but for the rich members or the benefactors of Luke's Christian community, whom Luke expects to exercise stewardship of the material possessions entrusted to them with sincerity and faithfulness for the benefit of other and poorer members inside (and outside) the community.

d. *Summary and Conclusion*

To sum up what I have discussed thus far, in narrating the parable of the faithful and wise steward, Luke, first, appears to define the duty and role of a steward as a unique sort of slave who is entrusted with material possessions by a master and takes charge of them; secondly, with respect to the attitude of a steward, he describes one whose belongings are not his own but his master's. A steward is not to dispose of them at his own will and for his own sake, but to use them entirely according to the will and order of his master. Thirdly, bearing in mind an eschatological crisis which may happen all of a sudden, a steward is to carry out his duty with alertness, because his position as steward does not continue for good but can be put under examination at any time. Fourthly, a judgment will come eventually but will vary according to the conduct of the stewards. Finally, as regards the matter of the addressees of this parable, it has been argued that it is more likely that the steward does not represent the Apostles or church leaders, but all disciples. However, as Luke's interest lies in those who are given or entrusted much, it is concluded that this parable is intended especially for the rich members of Luke's community.

3. *The Parable of the Unjust Steward (16.1-13)*

a. *Problems of Interpretation*

Historically this parable of the Unjust Steward in Luke has long been recognized as one of the most enigmatic passages in the New Testament. For this reason it has been labelled a *crux interpretum* at least from the period of A. Jülicher.[52] So from the turn of this century up to now, for nearly 100 years, a wide range of interpretations have emerged claiming that they have presented solutions to the problems we face in construing the parable. However, the fact that despite such a huge flood of interpretations new attempts have still come out continuously setting

---

52. B. Heininger, *Metaphorik, Erzählstruktur und szenischdramatische Gestaltung in den Sondergutgleichnissen bei Lukas* (Münster: Aschendorff, 1991), p. 167.

forth new perspectives, appears to demonstrate that all the interpretations introduced up to now are inadequate to solve the problems. Therefore, it might seem that there is no complete answer to the problems of this parable.[53]

In this context, since our major concern in dealing with this parable is to explore stewardship in relation to the theme of material possessions, to discuss all the articles and books on this parable published up to now would take us beyond our limit. Thus in what follows it would be helpful for us to restrict the focus of this study to discerning the main force of the parable for Luke and considering what is related to the theme of stewardship and possessions.

What are the problems which cause embarrassment in interpreting the parable? Broadly speaking, there seem to be two major problems. First, how can the master[54] applaud the bad steward who wastes the master's capital and commits other immoral activities, such as forgery

53. J. Kloppenborg, 'The Dishonoured Master', *Bib* 70 (1989), pp. 474-95 (474), says, 'In the ninety years since the publication of Adolf Jülicher's monumental study on the parables of Jesus there is hardly a consensus on any single aspect of this parable'. Cf. W. Loader, 'Jesus and the Rogue in Luke 16.1-8a: The Parable of the Unjust Steward', *RB* 96 (1989), pp. 518-32 (518-19). A history of interpretation of this parable is finely arranged by Fitzmyer, *Gospel*, pp. 1102-104, and M. Krämer, *Das Rätsel der Parabel vom ungerechten Verwalter* (Zürich: Pas-Verlag, 1972), pp. 260-72, and for a more recent one, see Ireland, *Stewardship*, 5-47. Cf. L.J. Topel, 'On the Injustice of the Unjust Steward', *CBQ* 37 (1975), pp. 216-27 (216).

54. Here to avoid an excessive digression, I follow an assumption which is largely accepted by scholarship in this field that ὁ κύριος in v. 8 is the master of the parable. However, a group of scholars, such as Jeremias (*Parables*, pp. 45, 182), Dodd (*Parables*, p. 17), A.M. Hunter (*Interpreting the Parables* [London: SCM Press, 1960], p. 100), and Schmithals (*Lukas*, p. 168), are of the opinion that ὁ κύριος in v. 8 refers to Jesus.

But this argument has been refuted by the majority of scholars in this area. It would mean that the parable ends at v. 8a and Jesus' sayings are appended from v. 8b to v. 13. Cf. Fitzmyer, *Gospel*, pp. 1095-97; B.B. Scott, 'A Master's Praise: Luke 16.1-8a', *Bib* 64 (1983), pp. 173-88 (175-77); D.O. Via, *The Parables* (Philadelphia: Fortress Press, 1967), p. 156; Loader, 'Rogue', p. 522; P. Gächter, 'The Parable of the Dishonest Steward after Oriental Conceptions', *CBQ* 12 (1950), pp. 121-31 (130); C.T. Wood, 'Luke xvi. 8', *ExpTim* 63 (1951-52), p. 126; C.B. Firth, 'The Parable of the Unrighteous Steward', *ExpTim* 63 (1951-52), pp. 93-95 (93); D.M. Parrott, 'The Dishonest Steward (Luke 16.1-8a) and Luke's Special Parable Collection', *NTS* 37 (1991), pp. 499-515 (502); Topel, 'Injustice', p. 218; D.R. Fletcher, 'The Riddle of the Unjust Steward: Is Irony the Key?', *JBL* 82 (1963), pp. 15-30 (16-17); T.W. Manson, *Sayings*, p. 292.

and fraud, causing financial damage to his master (v. 8)? Secondly, can it be imagined that Jesus (or Luke) invented and used this kind of parable of a negative nature in order to deliver a positive lesson, whether it be fiction or a reflection of reality (v. 9)? With regard to these fundamental issues, there have been two differing lines of interpretation according to which we can classify various explanations which have emerged up to now:[55]

(1) The first line of interpretation comes out of an intention to delineate the steward in a positive light, on the grounds that the master praises him and Jesus also recommends his conduct to his disciples in vv. 8-9. In general, this view itself can be divided into two categories: one is a theory of interest proposed by J.D.M. Derrett, and the other is that of the steward's commission, suggested by J. Fitzmyer.

First, let us examine the theory of usury proposed by Derrett, an expert in oriental law.[56] His argument is based on the interpretation of the Old Testament and the Mishnah regarding the regulations against usury among the Jews. According to the regulations, usury was rigidly prohibited among the Jews, but in the New Testament times the rule was not properly put into practice, so usury itself became rather prevalent but in secret. Relying on this laxity of the regulations on usury in the later period, Derrett argues that the steward of the parable is a sort of legal agent dealing with interest-bearing loans on behalf of his master who does not want to be involved in such transactions because they are forbidden by the law. This explanation of Derrett leads to the suggestion that the amount of debt the steward rebates to the debtors is actually the interest component of the loan that is charged contrary to Jewish law, so that it is illegal gain owed to the master. In this situation, since to collect interest by way of usury among the Jews violates the law, there is little room for the master to manoeuvre except to approve the steward's action. By doing so, the master wants to show himself to the public as a benefactor at the cost of some financial loss.[57] Thus, Derrett claims, the steward's conduct to take off the illegal interest for the

55. Cf. Parrott, 'Collection', p. 499.

56. J.D.M. Derrett, *Law in the New Testament* (London: Darton, Longman & Todd, 1974), pp. 48-77. Those who hold similar views to Derrett's theory are as follows: Caird, *Luke*, p. 187; I.H. Marshall, *Commentary*, pp. 613-17; Firth, 'Unrighteous Steward', pp. 93-95.

57. Derrett, *Law*, p. 72.

purpose of making friends is legitimately law-abiding, which drives the master to acclaim his steward, although reluctantly.

Despite his assumption of farm tenancy as the background of this parable which has been a dominant theory among scholars, Fitzmyer's opinion on this issue is by and large on the same track as Derrett's, because he also tends to interpret this parable in light of the practice of usurious loans. A difference between the two theories is that for Fitzmyer the interest component suggested by Derrett is the steward's commission.[58] Thus, according to Fitzmyer's solution, the steward, an estate manager for an absentee landlord, who also handles the usurious loan with his master's sanction, turns out to forgo his share of the profits coming from business dealings, and since the master does not suffer any loss whatever, it is plausible that the master in v. 8 acclaims the way the steward handles his crisis to ensure his future security by making friends at the expense of his own profits, and Jesus in v. 9 recommends the action of the steward as a good way to cope with a crisis.[59] Taken together, these two theories have made valuable contributions in some aspects to a better understanding of this parable, so for some time they have enjoyed a rather good reputation in this area.[60]

---

58. Fitzmyer, *Gospel*, p. 1101. This hypothesis of Fitzmyer was initially proposed by M.D. Gibson in 1903 ('On the Parable of the Unjust Steward', *ExpTim* 14 [1903], p. 334), but did not attract much attention at that time. Half a century later in 1950, however, P. Gächter, picking up this assumption again, developed Gibson's main idea in his article, 'Oriental Conceptions', pp. 121-31, and it was finally J. Fitzmyer who in 1974 made it fully blossom, embellishing the essence of the hypothesis, so that it appears to have become one of the most appealing theories in this area. Cf. W.D. Miller, 'The Unjust Steward', *ExpTim* 15 (1903), pp. 332-34.

Others who take similar approaches to this are J.A. Findlay, *The Gospel according to St Luke* (London: SCM Press, 1937), p. 177; Ellis, *Luke*, pp. 200-201; Moxnes, *Economy*, p. 140. Meanwhile, Wood, 'Luke xvi.8', p. 126, sets forth a slightly different solution, presupposing that the steward broke the law: 'the steward was normally given a certain discretion to remit some portion of the rent, if the tenant could plead a bad crop or family misfortunes'.

59. Apparently Fitzmyer, *Gospel*, pp. 1095-104, seems to combine into one the motif of almsgiving noted in Derrett's argument and that of eschatology proposed by Jeremias. However, in fact, he appears sceptical about the motif of almsgiving as a point of this parable, and to feel more comfortable with that of eschatology. As for the motif of eschatology, however, Kloppenborg encouraged by J.D. Crossan ('The Servant Parable of Jesus', *Sem* 1 [1974], pp. 17-62 [46]), notes, 'Yet nothing in the parable evokes an apocalyptic situation' ('Dishonoured Master', p. 478).

60. Cf. Kloppenborg, 'Dishonoured Master', pp. 486-87.

However, a few drawbacks have been pointed out in criticism of these theories. First, there is no explicit reference at all in the given text to the commission or the interest on which the proponents of these theories depend in construing the parable.[61] In other words, as far as the text goes in vv. 5-7, there is nothing to suggest that a part of the debts belongs to the steward; rather, the whole of the debts is owed to the master.[62] In addition, it is to be noticed against Fitzmyer that a recent study of the contemporary loan system of Egypt performed by Kloppenborg shows us that 'there is *never* any indication of how, if at all, the agent is to be remunerated... there was no uniform means for the remuneration of household managers'.[63] Against Derrett's argument as well, Kloppenborg also suggests an important criticism: it was not secret but public practice that the laws prohibiting usury among the Jews were not kept properly at that time.[64] So Derrett's argument that the action performed by the unjust steward is law-abiding misses the point of the parable, because such laws did not exist any more in reality. Parrott also criticizes these theories, stating that they made a mistake because they relied upon wrong literary evidence which was 'codified' not in the early first century CE but in the early third century CE.[65] Secondly, if these theories are to be accepted, there seems to be no reason why the steward is described as τῆς ἀδικίας in v. 8 at the end of the parable;[66] rather he could suitably be called δίκαιος because he

61. Cf. Kloppenborg, 'Dishonoured Master', p. 481; Parrott, 'Collection', p. 503.

62. Scott, 'Master's Praise', p. 177.

63. Kloppenborg, 'Dishonoured Master', p. 481. Cf. Cicero, *Rep.* 1.61. K.E. Bailey (*Poet and Peasant and Through Peasant Eyes* [Grand Rapids: Eerdmans, 1988], p. 90), also argues against Fitzmyer in particular that 'according to Jewish Law, if an agent buys for less or sells for more than the price specified by the principal, the extra profits belong to the principal, not to the agent'. Note should be taken of v. 5 that the debt is owed to the master, not the agent.

64. After examining literary evidence about loan agreements in Egypt and Palestine involving Jews, Kloppenborg, 'Dishonoured Master', p. 484, attacks the assumption shared by Fitzmyer and Derrett that 'Jewish lenders in general felt at least occasional compulsion to observe the biblical injunctions on usury *and* that the audience of Jesus' parable would recognize this', and argues that 'the prescription against usury in Deut. 15,7-8; 23,20-21; Exod. 22,2 and Lev. 25,36-37' was ignored. For more details, see Kloppenborg, pp. 484-86. Cf. Firth, 'Unrighteous Steward', p. 95.

65. Parrott, 'Collection', p. 503.

66. Topel, 'Injustice', p. 219; Fletcher, 'Riddle', p. 22; Parrott, 'Collection',

gives up either his own profit, that is, the commission, or the illegal gain from usury, in order to help his neighbours in need.[67] Therefore it is less likely that we can have confidence to accept these theories as a right answer to the problems which arise from interpreting this parable.

(2) The second (and traditional) view is that the unjust steward is wrong throughout, leaving nothing good in his conduct. Older versions of this interpretation generally failed to take into account the legal and socio-economic situation presupposed in this parable, whose consideration made Derrett's and Fitzmyer's approaches appear so convincing. However, the more recent approach of Kloppenborg both applies socio-economic knowledge to the interpretation of the parable and exposes the weakness in Derrett's and Fitzmyer's theories. Even though it is regretted for our case that his main theme is not related to almsgiving nor the theme of material possessions, but to 'a challenge of the social codes of honour and shame',[68] yet his handling of the theme of material possessions that is our concern here seems to be fairly persuasive, because it came into existence after his extensive review and examination of the major hypotheses which have been submitted to date in this field, such as those of Jeremias, Fitzmyer and Derrett.[69]

If we follow his theory, the explanation of the parable would be as follows: The unjust steward is informed of his dismissal by his master due to his mismanagement of his master's capital and property,

p. 503. H. Kosmala's point ('The Parable of the Unjust Steward in the Light of Qumran', in *Studies Essays and Reviews* [Leiden: E.J. Brill, 1978], II, pp. 17-24) that ὁ οἰκονόμος τῆς ἀδικίας in v. 8 implies just a steward belonging to this world seems unsatisfactory because it does not take into account the immediate relation between this phrase and the parable in the context (cited from Loader, 'Rogue', p. 526). Fitzmyer unnaturally confines the 'injustice' to the allegation of vv. 1-2.

67. Loader, 'Rogue', p. 526. Parrott, 'Collection', p. 501, holds that attempts to portray the unjust steward in a favourable light 'gloss over the criminal act of the steward' (cf. pp. 502-503). Cf. Scott, 'Master's Praise', p. 177; Topel, 'Injustice', p. 218.

68. Kloppenborg, 'Dishonoured Master', p. 494. Scott, 'Master's Praise', is also in this line of interpretation: 'Now the parable challenges the reader's implicit world by challenging the way justice operated in that world. The parable presents a counter-world to the reader's normal world' (p. 187).

69. Although D.M. Parrott's article, 'Collection', is more recent in this area among the articles available to me, it is some distance from our concern because it focuses mainly on the theme of forgiveness, so does not have much to do with the motifs of almsgiving and wealth.

but instead of repentance, by reducing at his disposal a large amount of debt which the debtors owe to his master,[70] he engages in further misconduct by dispersing his master's wealth for the purpose of preparing his own future after being sacked. Nonetheless, although this wrongdoing committed by the unjust steward causes the master to lose more of his capital, the master acclaims the way his steward overcomes his crisis, since he makes friends for his future by giving away to those in need some of the material possessions of which the steward is still in charge. Kloppenborg is particularly interested in the way that the master's surprising response at the end overturns cultural expectations of his concern for his own honour.

There is one element that these two differing views share in common, that is, the fact that the master praises the unjust steward. But this fact drives those in the second category to face a seeming contradiction: how can the master recommend such a rogue? Thus regarding this dilemma proponents of these theories have suggested a variety of ideas to solve this problem,[71] such as 'irony',[72] 'injustice',[73] and 'controversy'.[74]

70. 100 baths equal 1000 denarii, and 100 cors equal 2500 denarii. What is interesting in this figure is that the amount the steward reduces on behalf of the debtors is nearly the same in value (Jeremias, *Parables*, p. 181).

71. By and large, these group of scholars share a view in common that Jesus in the Gospels is seen 'to shock people and so break open their awareness for new insight' (Loader, 'Rogue', p. 532); Fletcher, 'Riddle', p. 24, says, 'In the kingdom most of the conventional standards and values of man's society are upended'; Topel, 'Injustice', p. 225, states that '"laws" like Jesus' violate our human traditions and concepts of the justice of well-ordered society. They are unjust.'

72. Assuming φρονίμως . . . φρονιμώτεροι (v. 8) as having 'a lightly scornful or derogatory overtone', Fletcher, 'Riddle', pp. 27-30, argues that irony is the key to appreciate properly the meaning of the parable. His point of argument can be noted in the following passage: 'The sons of this world are shrewd; they are sharp and clever in a way which those who are sons of light are not to envy, and even less to try to emulate. You cannot keep pace with the cleverness, the kind of astutely self-interested dealing admired in the present world, and still be a citizen of the kingdom of God. The two do not mix. Jesus makes the point ironically; then he makes it in a very explicit and unmistakable statement' (p. 28).

73. The intention of Topel's article is, as he admits ('Injustice', p. 217 n. 4), to publicize Fritz Maass's main point in his interpretation of this parable: 'Maass calls attention to the fact that the steward is called unjust by the lord precisely in the act of praising him (vs. 8), and then proceeds to speak of forgiveness in a way which seems 'unjust' to ordinary human judgment as the most profound meaning of the parable' (p. 217).

74. Loader, 'Rogue', regards this parable as one of the parables reflecting contro-

(3) Now then, bearing in mind this result of our survey of the previous work done in this area, let us examine a couple of points which have been referred to earlier as the problems which make this parable difficult to interpret.

First, how can the master applaud such a rascal? To answer this question, what is to be noticed initially is that it is not the unjust steward himself but his way of behaviour that attracts the praise from the master.[75] This aspect derives from ὅτι φρονίμως ἐποίησεν in v. 8. In other words, the unjust steward himself is not wise but *acts* wisely.[76] Although he acts unjustly, he acts prudently, and it is his prudence rather than his injustice which is praised by his master. Or, to put it another way, although the *content* of the steward's behaviour is unjust, its *mode* is prudent and it is the mode which attracts the master's admiration. Then we now come to see that the content of the steward's behaviour is depicted in a negative light throughout the parable.[77] But this

versy related to other major motifs noted in Luke, such as the motifs of reversal, debt, the master and slave relation, and authorized and unauthorized agency. In this category, he includes almost all parables in Luke. This assertion of his is, as he implies, in fact based on allegorical interpretation focusing on Christology (pp. 521-31). His main thesis in his article is as follows: 'It is to be read in the light of the opposition he [Jesus] faced from those who objected to him as a rogue, a would-be servant of God, who operated without proper authority in offering acceptance and forgiveness to sinners' (p. 519).

75. Plummer, *Luke*, p. 385.

76. Relying on this point, Gächter, 'Oriental Conceptions', p. 124, contends that the action of rebate taken by the steward was not dishonest, and he was called dishonest 'before he performed his last measure' (cf. Gächter, p. 131; Firth, 'Unrighteous Steward', p. 95). If we are allowed to follow this theory, the steward is dishonest and unfaithful so as to waste his master's capital, but his subsequent action should not be regarded as such, since it is either law-abiding or to give up his own profits for the benefit of those in need. This contention of Gächter results from his inclination for the theory proposed by Gibson, which I have already rebutted after serious discussion.

Regarding this point, Parrott, 'Collection', p. 504, claims that 'διασκορπίζων (v. 1) in itself connotes criminal activity' (cf. Topel, 'Injustice', pp. 217, 219; Fitzmyer, *Gospel*, p. 1100). In relation to this, Topel, 'Injustice', pp. 219, 226, holds that the praise of the master for the prudence exercised by the unjust steward to escape his predicament was 'the meaning of the parable in the earliest tradition', and other applications have been added to it. Cf. Jeremias, *Parables*, pp. 47, 182; Loader, 'Rogue', pp. 520-21; Fletcher, 'Riddle', pp. 15-17; Dodd, *Parables*, p. 17.

77. On the basis of reader–response criticism, Scott, largely relying upon vv. 1-2, particularly the word, διεβλήθη in v. 1, suggests that the master is a villain and

observation leads us to ask the question why Jesus uses such an immoral figure in giving an ethical lesson to the relatively moral disciples (v. 1). Can it be justified? To our common sense it is right that a good goal should be accompanied by a good method. With regard to this objection, Williams's suggestion appears to afford a sustainable answer:

> This difficulty disappears, once it is realized that we are dealing here with a sort of *a fortiori* argument. In two other passages of the third gospel, the behaviour of evil persons is treated as relevant to some issue under discussion. In neither of these cases is the wicked man held up as an ideal; rather, the thought is: 'If such-and-such a principle applies even in the relationships between evil men, will it not apply all the more in the relationship between God and the faithful?'[78]

Following the first question, we raise a second: how does the unjust steward then act so prudently that the master is able to recommend him? A brief answer may be found in the fact that by making good use of material possessions which are still entrusted to his care, that is, by distributing them to those in need, though from selfish motives, the unjust steward prepares his future well in the expectation that the friends, that is, the debtors, would welcome him into their houses. Since this must be a central point in this parable, I shall now discuss this point further in order to explore fully the message Luke would originally have intended to convey to his readers.

b. *The Model Intended by Luke*
In order to discuss properly the key point of this parable it appears that three elements are to be explored: the context, the meaning of the debt (ὀφείλω), and the reciprocity ethic. First, let us look into the context around the parable. As far as the context is concerned, it seems that

the steward is 'a victim of the rich man's injustice' (p. 185). Thus he seeks to portray the master as bad and the steward as good, depending upon his basic assumption that 'A stereotyped animosity between masters and servants is common in Jesus' parables' (p. 180).

Against this argument, L.M. Friedel ('The Parable of the Unjust Steward', *CBQ* 3 [1941]), pp. 337-48 (338), produces a good counter-argument, stating that the fact that the steward did not try to defend himself would mean that the charges put forward against him were true. Cf. Bailey, *Poet*, pp. 97-98.

78. F.E. Williams, 'Is Almsgiving the Point of the "Unjust Steward"?', *JBL* 83 (1964), pp. 293-97 (294). For the two passages which have an *a fortiori* argument, he refers to Lk. 11.13 and 18.6. Cf. Gächter, 'Oriental Conceptions', p. 131; Firth, 'Unrighteous Steward', p. 95.

prior concern should be accorded to the passages that follow the parable (vv. 9-13). They are generally acknowledged as Luke's own commentary on the parable revealing his intention to show his readers how to interpret the parable.[79] What interests us in these passages is that they show that the focus of this parable is not the behaviour of the master, as Kloppenborg,[80] Scott,[81] and Loader[82] argue, but that of the unjust steward,[83] because they are mainly concerned with the motif of wealth.[84] This is particularly disclosed at v. 9—the action taken by the unjust steward to ease the debtors of their financial burden is identical to the implication of v. 9, because it would mean that he makes friends by means of unrighteous Mammon.[85] In consequence, there is good reason

79. Cf. Kloppenborg, 'Dishonoured Master', p. 475: 'Besides, the implication of v. 9 that wealth is both a serious threat to Christian faith if it is mishandled, and a means of benefaction and reconciliation is so congenial to Lukan editorial interests that it is quite likely that v. 9 is a Lukan commentary on v. 4.' Cf. Topel, 'Injustice', p. 220. A large percentage of the discussion of this parable in recent scholarship is concerned to uncover the 'original meaning' of the parable as spoken by Jesus as in its pre-Lukan form. But *our concern* is with Luke's understanding and use of this parable, and for this purpose the appended statements in vv. 9-14 are crucial.

80. Focusing on v. 9, Kloppenborg, 'Dishonoured Master', p. 479, seems to believe that he obtains a ground on which to shift the focus of the parable from the steward to the master. But this observation appears to ignore unduly the implication of v. 9 which he has suggested is 'a Lukan commentary' (p. 475), and that of the other inserted passage, i.e. vv. 10-13, which deals mainly with the use of material possessions of which an example is shown in the activity of the steward in the parable. Cf. B. Byrne, 'Forceful Stewardship and Neglectful Wealth: A Contemporary Reading of Luke 16', *Pacifica* 1 (1988), pp. 1-14 (4-5).

81. Scott, 'Master's Praise', pp. 187-88.

82. According to their argument, the parable is to be explicated as follows: This activity done by the steward means great financial damage to the master, but is a great favour to the debtors, so that the master can be acclaimed as a benefactor by them and the community as well. Of course, the master, if he wants, is able to regain by force the amount that his steward rebates for the debtors, but it would mean to deprive him of honour and reputation which has already been earned from his steward's action. In a situation like this, it would be likely that the master feels forced to approve the steward's action in order to save his honour and reputation, which would have been highly important in an ancient society where honour and respect is highly cherished among the wealthy and those in power.

83. Gächter, 'Oriental Conceptions', p. 122.

84. Byrne, 'Forceful Stewardship', pp. 4-5.

85. The material possessions he uses for this purpose can be rightly called 'ἀδικίας', for they are not his but his master's (cf. ἀλλότριον in v. 11). This point

to hold that the action taken by the unjust steward can be referred to as equivalent to almsgiving.[86]

Then what can we say about vv. 10-13? At first glance, the focus of these verses appears to deviate from the main point of the parable.[87] In other words, if we tend to interpret the parable in terms of vv. 8-9, then the implication of these passages might seem to be opposite to that of the parable, since vv. 10-13 appear to understand the parable in a negative way, whereas vv. 8b-9 suggests it contains, in at least some features, a positive model to be imitated.[88] As regards this aspect, however, Byrne's interpretation seems to be plausible:

> Within the literary unity of the whole, however, the notion of stewardship stated in vv. 10-12 undergoes transformation. Paradoxically, in the broad Christian perspective the Rogue Steward becomes the Faithful Steward. True stewardship involves precisely his unscrupulous casualness with respect to wealth. Throw it away to the poor in order to ensure heavenly

derives from the fact that the steward uses them unlawfully, not following the rule he should keep as a steward. Cf. Williams, 'Almsgiving', p. 295; Parrott, 'Collections', p. 500.

86. Moxnes, *Economy*, pp. 142-43; I.H. Marshall, *Commentary*, p. 621; Grundmann, *Lukas*, p. 321. Cf. Ireland, *Stewardship*, pp. 105, 115. In opposition to the idea of almsgiving as a main motif of this parable which he considers to be merely 'self-interested philanthropy', Fletcher, 'Riddle', p. 25, argues that 'the thrust of these sayings is to focus the disciple's interest and concern on the kingdom of God'.

However, his contention seems to result largely from an inadequate appreciation of the immediate context of the parable, such as the appended sayings of Jesus (vv. 9-13) and the Parable of the Rich Man and Lazarus.

87. Fletcher, 'Riddle', p. 21.

88. Williams, 'Almsgiving', p. 296, tries to explain this apparent contradiction as follows: 'The gentile auditor (let us say) would tend to fix upon the steward's immorality, rather than upon the act *per se* of giving away money, as the story's focus, and would try from this point of view to draw the moral. Verses 10-13 are a commentary attempting, with some difficulty, to do this.'

Meanwhile, focusing on the theme of 'prudence and justice' as a key point of the parable, Friedel, 'Unjust Steward', appears to seek an answer to the contradiction by means of contrast: 'While the lesson of prudence is illustrated by the similar conduct of the steward, that of justice is introduced by the contrary justice-defying example of the same person. There is no room for any doubt that the lesson of justice contained in verses 10-13 forms an integral part of our parable. For the steward's prudence, which is divorced from justice, is the dark background on which our Lord makes the unsullied immaculateness of the inseparable Christian virtues of prudence and justice stand forth in bold and sharply contrasted relief' (p. 347).

credit. Money or 'mammon' becomes a rival master. Only when its claim
is wholly rejected can one faithfully serve God (v. 13).[89]

If this point is properly taken into account, Byrne's contention that
the entire context of vv. 1-16 displays 'an ultimately coherent teaching
about wealth' does not appear unreasonable, even if some internal tensions remain.[90] Moreover, we should not fail to recognize the significance that the parable of the Rich Man and Lazarus has in contrast to
this parable.[91] The reaction of the Pharisees (16.14)[92] to Jesus' teaching, 'You cannot serve God and Mammon' (16.13), appears to connect
the parable of the Unjust Steward and the parable of the Rich Man and
Lazarus. Many commentators, taking note of the relation between the
two parables, have suggested that in terms of the right use of wealth
the parable of the unjust steward presents at least a partially positive
model to be emulated, whereas the parable of the Rich Man and Lazarus
introduces a wholly negative model to be eschewed.[93] In this sense, it
has also been claimed that Luke 16 as a literary unit has a continuity of
one theme, that is, the right use of material possessions.[94]

Secondly, in this connection it is worth considering the system of reciprocity that is said to have been prevalent in the Graeco-Roman world

89. Byrne, 'Forceful Stewardship', pp. 4-5.

90. Byrne, pp. 4-5. Cf. Tannehill, *Narrative Unity*, pp. 130-31; Talbert, *Reading Luke*, pp. 153-55.

91. Talbert, *Reading Luke*, p. 153; Tannehill, *Narrative Unity*, pp. 130-31; Pilgrim, *Good News*, p. 129.

92. By Lk. 16.14 where the Pharisees depicted as lovers of money are sneering at Jesus, we may assume that Luke represents them as present when Jesus tells the story. So they are most likely to have heard the Parable. Thus as in the parable of the Great Banquet, the Pharisees, the rich man in disguise, to whom Jesus' teaching is addressed, would be regarded as representative of the wealthy in Luke's community. Therefore it leads us to the conclusion that the Lukan Jesus points out critically the inconsistency in the lives of those who love money, living in luxury, and thinking that being a descendant of Abraham guaranteed salvation. Cf. Schmidt, *Hostility*, pp. 155-57.

Meanwhile, Mealand (*Poverty*, pp. 46-49), Caird (*Luke*, p. 191), T.W. Manson (*Sayings*, pp. 296-301), and Hunter (*Parables*, pp. 83-84), suggest that the parable is addressed to the Sadducees because they deny the resurrection and the life after death. This would be a helpful suggestion indeed, if the immediate context directly or indirectly referred to them. Presumably they are talking about the *Sitz im Leben Jesu*.

93. Talbert, *Reading Luke*, p. 159; Williams, 'Almsgiving', p. 294; Topel, 'Injustice', pp. 221-22; Plummer, *Luke*, p. 390.

94. Byrne, 'Forceful Stewardship', pp. 2-3.

around Luke's time.[95] This ethic dictates that to help one's friends financially means in fact to lend money to them, and the recipient must give back the benefits he received to his friends later when needs will have occurred to them. In view of this ethic, we can see that the unjust steward appears to act prudently because he helps the two debtors in great need reducing a large amount of debt, which in fact means that he lends a great deal of money to them for which the two debtors should feel a responsibility to reciprocate. This idea to help those in need and the poor in any manner is echoed in Lk. 14.12-14, and reiterated in the Parable of the Great Banquet in Lk. 14.16-20 which exploits this motif. Thus the unjust steward can be presented as a model who makes use of material possessions in a right way by distributing them to those in great debt. Therefore, it would appear that the master acclaims the way the steward deals with his crisis in v. 8, whereas Jesus recommends his handling of possessions for the purpose of almsgiving.[96]

In this connection, we should ask who the φίλους are in v. 9: 'And I tell you, make friends for yourselves by means of unrighteous Mammon, so that when it fails they may receive you into the eternal habitations.' Some assert with respect to this word that it does not imply the recipients benefited by the steward, but the angels as circumlocution for God, that is, God himself.[97] But it should be considered that in the context the subject of δέξωνται is φίλους in the principal clause, and nowhere in the New Testament are the angels depicted as φίλοι.[98] Thus if we cannot find such an example in the New Testament, particularly in Luke's work, then it could not be argued to be a clue to interpretation of φίλους in this passage.

But when we compare δέξωνται in 16.9 with δέχομαι in 9.5, 48 (compare Jas 4.45), 'possibly the φίλοι are to be understood as procur-

95. Kloppenborg, 'Dishonoured Master', p. 491; Karris, 'Poor and Rich', pp. 120-21; Gächter, 'Oriental Conceptions', p. 130; Moxnes, *Economy*, pp. 141-43.

96. Williams, 'Almsgiving', pp. 293-94, presents a different solution as regards the motive by which the steward helps the debtors, which comes from the biblical evidence: 'eschatological self-interest'. Thus arguing that some passages in the Synoptic Gospels referring to almsgiving 'make frequent use of this type of motivation', he enumerates Lk. 6.38, 12.33-34, 14.13-14, 16.19-31, and 18.22, for this category into which he puts this parable.

97. Jeremias, *Parables*, p. 46; cf. Grundmann, *Lukas*, p. 321.

98. Schweizer, *Luke*, p. 126, argues that 'in the rabbinic writings, the third person plural is often used periphrastically for God'. Nonetheless it seems hardly feasible that his principle can apply directly to the New Testament.

ing the reception'.[99] When we take this position on φίλους, what v. 9 makes manifest is that if a steward helps those in need by means of wealth entrusted to him, they who cannot recompense in this world would witness to his good behaviour in that world and welcome him (δέξωνται).[100] This idea can also be detected in the Parable of the Great Banquet which follows Jesus' exhortation about this: 'when you give a feast invite the poor, the maimed, the lame, the blind, and you will be blessed, because they cannot repay you. You will be repaid at the resurrection of the just' (Lk. 14.13-14).[101]

Thirdly, it is worth asking who the beneficiaries in the parable are. Most have taken the background as farm tenancy, with the steward as an estate manager and the debtors as impoverished tenants. It is possible to argue, against this, that the large sums of money involved suggest wealthy merchants or traders rather than poor farmers.[102] Since the parable itself gives such scanty detail, it is impossible to be sure. But even in the latter case, the relief of debt is so large as to mean, in effect, a form of almsgiving.

Therefore, it may be noted that in Luke's mind the stress of this parable is laid on the right use of material possessions entrusted to the steward,[103] the best way of which is to distribute it for helping the needy, which in turn may be regarded as heaping up treasure in heaven (16.9; compare 12.33).

c. *The Steward Figure*

With regard to stewardship, we are able to notice some important elements linked to it which I have already drawn from the previous parable. First, here is the finiteness of stewardship: the steward is seen as not having any possessions and property of his own, but as taking care of his master's capital and property until the master suddenly summons

---

99. Plummer, *Luke*, p. 386. In this sense, v. 9 may mean that the best way of the use of material possessions is to provide help for the needy.

100. F.W. Farrar, *St Luke* (Cambridge: Cambridge University Press, 1899), p. 265; Byrne, 'Forceful Stewardship', pp. 4-5.

101. Counting on rabbinic literary evidence, such as *P. Ab.* 4.11 and *B. Bat.* 10a, Williams, 'Almsgiving', p. 295, suggests an interesting idea that φίλοι are alms-deeds themselves personified. But since this view lacks textual evidence from Luke's work, it appears to be pressed too much.

102. Kloppenborg, 'Dishonoured Master', p. 482.

103. Ireland, *Stewardship*, p. 217.

him to turn in the account of his stewardship (vv. 1-2). Thus what matters is to make use of his opportunity during the period of his being a steward, and there is a reward according to the result of his work—either praise or punishment. In support of this thought, we also find a significant point as regards stewardship in v. 12, a part of Jesus' teaching on wealth that constitutes the second half of this story (vv. 9-13). Our attention is drawn here to the word, τὸ ἀλλότριον, which means something belonging to someone else.[104] This word reminds us of the property and possessions entrusted to the steward in vv. 1-2, of which he turns out to be unfaithful in his management by squandering. Thus it is probable that this word can be thought of as a technical term to reveal Luke's notion of stewardship: what a steward possesses is not his at all but another's, that is, his master's. There is nothing of his own.[105]

Secondly, the steward in this parable initially displays a bad image of a steward, because he squanders his master's property and assets by using them at his own will. Such a steward who wastes wealth entrusted to him at his disposal cannot be a true steward, and finally should be dismissed from his position. This negative portrait of the steward also appears to tally with that of the unfaithful steward in the previous parable in Luke 12, which eventually costs them their stewardship (v. 2).

Since these two lessons are found in Luke 12 as well, it may be concluded that these indicate a developing consistency in Luke's idea on stewardship. In consequence, these double pictures of the stewards in both parables enable us to confirm that the elements mentioned above are basic and principal to stewardship. In addition to these points, the recurrence of φρονίμως (v. 8 = 12.42, adjective) might be an index of Luke's intention to include 'prudence' as an indispensable element that is required of a good steward.

---

104. 'Earthly wealth is not only trivial and unreal; it does not belong to us. It is ours only as a loan and a trust, which may be withdrawn at any moment. Heavenly possessions are immense, real, and eternally secure' (Plummer, *Luke*, p. 386).

Grundmann, *Lukas*, p. 322, also makes this point: 'Das irdische Gut, so wird im tritten der Sprüche ausgeführt, ist ein Gut, das dem Menschen nicht zu eigen gehört, weil er es lassen muß; es ist fremd und bleibt ihm fremd, aber die ewige Gabe Gottes soll ihm zu eigen gehören.'

105. Cf. Ireland, *Stewardship*, pp. 110-11; Schmidt, *Hostility*, p. 155; Talbert, *Reading Luke*, p. 155; Morris, *Gospel*, pp. 249-50; Geldenhuys, *Gospel*, p. 417; I.H. Marshall, *Commentary*, p. 623. Among those mentioned here Marshall and Talbert refer explicitly to 'the idea of stewardship'. Here τὸ ὑμέτερον may mean the reward that the Master would give a faithful steward at the end.

Finally, there is one thing which interests us in regard to stewardship, that is, Luke's use of a variety of terms explicitly indicating steward-ship, such as οἰκονόμος (vv. 1, 3, 8 = three times), οἰκονομία (vv. 2, 3, 4 = three times), and οἰκονομέω (v. 2). The frequency of Luke's use of related terms in this single passage (unique to Luke) shows that Luke has particular interest in this motif.

d. *Summary and Conclusion*

Taking together what I have discussed thus far, we may summarize as follows: The unjust steward in this parable, to overcome the crisis con-fronting him, invests the material possessions of another, that is, his master, in making friends by way of helping those in need with an ex-pectation, according to the reciprocity ethic prevailing at that time, that they will later accept him into their houses once he has been stripped of his stewardship. Thus, although the action itself is unjust, both the prudent mode of action and its final result, the relief of people in need, might be understood by Luke as a model for believers to follow in handling wealth entrusted by God.[106] In this sense, it is reasonable that the master applauds his way of using possessions for the purpose of almsgiving, and Jesus himself recommends it as a way that Christian believers as stewards should follow in managing wealth given and en-trusted by God. In conclusion, when we seek out Luke's particular emphatic aspect of stewardship in this parable, it is suggested that that is an exhortation as to how a steward uses his possessions rightly.

4. *The Parable of the Ten Minas (19.11-27/Mt. 25.14-30)*

a. *The Composition of the Parable*

It has long been in dispute whether or not this parable in fact consists of two parables, such as the parable of the ten minas and that of the throne claimant or the rejected king. The opinions of scholars are by and large divided in this matter: one side argues that the so-called para-ble of the rejected king cannot be regarded properly as a parable, but just as an additional expansion,[107] while the other side claims that two

---

106. Cf. Kloppenborg, 'Dishonoured Master', p. 475; Schweizer, *Luke*, p. 255.

107. Creed, *Gospel*, p. 232; T.W. Manson, *Sayings*, p. 313. Bultmann and Schulz also are of this opinion (I.H. Marshall, *Commentary*, p. 701). However, Plummer, *Luke*, p. 437, takes this parable in its present form as a whole unit which maintains a consistency, while, Evans, *Saint Luke*, pp. 668-69, holds that the passages added to

separate parables are fused together into one.[108] However, it seems to be agreed that, in its present focus at least, the parable has two motifs: the meaning of discipleship and the rejected king. As to the meaning of discipleship, scholars point out the faithful and profitable service of those who are given responsibilities, whether they are the Jewish leaders or the Apostles. On the other hand, as to the motif of the rejected king, it is suggested that Luke's effort to correct a misunderstanding of the *parousia* is to be noted.

In addition, there is another unsolved problem in this parable: is this parable of the ten minas in Luke to be considered as a variant version of the parable of the talents in Matthew? In this regard, opinions do not appear to be unified. One group is in favour of 'one original parable that lies behind the two versions',[109] suggesting 'Q' material as a common source, whereas the other group is against that view, and claims that the two parables in Luke and Matthew are 'accurate reports of two different parables and not two reports of the same parable'.[110] In this context, what appears to matter to my case here is not to decide which view is right, but to appreciate the story as it is presented here in Luke.[111]

b. *A Stewardship Parable?*
In order to explore the meaning of this parable, it would be helpful to deal with the question as to why this parable of the ten minas is to be discussed here under the rubric of Lukan stewardship. Thus, first of all, this question ought to be tackled before we proceed further.

---

the main parable are made of Luke's literary work 'to give it [the parable] a new framework and a fresh point'. Cf. Drury, *Parables*, p. 156.

108. Jeremias, *Parables*, p. 59; J.D. Crossan, *In Parables* (New York: Harper & Row, 1973), pp. 100-101. Ellis, *Luke*, pp. 222-23, regards this parable as 'a double parable that carries two motifs'. Fitzmyer, *Gospel*, pp. 1230-31, finely classifies commentators' opinions on this matter and lists scholars who belong to each group.

109. I.H. Marshall, *Commentary*, p. 701.

110. Plummer, *Luke*, p. 437; Ellis, *Luke*, p. 222; Kistemaker, *Parables*, p. 139. Crossan, *In Parables*, pp. 100-101, contends, doubting such a common source as 'Q', that Luke and Matthew resort to 'their own special and independent sources'. Meanwhile, Jeremias, *Parables*, p. 58, asserts that the parable of the ten minas has come down in three versions: Lk. 19.12-27, Mt. 25.14-30, and the Gospel of the Nazarenes.

111. For lists of scholars on both sides, see Fitzmyer, *Gospel*, p. 1230.

It is clear that in this parable there appear no terms explicitly related to stewardship. Nevertheless this does not seem to me to be against our case, because even though specific terms are not employed here, the servants in this parable are in many ways analogous to the stewards in the previous parables in terms of role and function. The following are to be pointed out as similarities between the servants here and the stewards there:

(1) As in the parables of chs. 12 and 16 the stewards are entrusted with wealth and put in charge of it by their masters, so the servants in this parable are also assigned a portion of capital temporarily[112] during their master's journey, in order to take care of it.

(2) The three parables show consistency in assessing the work done by the servants: with respect to judgment of the unfaithful servants the three stories deprive them of their position as steward (12.46/16.2/ 19.24); with respect to the commendation of the faithful servants, two parables give more assets and responsibilities to those who prove that they can make full use of wealth and property entrusted to them (12.44/ 19.17, 19).[113] In this context, it is also worth noting that the phrase, πιστὸς...ἐν ἐλαχίστῳ, is shared by two of the parables (19.17 and 16.10), which exhibits explicitly a connection between the two parables.[114]

(3) In the light of the behavioural attitude required of a steward, the two servants who increase their master's capital in this parable would ultimately be comparable to the steward who discharges his duty faithfully following his master's will (12.43-44), because they cannot increase their master's capital if they do not execute their obligations faithfully. On the other hand, the servant who, too afraid of his master's harsh character, earns no profit for his master would likewise be comparable to the steward who squanders his master's assets (16.2), or abuses his position in beating fellow servants, eating, and drinking (12.45), because he does not carry out his duty faithfully according to his master's will and order.[115]

---

112. ἐν ᾧ ἔρχομαι of v. 13 may be thought of as showing the temporality of their position as stewards.

113. Schmidt, *Hostility*, p. 160. Cf. Drury, *Parables*, p. 156.

114. Schmidt, *Hostility*, p. 160.

115. It might appear that the third servant does not do anything wrong, and in fact he accuses his master of his severity because he takes up what he did not lay down and reaps what he did not sow (v. 21), which his master himself admits, too (v. 22). In this connection a question may arise; why then does the master condemn the third

(4) It has been said that this parable of the ten minas, reflecting an actual historical fact,[116] was taught at the time when the people thought that the Kingdom of God was about to appear as Jesus approached Jerusalem. It would appear that from recent Jewish history integrated into the parable, Luke intends to teach his contemporaries a lesson concerning the coming of the Kingdom of God. This theme of *parousia* appears in the introduction, in which Jesus cautions that the consummation of God's reign is not imminent (19.11). According to Luke's introduction the parable is designed to correct the false expectation of God's reign, and to teach that an interim is to occur between his first and second coming[117] and that this interval before the *parousia* will be a time of testing, that is, a period of probation, and according to the quality of their work during that interval, people will be judged as the ten servants are judged in this parable.[118] Here we note the eschatologi-

---

slave? The text shows that the basis of the condemnation is that if the slave knows what sort of a person his master is, e.g. a person who is so strict as to take up what he did not lay down and reap what he did not sow, and also that he is a slave of such a person, he must do anything to get profit for his master at all costs, behaving as his master does (Evans, *Saint Luke*, p. 667; cf. Seccombe, *Possessions*, p. 192).

The other point of significance as regards the misbehaviour is that he takes no heed of his master's command that appears in v. 13: 'Trade with these till I come'. Here πραγματεύσασθε implies 'to carry on business, especially as a banker or a trader' (Plummer, *Luke*, p. 439). Whether his master is strict or not, as slave the slave must act upon his master's will and order. But he fails to do this, so there is nothing wrong with his master's punishment.

116. In 4 BCE, Herod the Great had died and his son, Archelaus, journeyed to Rome hoping to receive the title of King of Judaea. He was followed by a Jewish embassy of 50 persons who told Augustus that they did not want Archelaus to be their king because of his tyranny. But Archelaus was appointed as ethnarch of Idumaea, Judaea, and Samaria, and heard a promise that if he would rule well he would obtain kingship. Afterwards, when he returned to Judaea he wreaked bloody revenge on the people, which has never been forgotten. Eventually he was replaced by a Roman governor, and Pontius Pilate was the fifth of these governors (Josephus, *War* 2.80; *Ant.* 17.299-300).

117. I.H. Marshall, *Commentary*, p. 702; Hunter, *Parables*, p. 81.

118. Creed, *Gospel*, p. 232; Jeremias, *Parables*, p. 59. In this connection, Danker, *Jesus*, p. 193, asserts that 'The parable also summarizes Luke's doctrine of the two-phase Kingdom. Luke does not deny that Kingdom is present reality, but he uses the parable to correct a misunderstanding of the imminent *parousia*'. Meanwhile, Schweizer, *Luke*, p. 292, argues that 'Luke's concern is not with its delay but with its presence and above all with what the community does in the interim'.

cal feature observed in the parables of stewards in chs. 12 and 16.[119] Thus in keeping with them, in the parable of the ten minas, it is noted that in discharging his stewardship, a steward should be on the alert and faithful to his job because the interim is a time of probation, and after that there is a judgment according to his work.

(5) To sum up, even though specific terms are not used by the author in this parable in relation to stewardship, in view of the features that we have observed in the previous two parables with regard to stewardship, this parable of the ten minas appears to be connected with the stewardship motif in Luke's mind.[120]

c. *The Point of the Parable*

Having discussed similarities between this parable and the previous parables as regards stewardship, now we may have to take into consideration a point of difference between them, that is, the duty which the servants here and the stewards there are supposed to perform. In this parable the obligation of the servants is not only just taking care of assets and property consigned to them but also making gain out of them for the benefit of their master, while in the forgoing parables the stewards are not expected to trade in order to earn profit but just to look after the assets and capital their masters put into their hands. It is too hasty to conclude from this difference that we should construe this parable in a different and separate way from the preceding parables. Rather it may be asserted that this difference we have noticed in comparing with its precedents broadens our understanding of Lukan stewardship, because this discrepancy is added as a new element of stewardship to the features observed in the forgoing parables. That is to say, it would seem that in Luke's mind a steward is supposed not only to carry out faithfully his responsibility of taking care of the property and capital assigned to him, but also where appropriate to make some profit out of the assets and material possessions his master entrusts to his care.

In the interpretation of this parable many a scholar is inclined to give it a spiritual application, regarding the minas as spiritual gifts or

119. Cf. Dodd, *Parables*, p. 120; Jeremias, *Parables*, p. 63.

120. Schmidt, *Hostility*, p. 160, recognizes this point accurately saying that 'Within this context, it is evident that stewardship of possessions is a fundamental criterion for judgment: 19.17 is an unmistakable echo of 16.10-11'.

talents of some kind, rather than as a token of a financial reality.[121] But scant evidence seems to be found in favour of such a spiritual inter- pretation. Rather ἀκουόντων δὲ αὐτῶν ταῦτα in v. 11 reveals that this parable is closely connected to its precedent, that is, the Zacchaeus incident.[122] Thus Drury explicates the relation of two stories as follows:

> Zacchaeus the publican had done well out of his business and was able to give half his goods to the poor as well as restoring fourfold to those whom he had swindled: something like the two servants in the parable who increase their capital by enterprise.[123]

And in addition, when we take into account Luke's particular interest in the literal reality of poverty (6.20; 16.20-21) and his consistent concern for the poor, the outcast, and the underprivileged throughout the Gos- pel,[124] a spiritual interpretation of the minas in this parable may be thought of as missing his intention. In regard to this point, Flender states against the allegorical application of this parable: 'In Luke 19,13 the work demanded of the disciples could easily be equated with missionary service. But as I see it, it means primarily action in the world . . . Luke wishes to emphasize the importance of secular activity.'[125] This result may apply to the other parables of stewardship in Luke 12 and 16.[126]

---

121. In line with this, focusing on the third servant, they tend to see this parable as directed against the Jews, or the religious leaders, the scribes in particular (Jeremias, *Parables*, pp. 61-62), or the Pharisees (Caird, *Luke*, p. 210), who failed to utilize the spiritual gifts which God has entrusted to them, such as the Word of God, the grace of God, and the gifts of the Holy Spirit (Seccombe, *Possessions*, p. 191).

122. Bengel, *Gnomon*, II, p. 176; Plummer, *Luke*, p. 438; Seccombe, *Posses- sions*, p. 191; Drury, *Parables*, p. 155.

123. Drury, *Parables*, p. 155.

124. Lk. 4.18-19; 7.21-22; 14.13-14, 21; 16.20-21, etc.

125. Flender, *St Luke*, p. 77.

126. Cf. Seccombe, *Possessions*, p. 193. One may say that this interpretation of the parable of ten minas does not take account of the matter that the profit made by the two servants is given to the master, not to the poor. But for my argument here it is not important to whom the profit accrues (is it for the master, v. 23? but in v. 25 the slave still has the ten minas); that is really beside the point. The details of the parable are literal financial affairs. Almsgiving is more clearly specified elsewhere, and dealt with later in this book.

5. *Summary and Conclusion: The Strategic Importance of the Three Parables and their Interconnection with Wealth Material*

Thus far in relation to stewardship as one of the major themes of Luke's Gospel, we have examined three stories, all of them parables, one after another. Each of them may be reckoned as containing important ideas on stewardship, and as a result of our investigation a few crucial elements almost common to the three parables in regard to stewardship have been identified. Now it will be convenient for us to organize them systematically, so that we may look at Luke's view of stewardship as a whole.

(1) *Role and Function*: In Luke's mind a steward is a slave whom his master entrusts with, and leaves in charge of, his assets and material possessions (12.42; 16.1; 19.13). Thus it is discovered that he has nothing of his own and all he has belongs to his master.

(2) *Assessment*: It seems necessary that stewardship entails an assessment. According to the result of their work, a faithful steward will be commended and given opportunity for wider service and larger responsibility (12.44; 16.8a; 19.17, 19), while an unfaithful steward will be reproached and deprived of his position, that is, the opportunity to serve (12.46; 16.2; 19.24, 26).

(3) *Demeanour*: Since the wealth of a master is entrusted to a steward provisionally, the position of steward is to be reckoned within a fixed timescale. This element of stewardship is closely related to the eschatological feature consistently revealed in the three parables. Stated simply, in carrying out his duty, the primary thing which a steward should keep in mind is that his position is not permanent but provisional, so that it will end at any time when demanded by his master (12.43, 46; 16.2; 19.13, 15). Thus what is required of a steward is that during the period of his stewardship, that is, a period of probation, he should carry out his duty prudently, and be on the alert, being aware of the day when his work will be judged.

These three points singled out above are explanatory of Luke's idea of stewardship in general. Now in what follows, bearing in mind these basic elements of Lukan stewardship, we will concentrate on Luke's application of these ideas of stewardship to the areas in which he would have been much interested.

Apart from these three parables, it seems that direct and explicit references to stewardship do not occur any more in the Gospel. However, it cannot be said that the three parables are all there is about stewardship in Luke's Gospel, because it is probable that although explicit references to stewardship may not be found any more, the stewardship theme continues to be present in the Gospel in a somewhat different way.

In this connection, we should not overlook the arrangement of the material made by the author that those parables occur three times at regular intervals, for example, chs. 12, 16, and 19: in other words, we may state that the parable of stewardship repeats itself on three occasions—among which the material related to wealth is scattered here and there. Hence it could be argued that such an intermittent repetition is to be regarded as thoughtfully arranged by the author in order to express his idea of stewardship more overtly by this literary device. In short, the fact that a number of references to material possessions are dispersed throughout the Gospel centring on the three parables could be reckoned as indicating the relevance of the stewardship motif to that of wealth, which appears Luke's main concern in this material.[127] Therefore, in what follows, I shall examine Luke's application of these basic ideas of stewardship to the motif of material possessions which is largely divided into two major categories: instruction concerning the right use of wealth and warning about the wrong use of wealth.

127. Cf. Seccombe, *Possessions*, pp. 190-94; Schmidt, *Hostility*, pp. 145-60.

Chapter 6

STEWARDSHIP OF WEALTH

With regard to this subject, we can find a great deal of material in Luke–Acts which far exceeds that in Mark and Matthew in quantity. But one thing which should be stated at the outset to avoid being misleading is that not all the material I will discuss from now on is focused primarily on this motif, because in some cases the motif appears secondary to the main subject. This does not surprise us because it is plain that the motif of instruction on the right use of material possessions in Luke–Acts cannot be claimed as the sole concern in Luke's theological thoughts. Rather it may be safe to remark that this motif of almsgiving is to be acknowledged as one of the main theological ideas that Luke bears in mind when writing his works. In view of this position, therefore, I will pick up and deal with any material which refers to the motif at issue in any circumstance, even though it appears secondary.

1. Proper Stewardship of Wealth (The Right Use of Wealth)

a. The Ethical Teaching of John the Baptist (3.10-14)
It is remarkable that in contrast with the other Evangelists, Luke records more material as regards the teaching of John the Baptist. Among the material in question, Lk. 3.10-14 which we are dealing with here is peculiar to Luke, so it adds extra weight to Luke's case for the motif of the right use of wealth.[1]

The ethical teaching issued by John the Baptist is in fact presented as a reply to the multitude's question 'what then shall we do?' (v. 10). This question, however, is also a sort of response to the sermon of John the Baptist, which is tinted with imminent eschatology and so demanding of the production of good fruits as to make them ask the question.

---

1.   Fitzmyer, *Gospel*, p. 464; I.H. Marshall, *Commentary*, pp. 141-42; Pilgrim, *Good News*, p. 143.

John replies, 'He who has two coats, let him share with him who has none; and he who has food, let him do likewise' (v. 11). Here what arrests our attention is the expression, τῷ μὴ ἔχοντι, which Luke uses to depict those who do not have the most basic and essential necessities in the daily life of human beings, such as clothing and food. In fact, they are none other than the destitute.[2] In relation to this aspect, the word μεταδίδωμι (v. 11) which is only used here among the four Gospels,[3] is also to be appreciated properly, because it seems to express Luke's emphasis on distribution of wealth to the poor.[4] Thus it may not be overstated that the Baptist's sermon to the multitudes is in reality to be understood as an exhortation to give alms to the poor and needy,[5] which is also in line with 'Luke's description of the shared economic life of the early church in Acts'.[6]

With the presupposition that this context reflects the social situation of Palestine, Schottroff and Stegemann claim that the ὄχλος to whom this sermon is addressed are poor, and that in view of Isa. 58.7 the poor who have two undergarments (χιτών) should share one of them with those who have none. In other words, the poor people, they argue, are 'exhorted to solidarity among themselves'.[7] Although this identification of the crowd as 'the poor' is open to question,[8] their conclusion

2. Cf. Ernst, *Lukas*, p. 144.
3. Among four occurrences of this word in the New Testament, Rom. 1.11; 12.8; Eph. 4.28; 1 Thess. 2.8, on two occasions, i.e. Rom. 12.8 and Eph. 4.28, this word is employed directly for implying almsgiving, but on the other two occasions it still has the meaning of sharing (I.H. Marshall, *Commentary*, p. 142).
4. Cf. Fitzmyer, *Gospel*, p. 465.
5. Ernst, *Lukas*, p. 144, recognizes John's exhortations as radical and practical: 'Johannes fordert radikal, aber nichts Außergewöhnliches, wie etwa Jesus in der Feldrede (Lk 6,29)... Für das Verständnis des Lk zeigt sich die von Johannes verlangte Umkehr im praktischen Alltagsleben'.
6. Pilgrim, *Good News*, p. 144.
7. Schottroff and Stegemann, *Hope*, p. 108.
8. According to Plummer (*Luke*, pp. 90-91) and Creed (*Gospel*, p. 52), χιτών is regarded as less necessary than ἱμάτιον which is indispensable to the people of Palestine (cf. Lk. 6.29; Acts 9.39; Mt. 5.40; Jn 19.23). This point leads us to think of the following logic: if anyone owns two undergarments that are not absolutely essential for daily living, then it seems difficult to label him as poor in the proper sense. Rather it may be possible to regard him as better off because he owns *two* undergarments which are not fundamental. It does not mean that the ὄχλος referred to here are rich, but that they are not poor as Schottroff and Stegemann insist (*Hope*, pp. 107-108). If we take into account the word ὄχλος which may possibly embrace

can, in general, be sustained. They contend that this lesson drawn from a historical situation is applied to the ordinary folk of Luke's contemporary situation. 'Thus the caritative activity of ordinary people takes the concrete form of solidarity and a readiness to help others even needier than themselves'.[9]

The second and third questions issued by the tax collectors and the soldiers respectively in vv. 12 and 14 appear to be in accordance with that of the multitudes in terms of a response to John's eschatological sermon. John's commands to the tax collectors and the soldiers appear to protect the poor and the powerless from being extorted and exploited.[10] In addition, there is one thing which still needs to be considered. Luke does not record John's ascetic mode of life which Mark (1.6) and Matthew (3.4) do in their versions. As for the reason for this omission, Fitzmyer's suggestions appears to be reasonable: it is 'because of the emphasis put here on ethical reform and concern for one's neighbor'.[11]

These three points being taken into account, it seems plausible for us to regard the first answer to the multitudes as the basic principle of almsgiving, and the second and third answers as extended application of the stated principle to more specific situations that people face individually in their own circumstances.[12]

Finally having said this, we should not fail to recognize that Luke intends to show his readers that as far as the motif of the right use of material possessions is concerned, John the forerunner of Jesus the Christ (vv. 16-17; 9.20) holds pace with Jesus whose ethical teaching on the motif at issue will be discussed in what follows.[13] In other words, we can state that there appears to be a continuity between John the Baptist and Jesus in view of the theme of the right use of possessions.[14]

---

all classes of people at that time, we may suggest in all likelihood that this sermon of John the Baptist is addressed to all people, but in fact specifically to those who are a little more affluent so that they can give a spare undergarment and food to those in need.

9. Schottroff and Stegemann, *Hope*, p. 109; Pilgrim, *Good News*, pp. 143, 146.

10. Pilgrim, *Good News*, pp. 145-46; cf. Beck, *Character*, pp. 43, 193.

11. Fitzmyer, *Gospel*, p. 469.

12. Schweizer, *Luke*, p. 73; cf. Evans, *Saint Luke*, p. 240.

13. John's designation, διδάσκαλος, used by the publicans can also be pointed out as a link between Jesus and John, because it is later applied to Jesus (7.40; 9.38; 10.25; 11.45; 12.13; 18.18; 19.39; 20.21, 28, 39; 21.7).

14. Cf. Tannehill, *Narrative Unity*, pp. 50-51.

b. *Give to Everyone who Begs from You (6.27-38)*
This part of the Sermon on the Plain has parallels in Matthew, which
may drive us to think of a common source, such as 'Q', to which Luke
and Matthew might have resorted, but it is not a simple matter to be
firmly established.[15] Even if we admit that both Evangelists drew these
passages from the same fountain, Luke's additions and differences, for
example, vv. 34-36, from the Matthaean version (Mt. 5.39-42) appear
to make Luke's case here quite different from that of Matthew.[16] In
fact, Matthew has just two references (vv. 40, 42) in relation to giving
or lending to other people. On the other hand, Luke appears to be consistent in pursuing his aim in this section which is to develop the theme
of generous giving.

This section consists of three threads of themes bound together which
prescribe the attitude of Jesus's disciples: ἀγαπᾶν (vv. 27-28, 35),
ἀγαθοποιεῖν (vv. 31-33), and δανείζειν (vv. 34-38).[17] What emerges
prominently among these three closely related themes is Jesus' exhortation to give away or lend without expecting to get any recompense
(vv. 30, 34-35), because Matthew does not mention this particular
point at all in his Gospel.[18] This key theme is repeated again in v. 38,
which is introduced as a conclusion of the material ranging from vv.
27-37.[19] But unlike the previous sayings encouraging to give and lend

15. I.H. Marshall, *Commentary*, pp. 257-58.
16. Cf. Evans, *Saint Luke*, pp. 335-36.
17. Degenhardt, *Lukas*, p. 55. Although it seems a little forced, Talbert's categorization of these passages into four thought units appears tolerable (*Narrative Unity*,
p. 69): '(a) 6:27-28 = love, do good, bless, pray, (b) 6:29-30 = strikes, takes away
your cloak, begs, takes away your goods, (c) 6:32-35 = the first three—if you love,
if you do good, if you lend—are balanced by the fourth—but love, do good, lend,
(d) 6:37-38a = negatives—judge not, condemn not—balanced by two positives—
forgive, give—followed by a summary, vs, 38b.' Cf. Fitzmyer, *Gospel*, pp. 637-
41; Evans, *Saint Luke*, pp. 324-25.
18. Pilgrim, *Good News*, p. 137.
19. Talbert, *Reading Luke*, p. 69. Apparently v. 37 does not seem congruous with
the context, which appears to sever itself from the theme of giving away stressed
continuously from v. 27 to v. 36. However if we take v. 37 as meaning not to take to
court those enemies who extort and take away, the problem of discontinuity in flow
of the giving away theme might be solved. And when we note that the theme recurs
at v. 38, and that μέτρον (v. 38) is 'associated with giving rather than judging, as in
Matthew 7:2' (Schweizer, *Luke*, p. 126; Creed, *Gospel*, p. 96), v. 37 seems merely
to reflect Luke's source without any specific emphasis. If Luke intended to stress
judging, he should have related v. 37 directly to μέτρον, as Matthew did.

without expecting repayment (v. 35), here the reward for such an act is recorded. The reward referred to here is not material and earthly but spiritual and heavenly, on the grounds of v. 35b, 'your reward will be great, and you will be sons of the Most High'.[20] This second half of v. 35 is substantially in keeping with the first half of v. 35, 'expecting nothing in return', that is, to expect a reward in heaven would mean not to expect repayment on earth. In other words, it means that a Christian disciple is supposed to give and share generously what he has of his own with others in need.[21] This meaning of v. 35 is in fact repeated emphatically in v. 36 in the form of 'mercy', and Luke's import in this verse will be revealed when v. 36 is compared with Mt. 5.48, 'You, therefore, must be perfect, as your heavenly Father is perfect'. What is outstanding in this comparison is that the concept of perfection in Matthew is matched by that of mercy in Luke, which tallies perfectly with Luke's care for the poor and needy. When these points mentioned above are considered, these sayings of Jesus can be thought of as an admonition to distribute one's own possessions as almsgiving to those in need.[22]

This phenomenon may tell us that this instruction of Jesus reflects the contemporary situation of Luke's community, concerning which we have already drawn a conclusion that it may have been in urban circumstances highly influenced by Graeco-Roman culture. We know from the ancient literature at Luke's time that a sort of IOU system, 'das Prinzip der Gegenseitigkeit', was prevalent throughout the Roman Empire.[23]

Meanwhile, Degenhardt, *Lukas*, pp. 56-57, binds vv. 37-38 together, claiming that they describe 'die barmherzige Grundhaltung des Anhängers Jesu', and Fitzmyer, *Gospel*, p. 641, also holds, 'Mercy in judging should lead also to generosity in giving, and so the foursome [two prohibitions and two commands] is united'.

20. Cf. Pilgrim, *Good News*, p. 138; I.H. Marshall, *Commentary*, p. 267.

21. Tannehill's assertion (*Narrative Unity*, p. 209) that the thrust of Jesus' commands is total renunciation like that of the apostles is a mistaken interpretation.

22. Cf. Tannehill, *Narrative Unity*, p. 209.

23. H. Bolkestein in his masterpiece, *Wohltätigkeit und Armenpflege im vorchristlichen Altertum* (Utrecht: A. Oosthoek, 1939), made a clear statement: 'das Prinzip der Gegenseitigkeit hat eine der Grundlagen des sozialen Verkehrs der Griechen gebildet' (cited by W.C. van Unnik, 'Die Motivierung der Feindesliebe in Lukas 6.32-35', *NovT* 8 [1966], pp. 284-300 [291]). Cf. S.C. Mott, 'The Power of Giving and Receiving: Reciprocity in Hellenistic Benevolence', in G.F. Hawthorne (ed.), *Current Issues in Biblical and Patristic Interpretation—Studies in Honor of M.C. Tenney* (Grand Rapids: Eerdmans, 1975), pp. 60-72.

Thus Jesus' exhortation here is in head-on collision with the current ethic which in Luke's eyes has no love and mercy in reality, and so should be abolished at least among Christians.[24] In other words, it can be said that for Luke the expectation of reciprocity is not the right attitude which Christians ought to hold; instead he recommends his congregation to give or lend generously expecting nothing in return.

This recommendation of generosity is in keeping with John the Baptist's exhortation to share material possessions with destitute people, although the motif of almsgiving does not seem to come to the fore explicitly. So we would conclude that in the sayings of Jesus ranging from 6.27 to 6.38 the continuity of Luke's thought on almsgiving is found once again with clarity.

c. *The Anointing Incident (Lk. 7.36-50)*

This incident in Luke appears to be similar to that in Mark and Matthew, because the basic facts seem identical: first, Jesus is invited by Simon to a meal, and secondly, a woman pours ointment on Jesus. Despite these basic similarities, however, we can also observe a few differences between Luke and Mark, which are so significant as to offer the grounds to suggest that the two stories are not identical:

(1) The contexts are different. The setting in which the Lukan story is placed is totally different, because the Markan story is placed in the passion narrative, being related to the salvific death of Jesus, whereas the Lukan narrative is seen to be linked to the preceding story by means of criticism against the Pharisees who along with the scribes criticize Jesus for being a friend of tax collectors and sinners (Lk. 7.30, 33-34/7.39).[25]

(2) The process of the narratives is different. The woman in Luke who is introduced as a sinner pours the ointment on Jesus' feet, weeping, wetting his feet with her tears, and wiping them with her hair (Lk. 7.38), whereas the woman in Mark, who is not a sinner, pours the

---

From this assertion van Unnik starts to build his argument that the Lukan Jesus criticises sharply this Greek moral of reciprocity, which leads into Luke's motif of *Feindesliebe* in Lk. 6.32-35 (van Unnik, 'Motivierung', pp. 284-300). We will discuss this feature at length in Chapter 8.

24. Jesus' sayings in 6.27-38 'are a two-printed attack on reciprocity as a governing principle in human relationships' (Talbert, *Reading Luke*, p. 73; cf. p. 75).

25. Tannehill, *Narrative Unity*, pp. 116-17, 177.

ointment of pure nard, on Jesus' head, without weeping, wetting, and wiping (Mk 14.3).

(3) Following these discrepant points, each account turns out to develop its own theme: the Lukan story concerns the forgiveness of sin, with the help of an additional parable, that is, the parable of two debtors (Lk. 7.41-43), and the ensuing conversation between Jesus and Simon (Lk. 7.44-47) that also speak of the motif, while the Markan story focuses on the redemptive death of Jesus (Mk 14.8). If the Lukan anointing account is to be recognized as different from that of Mark, then a question should be answered in this connection: why does Luke leave out another anointing story recorded in Mark?

The reason for this omission by Luke may be initially drawn from Luke's particular concern for the poor. Mark's account shows a conflict exists between Jesus and people around him, who are the disciples according to Matthew, as regards the woman's pouring expensive perfume on Jesus' head. They rebuke her harshly for her extravagant behaviour, appearing to mind the situation of the poor (Mk 14.5). But supporting the woman and praising her action toward him, Jesus says, 'For you always have the poor with you, and whenever you will, you can do good to them; but you will not always have me' (Mk 14.7). In this saying of Mark the poor are seen as less significant being contrasted with Jesus in terms of priority.[26] Consequently, it seems certain that Luke does not find this statement of Jesus appropriate to maintain his position as advocate of the poor and the destitute, and this is surely among the factors which drive Luke to omit this incident from his Gospel.[27]

26. Schottroff and Stegemann, *Hope*, pp. 109-11, use Luke's omission of this account in Mark to argue that there is no οἱ πτωχοί in Luke's community. For criticism of this argument see Introduction, 1.1.e.

27. 'The fact that Luke has omitted the narrative in Mk 14.1-9 at the corresponding point in his own Gospel is no proof that he regarded this story as identical with Mark's one . . . The two narratives deal with separate incidents and have different characters and purposes; it is unlikely that Luke has reworked Mk 14.1-9 or that Luke's tradition and Mark's tradition ultimately refer to one and the same incident' (I.H. Marshall, *Commentary*, p. 306). For another, differing, opinion on this matter, see Goulder, *Paradigm*, II, 403.

d. *The Devotion of the Galilaean Women (8.1-3)*

This narrative is very valuable in giving us an indication of how Jesus and his disciples' needs, that is, their means of livelihood, were met during their wandering lives. In these three verses we find a unique occasion in the record of the earthly ministry of Jesus that during their wandering lives Jesus and his band of disciples were followed and supported by a number of the Galilaean women out of their own possessions (v. 3).[28] Even though Jesus and his disciples were not seldom invited to meals by various classes of people of his time (5.29; 7.35; 10.38-42; 14.12), yet that they were supported financially particularly by women[29] in their daily living is recorded here only in the Gospels.

(1) We have to consider one aspect here that according to v. 1 Jesus and his disciples lived a wandering life without any settled abode, and it enables us to suppose that they were not well off.[30] This aspect would

28. Taking notice of this fact, B. Witherington ('On the Road with Mary Magdalene, Joanna, Susanna, and Other Disciples—Luke 8.1-3', *ZNW* 70 [1979], pp. 243-48 [244-45]), holds that 'But for her [a woman] to leave home and travel with a rabbi was not only unheard of, it was scandalous'. However, as I have argued earlier in Chapter 3, since there are no further references to women during Jesus' journey to Jerusalem while ample references to the Twelve and the Apostles are recorded, it is only a slim possibility that these women travelled all the way with Jesus and his apostles.

Having said this, we might have a guess like this: in order to serve Jesus and his Apostles, these women might have had a short break from daily household routine which their husbands might have allowed to them. Therefore, what I want to argue here is that they did not abandon their homes and families to serve, and to be with, Jesus, as Witherington insists.

29. Jesus' friendship with women is particularly noted by Luke, such that it is one of the characteristics of his Gospel (White, *Luke's Case*, pp. 79-81). In line with this, Tannehill, *Narrative Unity*, p. 139, contends that this fact of women's following Jesus with the Apostles in fact fulfils 'the commission which Jesus announced in Nazareth in an impressive way' (Lk. 4.18-19), that is, to preach the gospel to the poor and the oppressed and the excluded. See also Witherington, 'On the Road', pp. 244, 247. In this connection, Schmithals, *Lukas*, p. 101, says that 'Der vorliegende Abschnitt ist der zentrale Beleg für Lukas als "Evangelist der Frauen"'. Cf. Ellis, *Luke*, p. 127. See Lk. 23.49; 24.10; cf. Acts 1.14; 9.36-43; 16.11-15.

Meanwhile, Talbert, *Reading Luke*, pp. 90-93, dwells upon Luke's particular interest in the roles and ministries of women in his writings. His conclusion on this matter is that 'in the Lukan scheme of things, women often functioned side by side with men in Christian ministry, including the ministry of teaching' (p. 92). Contra Evans, *Saint Luke*, pp. 366-67.

30. Lk. 9.58 being taken into account with this episode, it is noted that Jesus was

be corroborated in the mission sermon of Jesus to his disciples when he sent them out to preach the Gospel (9.3; 10.4, 7): according to the Mission Sermon, the disciples' life during their mission travels seems to have been very hard, because they were supposed to rely on hospitality from those to whom they preached the Gospel.[31] In consequence, it may be assumed that even if they were not the poor of Luke's contemporaries in the strict sense, nonetheless it is true that they were poor in view of their actual lifestyle, that is, a wandering life expecting hospitality from others. Thus, in this context, it may not be an exaggeration to say that the action taken by these Galilaean women would be analogous to almsgiving.[32]

(2) Among those women referred to, the one who attracts particular attention is Joanna who also appears in 24.10, the wife of Chuza, Herod's steward, for she was from the upper circle of society.[33] From this we would imagine that she was wealthy and had a great deal of possessions.[34] It seems to me that it is of particular interest that Luke introduces Joanna along with other women, all of whom were healed from their illnesses by Jesus, since she can be a model for the rich people of Luke's community as to how the rich should use their wealth,[35] that is,

so poor as to be homeless, but what should be noticed is that Jesus and his disciples became poor voluntarily, not compulsorily.

31. Thus it may be assumed that 'Das Leben der Jünger ist ungesichert' (Degenhardt, *Lukas*, p. 201).

32. It is known that at the time of Jesus' ministry, rabbis were supported by people who listened to their interpretation of the Law, which was considered as a pious act. Thus Witherington, 'On the Road', p. 244, notes that 'it was not uncommon for women to support rabbis and their disciples out of their own money property, or foodstuffs'. Thus Luke's case for the Galilaean women here might be in line with this custom prevalent at that time. Cf. Plummer, *Luke*, p. 215. See also Talbert, *Reading Luke*, pp. 92-93.

33. This makes us infer that 'Jesus' influence and preaching was reaching even to high places' (Fitzmyer, *Gospel*, p. 698). Cf. Evans, *Saint Luke*, p. 366; Witherington, 'On the Road', p. 246.

34. Plummer, *Luke*, p. 216; Witherington, 'On the Road', p. 246; I.H. Marshall, *Commentary*, p. 317.

35. Sweetland, *Journey*, pp. 147-48. ἐκ τῶν ὑπαρχόντων (Lk. 8.3) distinguishes this passage from Mt. 27.55 and Mk 15.41, where the διακονεῖν might refer to mere attendance to him (Plummer, *Luke*, p. 217). 'Serving tables for the needy continues to be an important function in the early church (Acts 6.1-6)' (Tannehill, *Narrative Unity*, p. 138). Hence Talbert, *Reading Luke*, p. 91, makes the point that 'in this matter Luke manifests continuity with early Christianity generally'.

to distribute material possessions to the poor and needy. In addition to this, that this narrative is an actual example of almsgiving in practice, and that it is peculiar to Luke would make Luke's emphasis particularly clear.

We conclude that in this story unique to Luke where the women (who were rarely taken as religious models at that time)[36] provided out of their means for Jesus and his disciples (who would have been comparable to the poor of Luke's contemporaries), we find one practical incident in the first half of the Gospel in which Luke's concern for the poor and almsgiving is clearly demonstrated.

e. *The Parable of the Good Samaritan (10.29-37)*
There is no doubt that the main point of this parable peculiar to Luke is that to love one's neighbour is to be the person who is willing to help anyone in a predicament (v. 37),[37] although it includes implicit criticism against the hypocrisy of religious leaders such as a priest (v. 31) and a Levite (v. 32) of that time.[38] By this story it would appear that Luke intends to show that human needs matter more than religious ceremony or duty represented by the above two religious leaders.[39]

First, of particular interest in the parable is the fact that sacrificing his wealth and time, a Samaritan[40] helps the half-dead man stripped and

In relation to this aspect, Witherington, 'On the Road', p. 245, makes an interesting note that 'θεραπεύω in secular Greek means "to serve" and has the same meaning as διακονέω. Thus, we can see Luke's fondness for parallelism coming to the fore. Jesus serves these women by healing, and they in turn serve out of gratitude'.

36. Since women were equated with children with respect to capacity for knowledge of the Torah, women were refused to be taught, 'unless their husband or master was a rabbi willing to teach them' (Witherington, 'On the Road', p. 244), and so they were generally assigned a very inferior place (Morris, *Gospel*, p. 149; Danker, *Jesus*, p. 10).

37. Caird, *Luke*, p. 148: 'It is neighbourliness, not neighbourhood, that makes a neighbour.'

38. For dispute on this matter, see Evans, *Saint Luke*, pp. 468-69.

39. If the priest had touched the injured man then discovered that he was dead, he would be unable to perform any ceremony in the Temple for seven days, being considered ritually unclean. The Levite, an assistant in the Temple, may have avoided the body for the same reason (cf. Lev. 21.1-3). From this we can notice that they placed the duty of leading worship before a concern for suffering humanity, which can be called 'loveless religiosity' (Pilgrim, *Good News*, p. 142).

40. Why does the Lukan Jesus mention a Samaritan, an outcast to Jews, here instead of a Jewish layman, as his listeners were certainly expecting after a priest and

beaten by robbers. He uses costly oil and wine recognized as household remedies to salve the wounds, and takes him to an inn. There he cares for the man until the next day, paying the night's board and lodging,[41] and asks the innkeeper to take care of the man, promising that when he comes back he would pay any further expenses needed. Schweizer's comment on the Samaritan's behaviour seems to the point:

> It [vv. 34-35] is not mere emotion but finds expression in the considered use of medical help. In addition to the direct ministrations of love, there is also room for indirect love through financial contributions—as long as help is really given. There is neither heroic accomplishment—the helper leaves and goes about his business—nor neglect of what is necessary. The one who needs help is the only law governing what is done.[42]

Secondly, what is outstanding in this parable is the shift of Jesus' concluding question (v. 36). It is sometimes suggested that Jesus fails to answer the lawyer's question about the object of love (v. 29). Yet Jesus in fact directly addresses the question, that is, what really matters is not to simply know who my neighbour is but to become a neighbour to those in need, as the Samaritan does. Along with this, twice-repeated commands of Jesus, such as τοῦτο ποίει καὶ ζήσῃ (v. 28), and πορεύου καὶ σὺ ποίει ὁμοίως (v. 37), are seen to enforce the practicability in

a Levite? 'By this means the limited question of determining one's fellowman by nationality or religion is converted into a question of the neighbour who can meet us in every man' (Weeber), quoted by E. Linnemann, *Parables of Jesus: Introduction and Exposition* (London: SPCK, 1982), p. 54. Cf. Tannehill, *Narrative Unity*, pp. 179-80.

41. 'Since one denarius was the equivalent of a day's wage for a laborer, no little sum was involved' (Pilgrim, *Good News*, p. 142).

42. Schweizer, *Luke*, p. 186. See also Evans, *Saint Luke*, p. 471. Against this argument of Schweizer, J.T. Sanders, *Ethics in the New Testament* (London: SCM Press, 1986), p. 8, states as follows: 'The Samaritan's comportment cannot be possible to every man who, at any time, sees as the Samaritan sees; it cannot be possible to the one who, by his own choosing, decides to step into the Samaritan's world. The characteristic aspect of the Samaritan's behaviour is that it is not of this world.' Although there may be an element of truth in Sanders's viewpoint, it is clear that Luke (and Jesus) intended the example of the Samaritans to be taken seriously. To be sure, the ethic is strenuous (like the Sermon on the Plain), but not wholly unrealistic.

Meanwhile, Plummer's suggestion (*Luke*, p. 287) in relation to this matter appears interesting: 'Christ may have chosen a Samaritan for the *benefactor* [emphasis mine], as a gentle rebuke to James and John for wishing just before this to call down fire on Samaritans (ix. 54)'.

Luke's mind as respects his ethical admonitions.[43] Accordingly, these two points seem to be in line with Luke's concrete interest in almsgiving, so it is likely that Luke proffers this parable to the community as a good example closely attached to the right use of material possessions.[44]

In this connection, there is another point that it seems we ought to deal with. It is likely that the man attacked by robbers must have had some possessions before he was robbed (ἐκδύσαντες, v. 30), so might not have been poor originally. What matters in this parable, however, is not his past, that is, his situation prior to the incident, but his present, that is, his miserable and destitute situation after the attack. According to Luke's description of the robbed man, he is deprived utterly, even stripped and wounded critically (ἡμιθανῆ, v. 30). It would seem that Luke introduces the robbed man as the poor who needed others' help mentally and materially, and as the rich, though relatively, the good Samaritan who helps him making good use of his wealth in the way that in Luke's view material possessions should be used.

To conclude, we learn from one of the most famous parables in the Gospels that by means of the benevolent conduct of the Samaritan Luke intends to show the way material possessions should be rightly used, and in particular that they should be distributed for the sake of the needy and the poor.[45]

43. Taking notice of the fact that the present imperatives are employed here, Plummer, *Luke*, pp. 285, 289, paraphrases these verses as follows: 'Thou also habitually do likewise'. See also Talbert, *Reading Luke*, p. 121.

44. D. Juel, *Luke–Acts* (London: SCM Press, 1984), p. 91. Talbert, *Reading Luke*, pp. 120-26, regarding 10.25-42 as a thought unit, makes an interesting claim: 'The thought unit, 10:25-42, consists of an exposition of the two great commandments for disciples. To love one's neighbor means to act like the Samaritan. To love God means to act like Mary.'

I agree totally with the former view of his but as far as the latter view is concerned, I have some doubt. Is it really true that to love God is just to hear Jesus' words or to be his disciple without doing anything on behalf of him? In my opinion, although Martha receives a gentle indirect rebuke from Jesus because of her complaints about her sister, Mary, what is to be noticed here is that she tries to serve Jesus much (πολλὴν διακονίαν, v. 40), which must come out of her genuine love towards Jesus. Therefore, it appears unreasonable that to listen to Jesus is the only meaning of 'loving God'.

45. Pilgrim's conclusive comment on the implication of this parable seems to the point: 'The parable claims that love is not words, but deeds. And these deeds involve risks, sacrifices, and sharing of one's possessions. Any well-off reader cannot avoid the implication with regard to personal wealth. Where suffering is found, where the

f. *Give for Alms those Things which Are within (11.41)*
This verse is difficult to understand, so up to now various suggestions have been made, which generally fall into two categories. First,
τὰ ἐνόντα is to be interpreted as 'heart', being compared with the
Matthaean parallel (Mt. 23.26), that is, 'Purify the inside (heart), and
then all is pure for you'. This interpretation results from the argument that Luke's ἐλεημοσύνην is a mistaken rendering of an Aramaic
original correctly translated by Matthew.[46]

The second interpretation is that τὰ ἐνόντα symbolizes wealth in
general which one owns. According to this theory, τὰ ἐνόντα would
mean the contents that Pharisees have gained through ἁρπαγή, that is,
the ill-gotten gains.[47] Taken together, the second interpretation renders
this verse as follows: 'You should give alms out of the store you have,
and at once all that is yours becomes clean'.[48] In this context, if we take
into account the other examples which portray critical differences, such
as 6.37-38 and 12.33-34, as compared with their parallels (Mt. 7.1-2;
6.20), it is likely that the discrepancy noticed in v. 41 from Mt. 23.26
belongs to that category. In other words, the difference represents
Luke's emphasis on almsgiving which is constantly noted throughout
the Gospel.[49]

poor and needy exist, there lies an opportunity to make friends with our wealth and
to give from a deep sense of God's mercy' (*Good News*, p. 143).

46. The pioneer of this argument was Wellhausen who held that δότε ἐλεημοσύνην is due to a translator who mistook Aramaic דכה 'purify' for זכי 'give alms',
and that the conjecture is supported by Matthew who gives καθάρισον (Moule,
Idiom, p. 186; Caird, *Luke*, p. 158). C.F. Burney (*The Aramaic Origin of the Fourth
Gospel* [Oxford: Clarendon Press, 1922], p. 9), however, has shown that זכי can
mean both 'to give alms' and 'to cleanse' (cf. Moule, *Idiom*, p. 186). I.H. Marshall,
Commentary, p. 496, sides with Burney in arguing that 'In general Luke himself
shows no signs of Aramaic influence . . . the Aramaic basis for this conjecture remains
highly problematic'. Thus there is a possibility that Luke may have a mistaken rendering, but this needs further thorough explanation.

47. Ellis, *Luke*, p. 169; Schweizer, *Luke*, p. 200; Gooding, *Luke*, p. 232.

48. Following this position, Fitzmyer explicates this passage stressing almsgiving:
'Luke has used v. 40 as the equivalent of Mt. 23.26 and then freely added the further
recommendation about the contents to be given away as alms' (*Gospel*, p. 947). Meanwhile, consulting Rengstorf, Grundmann, *Lukas*, p. 248, suggests his exposition on
this passage like this: 'Nicht der Weg der Habsucht, sondern der Weg der Hingabe
führt dazu, daß für den Menschen alles rein wird'. Cf. Evans, *Saint Luke*, p. 505.

49. Goulder, *Paradigm*, II, p. 519, states, 'It [almsgiving] is the same practical
solution to the problem of money which Luke turns up with every time'. Cf.

g. *The Parable of the Rich Fool and the Following Sayings (12.13-34)*
This section is to be divided into two units: the first unit consists of
Jesus' conversation with a man who has a trouble with inheritance
(vv. 13-15) and the parable of the Rich Fool appended to it (vv. 16-
21), and the second unit is mainly Jesus' admonition to his disciples as
regards worry about earthly things (vv. 22-34). Accordingly, to proceed to interpret this parable properly, it would be necessary to look
into whether the first unit is related to the second unit, in other words,
whether there is a thematic unity between the two.

First, under the cloak of someone's request related to division of an
inheritance (v. 13), Jesus, apparently refusing to become an arbitra-
tor,[50] utters a proverbial saying at v. 15: 'a man's life does not consist
in the abundance of his possessions'. To expand this lesson further,[51]
Jesus gives a parable about the Rich Fool who is seen to worry about
craving more wealth, believing that his life consists in the abundance
of his possessions. And to conclude the conversation with the man and
the following parable, Jesus presents another proverbial saying at v. 21:
'So is he who lays up treasure for himself, and is not rich towards
God'. The thrust of the first half of this passage is that one's wealth
should not be stored up on earth for his selfish avarice,[52] but it is not
clear within the parable itself what it means to be εἰς θεὸν πλουτῶν. It
might be suggested that wealth should be used for some cultic purpose,
if this parable were not followed by the second pericope.[53]

Geldenhuys, *Gospel*, pp. 341-42; Tannehill, *Narrative Unity*, pp. 127-32; Schmidt,
Hostility, p. 145. In interpreting this parable, Seccombe, *Possessions*, p. 185, relates
Luke's concept of charity to the coming of the Kingdom in which money is to lose its
worth; in this circumstance, he claims that 'the sensible thing to do with it now is to
convert it into something which will retain value beyond the changing of the aeons,
namely the values of brotherhood and friendship'.

50. Pilgrim's (*Good News*, pp. 110-11) explanations as to why Jesus refuses to
be a mediator over the dispute is probable: 'No mediation of one dispute will solve
the deeper problem of the human heart' (p. 111).

51. Evans, *Saint Luke*, p. 520: 'The parable Luke then appends (*And he told them
a parable* is his form of introduction) is intended to reinforce the teaching of v. 15.'

52. From v. 17 to v. 19, the first person singular occurs eight times; ποιήσω
(twice), συνάξω (twice), ἔχω, καθελῶ, οἰκοδομήσω, ἐρῶ, and the pronoun μου
(four times). Cf. Plummer, *Luke*, p. 324; Morris, *Gospel*, p. 212. Meanwhile,
Talbert, *Reading Luke*, p. 141, claims that this first unit is designed to tackle the
problem of covetousness, which he argues was a problem before Luke as well as of
his contemporary time.

53. Some argue that originally this parable was 'an eschatological parable', of

Here comes the necessity for looking into what is said in the second unit. Jesus' sayings in this unit can be presented as an injunction not to worry about worldly things, that is, to discard the earthly cares of material possessions,[54] which appears in fact to tally with the force of v. 15, and also as an assurance that God will provide for his people what they need for daily living on earth. In consequence, we can say that as Pilgrim comments, the meaning of the first unit, v. 21 in particular, is spelled out in the second unit that follows immediately.[55]

Having pointed out features of both units, we may state that it is to be noticed that these two pericopes are not separate but closely attached by means of the theme of possessions.[56] In other words, the unity of contents should be acknowledged from 12.13 to 12.34 in view of the theme of wealth, for both the parable and the sayings refer to the same

which the key point is the crisis brought about by the approach of the Kingdom (Jeremias, *Parables*, p. 164; cf. Evans, *Saint Luke*, p. 521). However, in this regard, Pilgrim (*Good News*, pp. 112-13) makes a point that by adding v. 21 Luke attempts to relate this original meaning of the past to a new meaning of the present, which is 'to stop living for oneself before it is too late and start accumulating riches toward God'.

54. 'For the disciples' worldliness presents itself more often in an anxious attitude than in the materialism of the rich man' (Ellis, *Luke*, p. 176).

55. Fitzmyer, *Gospel*, p. 976, states in this regard that the second unit 'acts as a commentary on the parable of the rich fool'.

Meanwhile, Tannehill, *Narrative Unity*, p. 246, is of the opinion that since the second unit is addressed particularly to the disciples, it shows their hard and difficult situation of living because they left behind everything they had. Schottroff and Stegemann who appear very keen to sort out the addressees of Jesus' sayings, are also in line with this opinion (*Hope*, pp. 72-75, 80-82).

Against this view, we may raise two questions:

(1) If we have to follow this argument, it would be difficult to understand vv. 33-34, a dominical injunction of almsgiving, because the disciples who are supposed to depend upon 'the hospitality of strangers' seem to have nothing for charity (cf. 9.3; 10.4). Cf. Evans, *Saint Luke*, p. 531. To obtain an excuse for this point, Tannehill suggests that this instruction applies to 'all disciples who still have disposable property' (*Narrative Unity*, p. 246). It is unclear what 'disposable property' means here, when he has already pointed out that they left everything.

(2) As we have observed earlier, in Luke, μαθηταί are not to be identified with the Apostles who actually renounced their assets and capital, but with a large group of followers. Therefore, it seems that it is more natural to state that these sayings are intended for those with material possessions.

56. Talbert, *Reading Luke*, p. 140. Plummer, *Luke*, p. 329, also relates v. 21 to v. 33 by means of covetousness, stating that almsgiving is a way of being freed from covetousness, so that it does good to the giver as well.

motif, although their approaches to it may be slightly different. Or it can be presented in another way. That is, since the first unit (12.13-21) is peculiar to Luke, which means again that his special interest can be found in it, it would lead to the supposition that Luke puts emphasis on the wealth motif of the second unit (12.22-34) which has a Matthaean parallel (Mt. 6.25-34, 19-21), by adding his unique material before it which clarifies and strengthens the force of the following sayings.

Then what is Luke's emphasis here? To answer this question, it would be helpful to look at the final verses of this narrative. vv. 33-34, for the following two reasons: (1) They appear to be a conclusion not only to Jesus' sayings in the second unit (vv. 22-32) but also to the first unit (vv. 13-21), since they are placed at the end of the whole section.[57] (2) Luke shows particular interest in the motif of almsgiving which is introduced as a way for him to instruct how to use wealth rightly.[58] This point is clearly to be observed when Luke's version is compared with that of Matthew (6.19-20). As a result of this discussion, we are now able to suggest that in terms of the thematic unity 'being rich towards God' at v. 21[59] is possibly to be explained as 'giving alms to the poor' at v. 33.[60]

57. Talbert, *Reading Luke*, p. 142, also recognizes the importance of these verses in this section as a whole, stating that 'the section on possessions is climaxed by 12:33-34, a specific injunction to almsgiving'. Cf. Evans, *Saint Luke*, p. 525. Besides, as we can observe, from v. 35 onwards there occurs a new section.

58. Cf. Tannehill, *Narrative Unity*, pp. 247-48.

59. Degenhardt, *Lukas*, pp. 79-80, contends that 'being rich toward God' can be identical to benevolent behaviour: 'Die Mahnung V. 21 verschiebt den Akzent auf die Forderung nach richtigem Gebrauch des Besitzes, ihn nämlich nicht egoistisch zu verwenden, sondern durch ihn bei Gott reich zu sein, d.h. gute Werke damit zu tun.' Meanwhile, Evans appears correct in pointing out the fact that v. 21 'connects the "abundance" in the story with the avarice in v. 15' (*Saint Luke*, p. 523).

60. See also Evans, *Saint Luke*, p. 531; Talbert, *Reading Luke*, pp. 141-43; Creed, *Gospel*, p. 173; Pilgrim, *Good News*, p. 111; Fitzmyer, *Gospel*, p. 974. Since this verse occupies central position in the whole section, a variety of remarks and comments on it have been made, and the following are some of them which have a bearing on our topic here:

(1) πωλέω and δίδωμι of Jesus' admonition here occurs again at 18.22 (πωλέω and διαδίδωμι) in the Gospel, and appears in Acts in the form of fulfilment of this dominical injunction (Acts 2.45; 4.34-35). Thus this unique accent made by Luke appears to show a continuity between his two works in terms of the motif of almsgiving (Tannehill, *Narrative Unity*, pp. 247-48; cf. Fitzmyer, *Gospel*, p. 982).

(2) Degenhardt's claim that this dominical exhortation is intended for the church

In addition to this aspect, there is still one thing to discuss in this context. That is a relation between this whole section and the parable of the wise and faithful steward at vv. 42-48 in the same chapter, which we have explored in detail above as one of the key parables for the motif of stewardship. In view of the stewardship motif, it can be said that in the parable of the steward Luke presents as the Rich Fool in disguise the unfaithful steward who squanders his master's wealth.[61]

In doing so, it would appear that Luke intends to remind the rich members in his community that the wealth they possess temporarily on earth belongs to God, so that wealth entrusted by God should not be used for their selfish pleasure, that is, laying up treasure on earth, but for the sake of the poor and needy in the society, that is, being rich towards God.[62] As discussed earlier, it is most likely that v. 48 is an obvious description of the rich to whom the whole passage (12.13-34, 41-47) is addressed. In this sense, finally, the admonition towards the rich to give alms is shown as the main force of the whole passage including the Parables of the Steward and the Rich Fool.

h. *The Parable of the Great Banquet (14.12-24)*
Lk. 14.1-24, in sharing a single setting of table-fellowship,[63] depicts what happens when a Pharisee ruler invites Jesus to dine. The historical situation is continuous, but the contents of the incidents appear not

---

leaders in the community may be missing the point of the parable, because, as pointed out earlier in n. 55, it would not make sense that the disciples here can be identified with 'die Armtsträger' (*Lukas*, p. 87). I suppose that this contention of Degenhardt results from his basic assumption that the disciples are no other than the apostles in Luke's writings.

(3) It seems wrong to claim that v. 33 displays 'ascetic colouring' (Creed, *Gospel*, p. 175; cf. Schottroff and Stegemann, *Hope*, p. 75), because it is not asceticism but benevolence that is the issue in this verse and the whole section. This would be a corollary of what we have discussed above. See Plummer, *Luke*, p. 329, and note also his remark on σής which he supposes 'is a reference to costly garments'. Cf. I.H. Marshall, *Commentary*, p. 532.

61. Cf. Tannehill, *Narrative Unity*, p. 247; I.H. Marshall, *Commentary*, p. 521.

62. That the parable of the steward occurs in the same ch. 12 can also be attributed to the author's thoughtful arrangement of his material in order to accentuate his intention of encouraging his rich readers to use their material possessions faithfully, that is, to distribute them for the poor.

63. Talbert, *Reading Luke*, p. 196, suggests that 'the scene is a literary device' to bind together four separate traditions, such as vv. 1-6, vv. 7-11, vv. 12-14, and vv. 15-24. Cf. Creed, *Gospel*, p. 188; Ellis, *Gospel*, p. 191.

to be. In detail, vv. 1-6 record an argument between Jesus and the Pharisees regarding the healing of a leper on Sabbath, and vv. 7-11 record ethical teaching of Jesus about social manners at a meal.

Thus it appears that these two sections deal with differing subjects. But vv. 12-24 appear to deal with a single theme which concerns the right use of wealth and the interest in the poor and unfortunate of the community, so this section can be regarded as a unit on its own.

In v. 12 Jesus tells his host, a Pharisee leader, that when he holds a feast or a banquet he should not invite his friends, brothers, relatives, or rich neighbours with the hope of receiving in return invitations, but the poor, crippled, lame, and blind who are anyhow not able to repay the hospitality at all (v. 13)—then he would receive his repayment in the resurrection of the just (v. 14).[64] What is to be taken into account is that it is likely that the Pharisee and his invited friends to whom the teaching of Jesus is addressed in vv. 12-24 represent here those in Luke's community who have rich neighbours and who have means enough to provide meals and to invite their rich neighbours to their houses.[65] That he is ἄρχων, possibly a member of the Sanhedrin, may tell this point. In this connection Karris's remark on vv. 12-14 seems to be helpful to appreciate these sayings of Jesus:

> For this latter passage [14:12-14] to make sense it must mean that there are members in Luke's community who have the wherewithal to host festive meals. Luke 14:12-14 is addressed to them and goes against the common Graeco-Roman reciprocity ethic: put your friends in your debt, so that at some future time you can cash in on their IOU's.[66]

So the point of vv. 12-14 would be that the rich should help the poor and unfortunate in the community by making good use of their possessions, without expecting any recompense on earth (compare Lk. 6.35).[67]

---

64. Here we find that the reward in heaven is emphasized so greatly that it makes the reward on earth trivial and negligible. This point serves to elucidate Luke's idea of reward in general, which is characterized as spiritual and other-worldly (cf. 6.33-34; 18.22). Meanwhile, the excuses of the three invited guests will be discussed later in this chapter where the reprimands towards the rich will be dealt with at length.

65. Talbert, *Reading Luke*, p. 183.

66. Karris, 'Poor and Rich', p. 120; cf. Van Unnik, 'Motivierung', pp. 284-300.

67. In the Hellenistic society of Luke's time, it is said that the whole society was largely influenced by reciprocal relations which was able to be claimed at later date. A

Taking up the motif of the previous sayings, Jesus introduces the parable of the Great Banquet which is so picturesque that it serves well to enhance the force of his teaching manifested already in vv. 12-14.[68]

A certain man here invites many guests to his banquet who are possibly 'well-to-do people, large landowners',[69] but they in common reject the invitation for various private reasons. Thus instead of the invited guests, the host invites the poor, crippled, lame and blind (v. 21) and 'the homeless from the streets and the hedges of the vineyards' (v. 23). Thus it would be logical that 'the entire banquet-hall is filled with beggars'.[70]

In this context, it is remarkable that this list of the alternative guests is exactly the same that appears in v. 13, except for the inverted order of the blind and the lame. Besides, when we compare this parable of Luke's Gospel with its counterpart in Matthew's Gospel (22.1-14),[71] particularly the alternative guests who replace those initially invited between the two accounts,[72] it seems clear that Luke's insertion of those

---

prime example of this custom in Luke is to be found in the policy of the Unjust Steward (Lk. 16.3-7) which we have discussed earlier. So Jesus' sayings in Lk. 14.12-14 are rejecting the fundamental rationale of gift giving in this culture, so that they might be regarded as something akin to social revolution.

68. Relating the parable to Jesus' teaching in vv. 12-14, Beck, *Character*, p. 35, contends that the parable is introduced 'to give a foundation for the advice of vv. 12-14'.

69. Jeremias, *Parables*, p. 176. Taking into account the reciprocity ethic prevalent at that time, it is probable that in order to receive benefits in return, this host would have invited social equals who were so rich as to invite him back. So it seems possible to argue that the farmer (v. 19) who bought five yoke of oxen owns a vast track of land, most likely in excess of 45 hectares (111 acres), and similarly the man who bought a field (v. 18) and the man who just got married are also social equals.

70. Jeremias, *Parables*, p. 178.

71. It is in dispute whether the Matthaean version of the parable derives from the same source on which Luke may depend, or whether the two accounts are independent. For more detail, see Fitzmyer, *Gospel*, pp. 1050-54; I.H. Marshall, *Commentary*, p. 584.

72. Mt. 22.10 reads 'the bad and the good' as the replacement of those originally invited. In this connection, Creed, *Gospel*, p. 188, holds that 'Matthew gives the parable in a more developed and more allegorical form than that which appears here'. Jeremias, *Parables*, p. 176, is also of the opinion that as compared with Matthew, the list in Luke is original, 'essentially unchanged'. Cf. I.H. Marshall, *Commentary*, p. 590.

invited later is intentional,[73] for it corresponds to the guest list in
v. 13,[74] and a similar list appears elsewhere in 4.18 and 7.22. These
four passages that are scattered widely in the Gospel can be regarded
as a clear indication that Luke has a particular concern with the poor
and the unfortunate, the people who are religiously alienated,[75] socially
deserted,[76] and economically so helpless as to be dependent on others'
support.

It is probable that Luke may have known this sort of dire socio-economic situation at his time, so that he would have urged wealthy Christians in his community not to follow the attitudes that those affluent
outside the church cherished, but to behave quite differently, being
beneficial and generous to those who are poor and deserted. This point
may tally with the motif of v. 12, where Jesus' advice is that it is better
to invite the poor and needy than the rich who can reciprocate. In this
context, it should also be remembered against the background of this
parable that holding a feast or a banquet by wealthy patrons or benefactors at Luke's time was a way to help the poor, that is, to relieve their
hunger, in secular society outside the church. But it was used to show
their superior position, and it was too infrequent to be a permanent
solution to the problem of hunger.[77]

As regards the relationship between the parable and the sayings of
Jesus (vv. 12-14), some distinguish between them and interpret the former spiritually, and the latter literally.[78] As for the interpretation of
the parable, on the grounds that its background is the Kingdom of God
(v. 15), and that Jesus calls this banquet μου τοῦ δείπνου (v. 24), some
intend to understand this parable in the light of salvation history or
soteriology.[79]

73. Fitzmyer, *Gospel*, pp. 1049-50; Schweizer, *Luke*, p. 238; Schmidt, *Hostility*,
p. 148.

74. The exact agreement of the two lists in vv. 13, 21 leads Beck to insist that
'this cannot be accidental and justifies our concentrating on the economic condition of
the guests. Those who refuse are rich; those who accept are the poor who cannot
repay' (Beck, *Character*, p. 35).

75. Cf. Lev. 21.17-23; Degenhardt, *Lukas*, p. 100.

76. For the exclusion of such people, see 2 Sam. 5.8; 1QSa 2.5-7; 1QS 2.4-6.

77. We will return to this theme again in Chapter 8.

78. See Schmidt, *Hostility*, pp. 148-49.

79. Geldenhuys, *Gospel*, p. 393; Morris, *Gospel*, p. 235; T.W. Manson, *Sayings*,
pp. 129-30.

I do not deny this possibility.[80] But if we are to appreciate this parable of Luke appropriately, then we ought to take into account an eminent feature in Luke's theology, his emphasis on wealth and poverty. The conclusion we have already reached, in general, is that Luke's understanding of the poor and the unfortunate is neither spiritualized nor allegorized, of which the classical example is 6.20-21 (compare Mt. 5.3-10),[81] and its analogy is to be noted in 4.18 and 7.22. So if we bear this feature of Luke on wealth in mind, it would hardly be reasonable here to interpret the poor in a way that is unfamiliar with Luke.[82]

In relation to this point, Schmidt's argument that v. 13 must be understood primarily in a literal, material sense, while v. 21 primarily in a figurative, spiritual sense, appears untenable.[83] Is it really possible that Luke intends his readers to read almost identical verses in a different way one after another?

To conclude, this parable and the previous sayings of Jesus indicate that there is a profound gulf between the rich and the poor in Luke's community, and that although both of them share Christian faith in common, the rich still conduct themselves according to the customs of their contemporary culture in which the reciprocity ethic is predominant. Hence to correct their ingrained non-Christian attitude, and to awaken their brotherhood in Christ, Luke appears to intend Jesus' view on this subject to apply to relationships between the rich and the poor within his community.[84] Therefore it could be drawn from this discussion that to invite the poor in the parable is introduced as one example of the practice of almsgiving.

i. *The Parable of the Rich Man and Lazarus (16.19-31)*
As already mentioned above, the rich people in Luke's time sometimes proffered festive meals to the poor in order to make a display of their

80. See Fitzmyer, *Gospel*, p. 1053. The feast represents the Messianic Banquet. The important point is that (1) although this is an *eschatological* feast, it is not thereby spiritualized; that is to say, it is important to Luke that it is precisely the literally poor who benefit from the Messianic Banquet (cf. Lazarus and the Beatitudes); and (2) the context in Lk. 14 shows that the eschatological Messianic Banquet is meant to serve as a model for human behaviour here and now—in treatment of the poor.

81. Tannehill, *Narrative Unity*, pp. 64-65, 129; Fitzmyer, *Gospel*, pp. 248-49; Creed, *Gospel*, p. 191.

82. See Beck, *Character*, pp. 35-36; Cf. Seccombe, *Possessions*, pp. 31-32.

83. Schmidt, *Hostility*, p. 149.

84. Cf. Degenhardt, *Lukas*, p. 101.

superior position, wealth and name. It was a rare but very precious opportunity for the poor to satisfy their hunger. The background of this parable may reflect such social customs in Luke's contemporary society (v. 19). That the Rich Man holds sumptuous feasts καθ' ἡμέραν and is dressed[85] in purple[86] and fine linen, 'the most luxurious fabric of the ancient world',[87] indicates clearly how rich and wealthy he is. Despite his affluence, however, he does nothing to relieve the painful hunger[88] and disease of the poor Lazarus at his gate, who is covered with ulcers, too helpless to drive off dogs from licking his sores, and in such poverty that he would gladly eat the bits which fall from the Rich Man's table.

It appears that according to the text the Rich Man does not deserve his hellish torment for what he has done in his life on earth, but for what he has failed to do. That is to say, he neglects to love God and his neighbour, which is commanded of all Jews (Deut. 6.5; Lev. 19.18). This negligence of his obligations to help his poor neighbours is implied in the story, especially in the conversation between Abraham and the Rich Man (v. 25), because the Rich Man does not complain about his torment and request to be released from his punishment.[89] In his lifetime the Rich Man himself severs the spiritual ties with Abraham by ignoring the needs of his fellowman. Instead of loving his neighbour as himself, he lives neither for God, nor his fellow man, but for

85. ἐνεδιδύσκετο in v. 19, imperfect and frequentative, which denotes his habitual attire.

86. πορφύρα is said to be associated with 'royal or quasi-royal dignity' and to cost very much (T.W. Manson, *Sayings*, p. 296; Jeremias, *Parables*, p. 183).

87. T.W. Manson, *Sayings*, p. 296. Cf. Plummer, *Luke*, p. 391.

88. ἐπιθυμῶν in v. 21 with the infinitive (cf. 15.16; 17.22; 22.15) indicates Lazarus's unfulfilled desire, that is, 'eagerly and not receiving what he desired' (M.R. Vincent, *Word Studies in the New Testament* [Wilmington: Associated Publishers and Authors, 1888], I, p. 201). So Jeremias, *Parables*, p. 184, paraphrases this verse as follows: 'How gladly would Lazarus have satisfied his hunger with them (pieces of bread)'.

89. Plummer, *Luke*, p. 395. Contra Evans, *Saint Luke*, p. 615. Meanwhile, Jeremias's exposition of v. 25 appears to go beyond the given text (*Parables*, p. 185): 'What v. 25 really says is that impiety and lovelessness are punished, and that piety and humility are rewarded.' But we should recognize that the story concerns the wrong done by the Rich Man, rather than the piety and humility of Lazarus. Here we do not find that anything is said about the goodness of Lazarus, but God's partiality towards the poor, which is characteristic of the Old Testament and Jesus (Schweizer, *Luke*, p. 262).

himself, so that he pursues the goal of self-gratification.[90]

In this connection, the Lukan thought of v. 25 (ἀπέλαβες) virtually corresponds to the woes to the rich (6.24-25), on the grounds that the rich have received their consolation in this world, but shall hunger, mourn and weep in that world.[91] This correspondence demonstrates a continuity in Luke's concern for the poor and warning to the godless rich,[92] and also the reversal of fortune in the coming age which is also found in the Magnificat (1.53) and the woes to the rich (6.24-26; compare 18.29-30).[93] Therefore, once again, we are able to claim that the point of the parable is also 'the right employment of earthly possessions'.[94]

Now in this connection, it would be helpful to take into account the context, noting that Luke puts together this parable and the parable of the Unjust Steward in the same chapter.[95]

In the former parable, the Unjust Steward finally uses his entrusted wealth rightly for the welfare of the poor debtors, so that according to 16.9 he would have been received into the eternal habitations by the

90. H. Klein's definition of his sin seems to the point: 'Seine Schuld besteht also nach dem SLk darin, daß er nur seinen Reichtum sah und darin Genüge hatte' (*Barmherzigkeit gegenüber den Elenden und Geächteten* [Zürich: Neukirchener Verlag, 1987], p. 99). Cf. Mealand, *Poverty*, p. 47.

91. Against Jeremias's argument (*Parables*, p. 186) that the main point of the parable is to be found in the second part (vv. 27-310), Evans, *Saint Luke*, pp. 614-15, states as follows recognizing the relation between this parable (v. 25) and Luke's version of the Beatitudes: 'Moreover the verdict delivered in v. 25 so exactly reproduces the first of the Beatitudes and of the woes in $6^{20,24}$ that it stands in its own right with considerable force, and makes a point that is too emphatic to be merely a prelude to something else.' See also Pilgrim, *Good News*, pp. 114-15; Schottroff and Stegemann, *Hope*, p. 99.

92. With his basic position that the force of the parable is 'comfort to the poor and warning to the rich' (*Good News*, p. 119), Pilgrim expounds the second part of the parable as a warning directed to the wealthy. In relation to this aspect, one interesting point in his exposition is his view on Moses and the prophets in v. 29 that 'the requirement of charity toward the poor and needy stands at the heart of the Old Testament Law' (p. 118).

93. Mealand, *Poverty*, p. 48; cf. pp. 41-50; A. Verhey, *The Great Reversal: Ethics and the New Testament* (Grand Rapids: Eerdmans, 1986), pp. 15, 94; Evans, *Saint Luke*, p. 613; Pilgrim, *Good News*, p. 615.

94. Plummer, *Luke*, pp. 390, 392. Cf. Klein, *Barmherzigkeit*, p. 99.

95. The relation between these two parables has already been explored in the previous chapter, so here I just want to refer to key points of it directly.

help of his witnesses, that is, the recipients of his benevolence on earth. In the latter parable, however, the Rich Man uses his wealth solely in the interest of his selfish ends, so that, if we apply 16.9 to this case, he is not received into the eternal habitations, because no friend would witness to his benevolence on earth, and he eventually falls into hell, as described in 16.23.[96] In this sense, 16.9 can be regarded as a theme verse which plays an important role in unfolding the implication of both parables.[97]

Consequently, it becomes clear that these two parables present two contrastive steward models in terms of the right use of material possessions: the one is depicted as good and successful (the Unjust Steward), and the other as bad and a failure (the Rich Man). With this pair of models, it seems that Luke intends to proffer both encouragement and warning to his contemporaries, particularly the rich members like the Rich Man, the representative of those who spend their wealth for their selfish pleasure, but do not wish to use their material possessions for the sake of the poor and needy in their neighbourhood.

j. *The Incidents of the Rich Ruler and Zacchaeus (18.18–19.10)*

The narrative of the Rich Ruler is recorded in all the Synoptic Gospels, but the details differ. So the observation of the differences among them would be helpful for us to penetrate Luke's intention. Since the main point of this narrative concerns the adherence of the Rich Ruler to material possessions, rather than almsgiving or benevolence, as in the Parable of the Rich Man and Lazarus, detailed analysis will occur later in this chapter, and at the moment only references to the motifs of wealth and almsgiving are to be discussed.

First, what arrests our attention in the incident of the Rich Ruler is how Luke describes him, particularly in v. 23, which differs from the counterparts in Mark (10.22) and Matthew (19.22): περίλυπος (Luke)/ λυπούμενος (Mark and Matthew); πλούσιος σφόδρα (Luke)/κτήματα πολλά (Mark and Matthew). In general, Luke's words in this verse are stronger than those of Mark and Matthew.[98] περίλυπος seems to disclose the Rich Ruler's strong attachment to wealth and πλούσιος σφόδρα, his great amount of capital and assets.[99] This verse as a whole

---

96. Plummer, *Luke*, p. 390; Caird, *Luke*, p. 191.

97. Evans, *Saint Luke*, p. 611.

98. Evans, *Saint Luke*, p. 652.

99. His title, ἄρχων, absent in Mark and Matthew, also attracts our attention. It

shows how wealthy he is, but he does not want to break ties with his possessions, and as a result he turns out to refuse to sell his property on behalf of the poor. As an exemplary story, this description of the Rich Ruler would show harsh criticism against the rich members in the community, reluctant and hesitant to hand out some possessions to the poor. So this alteration by Luke as respects the description of the Rich Ruler might be deemed as one of his emphases.

Secondly, another point which should be noted is that in Mk 10.22 and Mt. 19.22 the Rich Ruler goes away (ἀπῆλθεν), but in Luke's version, since any such verb is left out, he is presumed to remain 'as the representative of the rich'[100] in the midst of Jesus' audience. Thus, it seems reasonable to hold that Jesus' teaching on the danger of wealth in vv. 24-25 is given to him personally, not only to the disciples as in Mark (10.23),[101] from which it could be drawn that in the Lukan community there were problems caused by the rich members.[102] Therefore these sayings of Jesus are likely to be regarded as an injunction as well as a warning to the rich members in Luke's community.

The significance of the incident of Zacchaeus must also be recognized for a full appreciation of Luke's theology of wealth and almsgiving.[103] In this story, our prime interest lies in v. 8 where Zacchaeus promises Jesus to give half of his wealth to the poor and to restitute fourfold what he might have defrauded other people of. His vow of charity and restoration is far beyond the limit and the requirement.[104]

may imply that he is a leader of the synagogue (cf. 8.41) or a member of the Sanhedrin (23.13, 35; 24.20) (I.H. Marshall, *Commentary*, p. 684). So this title can also be deemed as an indication of his great wealth (cf. 14.1; Creed, *Gospel*, p. 225). In this regard, Evans, *Saint Luke*, p. 649, points out a Lukan feature: 'For Luke wealth and exalted position tend to be synonymous (cf. 16[14f.]).'

100. Evans, *Saint Luke*, p. 649.

101. Note Luke's alteration here: ἰδὼν δὲ αὐτὸν. Cf. Mk 10.23; Mt. 19.23. See Evans, *Saint Luke*, p. 652.

102. Esler, *Community*, p. 185; Schweizer, *Luke*, p. 286; Schottroff and Stegemann, *Hope*, pp. 74-77.

103. Pilgrim, *Good News*, p. 129, evaluates the story of Zacchaeus 'as the most important Lukan text on the subject of the right use of possessions', and states that 'the Lukan theme of possessions here receives its fullest treatment' (p. 130). Cf. Schottroff and Stegemann, *Hope*, pp. 106-107.

104. 'A fifth of one's wealth and future income was considered the most that could be given away in charity. In cases of fraud, restitution plus twenty percent of the total taken was required (Lev. 5:16; Num. 5:7). Only stolen cattle were repair four or fivefold (Exod. 22:1; 2 Sam. 12:6)' (Schweizer, *Luke*, p. 291). So here we find that

What emerges outstandingly is that as a person of wealth and power, Zacchaeus exhibits his concern for the poor and those exploited by the authorities. Here τοῖς πτωχοῖς is not incidentally inserted, but rather well displays Luke's consistent interest in this class of the destitute and lowly in his community. In this context, it should be borne in mind that this is an incident of significance in Luke in which almsgiving, which the author eagerly wishes to be realized in his community, is materialized.[105] Thus it may not be an exaggeration that 'if he carries through [*sic*], he will no longer have the status, possessions or identity of the rich'.[106] Prior to this incident in the Third Gospel, only encouragement and exhortation to offer almsgiving on behalf of the poor are introduced, but it is in the incident of Zacchaeus that Jesus' admonition respecting this subject eventually comes into practice. This would be the key point that the account of Zacchaeus is likely to hold for our theme, and that this pericope is peculiar to Luke among the four Gospels would add extra weight to our case.

These two outstanding features found in this incident seem to be enough to display its significance in the Gospel. But besides this uniqueness, another important element in this narrative may be found in the

Zacchaeus goes far beyond normal practice, and binds himself to the law imposed on rustlers (Exod. 22.1), who were liable to a fourfold penalty for theft of sheep (Danker, *Jesus*, p. 172; Morris, *Gospel*, pp. 272-73; I.H. Marshall, *Commentary*, pp. 697-98; Derrett, *Law*, p. 284). In any case, what is remarkable is that both the amount given to the poor and the amount given in restitution exceed the limits of Jewish piety. In line with this, Pilgrim, *Good News*, p. 133, seems correct in stating that introducing Zacchaeus's example, 'Luke forcefully informs his readers that the new way of discipleship goes beyond what any law can require . . . a total commitment of one's wealth for the poor and needy'.

   In this connection, Schottroff and Stegemann's assertion that the act of Zacchaeus is to be taken as 'arithmetical form' appears incorrect (*Hope*, p. 109).

   105. If only the promise of Zacchaeus is taken into account without historical setting, it would be possible to regard v. 8 as a mere promise, rather than as an actual event in which almsgiving is materialized. If Zacchaeus only promised but did not practise it, the question as to why Luke wrote this incident, and what he intended in doing so, cannot be easily solved. Since v. 8 is a vivid expression of a convert's resolve, it is natural to think it actually happened (D. Hamm, 'Luke 19.8 Once Again: Does Zacchaeus Defend or Resolve?', *JBL* 107 [1988], pp. 431-37). Hence it would be reasonable to suppose that Zacchaeus becomes a living illustration of what the Lukan Jesus repeatedly states on the subject of wealth (Danker, *Jesus*, p. 192).

   106. J. O'Hanlon, 'The Story of Zacchaeus and the Lukan Ethic', *JSNT* 12 (1981), pp. 2-26 (19).

context in which it is placed. It is already known as one of Luke's literary devices that the middle section of the Gospel constitutes the Travel Narrative (9.51–19.27) which deviates entirely from the Markan order, and consists mainly of his unique material. The incident of Zacchaeus is the very last material peculiar to Luke in the Travel Narrative.[107] Accordingly, by placing the Zacchaeus incident which demonstrates in practice Luke's concern for almsgiving at the end of the Travel Narrative, Luke seems to succeed in throwing his theme into bold relief.[108] In other words, it can be said that the Zacchaeus incident is to be regarded as one of the most important in the Gospel, for in terms of literary artifice and contents it reveals effectively the author's intention concerning almsgiving and his interest in the poor in his community.

After we have examined individual features to be noted in these two accounts, it would be to our advantage to observe them in the sequence

---

107. On the grounds that Luke takes up the Markan order from 18.15, some hold that the view that the Travel Narrative ends at 18.14 (B. Reicke, 'Instruction and Discussion in the Travel Narrative', *SE*, I, pp. 203-16 [206]). But others argue that it ends at 19.44 for Jesus actually enters into Jerusalem at 19.45 (Ellis, *Luke*, p. 225).

As for the former argument, if we are to call the central section of the Gospel the Travel Narrative, it is necessary to consider the travel itself rather than the Markan order. Also 18.35 and 19.1 being considered, it is nonsense to assert that the journey ends at 18.14. As for the latter argument, when we take into account 19.29, 37, it is certain that Jesus and his disciples have almost arrived in Jerusalem. Bethany is situated about two miles SE of Jerusalem (Jn 11.18) on the eastern slope of the Mount of Olives, and Bethphage also on the Mount, just east of the summit and about a mile east of Jerusalem. In particular, in view of 21.37 and 22.39, the distance from Jerusalem to Bethany is not far enough to be called 'travel' as it is within the boundary of daily working. And when we remember that Mark is a major source of Luke's Gospel, it is unreasonable to hold that Luke did not know the material of Jesus' entry to Jerusalem in Mark (11.1-11).

In this sense, it is more likely that 19.45 does not mean that the journey finally ends there, but is simply an incidental part of the whole passage of Jesus' cleansing of the Temple. As regards the end of the Travel Narrative, Conzelmann asserts that with reference to Luke's geographical plan, 9.51–19.27 is a continuous section, in saying that 'the extent of the typical "journey references" supports his marking of the division' (*Theology*, pp. 63-64).

108. Pilgrim's position is similar to ours here. He holds that this account is 'the last event in Jesus' public ministry according to Luke' (*Good News*, p. 130), and in line with this he goes on to argue that 'the placement of this story at the end of Jesus' public ministry underlines its symbolic and summary significance for Luke's presentation of Jesus' mission'.

of the context in which they are placed, so that the flow of Luke's thought particularly concerned with the theme of wealth would be recognized properly. In my opinion, it seems clear that 18.18 to 19.10 constitutes a single thought unit in view of its literary structure and contents.[109] The narrative of the Rich Ruler (18.18-2) introduces a man who does not give up his wealth for the sake of the poor,[110] so that he turns out to decline to follow Jesus. Taking up this motif of the narrative, 18.24-30 describes the right attitude towards possessions and human relations which Jesus' disciples should take, and 18.35-43 depicts the healing incident of a blind man[111] which in Mark's Gospel, as already discussed above, plays an important role in presenting an example of good discipleship to Mark's community, and is used by Mark to criticize the spiritual blindness of the disciples.

Similarly, the incident of a blind man in Luke also plays a crucial role, though the perspective on it is different. In Luke's Gospel, the Rich Ruler is introduced as a model of stewardship failure who does not forsake his assets for the poor (18.22-23), and the story leads to the healing incident, and then Zacchaeus is introduced as a model of successful stewardship, a man who forsakes his assets on behalf of the poor

109. Seccombe, *Possessions*, pp. 131-34, interprets these two stories in the light of individual salvation, i.e. the salvation of the rich. He also regards Lk. 18.9–19.10 as a carefully framed section. In relating the Zacchaeus incident to that of the Rich Ruler, he argues that 'Luke not only affirms the possibility of the rich being saved, but provides an example of a rich man, who, unlike the ruler, joyfully embraced the Kingdom when it met him in the person of Jesus' (p. 134). Behind this argument, there lies McCormick's presupposition (B.E. McCormick, 'The Social and Economic Background of Luke' [PhD dissertation, Oxford University, 1960]) with which he agrees that 'one of Luke's characteristics is "a concern for the salvation of the rich"' (p. 131). Cf. Pilgrim, *Good News*, pp. 129-34.

Similarly, I.H. Marshall, *Commentary*, p. 677, regards 18.9–19.10 as 'the scope of salvation', and states that as the final story of this section, this story of Zacchaeus is meant to be a claim in the ministry of Jesus, and it brings out several notable features which Luke considered important, one of which is the meaning of discipleship in regard to wealth.

110. The description of the Rich Ruler and Zacchaeus as πλούσιος (18.23; 19.2) can be regarded as 'an intentional cross-reference' to relate one to the other (Seccombe, *Possessions*, p. 130).

111. In Mark, prior to this incident the worldly request of James and John is recorded. Luke's omission of this account in Mark may show his intention to sharpen his theme (cf. Danker, *Jesus*, p. 190).

(19.8).[112] In this context, the healing incident in Luke can be said to function as a bridge in the figurative sense connecting the narrative of the Rich Ruler with the Zacchaeus incident.[113] Through this analysis, we can suggest as an application to Luke's community that by this healing of a blind man, Luke intends, on the one hand, to reproach the rich in his community as the spiritually blind who are too attached to material possessions to distribute their material possessions for the poor, and on the other hand, to provide them with a good model of desirable stewardship of possessions—Zacchaeus, who is willing to practise Christian generosity towards the poor.[114]

What is contrasted between Luke and Mark in setting up an exemplary model is that in Mark one incident of healing a blind man, Bartimaeus, appears enough to reveal Mark's theme of discipleship, that is, the disciples should follow Jesus everywhere he goes, whereas an incident of healing a blind man in Luke does not appear enough to disclose Luke's theme of almsgiving sufficiently. Hence it leads him to add the Zacchaeus incident which is peculiar to Luke and fits his theme well. Then it appears that Luke attains to his goal by arranging and

112. Assuming Zacchaeus as a foil to the Rich Ruler who failed to follow Jesus' command to sell his possessions for the poor (Fitzmyer, *Gospel*, p. 1222), Ireland, *Stewardship*, p. 190, regards him as 'living illustration that an exception to 18.24-25 ("How hard it is") is always possible, "the mode for the miracle of grace" (18.27)'. Meanwhile, I.H. Marshall, *Commentary*, p. 691, relates the incident of healing a blind man and Zacchaeus to each other in view of the geographical location: 'In Luke the story [of the healing] is closely associated by means of the geographical location with the separate tradition of the conversion of Zacchaeus, so that we have a climax to the ministry of Jesus in his call to the poor and the outcast.' Cf. Creed, *Gospel*, p. 228; Fitzmyer, *Gospel*, p. 1222.

113. Cf. Fitzmyer, *Gospel*, p. 1222; Evans, *Saint Luke*, p. 660; Goulder, *Paradigm*, II, p. 673.

114. Karris, 'Poor and Rich', p. 123, also recognizes the contrast between the incident of the Rich Ruler and Zacchaeus in terms of the theme of wealth; 'This redacted story (19.1-10) contrasts to 18.18-30 as it shows that there may not be one dominant answer to the problems of possessions in the Lukan community. Zacchaeus is not to sell all; nor does he voluntarily give to the poor. It suffices that he donates half of his possessions to the poor'.

Meanwhile, O'Hanlon's notice ('The Story of Zacchaeus', pp. 9-11) of the Lukan context from 18.1 to 19.10 appears plausible. But it seems to me that he presses his point too far, because it is in the Zacchaeus incident that he attempts to find an excellent summary of many of Luke's major themes scattered in the Travel Narrative.

adding his material skilfully in such a way that his main theme is high-lighted. Consequently we can suggest that the good steward Luke wishes to introduce to his community is not like the Rich Ruler who is too blind owing to his excessive love of wealth to consider almsgiving to the destitute, but like Zacchaeus whose eyes are so opened that he might give half of his possessions to the poor. Thus Schottroff and Stegemann regard Zacchaeus as 'the paradigm of what Luke expects from wealthy Christians'.[115]

k. *Summary and Conclusion*
Thus far in this chapter we have discussed all material dealing with the matter of wealth in Luke which directly or indirectly refers to the motif of the right use of material possessions, that is, almsgiving, and Luke's concern for the poor and needy. Most of the passages discussed in this chapter consist of material peculiar to Luke (3.11-14; 8.2-3; 10.30-37; 12.13-21; 16.1-13, 19-31; 19.1-10), and the rest are the material which has its parallels in Mark and Matthew. However, to high-light his theme, Luke alters and adapts his sources of the Markan parallels (Lk. 3.11-14/Mk 1.9-11; Lk. 18.23/Mk 10.23) to be fit for his theme, and adds much material peculiar to him recorded predominantly in the Travel Narrative.[116] This feature of Luke's artifice is also found in the differences from the Matthean parallels.[117] Thus the result of this general review on the literary composition of Luke's Gospel shows us that in order to place emphasis on his theme, Luke relies on his unique material itself more than an alteration or adaption of the sources and traditions available to him.

With such findings we now conclude that all those sayings of Jesus are addressed by Luke to the rich and wealthy in his community in order to criticize their wrong attitude towards possessions, by means of the bad exemplary models, such as the Rich Fool, the Rich Man and the Rich Ruler, as well as to encourage them to do good to their poor neighbours by means of the good exemplary models, such as the Galilaean women, the Good Samaritan, and Zacchaeus. In addition to these exemplary models, a number of dominical admonitions are introduced

115. Schottroff and Stegemann, *Hope*, p. 107. Cf. Fitzmyer, *Gospel*, p. 1222.
116. 8.2-3; 10.30-37; 12.13-21; 14.12-14; 16.19-31; 19.1-10.
117. Lk. 6.27-35/Mt. 5.38-48; Lk. 11.37-41/Mt. 23.25-26; Lk. 12.33-34/Mt. 6.19-21; Lk. 14.21/Mt. 22.10.

to help us appreciate the meaning of the parables in which the exemplary models are mentioned.

The statistical findings also arrest our attention. Firstly, there occur many references to possessions and almsgiving in almost every chapter in the Travel Narrative (10, 11, 12, 14, 15, 16, 18, 19)—all except chs. 13, 17. Secondly, of all the verses of the Travel Narrative (9.51–19.27), that is, 407 verses, 182 verses (45 per cent)[118] are related to material dealing with the themes of wealth and almsgiving. This large percentage, larger than that of any other theme in the Gospel, at least in the Travel Narrative,[119] indicates apparently Luke's particular interest in that matter. In other words, it means that Luke is so enthusiastic about the theme as to collect the material unique to him and alter his sources and traditions as far as possible in order to throw his theme into bold relief.

We also have to pay attention to Luke's artifice seen in arranging and composing the structure of his material. In placing the incidents of the Rich Ruler, healing a blind man, and Zacchaeus consecutively at the end of the Travel Narrative, that is, in the conclusive part of this theme, Luke seems to increase his emphasis gradually to finally climax in the incident of Zacchaeus which materializes Luke's theme of almsgiving in a dramatic way. Therefore, along with the other elements, such as alteration, adaptation, and addition of his material, this skilful literary artifice exercised by Luke to attain his goal of emphasis should be properly acknowledged for a full appreciation of Luke's concern for the poor and almsgiving as well as stewardship of material possessions in the Third Gospel.

At this stage it would be useful to discuss two matters related to Luke's exhortation on the proper use of wealth. First, how much are the wealthy Christians in Luke's community expected to give in alms to the poor neighbours? Secondly, who are the alms for? Are they the poor Christians inside the community or the poor in general outside the community, or possibly both?

---

118. 10.30-37; 11.37-41; 12.13-34; 14.12-35; 15.11-32; 16.1-31; 18.18-30; 19.1-27.

119. The other themes that can be noted in the Travel Narrative are so varied that they cannot be easily categorized. Among those themes, repentance (15.1-32, in total 32 verses), and prayer (11.1-13; 18.1-14, in total 27 verses) are to be noticed, but as compared with material containing the wealth theme, they are far less prominent in terms of the proportion which they take in the Travel Narrative.

With respect to the proportion of alms to one's material possessions, we are supposed to examine the material in the Gospel where almsgiving is put into practice or Jesus' injunction of almsgiving appears. First, the Rich Ruler is commanded by Jesus to sell πάντα that he has and to distribute to the poor (18.22). Secondly, Zacchaeus is said to be willing to give τὰ ἡμίσια of his possessions to the poor (19.8). Except for these two occasions, there are no other accounts in the Gospel which refer explicitly to the amount of material possessions that should be given to the poor. Here what concerns us is that Jesus' exhortation toward the Rich Ruler to sell all he has for alms is not fulfilled, while Zacchaeus takes an initiative to give half of his assets to the poor. In view of this contrast, we may suggest that in Luke's view total renunciation for the purpose of almsgiving is not intended, Or, at least, in the light of these two incidents, we may state that no fixed amount or percentage of almsgiving to one's assets is formally introduced. Then it might be suggested that as we see in the accounts of Zacchaeus, the Galilaean women, and the good Samaritan, the amount or percentage of almsgiving to one's possessions is up to individuals who should make a decision on it voluntarily, not in any forced or legalistic way.

With respect to the recipients of the alms, it is unclear whether they have to be distributed to the poor inside or outside the Christian community, or both, since explicit references to this matter are not made in Luke–Acts. Thus it is worthwhile looking into the accounts one after another where the motif of almsgiving appears:

(1) In the Sermon on the Plain, we notice that there are no restrictions on the recipients to whom one is supposed to lend or give money (6.29, 30, 35, 38).

(2) In the case of the good Samaritan, we may infer that alms should also be given to the poor outside the community. This inference results from the fact that to the good Samaritan who helped the robbed man out of his means his beneficiary is in fact an outsider.

(3) The Parable of the Great Banquet also shows no bias towards the poor inside the community, but rather displays particular concern about the poor and homeless outside the fence of the community (14.23; compare v. 13).

(4) It is also unclear whether or not the poor to whom Zacchaeus might give half of his capital belong to the community (19.8); it is the same with the exhortations of John the Baptist (3.11) and Jesus (11.41;

12.33; 18.22), and Cornelius (Acts 10.2), where the acts of almsgiving appear to be highlighted.

(5) Lk. 8.3 is the only account in the Gospel where generous acts analogous to almsgiving are shown only to the people inside the community.

(6) The passages containing the motif of almsgiving in Acts (2.42, 4.32-37, 6.1-6 and 11.27-30) show that alms were given to the poor within the community.

(7) The account of Tabitha (Acts 9.36) is, however, somewhat different from any other account referred to above. The reason for this lies in v. 41b: 'Then calling τοὺς ἁγίους καὶ χήρας he presented her alive.' Bruce may be right in asserting that 'Luke does not mean that the widows could not be saints'.[120] Nonetheless, it should not be disregarded that Luke clearly referred to two groups, the saints and the widows separately. This aspect leads us to suppose that the widows might have been non-Christians, so that Tabitha helped not only the Christians inside her community but also non-Christians outside the community.[121] It is clear that in many passages in Acts the recipients of charity are members of the Church, but the Tabitha example still stands as indicating that it is not *restricted* to them.

When we take these points together, we can draw the following conclusions: first, there is no clear demarcation on the matter of the recipients of alms in Luke's writings, whether it should be given to the poor inside or outside the community. Hence, secondly, it seems possible to claim that almsgiving ought to be distributed to the poor and needy regardless of their membership of the Christian community. Above all, what seems to matter more than this conclusion in this chapter is that Jesus' commands concerning almsgiving are continued on from Luke into Acts.

2. *Improper Stewardship of Wealth (The Wrong Use of Wealth)*

The theme of the wrong use of possessions can be presented as one of the notable characteristics of Luke's theology on wealth and poverty,

120. Bruce, *Acts*, p. 212. Cf. I.H. Marshall, *Acts* (TNTC; Leicester: IVP, 1986), p. 180.

121. I.H. Marshall, *Acts*, p. 180. As we have examined in the survey of previous studies, Schottroff and Stegemann argue that 'Luke in fact has poor non-Christians in mind as the recipients of alms' (*Hope*, p. 110). For my criticism of this one-sided opinion, see Introduction, 1.1.e.

seen most clearly from a comparison of Luke with Mark and Matthew. We may say this, first, because more material describing the rich in a negative way is seen in Luke than in the other Synoptic Gospels, and secondly, because Luke changes the existing material where this theme is contained, and adds his own material, to put emphasis on it. The material dealing with the theme of the wrong use of wealth consists of altered material from Luke's sources as well as his unique material, but it is in the latter on the whole that this theme is found more frequently. Consequently, we can state that this theme of the wrong use of wealth is one of the important features of Luke's theology on wealth and poverty.[122]

In what follows I will discuss the material containing the theme of warnings, dividing it into three categories according to their outstanding features: adherence to wealth, waste of wealth, and hoarding of wealth. This division is made in order to give our discussion some precision. However, a certain amount of repetition and overlapping is inevitable in this kind of procedure.

a. *Introduction: The Woes to the Rich (6.24-26)*
Before examining each category, the woes to the rich[123] (6.24-26) are to be discussed at the outset as an introduction to the reprimand theme.

In the first place, we have to consider the role which these passages might play in developing the theme of warning to the rich in Luke's Gospel. It is worth noticing, above all, that this passage is peculiar to Luke, absent in Mark and Matthew, and constitutes an anti-thesis to the Beatitudes on the poor (6.20-23/Mt. 5.1-12). Before these passages, the material which can be mentioned in relation to the wealth theme is the sermon of John the Baptist (3.10-14), and the first sermon of Jesus (4.18-19). Thus, as far as the reprimand theme is concerned, these passages are introduced as the first material in Luke's Gospel.

---

122. Although the rich are not warned overtly for their wrong use of material possessions, we may infer it from the texts which refer to the misconduct of the affluent in handling their assets and capital. In other words, the wealthy are implicitly reprimanded and warned throughout the Gospel for their wrong use of wealth, such as waste, adherence, and hoarding, and also for their neglect of their poor neighbours.

123. The woe form is said to exist prior to Luke in the Gospel tradition, such as Mk 13.17; Mk 14.21; Mt. 23.23 (Lk. 14.12); Mt. 23.27 (Lk. 11.44). However, it is Luke who 'makes the most abundant use of it in the Synoptics (10.13; 11.43, 46, 47, 52; 17.1; 21.23; 22.22)' (Fitzmyer, *Gospel*, p. 636).

Although the teaching of John the Baptist in Luke (3.7-17) is different from that of Mark and Matthew, we may suggest that the basic structure of the material preserved in all three Gospels is in essence the same, and 3.10-14 is an addition by Luke[124] in order to accentuate his cherished intention, that is, the concern for the poor and needy. On the other hand, 4.18-19 and 6.24-26 (including 6.20-23) are totally different in both their contents and settings as compared with Mark and Matthew. As for the former (4.18-19), Luke's material is placed in the early stage of the ministry of Jesus, whereas those of Mark (6.1-6) and Matthew (13.54-58), at a considerably later stage, so that we would claim that Luke is responsible for this material. As for the latter (6.24-26), Luke's version is placed after Jesus' appointment of his disciples, and its background is the plain (6.17: ἐπὶ τόπου πεδινοῦ), whereas that of Matthew (5.1-12) occurs before Jesus' appointment of his disciples and its setting is the mountain (5.1: εἰς τὸ ὄρος). In consequence, while 3.10-14 is a simple addition to the given source material, which could be thought of as a kind of alteration, 4.18-19 and 6.24-26 can be accounted as totally new material. Therefore, being placed at the outset of all the other material, these two passages play an introductory role in developing two themes, that is, the blessings to the poor[125] and the woes to the rich, as well as occupying a guiding

124. The basis of this assertion is that this section may come from Luke's special source, since it is absent in Mark and Matthew (I.H. Marshall, *Commentary*, p. 142; T.W. Manson, *Sayings*, p. 253). Cf. Fitzmyer, *Gospel*, p. 464.

125. The list of the poor and underprivileged occurs five times throughout the Gospel, such as 4.18; 6.20-23; 7.22; 14.13, 21. It is true that these five lists are not always mentioned for the same purposes, for instance, 4.18-19 and 7.22 refer to the object to whom the Gospel is preached, 6.20-23 refers to the object to whom the blessings are given, and 14.13, 21 to the object to whom the invitation to the Messianic Banquet is offered.

Despite the apparent discrepancies, however, when we scrutinize the content of each list, it seems possible to draw from them a common theme, that is, the concern for the poor. This point would be derived from the following two respects: First, οἱ πτωχοί is found in every list, and in a broad sense, the other groups, such as οἱ ἀνάπειροι, οἱ χωλοί, οἱ τυφλοί (14.13, 21), οἱ λεπροί, οἱ κωφοί (7.22), οἱ πεινῶντες, οἱ κλαίοντες (6.21), can be regarded as equal to οἱ πτωχοί. Secondly, the Gospel, that is, the good news, mentioned in 4.18-19 and 7.22 can be understood as meaning much the same as the invitation to the Messianic Banquet (14.13, 21), and if both (the gospel and invitation) may be expressed in another form, it would be 'the blessings to the poor' as in 6.20-23.

In this sense, the significance which 4.18-19 has in the Gospel, including those

position to show the way to understand and interpret the following material related to these two themes.[126]

In view of the content, this unit (6.24-26) does not seem so much to explore the theme of wealth and poverty as to express hostility towards the rich. This aspect becomes more apparent when it is contrasted with its preceding verses (6.20-23; compare 4.18), that is, the unconditional blessings to the poor. Then, does it mean that the rich should be cursed only because they are rich, whereas the poor are blessed just because they are poor?

To solve this seemingly difficult problem, it would be helpful to look at this passage in the perspective of all the material in Luke related to wealth, rather than to consider it alone as a separate unit. As already discussed in the section on almsgiving, the Rich Fool (ch. 12), the Rich Man (ch. 16), the Rich Ruler (ch. 18) and Zacchaeus (ch. 19) are presented as the typical exemplars of the rich, whereas only one individual, Lazarus (ch. 16), is presented as a typical exemplar of the poor. Besides Lazarus, the exemplars of the poor are introduced in the form of the collective, such as οἱ ἀνάπειροι, οἱ χωλοί, οἱ τυφλοί (14.13, 21), οἱ λεπροί, οἱ κωφοί (7.22). What is interesting to note in these two types of exemplars of contradistinction is that the exemplars of the rich are presented individually and more frequently than those of the poor, and each case shows different aspects which generally rich people are inclined to possess, that is, hoarding of wealth (the Rich Fool), waste of wealth (the Rich Man), and adherence to wealth (the Rich Ruler). Conversely, in the case of the exemplar of the poor, it seems that the various delineations of the poor referred to above can converge on to one specific individual, Lazarus, because he is πτωχός as well as

lists, is that in the light of the concern for the poor and needy, it plays an introductory role, and takes the form of a prophetic proclamation which is to be realized and confirmed in the ensuing material. Thus Creed, *Gospel*, p. 66, points out the significance of this narrative as follows: 'Its real function is to introduce the main *motifs* which are to recur throughout the Gospel and the Acts, and this it does with great effect.' I.H. Marshall, *Commentary*, pp. 177-78, also describes it as of 'programmatic significance', and also recognizes that 4.18-19 contains many of the main themes of Luke–Acts *in nuce*. Thus the theme of blessings to the poor may be included as one of the main themes. Cf. Conzelmann, *Theology*, p. 34; Creed, *Gospel*, p. 65; Johnson, *Literary Function*, p. 91; F.W. Horn, *Glaube und Handeln in der Theologie des Lukas* (Göttingen: Vandenhoeck & Ruprecht, 1983), p. 171; Fitzmyer, *Gospel*, p. 248; Karris, *Artist*, pp. 32-33; Talbert, *Reading Luke*, p. 54.

126. Cf. Pilgrim, *Good News*, pp. 103-107.

εἰλκωμένος (v. 20), which, along with ἐπιθυμῶν χορτασθῆναι (v. 21),[127] would mean that he is a disabled man (οἱ ἀνάπειροι), so that he can be regarded as in the same category of οἱ ἀνάπειροι, οἱ χωλοί, οἱ τυφλοί, οἱ λεπροί, and οἱ κωφοί. In this sense, it may be assumed that Lazarus is presented in Luke's Gospel as the typical exemplar of the poor who can represent the various kinds of the poor at Luke's time.[128]

In relation to this point, another point of significance to be noted here is that most of the rich people who appear in the Gospel are depicted as cursed,[129] whereas Lazarus, the typical model of the poor, is blessed. In this connection, we may claim that 6.24-26, along with 4.18-19, appears as a prophetic proclamation which is to be realized in what follows in Luke, as Acts 1.8 does in the Acts of the Apostles,[130] and in terms of structure, it plays a crucial and emphatic role placed at the head of the Gospel. In consequence, we could suggest that 6.24-26 does not

127. ἐπιθυμῶν with the infinitive (cf. 15.6; 17.22; 22.15) indicates an unfulfilled desire (Vincent, *Studies*, I, p. 201). Thus from this phrase and the appearance of οἱ κύνες in v. 21, it may be derived that οἱ κύνες could have eaten the pieces of bread fallen from the Rich Man's table, before Lazarus could have moved to it. It may mean that he was a cripple. Regarding this point, Jeremias, *Parables*, p. 184, puts it plausibly: 'The dogs are wild, roaming street-dogs who cannot refrain from nosing the helpless, scantily-clad cripple'.

128. Cf. Tannehill, *Narrative Unity*, p. 186.

129. For instance, we can point out several cases, such as 1.52 in the Magnificat, the woes to the rich in 6.24-26, the Rich Fool in 12.13-21, the initially invited guests in the parable of the Great Banquet (14.17-24), the Rich Man in 16.19-31 and the Rich Ruler in 18.18-27.

In this regard, the significance which the incident of Zacchaeus has in Luke's theology on wealth and poverty should be acknowledged once again. That is, among the material dealing with the motif of wealth, this incident is unique, for no hostility towards the rich can be found, and almsgiving is actually materialized. Accordingly, as I have already argued, it is introduced as a definite conclusion of all the material dealing with wealth and poverty in the Gospel.

130. In Acts we can note that the prophetic announcement of the risen Jesus (1.8) is realized actually in the historical context. Hence Bruce, *Acts*, p. 39, states that 'it has been often pointed out that the geographical terms of v. 8 provide a sort of "Index of Contents" for Acts'. See also I.H. Marshall, *Acts*, p. 61; W. Neil, *The Acts of the Apostles* (NCB; London: Oliphants, 1973), p. 66.

Therefore, we may suggest that these three passages, such as Acts 1.8, Lk. 4.18-19, and Lk. 6.24-26, play the same introductory roles in presenting their particular themes.

mean that the rich are cursed only owing to their wealth,[131] and the poor are blessed only owing to their poverty,[132] but rather indicates a possibility which may be actualized in practice.[133] But such a possibility, in being confirmed in the ensuing material, turns out to be an actual fact.[134] Therefore this passage may be regarded as a suggestive prophecy at the outset of the Gospel, and at the same time can be presented as an actual fact in terms of the Gospel as a whole.

Here we find once again Luke's literary artifice seen by his arranging material in a way suitable for his aim. That is to say, by placing one of his theme passages, 6.24-26, at the head of the Gospel in the form of a prophetic announcement, and then confirming it gradually in the ensuing material, Luke effectively provides his readers with his intended theme.

b. *Adherence to Material Possessions*
1. *The Parable of the Great Banquet (14.16-24)*. The first case in which an example of adherence to possessions can be pointed out is the three rich invited guests who appear in the parable of the Great Banquet. Among the three, at least two guests (vv. 18, 19) reject the invitation to the feast, for they lay more emphasis on their wealth—the field and five yoke of oxen—than on participation in the feast.[135] But in fact, their excuses are transparently thin and false because the acts of the two invited guests are described in the aorist (ἠγόρασα, vv. 18, 19), referring to an act just completed.[136] So it seems strange that inspection should follow rather than precede the purchase.[137] Besides, everyone in Luke's day knew the prevailing custom of honouring an invitation of others to a feast, and also that to refuse a second invitation constituted

131. In the Gospel we find the examples of the rich who are not cursed in spite of their wealth, such as Zacchaeus, the Galilaean women, Joseph of Arimathea (23.50). Therefore, Pilgrim, *Good News*, p. 77, states that 'it is not just poverty or riches per se that is blessed or condemned, but poverty in the context of trust in God and riches in the context of rejection of God'. Cf. R.F. O'Toole, *The Unity of Luke's Theology* (Delaware: Michael Glazier, 1984), p. 129; Schnackenburg, *Teaching*, p. 125.

132. Cf. Schnackenburg, *Teaching*, p. 128.

133. Danker, *Luke*, p. 83.

134. Cf. Schweizer, *Luke*, p. 287.

135. Cf. Danker, *Luke*, p. 166.

136. M. Black, *An Aramaic Approach to the Gospels and Acts* (Oxford: Clarendon Press, 1967), p. 129.

137. Morris, *Gospel*, p. 234.

an outright insult to the host to such a degree that among Arab tribes it was the equivalent of a declaration of war.[138] So the invitation had to be honoured as if it were a command, but those invited in this parable appear to decline it deliberately. Thus it could be drawn from this rejection that their adherence to wealth prevents them from taking part in the feast.

Compared with the Matthaean version (Mt. 22.1-14), as discussed above, it can be noted that the excuses of the guests are highlighted in Luke's Gospel. In Matthew, the first two excuses they proffer for not responding to the invitation are shorter and simpler than those in Luke, and the third is totally different.[139] And it is also improbable that the guests in Matthew are rich, or their excuses relevant to the wealth theme, as in Luke. Thus this comparison between the versions of the two Synoptists shows that the theme of possessions here, the theme of adherence to wealth in particular, is more stressed in Luke than in Matthew.

In view of vv. 15, 24, this banquet is not so much a mere earthly banquet as the Messianic Banquet,[140] which is more clearly expressed in the Matthean parallel (Mt. 22.1-14). When we take this point into account in interpreting this parable, the rejection of the prospective guests would be very significant because they may never be allowed to enter the Messianic Banquet, that is, the Kingdom of God.[141] In other words, they are destined to lose their spiritual salvation.[142] Conse-

138. Plummer, *Luke*, p. 360.

139. Cf. Schweizer, *Luke*, p. 238; L.T. Johnson, *Literary Function*, p. 146.

140. Jeremias, *Parables*, p. 69, holds that Luke regarded the supper in this parable as the feast of salvation (Creed, *Gospel*, pp. 191-92; Ellis, *Luke*, p. 194). Cf. Grundmann, *Lukas*, p. 299; Schmithals, *Lukas*, pp. 159-60; I.H. Marshall, *Commentary*, p. 591; Hunter, *Parables*, pp. 56-57.

141. Relating the excuses of those invited to the law prescribed in Deuteronomy, Evans, *Saint Luke*, p. 574, remarks that 'while couched in scriptural language of permissible exemptions from duty, the excuses are probably intended, when taken together, to show the power of economic and social attachments to stand in the way of answering the summons to the Kingdom'. Cf. Danker, *Luke*, p. 165; Schweizer, *Luke*, p. 237.

142. At 13.25-30 there also appear some who miss the feast. The difference between these passages and 14.16-24 is that those in ch. 13 miss it unintentionally, whereas those in ch. 14, intentionally. They are invited to come, and summoned at the appointed hour to take their seats, but deliberately decline the invitation (Gooding, *Luke*, pp. 267-68).

quently, it would appear that they are to lose their spiritual salvation owing to their adherence to wealth. Marshall's comment on this matter seems to the point:

> All three excuses are concerned with the details of commercial and family life, and fit in with the teaching of Jesus regarding the danger of letting love of possessions or domestic ties interfere with total commitment to the call of discipleship; they do not need to be allegorized in order to be interpreted outside the parable.[143]

In this parable, it may be seen that two major themes are mixed into one plot. The first theme concerns almsgiving, which I have already discussed above, and its application is that when holding a feast, one should invite the poor and underprivileged in the society rather than the rich, because otherwise a person might lose their reward in heaven (14.14). The second theme concerns adherence to wealth discussed here, and reveals ostensively the severity towards the rich, providing the examples of the invited guests who reject the invitation owing to their excessive adherence to material possessions.

To conclude, in making use of the two themes in the story, Luke appears to advise the rich members of his community not to adhere to their wealth as those invited do in the parable, which might result in the loss of their spiritual salvation, but to distribute their wealth to the poor and outcasts, which would result in a heavenly reward.

2. The Incident of The Rich Ruler (18.18-30). In the above, we have already noted by contrast with the parallels of Mark and Matthew that the Rich Ruler's wealth recorded in Luke is greater than that in Mark and Matthew (πλούσιος σφόδρα; v. 23), which would reveal Luke's particular concern with problems of the rich. This feature may be corroborated from the facts that he was an ἄρχων (v. 18), and that he became very sad (περίλυπος; v. 23) on hearing Jesus' exhortation to sell all his material possessions and to give the proceeds to the poor.[144]

---

143. I.H. Marshall, *Commentary*, p. 588.

144. περίλυπος is stronger than λυπούμενος in Mk (10.22) and Mt. (19.22).

In this regard, Plummer, *Luke*, p. 424, interestingly compares this case of the Rich Ruler with that of the first disciples in terms of their response to Jesus' call (5.11): 'he [the Rich Ruler] possessed a great deal more than a boat and nets; and Peter, James, and John were not told to sell their boats and nets and give the proceeds to the poor; because their hearts were not wedded to them'. Cf. Fitzmyer, *Gospel*, p. 1200.

Among those points referred to, περίλυπος might indicate that he appears to adhere to wealth more seriously in Luke than in Mark and Matthew.[145] In consequence, according to Jesus' saying in vv. 24-25, the Rich Ruler, unlike Zacchaeus, may not inherit eternal life nor enter into the Kingdom of God if he insists on adhering to his wealth.[146]

One respect which should be borne in mind in this incident is that it is not a parable but an actual event. So it is highly likely that the significance which this incident had would have been more obvious to Luke's audiences than that of parables and sayings.[147] Moreover, since Zacchaeus is introduced by name, while the ruler is not, it seems possible to suppose that though the ruler and Zacchaeus were both representatives of the affluent members of Luke's community, since the ruler failed to follow Jesus' exhortation, his name is not introduced, but on the other hand since Zacchaeus succeeded in coping with financial matters, his name is introduced as a good example of stewardship of wealth.[148] To put it another way, in throwing into bold relief the Rich Ruler's adherence to wealth more than Mark and Matthew, Luke seems to warn the wealthy members in his community about the danger which may result from adherence to material possessions, that is, the loss of spiritual salvation.[149] That this danger is also mentioned in ch. 14, that is, the parable of the Great Banquet, may reveal the continuity of Luke's idea on punishment following the improper stewardship of wealth.

c. *Waste of Material Possessions*
This section deals with three parables which explore the theme of warning about the waste of possessions: the parables of the Prodigal Son

---

145. Goulder, *Paradigm*, II, p. 673, makes a contrast between the responses of the Rich Ruler and the blind man (18.35-43), stressing his grief because of this wealth. Cf. Evans, *Saint Luke*, p. 652.

146. 'Daher [18.3; cf. 16.14ff.; 18.9-14] muß, wer in die Herrschaft Gottes eingehen will, sein Herz von der Gebundheit an dem Besitz lösen' (Grundmann, *Lukas*, pp. 354-55). Cf. Schmithals, *Lukas*, p. 182; Caird, *Luke*, p. 205.

147. Ernst, *Lukas*, p. 503: 'Es darf vermutet werden, dab die Gemeinde, an die er sich wendet, in diesem Punkte besonders anfällig war'.

148. Seccombe, *Possessions*, p. 131, asserts that in Luke's mind Zacchaeus was someone of importance, and likely to be significant to his readers, 'because his readers had some knowledge of him, or even possibly because he was the kind of person with whom they could identify'.

149. Seccombe, *Possessions*, pp. 131-32.

(15.11-32), the Unjust Steward (16.1-13), and the Rich Man and Lazarus (16.9-31). What is to be mentioned at the outset is that in the three parables this theme of waste of wealth is not a main but a subsidiary motif which by backing up the main motif increases its effect. Nonetheless its weight in each parable as such is not to be taken lightly. Rather it has its own significance as a subsidiary theme, and at the same time it plays an important role by contributing to the formation of Luke's theology on the major theme of wealth and poverty.

1. *The Parable of the Prodigal Son (15.11-32).*[150] As the context of ch. 15 shows, the theme of this parable is mainly focused on repentance, along with the preceding two parables, that is, the parables of the lost sheep, and of the lost coin (vv. 7, 10, 32). But here our attention is on the wrong attitude of the younger son towards material possessions as a subsidiary motif.

It has been generally noted that when an Eastern father died his property was divided so that the eldest son was given a double share and each of the other sons received a single share.[151] Knowing that the bulk of the property would remain with the eldest, the younger sons sometimes asked for their inheritance, converted it into cash, and went off to make their own way in the world.[152] In this story the younger son did just like other youths of that time so that he asked for his share, sold the property and left home. In the time of Luke many young Jews are said to have gone away to try their luck in foreign countries. But instead of investing his money,[153] he 'squandered his property in loose living' (v. 13) and 'devoured his living with harlots' (v. 30). In the light of Luke's idea on the theme of wealth, such behaviour of the younger son seems striking and provocative to him because contrary to his intention that material possessions should be used for the sake of

150. Jeremias, *Parables*, p. 128, holds that this parable is not an allegory, 'but a story drawn from life' (cf. Linnemann, *Parables*, p. 74; Hunter, *Parables*, p. 61).

151. For more detail of share of inheritance in the Middle East in ancient times, see Jeremias, *Parables*, pp. 128-29. Cf. 12.13-14.

152. Emigration from Israel to the Diaspora was very common, because 'Palestine, visited by frequent famines, was not able to support the people of Israel, and anyone who wanted to get on had a better chance in the great trading cities of the Levant' (Linnemann, *Parables*, p. 75). It has been estimated that about eight times as many Jews (four million) lived in the Diaspora as in Israel (half a million) (Jeremias, *Parables*, p. 129).

153. I.H. Marshall, *Commentary*, p. 608.

the poor and needy, the younger son lavished his wealth only on his selfish interests of pleasure.

In line with this, the content of the younger son's behaviour should also be noted. According to the text, he is depicted as a model of the sinner who should repent, but it should be borne in mind here that he is not a sinner in the sense of having transgressed religious ordinances and commandments (v. 21). The content of his wrongdoing consists of having used his wealth in a wrong way. This assertion is based on the facts that his wrongdoing is described only in two verses (vv. 13, 30), and they merely point out his wrong use of wealth, that is, his dissipation of the share of the inheritance. Hence Evans puts this point as follows:

> . . . the sin of the younger against his father (v. 18) may have been in his having left home before the father's death. There is, however, no suggestion of disapproval in v. 12, and in v. 30 it is the dissipation of the father's wealth that constitutes the wrong against him.[154]

Accordingly, his sin is not so much specifically ritual,[155] as moral, in his wrong use of his wealth. In consequence, it seems natural that his repentance should be concerned only with his extravagant living (vv. 18, 21; compare vv. 13, 30). In relation to this, what deserves our concern is v. 21a: 'Father, I have sinned against heaven and before you'—his misdemeanour is, according to vv. 13, 30, to have squandered possessions, for to dissipate wealth can mean to sin against God. Thus Grundmann states that 'seine Sünde besteht in der Untreue gegenüber dem ihm vom Vater zum Leben anvertrauten Gut'.[156] In this sense, we may suggest that in Luke's mind to dissipate wealth is to

154. Evans, *Saint Luke*, p. 592; L.T. Johnson, *Literary Function*, p. 161; cf. Fitzmyer, *Gospel*, pp. 1088, 1091.

155. It may be possible to say that on the basis of v. 15, the younger son committed a ritual sin, because feeding pigs was strictly forbidden by the Jewish law, and in having been in the employ of a Gentile, 'he must have been forced to renounce the regular practice of his religion' (Jeremias, *Parables*, p. 129; cf. Linnemann, *Parables*, p. 76). However, this argument is not substantiated by the text itself. What is crucial here is explicit references to his wrongdoings, that is, dissipation of material possessions. Consequently, as regards defining the younger son's sin, it may be wise to consider the meaning explicitly exposed in the text rather than implicitly hidden.

156. '. . . his sin consists in his unfaithfulness to the wealth entrusted to him by his father'. Grundmann, *Lukas*, p. 312.

sin against God, and in this he has particularly in view the rich Christians in his community.[157] Applying this to the situation of Luke's community, it would appear that Luke in this parable warns the rich not to squander their wealth, pointing out that those rich frittering away their wealth in the interests of selfish pleasure are committing a sin against God.

Here it would be useful to look into the sequence of the narrative in this context, that is, the parable of the unjust steward immediately follows this parable by the link of δέ (16.1), and διασκορπίζω (διεσκόρπισεν—15.13; διασκορπίζων—16.1) is used in both parables. Grundmann recognizes this interrelation between the two parables:

> Der Zusammenhang mit der Erzählung von den beiden Söhnen ist durch die Zusammenstellung erwiesen; sie wird durch die zweimalige Verwendung von διασκορπίζειν 15,13 and 16,1 kenntlich gemacht: Verschleuderung anvertrauten Gutes bindet den jüngeren Sohn und den Verwalter zusammen.[158]

On these grounds, it might be possible to say that Luke would have been interested to relate both parables to each other by means of the theme of wealth, here particularly the theme of waste of wealth. Therefore, in this sense, we may suggest that this parable situated in between 15.3-10 and 16.1-13 takes a transitional character, because it contains both themes, that is, repentance and waste of wealth, and the following parable takes up one of the two themes, that is, the theme of wealth and poverty, to mould another crucial motif of the wealth theme: almsgiving.[159]

157. There is no doubt that the background of this parable is an affluent farm of which the owner, the father, has slaves, hired men, and cattle as well as a large field. Cf. Goulder, *Paradigm*, II, p. 613.

158. 'The relationship to the parable of the two sons is shown by means of edition; it is evidently revealed through two uses of διασκορπίζειν 15.13 and 16.1: dissipation of entrusted wealth binds the younger son and the steward together'. Grundmann, *Lukas*, p. 317. See also Ernst, *Lukas*, p. 462; Beck, *Character*, pp. 28-29; I.H. Marshall, *Commentary*, p. 608; Fitzmyer, *Gospel*, p. 1100; H. Hendrickx, *The Parables of Jesus: Studies in the Synoptic Gospels* (London: Geoffrey Chapman, 1986), p. 170. Meanwhile, Schmithals, *Lukas*, pp. 167-68, also connects this parable with its precedent and 14.25-35 by way of the motif of 'Armenfrömmigkeit', which he defines as follows: 'Wer Gott ausschließlich dient, hat mit seinem irdischen Besitz den Mitmenschen zu dienen'.

159. Fitzmyer, *Gospel*, p. 1095; cf. Hendrickx, *Parables*, p. 170.

Finally, in relating the theme of this parable to stewardship, it is probable that here the prodigal son who frittered away his possessions in pursuing his selfish pleasure is introduced as a model of a bad steward of material possessions.

2. *The Parable of the Unjust Steward (16.1-13).*[160] As already pointed out in the discussion of the parable of the Prodigal Son, both parables can be thought of as having the same subsidiary theme. That is, in the parable of the Prodigal Son, dissipation of wealth is introduced as a subsidiary theme with repentance as a main theme, whereas in this parable dissipation of possessions is also presented as its subsidiary with almsgiving as the main theme. So in the light of the subsidiary, both parables are under the continuity of the same idea, which δὲ καὶ (16.1) clearly indicates.[161]

In this parable the only thing pointed out as the wrongdoing by the steward is dissipation of his master's wealth (v. 1). So he faced dismissal from his position as steward (vv. 2-3).

That the steward in question is described as ἀδικίας also arrests our attention (v. 8a). If we take the view of our earlier conclusion about the main theme of this parable, that is, almsgiving, it seems unreasonable to depict him as ἀδικίας (v. 8). Rather, since he uses wealth entrusted to him in a right way, he should be depicted as δίκαιος. Then why is he described as ἀδικίας? The answer to this query might be derived from the previous parable because this parable shares its subsidiary motif with the precedent.[162] In the parable of the Prodigal Son, the younger son admitted that his wrongdoing of having lavished his wealth is a sin committed against heaven and his father (v. 21). This might reflect Luke's thought that to squander possessions is to commit a sin against God. In this sense, when we look into this parable, the steward who dissipated his master's capital can also be regarded as having sinned against God and his master, so that it would be reasonable to describe

160. Since we have discussed this parable at length in Chapter 5, here only the main point related to the topic at issue will be dealt with.

161. See n. 158.

162. The steward here is also charged with what the younger son does in 15.13. Thus in terms of dissipation of material possessions, the continuity is found between the two parables. Cf. Grundmann, *Lukas*, p. 317; Ernst, *Lukas*, p. 595; Danker, *Luke*, p. 173; Ellis, *Luke*, p. 200.

him as ἀδικίας.[163] Thus this word does not apply to the steward's actions towards the debtors. It also characterizes the steward's earlier life when he squandered his master's assets. In other words, it is partly because of his previous career of shady deals that he is called ἀδικίας in 16.8.[164] This aspect hidden in both parables would be a reflection of the author's intention to stress waste of wealth as well as to warn his readers of its danger.[165] In terms of stewardship, it is true that it constitutes a serious sin for the person who is allowed to manage the property entrusted by his master to fritter it away in regarding it as his own. Summing up the above discussions, the particular emphasis which Luke imposes in the parable is that to dissipate capital and property is ἀδικίας, and would result in the crisis of catastrophe.

3. *The Parable of the Rich Man and Lazarus (16.19-31).* Even though διασκορπίζω (15.13; 16.1) does not occur in this parable as in the previous parables,[166] v. 19 clearly indicates the extravagant living of the Rich Man, which can be depicted as dissipation of wealth. The impression from this verse is that he lived a luxurious life and indulged in pursuing his selfish pleasure (εὐφραινόμενος; v. 19). Although it may be admitted in some degree that he would wear πορφύραν and βύσσον (v. 19) in accordance with his wealthy status, nevertheless it is clearly dissipation of wealth to have a feast καθ' ἡμέραν (v. 19).[167] And when we look at v. 25 in this perspective, it may be found that criticism against the prodigal and extravagant living of the Rich Man is implied in v. 25: ἀπέλαβες τὰ ἀγαθά σου.[168] Consequently, the major reason why he fell into Hades is that in his lifetime he received his good things (v. 25), which would have resulted from his affluent wealth.[169] In

163. Talbert, *Reading Luke*, p. 154; Beck, *Character*, p. 29.
164. Kistemaker, *Parables*, p. 232; Fitzmyer, *Gospel*, p. 1100.
165. Jeremias, *Parables*, p. 47. Cf. Ernst, *Lukas*, p. 600.
166. But it should be noticed that two parables in ch. 16 are introduced by the same sentence; ἄνθρωπός τις ἦν πλούσιος (v. 1) / ἄνθρωπός δέ τις ἦν πλούσιος (v. 19). It would demonstrate Luke's intention that the two parables are to be homogenous.
167. Cf. Grundmann, *Lukas*, p. 327; Ernst, *Lukas*, p. 473.
168. Cf. 6.24. Fitzmyer, *Gospel*, p. 1133; cf. Grundmann, *Lukas*, p. 327.
169. Grundmann, *Lukas*, p. 329. In explicating the reason why the Rich Man was put in Hades, Mealand, *Poverty*, p. 32, focuses his attention on the motif of a reversal of fortune which he asserts matches the outlook of the woes and that of the Magnificat, while relegating a critique to the Rich Man to a secondary. But when we

other words, it means that in his lifetime he pursued his selfish pleasure by using up his possessions sumptuously.

Here what arrests our attention is that the Rich Man who frittered away his wealth luxuriously but never gave alms to Lazarus fell into hell. We have noted in the previous parables that dissipation of wealth is described as ἀδικίας (16.1) and ἁμαρτία (15.21). But in this parable such a judiciary description does not appear. Instead the direct result of his wrong acts on earth is recorded. So from this story is found that to squander wealth can be a sin that leads anyone to fall into hell. This could be an oriental hyperbole. But it is reasonable to suppose that such overt acts of the Rich Man represent a general tendency which we may find in the attitudes of the rich. That is to say, behind such overt acts of the Rich Man lies a possibility that more wrongdoing was bound up in his waste of wealth and rejection of almsgiving, which eventually led him to fall into hell. Thus this story would have been a formidable warning[170] to the wealthy who spend their capital sumptuously but never give alms to the poor and needy in the community.[171]

It should be noted that 15.11–16.31 constitutes a unit in terms of the theme of wealth.[172] This unit is mainly composed of three parables, and each parable has a main and a subsidiary theme respectively: in the case of the Parable of the Prodigal Son, repentance is primary and dissipation of wealth is secondary; in the case of the Parable of the Unjust Steward, almsgiving is primary and dissipation of wealth is secondary; in the case of the Parable of the Rich Man and Lazarus, dissipation of possessions is primary and almsgiving is secondary. Thus it turns out that each parable consists of a double motif structure, that is, a main theme and a subsidiary. This point could be regarded as another token of excellent literary artifice by the author of the Third Gospel.

face up to the text of the parable itself and the context surrounding it, i.e. the parable of the Unjust Steward, rather than taking into account the material remote from this story, it seems apparent that the reason why the Rich Man was thrown into Hades is his neglect of concern for his poor neighbours.

170. Plummer, *Luke*, p. 390; Mealand, *Poverty*, p. 47; Schmidt, *Hostility*, p. 157.

171. Binding together the two parables in ch. 16, A. Schlatter (*Das Evangelium des Lukas* [Stuttgart: Calwer, 1960]), p. 376, makes a statement which expresses succinctly its point: 'Gib, so sagte die erste Erzählung, so rettest du dich; behalte und geniebe, so verdirbst du dich, sagte die zweite'.

172. Ernst, *Lukas*, p. 472; Fitzmyer, *Gospel*, p. 1095.

c. Hoarding of Wealth: The Parable of the Rich Fool (12.13-21)

This parable which we have already discussed in the chapter on alms-giving is briefly dealt with here in relation to the theme of warning on the hoarding of wealth. Among the material dealing with the theme of wealth, only this parable takes a different aspect of the theme distinguished from the themes of adherence to and dissipation of wealth, and focuses on hoarding of wealth. The evidence which buttresses this argument can be found in the text in which the words related to hoarding are introduced with three different forms: συνάξω (vv. 17, 18), κείμενα (v. 19), and θησαυρίζων (v. 21). That these words related to hoarding are used four times in this story may indicate the significance which this parable has in relation to the theme at issue. Thus the Jerusalem Bible entitles this parable as 'on hoarding possessions'.

Responding to someone's request that Jesus should be a judge over dividing the inheritance, Jesus says in v. 15 that 'A man's life does not consist in the abundance of his possessions'. After that, in order to explain this point more clearly, the Lukan Jesus presents this parable of which the conclusion is introduced in v. 21. Verses 15 and 21 being taken together, consequently we may paraphrase v. 15 as follows: 'A man's life consists in being rich towards God'. The opposite case of this paraphrase is, as v. 21 shows clearly, to be rich towards himself, that is, hoarding material possessions only for his own comfort and pleasure in this world.[173]

Here we can notice that Luke criticizes the hoarding of wealth on earth which the Rich Fool wants to use for his pursuit of physical pleasure,[174] by stating that God will summon his soul on that night. In view of 12.33 which lies in the same context as this parable,[175] Luke's intention here would be that the affluent Christians in his community should not amass any material possessions on earth for the sake of their selfish pleasure, but distribute them to the poor who do not know where

173. Cf. I.H. Marshall, *Commentary*, p. 521. Along with this, the excessive selfishness of the Rich Fool which can be found in the fivefold use of μου should be taken into account to appreciate this fully. Thus it may be that selfishness and hoarding wealth is a pair of concepts bound together so as to express the folly of the Rich Man in this parable. Cf. Plummer, *Luke*, p. 324; Hendrickx, *Parables*, p. 101; Ernst, *Lukas*, p. 400.

174. Karris, 'Poor and Rich', p. 120.

175. Grundmann, *Lukas*, p. 258, holds that an answer of the question of 'das Reichwerden auf Gott' in v. 21 is given at v. 33. And Danker, *Jesus*, p. 252, states that v. 33 is after all a commentary on v. 21.

their next meal may come from. Regarding this setting of the parable and Luke's warning, Ernst affords us a pointed comment:

> Vielleicht stehen hinter dem Wortspiel aktuelle soziale Fragestellungen des Gemeindelebens. Begüterte Christen werden auf die Gefahren des Wohlstands hingewiesen und daran erinnert, dab sie die Anwälte der Armen sein sollen (vgl. Lk. 12,33; Mt. 6,19; Apg 2,45; 4,34).[176]

d. *Conclusion*

In this section, I have investigated the theme of the wrong use of wealth in Luke's Gospel, classifying the material into three categories: adherence to, waste of, and hoarding of, material possessions. This investigation has shown that Luke preserved quite a few pieces of material unique to him where such wrongdoings committed by the wealthy concerning the use of wealth are explicitly revealed—the parables of the Rich Fool, of the Prodigal Son, of the Unjust Steward, and of the Rich Man and Lazarus—and also rewrote his source material for the sake of his emphasis on this motif, that is, the parable of the Great Banquet and the account of the Rich Ruler. It seems likely that the intention which lies behind this edition of Luke was not unrelated to his concern about the poor and the rich in his community, when we take into account his view on wealth and poverty as a whole. Therefore, we would conclude that Luke intended to criticize the wrong use of wealth by the rich Christians in his community,[177] which is for Luke a clear token of improper stewardship of wealth.

Now that we have identified Luke's idea of proper and improper stewardship of wealth in the Gospel thus far, it is time for us to look at

---

176. 'Behind this expression [wordplay] there seems to have been actual social problems concerning the communal life. Wealthy Christians were warned of the danger of wealth, and demanded to remember that they should be patron of the poor (cf. Lk. 12.33; Mt. 6.19; Acts 2.45; 4.34).' Ernst, *Lukas*, p. 400; cf. Fitzmyer, *Gospel*, p. 972. Referring to Tobias's story in Tobit 7.9-11 and arguing that 'there is no allegory in this story at all', Drury, *Parables*, p. 137, reckons this parable as 'a real incident in the ordinary world, the moral force of which is intelligible to common sense'.

177. Describing Luke as 'the evangelist of the rich and the respected', Schottroff and Stegemann, *Hope*, pp. 87-92, argue that Luke presented the material relating to this motif in order for the rich and the respected 'to convert and to be reconciled to the message and way of life of Jesus and his disciples' who became voluntarily poor to participate in the present *basileia*. This view of Schottroff and Stegemann is shared by Pilgrim, *Good News*, pp. 103-22. Cf. Ireland, *Stewardship*, pp. 175-80.

Acts, because it seems natural to imagine that if Acts is written by the same author as that of the Gospel, his idea of stewardship should also be present in his second book for the sake of the continuity of the author's intention.

Chapter 7

THE ALMSGIVING MOTIF IN ACTS

In this chapter, I shall further pursue my exploration of the motif of almsgiving into Acts, bearing in mind the result that we have obtained in our study of that motif in the Gospel. By doing so, I hope to discover whether there is a thematic continuity between the Gospel and Acts in terms of the motif of almsgiving which for Luke is the proper way to practise stewardship of wealth. In order to carry out this task, the procedure I shall take is, first, to examine some examples where almsgiving is put into practice in actual circumstances, and then secondly to explore particularly the two summary passages which afford us valuable information as regards the communal life of the Early Church, which Luke probably intended to introduce to his congregation as a model to be emulated in their church life. Thirdly, I shall examine the problem of continuity between the Gospel and Acts in terms of the almsgiving motif, bearing in mind the findings from discussion of the first two sections. And finally, I shall append a detailed excursus on the subject of the similarities and dissimilarities between the Jerusalem Community and the Qumran Community in terms of their common funds and meals, because some argue that there are close links between the two communities.

1. *Examples of Almsgiving in Acts*

When we look at the book of Acts, we see that there are no direct and clear exhortations towards the rich to give alms to the poor such as are often found in the Gospel. Instead, we can find some passages in the summaries in which the motif of almsgiving is clearly observed (2.42-47; 4.32-37), and a few accounts where acts of almsgiving and charity performed by individuals and a church are recorded. Since the summary passages will be discussed at length later on, here my attention is given to such individual cases as Tabitha, Cornelius, the Antioch Church, and a saying of Jesus on almsgiving.

a. *Tabitha (9.36-43)*

Luke describes a unique incident[1] in which Peter raised from the dead by prayer, Tabitha, a female disciple who was well known for her good works and almsgiving (v. 36). This description of Tabitha's generous behaviour arrests our attention in dealing with the motif of almsgiving. It would seem that such a benevolent attitude from Tabitha drove the other disciples to summon Peter who was then at Lydda near Joppa, when we take into consideration the fact that all the widows wept for Tabitha and showed Peter coats and garments that she made for them (v. 39).[2] These widows had clearly been helped by Tabitha financially, since widows of that time were usually dependent upon the goodness and charity of the more affluent.[3] Bruce rightly makes this point: 'Widows are mentioned here, as in Ch. 6.1: as the natural recipients of charity, not as members of a special order attached to the church, such as we find later in 1 Tim. 5:3.16'.[4] It appears, then, that Tabitha's acts of benevolence towards the poor widows made her worthy to be brought back to life.[5] Luke may have recorded this story

1. Another incident of resuscitation is reported at 20.7-12 which is about Eutychus who fell to the ground from the third storey because of his deep sleep, while Paul was delivering his sermon.

However, these two cases do not seem to belong to the same category, first because Eutychus here appears to be a bad model to be shunned, and secondly because Eutychus was not resuscitated by prayer and the word of command (cf. I.H. Marshall, *Acts*, p. 180). Therefore, we may call the case of Tabitha unique from these viewpoints.

2. The middle voice of ἐπιδεικνύμεναι may show that the widows were actually wearing the coats and garments which Tabitha made for them (Bruce, *Acts*, p. 212; I.H. Marshall, *Acts*, p. 179).

3. R.P.C. Hanson (*The Acts* [New Clarendon Bible; Oxford: Clarendon Press, 1967], p. 118), makes an interesting remark in explaining why the widows wept, i.e. 'because they were poor folk who had been deprived by Tabitha's death of her charity'.

4. Bruce, *Acts*, p. 212. Cf. Hanson, *Acts*, p. 118; G.A. Krodel, *Acts* (Augsburg Commentary on the NT; Minneapolis: Augsburg, 1986), p. 185; I.H. Marshall, *Acts*, pp. 179-80.

5. Regarding as redaction Luke's description of Tabitha as 'full of good works and acts of charity' in v. 36b and the references to the clothes in v. 39b, G. Lüdemann, *Early Christianity according to the Traditions in Acts: A Commentary*

of Tabitha to emphasize the significance of benevolence, such that Tabitha got her life back because of the good works and alms she had contributed towards the poor.[6]

b. *Cornelius (10.1-48)*

In the account of the first conversion of a Gentile, Cornelius, a Roman centurion, is recorded here to have been a God-fearing Gentile and to have given alms to the people (τῷ λαῷ, the people of Israel[7]) liberally (πολλάς; v. 2) so that God remembered it along with his prayers (vv. 4, 31)[8] and also the whole Jewish nation spoke well of him (v. 22).[9] In other words, Cornelius earned recognition by God and his neighbours for his pious faith and benevolent acts towards those in need.[10] In this respect, the almsgiving that Cornelius put into practice made him worthy of divine approval. Up to this stage, we have seen not a few dominical exhortations on almsgiving and implementation of them by some individuals in Luke–Acts, but we have not had an opportunity to observe what the practice of almsgiving might bring about. From this narrative, however, we can clearly see God's acknowledgment of Cornelius's generous almsgiving and prayers which eventually resulted in the Jerusalem church's approval of evangelism to the Gentiles. Thus we see that the generous acts and prayers of Cornelius brought about God's approval, and it became a historical momentum which enabled

(London: SCM Press, 1989), p. 121, observes that 'this is how the woman is meant to be shown worthy of the miracle (cf. Lk. 7.2-5; 7.12; Acts 10.2, 4)'. Bengel's comment also seems to support this point: 'These works, consisting in the making of garments, were estimated at a high value, and recompensed with a great reward' (*Gnomon*, II, p. 598). Cf. Haenchen, *Acts*, p. 339; I.H. Marshall, *Acts*, p. 180.

6. Cf. Krodel, *Acts*, p. 185.

7. H. Conzelmann, *Acts of the Apostles* (Philadelphia: Fortress Press, 1989), p. 81.

8. Cf. Ps. 141.2; Tob. 12.12; Sir. 50.16; Phil. 4.18.

9. On this point, we might suppose that Jesus' command in Lk. 16.9 is echoed here in the narrative of Cornelius and that of Tabitha as well (9.39, 41), because both figures in Acts appear to have made friends by means of their material possessions, and were in turn recompensed; the friends of Tabitha helped her to be brought back to life, while Cornelius's friends helped him to be accepted into the Christian church.

10. Thus Bengel, *Gnomon*, II, p. 599, puts this notion like this: 'Among many of the Jews there was at that time great poverty. God repaid the debt of the poor, in their stead. The grace of God towards Israel recompenses the favour of Cornelius towards Israelites.' Cf. Beck, *Character*, p. 111; O. Cone, *Rich and Poor in the New Testament* (London: A. & C. Black, 1902), p. 146. See also 2.47. Cf. 4.21; 5.13.

the mother church to recognize the Gentile mission on an official level. Therefore, we can state that Luke would have sought to show his church how momentous it could be to practise almsgiving as commanded by Jesus.

c. *The Antioch Church (11.27-30)*[11]

Just as some individuals performed almsgiving out of their means, so we should note the case of the Antioch church, where Agabus, a prophet, prophesied a great famine over all the world (v. 28), which Luke wrote had taken place during Claudius's reign (41–54 CE). However, it is acknowledged that there was no worldwide famine during the entire period of the Empire, but bad harvests and frequent famines were reported to have occurred at various places during Claudius's reign.[12] In line with this, it is also reported that there was a famine in Judaea during 46–48 CE, so, according to Josephus, Queen Helene of Adiabene sent grain from Egypt to relieve the poor and hungry in Jerusalem.[13] To respond to this hardship which would have affected the Christians in Jerusalem as well, the Antioch church decided to send relief (διακονία[14]) to the brethren in Judaea and appointed Barnabas and Saul to carry out this task. Thus we may suggest that this famine relief of the Antioch church could be reckoned as an act of almsgiving of a different sort, that is, benevolence of an institution with wealth towards an institution in need.[15] Consequently, from this unique incident in Acts, we may observe that the scale of the practice of almsgiving is broadened so as to accommodate the need of a church in

11. Cf. Acts 12.25; 24.17.

12. Suetonius, *Claud.* 18.2; Tacitus, *Ann.* 12.43; Dio Cassius, *Rom. Hist.* 60.11; Orosius, *Hist.* 7.6.17. Cf. Haenchen, *Acts*, p. 374; Bruce, *Acts*, pp. 243-44; Lüdemann, *Traditions*, p. 135.

13. Josephus, *Ant.* 3.15.3; 20.2.5; 20.5.2. With respect to this famine in Judaea, J. Jeremias ('Sabbatjahr und neuetestamentliche Chronologie', *ZNW* 27 [1928], pp. 98-103), argued that the famine would have been very severe because it 'coincided with the effects of a fallow year' which the Jews kept faithfully according to the laws.

14. Paul also names his collection διακονία (1 Cor. 16.15; 2 Cor. 8.4; 9.1, 13; Rom. 15.31).

15. Labelling this event 'interchurch relief', Krodel, *Acts*, p. 210, makes a good point by stating that 'the new Jewish-Gentile Community . . . expressed anew the ideal of the Jerusalem Church (cf. 4.35-35) by helping to feed the hungry and needy there'. Cf. I.H. Marshall, *Acts*, p. 204.

trouble, and would possibly conclude that acts of almsgiving should be directed not only to individuals but also to Christian communities which may happen to be poor and so depend upon others' financial support.

d. *Jesus' Command (20.35)*

A single passage to which we now turn with expectation is 20.35 which is a part of Paul's farewell sermon to the elders at Miletus. Here Paul gives them an exhortation to help the weak quoting the Lord's command: 'it is more blessed to give rather than to receive'.[16] In this context (vv. 33-35), it seems that the weak (οἱ ἀσθενοῦντες) here would imply the poor in terms of the weakness of finance,[17] so that this injunction of Paul is in fact to be regarded as that of almsgiving. This interpretation of v. 35a seems reasonable because the implication of Paul's advice is in accordance with that of Jesus' command which follows immediately. Krodel takes cognizance of this point as follows:

16. We know this dominical saying does not appear verbatim in the New Testament or the early Christian literature, and the phrase, μακάριόν ἐστιν μᾶλλον διδόναι ἤ λαμβάνειν, is reminiscent of a Persian axiom. According to Thucydides, *Hist.* 2.97.4, it is known that in the Persian empire the kings gave rather than received presents (cf. Xenophon, *Cyr.* 8.2.7). Besides these passages, a number of phrases which contain similar motifs appear in both Greek and Roman literature (Plutarch, *Mor.* 173d, 182e, 778c; Seneca, *Ep.* 81.17).

However, as Hanson (*Acts*, p. 206) argues, there is no reason why Jesus should not have quoted or adapted a Greek proverb, if the cultural influences of Hellenism in Palestine are taken into account. Here μακάριον clearly speaks of a Jewish rather than a Greek style of expression, and in *Didache* 1.5 we can find an echo of this phrase: 'To everyone who asks you, give and do not require it back! For the Father wills that to all be given from one's own gifts of grace. *Blessed is he who gives* according to the commandment, for he is blameless. *Woe to him who takes.* To be sure, if anyone suffers want and so takes, then he will be blameless.'

In addition to this, in Lk. 6.38, 11.9-13, 14.12-14 and Jn 13.34, the spirit of this phrase is manifested (Bruce, *Acts*, p. 418; Pilgrim, *Good News*, p. 159; cf. Neil, *Acts*, p. 215. Therefore, there is much more to be said for its authenticity than Conzelmann (*Acts*, p. 176) allowed.

17. Schottroff and Stegemann, *Hope*, p. 111. Cf. Krodel, *Acts*, pp. 94, 392; I.H. Marshall, *Acts*, p. 336; Pilgrim, *Good News*, pp. 158-59; Beck, *Character*, p. 531; Sweetland, *Journey*, p. 188. Cf. Eph. 4.28.

It is probable that the background of this saying was a Hellenistic proverb
(Thucydides, 2.97.4, Plutarch, *Moralia* 173D) which became Christian-
ized and which Luke understood in analogy to Jesus' injunctions concerning
almsgiving (Lk. 6.30, 34-35, 38).[18]

It is also to be noticed that this saying of Jesus is unique, since no other
sayings of Jesus appear quoted in Acts and also no explicit command on
almsgiving is recorded in Acts. Thus in this sense, it can be said that this
last saying of Jesus in this regard may have been recorded here by Luke
as a summary of a series of Jesus' teachings on almsgiving which thus
appear prominently throughout Luke–Acts. In this regard, Pilgrim's
comment appears appropriate:

> We find this word from the Lord, 'It is more blessed to give than to receive',
> to be a most fitting conclusion to Luke's presentation of the theme of
> wealth and poverty and the proclamation of good news to the poor.[19]

2. *The Summary Passages (2.43-47; 4.32-35)*

Among those passages referred to above in relation to the actual practice of almsgiving, two passages in particular need to be considered,
2.42-47 and 4.32-37, which present brief summaries that the early
Christians shared their goods in common and also that there was none
needy among them.[20]

Since there is no explicit mention of almsgiving, or exhortations to
almsgiving, it might seem that they are not to be involved in this topic.
But they do refer to sharing goods in common among the members of
the Jerusalem Christian community and giving to those in need. So several issues need careful attention here: why did Luke insert these two
summaries while describing the communal life of the Early Church,
how significant are these summaries in the realm of Luke's theology of
wealth and poverty, and finally, how are they related to the exhortations in the Gospel? In answering these questions, we need to investigate

18. Krodel, *Acts*, p. 392. Cf. Bruce, *Acts*, p. 418. R. Pesch, *Die Apostelgeschichte*
(Apg 13-28) (EKKNT, 5.2; Zürich: Benzinger Verlag, 1986), p. 206, claims that
Luke understands this saying of 20.35 in connection with Jesus' social sermon in
Lk. 6.30-46 and 10.30-37.

19. Pilgrim, *Good News*, p. 159.

20. There are further summaries about the growth and situation of the Early
Church in Acts, such as 5.12-16; 6.7, 9.31, but they do not provide us with knowledge as regards the economic life of the early Christian community.

the literary and historical influences on Luke's descriptions of the communal life in Jerusalem.

a. *Echoes of Old Testament and Greek Utopian Ideals*
In general, it has been said that these summaries are introduced by Luke as fulfilment of a scriptural prophecy, Deut. 15.4, as well as 'the realization of the Greek ideal of community', that is, Greek Utopianism.[21] Thus it would be useful to look at this aspect in detail.

It is to be noticed that Deut. 15.4 (LXX, οὐκ ἔσται ἐν σοὶ ἐνδεής) is in fact echoed in 4.34.[22] At first Luke recognized this prophecy related to inheritance of land, and then showed how this feature of the eschatological prophecy of salvation is fulfilled in the early Christian community.[23] Some argue that this description, οὐδὲ γὰρ ἐνδεής τις ἦν ἐν αὐτοῖς, is idealized by the author,[24] but if we suppose that there was a sort of a common fund for charitable purposes, as described in the summaries in Acts,[25] it would not be hard to suppose that from this common fund all needs of the poor in the early Christian Community were sufficiently met, even if we cannot be sure of how long it lasted.[26]

21. Haenchen, *Acts*, p. 233; D.L. Mealand, 'Community of Goods and Utopian Allusions in Acts II-IV', *JTS* 28 (1977), pp. 96-99; Degenhardt, *Lukas*, p. 165; Conzelmann, *Acts*, p. 36; R.M. Grant, *Early Christianity and Society* (London: Collins, 1978), p. 100; I.H. Marshall, *Acts*, pp. 108-109; Pilgrim, *Good News*, pp. 151-52; Countryman, *Rich Christian*, p. 80; Schottroff and Stegemann, *Hope*, p. 118; M. Hengel, *Property and Riches in the Early Church* (London: SCM Press, 1974), p. 31; L.T. Johnson, *Sharing Possessions: Mandate and Symbol of Faith* (Philadelphia: Fortress Press, 1981), p. 128; H.J. Klauck, 'Gütergemeinschaft in der klassischen Antike in Qumran und im neuen Testament', *RevQ* 11 (1982–84), pp. 47-79 (69-70); Krodel, *Acts*, p. 117.
22. Haenchen, *Acts*, p. 231; Conzelmann, *Acts*, p. 36. We also find this motif in classical authors. Cf. Seneca, *Ep.* 90.38.
23. Klauck, 'Gütergemeinschaft', p. 74; Haenchen, *Acts*, p. 233.
24. For instance, Krodel, *Acts*, p. 117, views v. 34 as 'an unrealistic idealized picture', by which 'Luke challenged his readers to look at their own possessions in a new way and to see to it that there be **not a needy person among them in their community** [his bold]' (cf. p. 94). Conzelmann, *Acts*, p. 24, also rejects the historicity of this event in the Early Church, ascribing it to an idealized picture.
25. 2.45; 4.34-35; 5.2; 6.1.
26. Klauck, 'Gütergemeinschaft', pp. 69-70, infers that this idealized situation is the result of a certain process, which seems to imply a common fund: 'Der eingangs behauptete Idealzustand ("kein Bedürftiger") ist erst das Ergenis eines Prozesses'.
Apart from this prophecy, Klauck refers to a few words and phrases, such as 'ἐπὶ

The Greek ideal of Utopia appears in the summaries in the form of phrases, such as καρδία καὶ ψυχὴ μία, and (ἄ)παντα κοινά, or οὐδὲ(ν) ἴδιον, which are found frequently in Greek literature since Plato. First of all, as regards καρδία καὶ ψυχὴ μία (4.32), in Graeco-Roman writings, the phrase, ψυχὴ μία, does not seldom appear, describing a vital characteristic of the life of the Pythagorean communities as the prototype of an ideal community,[27] and is also cited as a proverb frequently in many writings of Greek and Latin literature.[28] It is known that the phrase, ψυχὴ μία, like *animus unus* or *mens una* or *spiritus unus* in Latin literature, was used to indicate 'real friendship'.[29] καρδία καὶ ψυχὴ also has some echoes of the LXX, because 'heart' and 'soul', as juxtaposed, appear frequently in the Old Testament, particularly in Deuteronomy, in the expression of 'with all thy heart and with all thy soul'.[30]

τὸ αὐτὸ' (2.43, 47), 'zu-Füße-legen' (4.35, 37; 5.2), νοσφίσασθαι (5.2, 3), in the summaries and the two individual incidents (Barnabas and Ananias) which have, he holds, some connection with the Old Testament. By presenting this evidence, he seems to contend that Luke made use of some Old Testament words and phrases (p. 74). This means that while writing the summaries and the two individual episodes, Luke did not solely depend upon Hellenistic ideals, but also on the Old Testament very deeply.

27. Iamblichus, *Vit. Pyth.* 30.167; Diodorus Siculus, *Bib. Hist.* 10.3, 5; Cicero, *De Off.* 1.17.56.
Possibly here problems may arise with regard to the connection between the late biographies written by Diogenes Laertius, Porphyrius, Iamblichus (3 CE) and original tradition about the Pythagorean community (6 BCE). A major clue to solve these problems is likely to be that the language about wealth in Plato is fairly similar to that in the late biographies, which appears to indicate a continuity between authentic tradition and the late biographies. When we look into this maxim in Plato, from the perspective of this continuity, it may be revealed that Plato himself relied on the Pythagorean tradition (L.T. Johnson, *Sharing*, pp. 139-40).

28. Diogenes Laertius, *Lives* 5.1.20; Diogenes Cynicus in *Stob.* 2.33.8; Plutarch, *Mor.* 478c (*De fraterno amore*); Aristotle, *Eth. Nic.* 1168b; Cicero, *De Am.* 25.92. Here it would not be irrelevant to note that Plato is said to regard humanity as a single entity (*State.* 274e; Gorgias, 507e-8a; cf. H.C. Baldry, *The Unity of Mankind in Greek Thought* [Cambridge: Cambridge University Press, 1965], pp. 76-77).

29. D.W. Van der Horst, 'Hellenistic Parallels to Acts', *JSNT* 35 (1989), pp. 37-46 (46); cf. A. Otto, *Die Sprichwörter und sprichwörtlichen Redensarten der Römer* (Leipzig: Teubner, 1890), pp. 25-26. Cicero, *SRosc.* 48.7: 'animus unus'; Silius Italicus, *Pun.* 11.307; Zeno of Verona, *Serm.* 2.27.10: 'mens una'.

30. Deut. 6.5; 10.12; 11.13; 13.3; 26.16; 30.2, 6, 10, etc. Cf. Klauck, 'Gütergemeinschaft', p. 74.

Secondly, it is to be noticed that 'among friends everything is common property' (κοινὰ τὰ φίλων) which is also a Cynic–Stoic–Pythagorean ideal, and is fairly close to 4.32b: οὐδὲ εἷς τι τῶν ὑπαρχόντων αὐτῷ ἔλεγεν ἴδιον εἶναι, ἀλλ᾽ ἦν αὐτοῖς ἅπαντα κοινά. It is said that in the Pythagorean communities which are considered the origin of this sort of common life, nobody claimed anything as his own possession, but everything was held in common among the members of the community.[31] This phrase appears frequently in Greek literature since Plato, as an indication of a feature of the ideal society.[32]

Thirdly, along with those two major phrases, οὐδὲν (or μηδέν) ἴδιον[33] is also introduced by Plato to describe an ideal state in the utopian passages in Greek literature.[34]

To sum up, that many Greek and Roman writers used such phrases as καρδία καὶ ψυχὴ μία, παντα κοινά, and οὐδὲ(ν) ἴδιον, may show their wishes that 'in some long vanished golden age, or in distant climes, or in some ideal future state people had shared, or did share, or would share, everything in common'.[35]

31. Iamblichus, *Vit. Pyth.* 30.167-68 (6.32.2; 19.92.21). There lie several factors behind this maxim. One of the three classic vices of Hellenistic morality is φιλάργυρια (cf. Lk. 16.14). Greek philosophers found that φιλάργυρια made people compete bitterly with each other and society to be divided by dissent. They also noted that in the relationship between friends there was no competition, which drove them to recognize that an ideal relationship in human society is the relationship between friends (L.T. Johnson, *Sharing*, pp. 119-20).

32. Plato, *Resp.* 4.424a; 5.449c; *Leg.* 739c. This phrase is also found in the following writings of Graeco-Roman literature: Aelius, 16.241; Aristotle, *Eth. Eud.* 1237b; *Eth. Nic.* 1159b; 1168b; *Pol.* 1263a—Aristotle's criticism of Plato's idea is that the possessions of friends ought to be common in use but not in ownership (cf. Euripides, *Androm.* 376-77); Clement of Alexandria, *Strom.* 1.12.122; Diogenes Laertius, *Lives* 4.53; 8.10; 110.11; Libanius, *Ep.* 1209.4; 1537.5; Olympiodorus, 4.88; Philo, *Vit. Mos.* 1.156-57; Plutarch, *Mor.* 490e; 644c; 767d; Theophrastus, 10.75.1; Cicero, *De. Off.* 1.16.51, 'amicorum esse communia omnia'; Ps.- Clem., *Recog.* 10.5.

33. Plato, *Criti.* 110d; *Resp.* 416d; 464d; 543b; *Tim.* 18b; cf. Diogenes Laertius, *Lives* 8.23.

34. It is remarkable that in one passage in Iamblichus we find a collection of words and phrases similar to those referred to in the summaries (*Vit. Pyth.* 167-68).

35. Mealand, 'Utopian Allusions', p. 98; Cf. Klauck, 'Gütergemeinschaft', p. 73; Aristotle, *Pol.* 1263a. Aristotle wrote:

If these facts are allowed for, it would seem sensible to hold that as a writer influenced by contemporary Hellenistic culture, Luke would have been familiar with those utopian words and phrases in Greek literature and would have taken them into account when he intended to present the Gospel to his Hellenistic readers. So in this sense, we may suggest that in 2.44-45 and 4.32-35 where he fused the proverbial passages expressing Greek ideals with Old Testament tradition,[36] Luke was placing the early Christian community at Jerusalem in the context of Hellenistic–Roman communal sharing, depicting it as fulfilling some of the Greek Utopian ideals, so that a Hellenistic congregation who would understand Luke's allusions to the Greek Utopian ideals might feel at home with this message of a newborn religion from Palestine.[37] Klauck puts this motif as follows:

> Man wird aber festhalten: Lukas wollte seinen hellenistischen Lesern zeigen, daß all die Träume und Wunschgebilde hellenistischen Sozial-denkens in der christlichen Urgemeinde vorbildlich verwirklicht wurden.[38]

To sum up, we find in these brief summaries that Luke intended to portray the nascent Christian community, 'as fulfilling the hopes, the promises, and the ideals, not only of Deuteronomy, but also that of the same Greek Utopianism'.[39]

> Such a system exists even now in outline in some states, showing that it is not impracticable, and especially in the ones that are well-administered parts of it are realized already and parts might be realized; for individuals while owning their property privately put their own possessions at the service of their friends and make use of their friends' possessions as common property; for instance in Sparta people use one another's slaves as virtually their own, as well as horses and hounds, and also use the produce in the fields throughout the country if they need provisions on a journey (*Pol.* 1263a.30-40).

36. Schottroff and Stegemann, *Hope*, p. 118; Haenchen, *Acts*, p. 231.

37. In relation to this feature of the summary passages, Horn, *Glaube*, pp. 47-49, claims that Luke did not idealize poverty itself here, but rather appealed to the well-to-do Christians in his community to help them recognize the importance of almsgiving for the sake of 'die Einheit der seine Gemeinde'.

38. 'However, one should understand that Luke wanted to show his Hellenistic readers that all the dreams and ideals of Hellenistic social thoughts are exemplarily put into practice in the Early Christian community'. Klauck, 'Gütergemeinschaft', p. 73.

39. Mealand, 'Utopian Allusions', p. 99; Haenchen, *Acts*, p. 233; Klauck, 'Gütergemeinschaft', pp. 72-74.

b. *Fanciful Idealization?*

Some deny that these idealistic conditions ever prevailed in the Jerusalem community and that Luke himself gave evidence of their failure.[40] The basis of this contention is that in 5.1-16 there is the notorious case of failure in making a common fund, and in 12.12, Mary, mother of John Mark, is described as still possessing a house of her own, which means that she had not sold it for the common purse; finally in 6.1-6 certain Hellenist widows in the original community were not provided for.[41] Those who insist on the above argument prefer to interpret the

40. Conzelmann, *Acts*, p. 24; Krodel, *Acts*, pp. 117-18. Regarding this matter, Haenchen, *Acts*, pp. 193-95, discussed a variety of suggestions which have been made to find out whether these summaries 'derived from a historically reliable source or from a worthless legendary source' (p. 193). His view on this aspect is that 'to us the summaries appear to flow entirely from the pen of Luke' (p. 195; cf. p. 233).

Meanwhile, Schottroff and Stegemann's position on this issue is in the middle, denying both options: 'the two passages [2.41-47; 4.32-37] do not give a historically faithful account of the primitive Jerusalem community, but neither are they simply idealizations of it on Luke's part. Rather, on the basis of information about the primitive community that we can no longer reconstruct, Luke here paints a picture of a Christian community as he thinks it should be' (*Hope*, p. 117).

41. Out of two incidents, Acts 6.1-6 and 5.1-11, Schottroff and Stegemann, *Hope*, draw a conclusion that there were 'social tensions between the respectable and those on whom they look down'. They argue that the widows of the Hellenists were not really poor, for in the Roman province the Hellenists were deemed as 'prosperous and respectable'. As evidence, they argue that the Hellenists 'were usually the first to receive Roman citizenship' (p. 118). So the widows of the Hellenists are asserted to be on a level with Ananias and Sapphira who were rich and prosperous Christians. The result of this argument is, therefore, that 'the respectable and prosperous', such as Ananias and Sapphira and the Hellenic widows, 'were undermining the ideal community' (pp. 118-19).

There may be some passages which refer to social tensions in the Gospel and Acts. But it is not likely that these incidents belong to such cases. In the case of the widows, there is clear textual evidence in favour of the fact that they were really poor. We see this from the use of the word διακονία. In Acts this root is employed seven times as a noun (1.17; 6.1, 4; 11.29; 12.25; 20.24; 21.19), and one time as a verb (διακονέω: 6.2). In most cases, it is used to mean ministry or service, but in two cases, i.e. 6.1; 11.29 (cf. 2 Cor. 8.4), it is used to mean *distribution of funds or food and relief*. In this connection, if the Hellenistic widows were not really poor, it was absolutely unnecessary for them to receive *daily* distribution of food. So in my opinion, using these two incidents as indicating social tensions as Schottroff and Stegemann do is too imaginative to be accepted in this context (cf. M. Hengel, *Between Jesus and Paul* [London: SCM Press, 1983], p. 16; H.W. Beyer, 'διακονία', *TDNT*, II, pp.

account of Barnabas in 4.36-37 as an exceptional case.[42] They assert that since it was exceptional, it did not reflect the common practice of the early Christian community as a whole. Thus they tend to regard the summaries as an exaggeration and a sheer idealization by the author from his 'socialist' point of view and that of his age.[43] In other words, they argue that here Luke is describing a picture of not what actually took place, but of what he thinks his community ought to be.

It must be conceded that there are a few words in these passages, such as οὐδὲν (or μηδέν) ἴδιον, and πάντα (or ἅπαντα) κοινά (2.44; 4.32), which represent an idealizing tendency in Luke's descriptions and make it impossible to deny that there is some degree of idealization. Nonetheless, major facts, such as selling property for the benefit of the poor in the community, sharing everything in common among the members of the community, and creating a common fund to relieve the poor in their difficulty, do not seem to be mere idealization.[44]

81-93). However, if the social tension may be understood in terms of cultural or racial perspectives, it is certainly present here.

42. Haenchen, *Acts*, p. 233.

43. Cone, *Rich and Poor*, pp. 143-58; Pilgrim, *Good News*, p. 148; Conzelmann, *Acts*, p. 24; Esler, *Community*, p. 196. L.T. Johnson, *Sharing*, p. 129, also asserts that the summaries can be seen as idealized, but his reason for that is different. He argues that Luke did not expect that a strict community of goods could be practised in later Christian communities.

In terms of a community of goods, his point may be right, but in the light of the exhortation to almsgiving, his argument cannot stand. For critical judgments on the practice of community of possessions themselves, see L.T. Johnson, *Sharing*, pp. 131-32.

44. Schottroff and Stegemann, *Hope*, view the distribution of wealth and goods among the members of the Early Church as 'an equalization of ownership', and argue that Luke 'thinks of the equalization in simple arithmetic terms' (p. 119). But it is doubtful that distribution according to the need of each one should be regarded as 'an equalization in simple arithmetic terms'.

What is to be recognized here is not an equalization, but the fact that they shared everything in common (πάντα κοινά). The ultimate aim of distributing according to the need of each person is not to equalize the poor with the rich, but to care for the poor who could not have survived without help from the wealthy.

In this context, when the meaning ἰσότης (ἴσος) is examined, what is revealed primarily is not an equality of size or number, but an equality of value or force, which is sometimes equally significant. For instance, ἰσότης can mean 'fair distribution' in terms of the Greek political and legal structure, and so in the Greek states it is a basic principle of democracy along with freedom (Aristotle, *Pol.* 1291b.35; 1279a.9) (G. Stählin, 'ἴσος/ἰσότης', *TDNT*, III, pp. 343-55 [346]). Such a notion of ἰσότης as

In relation to this, we might claim that there is every likelihood that historical fact lies behind this description.

As internal evidence for this claim, we may point out two incidents in Acts which are related to making the common fund, that is, the incidents of Barnabas (4.36-37) and Ananias and Sapphira (5.1-11). The story of Barnabas is here introduced as a typical concrete case, showing how the early Christians at Jerusalem in fact pooled their wealth into the common fund, while that of Ananias and Sapphira is here referred to as a failure to do this.[45] These two incidents appear to be rooted in history, because the cases bear the names of individuals involved, of whom Barnabas in particular later appears frequently in Acts as an apostle.[46] If we allow some measure of historicity here, we would be uneasy to accept the possibility that this communal life described in the summary passages is a purely idealized picture by the author.[47]

As for external evidence, if we compare the actual practice of the common life in the Qumran Community, one other contemporary Jewish group which is known to have adopted this way of life,[48] and

---

expressed in Greek society may be related to ἰσότης in 2 Cor. 8.13-14 where it is employed as criterion (ἐξ ἰσότητος) and as goal (ὅπως γένηται ἰσότης). From this examination it can be seen that what is emphasized in 2 Cor. 8.13-14 is the balance between the need of the poor on the one side and the superfluity of the rich on the other, which should be implemented by mutual assistance.

Therefore, from the above discussion we come to conclude that although ἰσότης can imply arithmetic equality, that is not the only meaning it has, and since it is used to mean qualitative equality, i.e. fair distribution, 'equalization in simple arithmetic terms' which Schottroff and Stegemann argue as regards distribution of wealth and goods among the early Christians seems hardly appropriate (cf. Pilgrim, *Good News*, p. 150; Neil, *Acts*, p. 93).

45. Here the incident of Ananias and Sapphira does not appear to contradict the features of the communal life of the early Christian community, because, according to 4.34, not all the members of the Early Church sold their property and gave their proceeds to the apostles, but only those who owned lands and houses. Thus the case may be regarded as a failure in terms of total devotion, but it is not to be regarded as a failure which destroys the entire system of the common fund as well as the communal life as a whole. This point will be discussed further later on when we come to compare the early Christian community with the Qumran community in terms of the common fund and meal.

46. 9.27; 11.2, 24-30; 13.2-4, 43, 46, 50; 14.12; 15.2, 12, 22, 26, 35-39.

47. See n. 37 above.

48. 1QS 1.12; 6.16-20. Contra Conzelmann, *Acts*, p. 24. Meanwhile, S.E. Johnson ('The Dead Sea Manual of Discipline and the Jerusalem Church of Acts', in

also what is said of the communal life of the Essenes,[49] it may well be that these remarkable features in the summaries actually took place in the Jerusalem community, at least in the early years of its life, whether or not the period during which they took place was short.[50]

Even if we acknowledge this fact of fulfilment in the early Christian community at Jerusalem, nonetheless, we do not need to conclude that Luke expected that it would necessarily be achieved in subsequent church situations. Even in the Jerusalem community itself, the 'ideal' may not have lasted long. Consequently, what we can conjecture with regard to this matter is that this fulfilment was attained only in the early period of the Jerusalem community,[51] and used by the author to encourage his readers to find a major source of inspiration in the communal life of the Jerusalem Christian community and to act in a similar way. Luke did not necessarily intend to encourage his community and subsequent Christian communities to establish a complete community of goods, but only that the exhortations to almsgiving given by Jesus should be fulfilled. Consequently, a community of goods itself does not appear to be essential. What really matters is rather that almsgiving was practised in a different type of communal sharing in a community of goods, such as that of the early Christian community.[52] This

K. Stendahl [ed.], *The Scrolls and the New Testament* [London: SCM Press, 1958], pp. 129-36), enumerates eight points of similarity between the Jerusalem church and the Qumran sect.

49. Josephus, *Ant.* 15.371. See the Excursus, below.

50. I.H. Marshall, *Acts*, p. 84; Contra Conzelmann, *Acts*, p. 24. Meanwhile, Klauck's conclusion regarding this element seems probable; 'Der Vergleich der Essenerberichte bei PHILO und JOSEPHUS mit den Texten aus Qumran hat erwiesen, daß auch unter vielfach überlagerten und verzerrten Traditionen verläßliche Nachrichten geborgen werden können. Angesichts dieses parallelen Sachverhalts wäre es ein methodischer Fehler, alle Angaben bei Lukas als unhistorisch über Bord zu werfen' ('Gütergemeinschaft', p. 76).

51. If we take into account the number of the early Christian community as noted in the early part of Acts (1.15 = 120; 2.41 = 3000; 4.4 = 5000, men only), it may be hard to think that the common life could function for long in such a large community. In this context, Klauck comments that 'Um die organisatorische Bewältigung der Gütergemeinschaft, die angesichts solcher Zahlen illusorisch bleiben muß, hat sich der Redaktor wenig gekümmert' ('Gütergemeinschaft', p. 69).

52. Horn (*Glaube*, pp. 39-49) argues that Luke intended to put emphasis on 'Almosenethik' by inserting καθότι ἄν τις χρείαν εἶχεν (2.45; 4.35) on purpose in each summary, a motif of almsgiving for the poor that is absent in the pre-Lukan traditions of the two individual episodes, i.e. 4.36-39 (Barnabas's contribution) and

means that Luke introduced an ideal at least partially attainable. Hence, Horn states this aspect clearly: 'die intendierte Sache bleibt trotz der idealisierendem Sprache praktikabel'.[53] In other words, we may suggest that Luke holds up the actual practice of the common life in which almsgiving was put into practice in the Jerusalem community 'as a mirror for his own community and hopes the latter will be guided by it'.[54]

c. *Relation of the Summaries to the Moral Imperatives*
The summaries, whether they are portrayals of actual historical circumstances or not, and the passages referring to almsgiving in Acts, may not be framed as imperatives like those exhortations in the Gospel. However it seems to me that although they do not take the imperative form, they actually play the same role in Acts. The ground for this argument is as follows: It is easy for Luke to employ imperatives in the Gospel, for he is introducing the person and ministry of Jesus who was regarded as the final authority in the early Christian community, since he was believed in as their Messiah and Lord. However, in Acts, the Apostles who would be the next final authority are depicted as witnesses of Jesus (1.8, 22; 3.15), and so they seem to be seen as ones who do not have their own messages, but only deliver Jesus' teachings,[55] at least as far as the motif of almsgiving is concerned.

Therefore, it would be quite appropriate for Luke to describe in Acts the fulfilment of Jesus' teachings on almsgiving rather than to introduce those of the Apostles time and again. In other words, it can be said that the fulfilment of Jesus' injunctions on almsgiving can be regarded as a refined form of imperative on almsgiving,[56] because it

5.1-11 (Ananias's and Sapphira's failure). In other words, according to Horn, what Luke wanted to point out in writing these incidents and summaries is an exhortation to the wealthy Christians of his community to give alms to the poor, which Luke desired to take place for the unity of the community: 'Was Lk von weiner Gemeinde erwartet, projeziert er paradigmatisch zurück in die Zeit der Urgemeinde' (*Glaube*, p. 43). Behind this statement of his lies Plümacher's assertion that 'die geschene Geschichte . . . fähig sein müsse, gegenwärtiges Geschehen inaugurieren und lenken zu helfen' (*Glaube*, p. 46).

53. '. . . in spite of idealized expressions the intended matter remains practicable'. Horn, *Glaube*, p. 36.

54. Schottroff and Stegemann, *Hope*, p. 118; cf. Krodel, *Acts*, p. 117.

55. For instance, 20.35.

56. In this context, one thing which attracts our attention is that ἐλεημοσύνη appears four times more in Acts (3.2, 3; 9.36; 10.2, 4, 31; 24.17) than in Luke

appears to be introduced by Luke as an example to be emulated by his community.[57]

3. *The Problem of Continuity between Luke and Acts*

Having examined the individual examples of almsgiving and the summary passages that allude to the practice of almsgiving in the Early Church, we now turn to the issue of continuity in this motif of almsgiving between Luke and Acts. It is interesting to observe that apart from 20.35, the dominical command that Paul quotes in his sermon, all the other cases we have discussed above describe the actual practice of almsgiving performed by some individuals and churches. We know from earlier discussion of this theme in the Gospel that there occur only two incidents in which Jesus' teaching on almsgiving is actualized among the followers of Jesus, that is, the Galilaean women and Zacchaeus, and the rest of the material related to the theme of wealth and poverty is comprised of Jesus' teaching and exhortation. In this context, we may suggest that these two incidents of the practice of almsgiving in the Gospel, functioning as a link between the Gospel and Acts in terms of the motif of almsgiving, foreshadow the full implementation of the teaching and exhortation on almsgiving later in the Early Church. Thus from this contrast between the Gospel and Acts, we may deduce that Luke wanted to show to his community that the disciples at the

(11.41; 12.33), although it may not be regarded as a definite factor in this matter. Nonetheless, it should be considered that the author's more frequent use of this word in Acts than in the Gospel can reveal something about his intent to accentuate the actual practice of almsgiving in Acts.

Meanwhile, after reviewing the usage of ἐλεημοσύνη in the Jewish and Hellenistic literature and the New Testament, R. Heiligenthal ('Werke der Barmherzigkeit oder Almosen?', *NovT* 25 [1983], pp. 289-301 [301]), concludes that 'Die Übernahme das pagan-friechischen Terminus für tugendhafte Tat (καλόν/ἀγαθόν) in die Sprache des helle-nistischen Judentums und des frühen Christentums vollzog sich unter Aufnahme und in Verschmelzung mit jüdisch-orientalischer Wertvorstellung, für die ursprünglich die Septuaginta den spezifischen Terminus ἐλεημοσύνη prägte'.

57. This point may also be related to the different nature of Luke's two-volume work, that is, the Gospel as record of the ministry and person of Jesus, and the Acts as history of the Christian movement. In this sense, it is supposed that there is not much room for imperatives in Acts, for it is designed particularly to sketch the growth of the Christian movement from Jerusalem to Rome.

time of the Early Church followed this command of Jesus faithfully,[58] so that the dominical teaching on almsgiving was fully kept and materialized in the lives of individuals as well as of churches. By doing this, Luke may have sought to encourage his readers to do the same thing in their circumstances emulating the examples set by the early churches and their individual members. In other words, what Luke really wanted to show was that since Jesus' teachings on almsgiving were actually implemented in the practice of the primitive Christian community, Luke's community should follow the exemplary model of its predecessor in distributing their wealth to the poor and sharing it with the destitute in their community. In this regard, introducing descriptions of the actual practice of almsgiving in Acts can be seen as a sort of positive injunction to almsgiving. So we can see here some continuity between the Gospel traditions and the early Christian community in terms of Luke's theology of almsgiving.[59]

4. *Excursus: Similarities and Dissimilarities between the Jerusalem Community and the Qumran Community*

In this section, I shall discuss similarities and dissimilarities between the Jerusalem community and the Qumran community, because it appears that these two communities may have shared similar patterns of life in a couple of aspects in the early period of our era. The discussion which follows will not be comprehensive, dealing with all the features of the systems and beliefs that were prevalent in the communities, but is confined to two major traits, a common fund and a common meal, which are most germane to our theme of almsgiving.

a. *The Qumran Community*
In many aspects the Qumran community was a unique society at that time. The people at Qumran, badly disillusioned by the corrupt religious leaders and the religious activities prevalent in Jerusalem around the Temple,[60] pursued independent lives, forming their own commu-

58. R.J. Cassidy, *Jesus, Politics and Society* (Maryknoll, NY: Orbis Books, 1978), pp. 147-48; cf. Pilgrim, *Good News*, p. 151.
59. Cf. Esler, *Community*, p. 169.
60. Such disillusion prompted them to interpret the Torah, Calendar and the Temple worship differently from orthodox Judaism (E.J. Pryke, 'Beliefs and Practices of the Qumran Community', *CQR* 168 [1967], pp. 314-25 [316-17]).

nity on an isolated site by the Dead Sea far from Jerusalem the capital city, in order to preserve their pure faith in the Torah and the commandments given to the chosen people like them. Their religious enthusiasm to keep their faith pure and undefiled was made manifest in their practical lives, so that religiously they ignored the official Temple and

replaced it with their own pattern of worship and kept a calendar different from the orthodox one, that is, the solar calendar, and economically, as mentioned above, they adopted a communal way of life, putting everything they possessed at the disposal of the community.

It is widely known that the people at Qumran surrendered their private property and possessions, and handed them over to the bursar of the community when they were admitted into full membership of the community. They did this in order to create a common fund.[61] From this pooled resource all the needs of members in the community were met evenly and properly. Consequently, it can be imagined that in that society there were neither poor nor rich, so everybody was equal in respect of economic life.[62] In short, it was a communal mode of life that the people at Qumran had in their remote community by the Dead Sea during the intertestamental period.[63] Here it is in this highly unusual

61. In the matter of private property, the Zadokite document indicates private ownership (CD9.10-16; 14.12-13), but the Manual of Discipline does not. Thus although the way of life in both organizations was not identical, what is common is that both of them had a system of common funds, out of which the poor, the orphans, the homeless and widows were provided for (G. Vermes, *The Dead Sea Scrolls in English* [London: Penguin Books, 1987], p. 15; Pryke, 'Beliefs', p. 319; cf. T.S. Beall, *Josephus's Description of the Essenes Illustrated by the Dead Sea Scrolls* [Cambridge: Cambridge University Press, 1988], pp. 126, 129).

62. In relation to this feature, Mendels contends that 'It must be emphasized that this concept of total cooperation and equality is exceptional in light of other ways of life proposed in antiquity' (D. Mendels, 'Hellenistic Utopia and the Essenes', *HTR* 72 [1979], pp. 207-22 [212]). However, as we can see clearly from the texts, all members of the Qumran sect were not equal in religious order and rank (1QS 5.20–6.8). Cf. G. Vermes, *The Dead Sea Scrolls: Qumran in Perspective* (London: SCM Press, 1988), pp. 90-92.

63. Some have raised an objection that there was private property at Qumran, and so it is more complicated than just to say that it was a society where a communism was actually put into practice (C. Rabin, *Qumran Studies* [Oxford: Oxford University Press, 1957], pp. 22-56; J.T. Milik, *Ten Years of Discovery in the Wilderness of Judaea* [London: SCM Press, 1959], p. 102). However, there is sufficient evidence that 'some form of community of goods was practised at Qumran, at least in the early

form of economic life at Qumran that we find a very similar pattern to that described in the summary passages of Acts at issue, 2.44-45 and 4.32-35.

b. *Relation of the Qumran Community to the Communities of Essenes*
In this context, it would be helpful here to distinguish the Qumran community from the communities of Essenes, for they do not appear to be precisely the same organization.

It is held by a number of scholars that the sectarians who deviated from mainstream Judaism and lived independently consisted of two types of organization: one is 'the enclosed celibate order' to which the Manual of Discipline is related, and the other is 'the open order' which has a connection with the Zadokite Document.[64] The former is known to have resided at Qumran, and the latter, on the other hand, to have been scattered in small towns and villages.[65] Philo said that the Essenes lived mainly in many towns of Judaea,[66] but Josephus argued that they resided in every town of Palestine.[67] According to Pliny, they avoided cities because they believed that inhabitants of cities were corrupt and immoral.[68]

In addition to this geographical difference, differences in other areas between the two groups are also to be pointed out.

First, a vitally different point is found in their religious attitude towards the Jewish cult. The town sect in the community revealed in the Zadokite Document criticized corruption of the priesthood in the Temple, regarding it as impure and illegitimate, but is still seen to have had a loose connection with the Temple. The desert sect at Qumran, as revealed in the Manual of Discipline, however, is seen to have had a more hostile attitude towards it, and to have cut off completely the connection with the Temple and the Jewish cult, for they were convinced that the Temple was 'a place of pollution where unlawful worship was

years of the life of the sect' (D.L. Mealand, 'Community of Goods at Qumran', *TZ* 31 [1975], pp. 129-39 [129]). Cf. Beall, *Essenes*, p. 45; A.R.C. Leaney, *The Rule of Qumran and its Meaning* (London: SCM Press, 1966), pp. 122-23; M.A. Knibb, *The Qumran Community* (Cambridge: Cambridge University Press, 1987), p. 126; Mendels, 'Utopia', p. 212.
    64. Pryke, 'Beliefs', p. 319.
    65. Vermes, *The Dead Sea Scrolls in English*, p. 15.
    66. Philo, *Apol.* 1.
    67. Josephus, *War* 2.124.
    68. Pliny, *Nat. Hist.* 5.73.

offered following an invalid calendar'.[69] Second, another difference
between the groups is found in the composition of the community
council: at Qumran it consists of three priests and twelve laymen,[70]
while at the sect of the Zadokite Document there are four priests and six
laymen.[71] Third, the laws of the Zadokite Document, in contrast to the
Manual of Discipline, include regulations regarding private property.[72]

When contrasting the desert sect with the town sect, Vermes argues
that one may at first find more differences than similarities between
the two sects, but despite the differences, the two groups of sectaries
were not totally separated but connected with each other in the light of
'doctrine, aims, and principles'.[73] Besides, on some grounds of literary and archaeological evidence, he contends that 'this was a single
religious movement with two branches'.[74]

c. *The Common Fund*
Of the two sectarian groups, our attention is here mainly directed to
the Qumran sect, because its similarities to the Jerusalem church have
often been commented upon, in the matter of its common fund and
common meals.

1. *Similarities*. Above all, what attracts our attention most in this
topic is that the people at Qumran made 'a common fund', as already
mentioned. In other words, it can be described as 'common ownership
of property', which means that discarding private property they shared
in common any property and possessions that they owned.[75] Here in

69. Vermes, *The Dead Sea Scrolls in English*, pp. 1-18; G. Vermes and M.D.
Goodman, *The Essenes according to the Classical Sources* (Sheffield: JSOT Press,
1989), p. 11. Cf. B. Gärtner, *The Temple and the Community in Qumran and the New
Testament* (Cambridge: Cambridge University Press, 1965), pp. 16-46.

70. 1QS 8.1-2.

71. CD 10.4-7.

72. CD 9.10-16; 14.12-13; Beall, *Essenes*, p. 45; G. Vermes, 'Essenes and History', *JJS* 32 (1981), p. 20. Concerning the Calendar that the Qumran Community
kept, see Milik, *Discovery*, pp. 108-13.

73. Vermes, *The Dead Sea Scrolls in English*, p. 16.

74. Vermes, *The Dead Sea Scrolls in English*, pp. 16, 17-18. For more detail of
similarities and dissimilarities between the Essenes and the Qumran sect, see the recent
monograph (1989) produced by Vermes and Goodman (*Classical Sources*).

75. 1QS 1.11-13; 3.2; 5.1-2; 6.17-22. Cf. 1QpHab. 12.9-10; Josephus, *War*
2.122; *Ant.* 18.20; Philo, *Hyp.* 11.2, 4; *Omn. Prob. Lib.* 76-77, 86. 'The strongest

this highly unusual form of economic life at Qumran, we find a very similar pattern to that described in the summary passages of Acts at issue, 2.44-45; 4.32-35.

Allowing for the historical context of both communities (Qumran and Jerusalem), it may be possible to argue that the Early Church at Jerusalem was influenced in one way or another by the Qumran system of economic life, for it would seem that the Qumran community in which in a sense there were no poor might have been seen by the early Christian community as an ideal society prophesied in the Old Testament (Deut. 15.4).[76]

The basis for this argument is that since Christianity was just newborn out of the womb of Judaism, it does not appear to have had strict organizations and regulations for maintaining its community,[77] and that since the Qumran community had existed just prior to the early Christian community, and, as pointed out previously, the two communities had in common a number of similarities, although different in some other respects, it would be difficult to exclude the possibility that the early Christian community was influenced by the Qumran community to some extent, particularly as far as the system of the common fund is concerned, as other aspects in the early Christian community, such as the tradition of almsgiving, were influenced by Judaism.

Following up the findings of his predecessors, such as H. Bardtke and W. Tyloch, M. Weinfeld makes a point that 'the organizational pattern of the Qumran sect, and likewise the penal code contained in 1QS are congruent with those of the cultic associations of Ptolemaic Egypt and of other regions of the Hellenistic and Roman world'.[78] For instance

---

bond joining the members together was an absolute common ownership of property' (E. Schürer, *The History of the Jewish People in the Age of Jesus Christ* [Edinburgh: T. & T. Clark, 1979], II, p. 565).

76. In addition to this, many similarities between the two communities have been taken note of in terms of various topics, such as the *eschaton* (H. Braun, 'The Qumran Community', in H.G. Schultz [ed.], *Jesus in his Time* [London: SPCK, 1971], p. 72; Pryke, 'Beliefs', pp. 196-99) and Messiah.

77. 'Organization was kept to a minimum, and in view of the intensive expectation of the return of Jesus, further forward planning was completely absent' (Hengel, *Property*, p. 34). Cf. F.F. Bruce, 'Jesus and the Gospels in the Light of the Scrolls', in M. Black (ed.), *The Scrolls and Christianity* (London: SPCK, 1969), p. 77.

78. M. Weinfeld, *The Organizational Pattern and the Penal Code of the Qumran Sect* (Göttingen: Vandenhoeck & Ruprecht, 1986), p. 7.

to support his argument, he enumerates such procedures as examination of the candidates for entry in the sect, approval of the candidates
by the votes of the assembly, and the registration of a member, which
are common both to the Qumran sect and the Graeco-Roman guilds
and associations. Although similarities between the organizations of the
Qumran community and contemporaneous Hellenistic communities are
to be noted, it should also be recognized that there are conspicuous differences between them, as Weinfeld himself reveals.[79]

In this context, it seems to me that it may be worth pointing out the
overlapping aspects between the Qumran community and the Graeco-
Roman guilds and associations in terms of the organization and the penal
code, but it should not be inferred that the Qumran community was
just one of those Hellenistic associations of that time. For, although in
Hellenistic associations we hear of mutual aid among the members of
an association and commands to care for the poor,[80] yet there was no
system of pooling individual property to create the common funds,
which are found uniquely in the Qumran community and the early
Christian community. Therefore, at least as far as the common fund is
concerned, some influence of the Qumran community on the early
Christian community is to be acknowledged.[81]

2. *Dissimilarities.* Although similarities are found in both communities, as far as the common fund is concerned, nonetheless it does not
mean that the Jerusalem community simply imitated and copied the
practice employed at Qumran. It seems to me that although the Jerusalem community might have been influenced by the Qumran way of
life, it did not simply emulate the Qumran practice, but adapted it for
its convenience in the interests of the welfare of its members. To support this assertion, I shall discuss a few discrepancies between the two
communities in what follows.

First, in terms of the motive for creating a common fund, while at
Qumran it was a means of maintaining its communal life in an isolated
region, it was an expression of loving care on behalf of the poor in
the Jerusalem community. In Acts there is only one concrete incident
recorded in which the common fund of the Jerusalem community was
used: daily distribution of food proffered to the widows in the commu-

---

79. Weinfeld, *Pattern*, pp. 46-47.
80. Weinfeld, *Pattern*, pp. 31-34.
81. Cf. Weinfeld, *Pattern*, p. 49.

nity (6.1). That widows were provided with a daily dole appears to correspond to the summary passages, 2.45; 4.34-35, which may be introduced as further evidence to define the purpose of the common fund.

There is another aspect of the common fund that makes this difference more obvious. Although it is not explicitly expressed in the summaries, we can imagine that one way in which the Christian common fund was used for financial support for the church leaders, that is, the Apostles, who left their jobs as fishermen, tax collectors, and so on, and thus were now penniless (3.6; 6.4). So it would not be hard to suppose that they were also provided with some financial help appropriate for their jobs as church leaders, as widows and other less fortunate people in the community might have been treated. It is obvious that this sort of fund cannot be regarded as almsgiving in the proper sense of the word. Therefore, here we are able to notice another important feature of the Christian common fund that does not have a direct parallel in the system of the common fund of the Qumran community.

Secondly, at Qumran the surrender of property was required of all members entering into the community, whereas, generally speaking, it was not required of all members in the Jerusalem community. For instance, in 12.12 Mary the mother of John Mark is seen to still have her own house in Jerusalem that accommodated a prayer meeting, that is, she did not sell it and hand over the proceeds to the community;[82] in 2.46, breaking bread is known to have been held in the houses of believers, and in 5.42 the early Christians taught and preached the gospel at home. From these accounts we can see that some members of the Jerusalem community did not in fact sell their houses.[83] This is despite the fact that the wording of 4.34 (ὅσοι) suggests a uniform practice. Thus we may conclude that not all of the members of the community sold their properties and handed them over to the community.[84]

---

82. Haenchen, *Acts*, p. 233. According to Meeks, that she had a house which accommodated meetings of worship and prayer at the time of the Early Church denotes that she must have been reasonably well-off (Meeks, *Urban Christians*, pp. 60-61).

83. As Haenchen points out (*Acts*, p. 233), this was 'entirely appropriate' because the primitive Church needed houses in which worship and common meals might be held. Cf. Klauck, 'Gütergemeinschaft', p. 69; Pilgrim, *Good News*, p. 150.

84. In relation to this aspect, some raise a different argument referring to Barnabas's surrender that the surrender of property is an obligation required of only *an inner group*, i.e. leaders of the church (contra this argument, see B.J. Capper, 'The Interpretation of Acts 5.4', *JSNT* 19 [1983], pp. 117-31 [122]). But here also, apart

In relation to this aspect, one thing which attracts our attention here is that κτήτορες χωρίων ἢ οἰκιῶν in 4.34 in general refer to the big landowners.[85] Then what may emerge from this fact is that the rich in the early Christian community created a common fund in having sold their houses or lands in order to help the poor like the helpless widows in the community. If this is the case, what is remarkable in the summary passages is that it is the exact fulfilment of what Jesus in the gospel exhorted the rich to do, so that the Jerusalem community had a common fund to give alms to the poor.

Thirdly, with respect to the surrender of property, there is also a difference between the two communities. According to the Rule of the Community, anyone who desires to enter into the Qumran community should bring all his property into the community,[86] and go through the probation period which normally takes more than two years.[87] During this period, his property is handed over to the treasurer of the community and placed in a blocked account.[88] After that, that is, at the end of a second year, if he is accepted as a full member, all of his property is finally mingled with the common fund of the community.[89] It is compulsory for all members without any exception. However, if a novice is deemed unsuitable, his property will be returned to him at the end of his probationary period.[90]

Conversely, in the Jerusalem community, first of all, the surrender of property is usually seen as not compulsory but voluntary.[91] This

form the Barnabas incident, no one like him can be found in Acts, which also makes this argument precarious.

85. Capper, 'Interpretation', pp. 121-22.

86. 1QS 1.12.

87. 1QS 6.13-23. Cf. Josephus, *War* 2.137-39.

88. 1QS 6.20. Cf. Josephus, *War* 2.122-23; Philo, *Apol.* 10.

This point is explained well in comparison to the system of the primitive Church in Capper's other article, '"In der Hand des Ananias. . ." Erwägungen zu 1 QS 6.20 und der urchristlichen Gütergemeinschaft', *RevQ* 12 (1985), pp. 223-36. Cf. Leaney, *Rule*, p. 196; P. Wernberg-Moller, *The Manual of Discipline* (Leiden: E.J. Brill, 1957), pp. 109-10.

89. 1QS 6.22.

90. In the other Hellenistic cultic communities, we hear that there were some admission procedures, such as oath on entry, registration, examination, decision by lot, and probationary period, but surrender of private property was seen only in the Qumran community (Weinfeld, *Pattern*, pp. 21-23, 78).

91. Josephus, *War* 2.122, 124-27; Philo, *Omn. Prob. Lib.* 77; Bruce, *Acts*, p. 113; I.H. Marshall, *Acts*, p. 84; Pilgrim, *Good News*, p. 149; Knibb, *Qumran*,

feature of the Christian community can be found in 2.44-45 and 4.32, 34 and also in two incidents such as the contribution of Barnabas (4.36-37), and of Ananias and Sapphira (5.1-11). From these incidents and passages we find that the early Christians were not forced to contribute their property to the community, but moved to merge their assets voluntarily as needs were encountered. So it seems right for Derrett to argue that 'The church did *not* have a rule that property should be legally pooled, should cease to be the legal asset of the proselyte'.[92]

Secondly, from those two verses, 2.44 and 4.32, we have the impression that the early Christians, filled with, and out of spiritual enthusiasm generated by the miraculous works of the Holy Spirit (4.31; 2.43; 4.33), desired to share their properties in common and to sell them with a view to meeting the needs of the poor fellow Christians in their community.[93] Since these acts seemed to be performed out of religious enthusiasm, and since they were still expecting the imminent *parousia* (1.5-6, 11), which might affect their attitude towards property so that 'capital would not be of great long-term value',[94] it would be probable that as compared with the Qumran community, regulations concerning the common fund in the primitive Christian community were not strictly organized.[95]

p. 82; L. Mowry, *The Dead Sea Scrolls and the Early Church* (Indiana: University of Notre Dame Press, 1966), p. 67.

92. J.D.M. Derrett, 'Ananias, Sapphira, and the Right of Property', in *Studies in the New Testament* (Leiden: E.J. Brill, 1977), p. 195.

93. Haenchen, *Acts*, p. 232, makes the point that the effect of the Holy Spirit led not only to the joyful and bold Christian proclamation, but also to Christian *koinonia* and communalism of goods. Cf. Bruce, *Acts*, p. 108.

94. Mowry, *Scrolls*, p. 67, holds a different position that since the Early Church did not manage the common fund as carefully as did the Qumran community, it had to face economical disaster, so that Paul collected relief funds from the Gentile churches. But when Acts 11.27-30 is taken into account, the poverty of the Jerusalem church does not seem to have resulted from the mismanagement of the common fund, but from the frequent famines during the reign of Claudius, among which the famine of Judaea around 46 CE was recorded as particularly severe (Haenchen, *Acts*, pp. 62-63; I.H. Marshall, *Acts*, p. 204). Josephus wrote about this Judaean famine as follows: 'It was in the administration of Tiberius Alexander that the great famine occurred in Judaea, during which Queen Helena bought grain from Egypt for large sums and distributed it to the needy, as I have stated above' (*Ant.* 20.101; cf. 20.51; 3.320).

95. Hengel's contrast of the Qumran community with the early Christian community with regard to organization of the common funds (*Property*, pp. 32-33) might

To conclude, these two features, that the surrender of property is voluntary as well as unorganized, make the system of the Jerusalem community quite different from that of the Qumran community. In addition to this aspect, it is to be borne in mind that at the Qumran community a novice shared material possessions with other members once-for-all on entry, whereas in the Jerusalem community the poor members were assisted regularly and continuously through the common fund which was gathered by way of the rich's voluntary contributions.[96]

With regard to these features of the Jerusalem community, Capper presents a unique argument that behind the incident of Ananias and Sapphira[97] lies a public and organized entrance procedure along with strict regulations about a novice's handing over property to the common funds of the community which are found in the Qumran community. His evidence for the argument is that those who sold their property laid the proceeds at the feet of Apostles (4.35, 37; 5.2). The entrance procedure, according to Capper, consists of two stages. The first stage is provisional, so if a novice wanted to leave the group after he had had a taste of communal life experiencing 'the possessions-lessness and the loss of independence discipleship involved',[98] he could ask to retrieve his property. Capper calls it 'an introductory catechetical

---

be helpful in this regard. Cf. Leaney, *Rule*, p. 122. I.H. Marshall, *Acts*, p. 84, also contends that 'We should not, therefore, conclude that becoming a believer necessarily entailed living in a tight-knit Christian community'.

96. Here notice should be taken of the tense of many verbs used in 2.45 and 4.34-35: ἐπίπρασκον, διεμέριζον (2.45); ὑπῆρχον, ἔφερον (4.34); ἐτίθουν, διεδίδετο, εἶχεν (4.35). All these verbs are imperfect. As generally known, the imperfect tense in Greek denotes a continuous or repeated activity, which is distinguished from the aorist tense that denotes a once-for-all activity. In line with this viewpoint, Haenchen, *Acts*, p. 192, reinterprets Acts 2.45 as follows: 'Whenever there is need of money for the poor of the congregation, one of the property-owners sells his piece of land or valuables, and the proceeds are given to the needy.'

97. Arguing that there is 'no historical kernel' in this story, Conzelmann, *Acts*, p. 37, regards this episode as one of 'popular and legendary stories', and also asserts that Acts 5.4 'is a description from the standpoint of conduct (sharing in love) rather than result (sharing of "property")'. In spite of this argument, as a parallel with Acts 5.1-2, he refers to the case of the Qumran community (1QS 6.24-25) which describes the punishment incurred by anyone who lies to the community as regards the surrender of his property to it.

98. Capper, 'Interpretation', p. 124.

phase',[99] which he asserts corresponds to Peter's remark to Ananias, 'while it remained unsold, did it not remain your own?' (5.4a).

The second stage is final commitment. If a novice decided to remain in the community, the proceeds that he brought to the community would be fully transferred and added to the common funds. Till then, even though he passed through the first stage bringing the whole sum of sold property to the community, legally it would still belong to him. This element is found in 5.4b, 'after it was sold, was it not in your power?'

For supporting evidence for his argument, he draws attention to the fact that the Qumran community and the Pythagorean community had also practised communal sharing of property and possessions, keeping the two-stage entrance procedure.

His argument is very interesting but seems too imaginative.

Against his argument, first of all, what I want to point out is that not all Christians were supposed to sell their property and bring the proceeds to the common resources of the community—for instance, the two cases, 12.12 and 2.46, referred to as evidence earlier in this chapter. Therefore, as Capper himself admits, it is likely that 'only the wealthier', such as Barnabas and Ananias, sold their property to contribute to the community.[100]

Secondly, with regard to the timing of Ananias's expression of intent to contribute, I agree with Capper in that the couple did not make a special vow, something like *korban*, the Jewish custom of dedication which Lake and Cadbury suggest.[101] From the text, we see that they made a decision to give a contribution to the community, and so were understood by the community to be giving all the money from that property.[102]

But when they actually purported to bring and lay their property at the Apostles' feet, they seem to have been tempted to retain part of the

99. Capper, 'Interpretation', p. 125.

100. Capper, 'Interpretation', p. 122. Cf. Haenchen, *Acts*, p. 233: 'only a few Christians can have possessed houses or real estate'.

101. Capper, 'Interpretation', p. 118.

102. This can be drawn from the fact that they sold a piece of property and brought part of the proceeds of what was sold. It reflects the typical nature of a voluntary contribution. Determination to contribute does not need to be made manifest, but would be made and kept inwardly. Since the decision to contribute was made inwardly in their own heart, it is natural that the proceeds should legally belong to them before and after the sale.

money when they saw it after having sold their property. It reflects the typical nature of the human mind in relation to wealth. In this sense, Peter's accusation to Ananias can be seen without the complexity which Capper tries to solve. But how did Peter know that the couple kept back part of the money? When we are reminded of the miraculous acts done through Peter by the Holy Spirit who made the couple die, it would not be impossible that the Spirit to whom Peter referred, accusing them of lying to Him, may have revealed to Peter their deception and embezzlement when they came to him. Consequently, we come to conclude that there was no two-stage entrance procedure related to handing over the property to the community. If it existed, there would have been only one procedure. The ground for this is that, except for the incident of Ananias, only 4.34 and the incident of Barnabas can be referred to as instances for Capper's argument, but there is nothing which can be drawn on to back up his argument.

Thirdly, the incident of Ananias does not describe a formal entrance procedure. The Jerusalem community was not such an enclosed sect as the Qumran community. It was open to everyone who might receive the Apostles' testimony to Jesus (2.41; 5.14), and it was not the Apostles but the Lord who brought people into the community (2.47). In this context, notice should be taken of the fact that the incidents of Ananias and of Barnabas are related to each other by way of δέ (5.1), so it should be recognized that 4.32 to 5.11 constitutes one whole story.[103] If this two-part story dealt with the entrance procedure, as Capper argues, the motif should be mentioned in the incident of Barnabas as well. But it is not. Consequently, it is safe to claim that it does not deal with an entrance procedure of prospective members, but rather how wealthy people among the members contributed possessions to the common funds of the community.[104] Thus surrender of wealth is not a condition of membership of the Christian community. Peter's question to Ananias on which Capper relies exclusively rather indicates this: 'while it remained unsold, did it not remain your own? After it was sold, was it not in your power?' (5.4).[105]

---

103. Derrett, 'Ananias', p. 194; I.H. Marshall, *Acts*, pp. 107, 111; Pilgrim, *Good News*, p. 152. Meanwhile, Haenchen, *Acts*, asserts that this story starts from v. 31: 'The summary properly begins with the imperfect *elaloun* in verse 31, the verse which describes the crucial event: they were all filled with the Holy Spirit . . . '.

104. Bruce, *Acts*, p. 108.

105. Leaney, *Rule*, p. 122.

Fourthly, Capper's argument concerning the incident of Ananias does not sufficiently clarify the charitable purpose of the common fund. There is a clear reference to distribution of money or food to the poor in 4.35 and 2.45. These two verses and 6.1, which refers to distribution of dole to the widows in the community, are introduced as the sole use of the common funds of the Jerusalem community in Acts. Thus, taking the story as a whole into consideration, the motive of charity in this text cannot be as easily dismissed as it is by Capper.

In my opinion, Barnabas is here introduced by Luke to the members of Luke's community as a positive model who practised Jesus' exhortation to the rich in the Gospel (Lk. 12.33), because he actually sold his property and gave the proceeds as alms to the poor through the common funds over which the Apostles had control, and Ananias and Sapphira, on the other hand, are shown as a negative model of people who sold their property but were trapped and choked by riches which Jesus warned against in the Gospel (Lk. 8.14; 18.22-23).[106] In this connection, we have pointed out the theme of stewardship to which Luke paid particular emphasis in his Gospel.

It would appear that Barnabas, Ananias and Sapphira were all entrusted by God with a certain portion of wealth, and as stewards, were expected to use it rightly and wisely according to the Master's will. Barnabas passed this test, but the couple failed.[107] In this connection, it seems to me that offering two modes of stewardship, one good and one bad,[108] Luke here still maintains his intention, as already expressed in the Gospel, that the well-off members of the community (like Zacchaeus and the Galilaean women) should be good stewards making right use of the wealth entrusted by the Master, and that the rich who forget their stewardship of wealth in the sight of God, being trapped by greed of material possessions, and hoarding or wasting them for their own sake, might be punished and excluded from the community (like the Rich Fool in Lk. 12, the Rich Man in Lk. 16, and the Rich Ruler in Lk. 18).

Therefore, here we are also able to detect a continuity throughout Luke's two-volume work with regard to the theme of stewardship.

---

106. That the couple broke 'the Spirit-centered unity of fellowship' by their greedy attitude to wealth would have been an obvious warning to Luke and his readers (Pilgrim, *Good News*, p. 153).

107. Cf. Lk. 8.14; 12.33; 18.22-23.

108. Derrett, 'Ananias', p. 194; Pilgrim, *Good News*, pp. 152-53.

d. *The Common Meal*

Attention should also be paid to the fact that both communities had customs of sharing a common meal among the members.[109] While the record as regards the custom of the common meal in the Jerusalem community is short and simple, that of the Qumran community is relatively long and detailed, so that much information can be obtained. In the communal life at Qumran, above all, we find that hierarchical order is regarded as important in the community,[110] and it is not confined to the matter of the common meal. At every meal the priest would bless the bread and new wine before and after the meal, and be the first to stretch out his hand for food. After that, the common meal would actually begin with all the congregation of the community following the same pattern of the acts done by the priest.[111] So along with the priority of the priest, the concept of hierarchical order is regarded as important in the custom of the communal meal at the Qumran community.

Secondly, 'equality of treatment' can be mentioned.[112] It means that including the priest, all members of the community are treated equally while eating and drinking. But in relation to this aspect of the common meal, what ought to be borne in mind is that at Qumran only the fully initiated members of the community may take part in the common meal. According to the Manual of Discipline,[113] a novice may partake in the common meal after a one-year probation, and after being a full member of the community, which needs at least a two-year probation, in the common drink which is fairly strictly regulated.[114]

---

109. Acts 2.42, 46; 20.7-11; 1QS 6.1-6; Cf. 1QSa 2.11-22; Josephus, *War* 2.129-33. In the matter of this common meal, the account of 1QSa is very similar to that of 1QS, except for the peculiar feature of the eschatological Messiah of Israel.

110. Regarding this element of the Qumran sect, B. Gärtner, *The Temple and the Community in Qumran and the New Testament* (Cambridge: Cambridge University Press, 1965), p. 8, notes that 'The strict hierarchy of the Qumran community resembles so closely the system observed among the temple priests that it is tempting to regard it as a reminiscence of the group which once broke away from the Jerusalem temple'.

111. 1QS 6.2-6.

112. Beall, *Essenes*, p. 59.

113. 1QS 6.22.

114. 1QS 6.20-21. 'From the rabbinic writings we know that the Pharisees believed that liquids were susceptible to ritual impurity to a higher degree than solid food, and that candidates for admission to the Pharisaic associations (*haburoth*) were not allowed

Among the full members of the community, however, there is no discrimination at all, that is, all members are treated equally and evenly, regardless of their order and rank as far as the meal is concerned, though offenders are treated differently.[115] In addition to these two respects, Josephus informs us of another aspect of the common meal at Qumran, which is frugality: 'one plate of one kind of food given to each'.[116] This aspect seems in line with their sobriety and abstinence, as well as the title, 'the poor', which they choose for themselves.[117]

Thirdly, it has been insisted that the common meal at Qumran was sacred in character and seen by the sectarians themselves as a cultic act because it took the place of the Temple sacrifice.[118] However, it is now widely acknowledged that the common meal at Qumran was not sacramental in character nor in essence a cultic activity. Concerning this facet of the common meal at Qumran, Schiffman offers us a clear-cut idea:

> There simply is no evidence that the 'meal' described in the Qumran passage cited above is a cultic or sacred meal. The purity of food and drink and the rituals associated with grace before and after meals were certainly widespread by this time, and in no way can it be said that every meal was sacred. All the motifs—purity, benediction, bread and wine, and the role of the priest—can be explained against the background of contemporary Jewish ceremonial and ritual practice.[119]

to handle liquids during the first stage of initiation. The same kind of attitude towards liquids underlies the legislation of the Rule' (Knibb, *Qumran*, p. 122). L.H. Schiffman, *The Eschatological Community of the Dead Sea Scrolls* (Atlanta: Scholars Press, 1989), p. 62. Leaney, *Rule*, argues that this regulation about the common drink is 'a safeguard of levitical purity' (p. 196; cf. pp. 191-94).

115. 1QS 6.24-25; cf. CD 14.20-21.

116. *War* 2.130, cf. 2.133; Philo, *Apol.* 11; Philo, *Hyp.* 11.5, 11; Diodorus Siculus, *Bib. Hist.* 2.59.1-3, 5. In keeping with this frugal diet, they are known to have worn their clothes and shoes until they fell to pieces (*War* 2.126).

117. 'The poor of the flock' (CD 7.20C).

118. M. Burrows, *More Light on the Dead Sea Scrolls* (London: Secker & Warburg, 1958), pp. 365-66; M. Black, *The Scrolls and Christian Origins* (Edinburgh: Nelson, 1961), pp. 102-15; Gärtner, *Temple*, p. 13.

119. *Scrolls*, p. 62. Cf. N.S. Fujita, *A Crack in the Jar: What Ancient Jewish Documents tell us about the New Testament* (New York: Paulist Press, 1986), pp. 151-52; E. Yamauchi, *The Stones and the Scriptures* (London: SCM Press, 1973), p. 138. For details, see Schiffman's full discussion on the topic, 'the non-sacral nature of the communal meals' (*Scrolls*, pp. 59-67).

The Jerusalem community is also known to have eaten a communal meal, but the passages that describe this practice in Acts do not give many details to us, so that we cannot really ascertain how the custom was practised in the Early Church at Jerusalem. What emerges from these passages is that when the early Christians met together in their homes for worship or whatever, they broke bread[120] and shared food, but wine is not mentioned. So it would not be easy to say whether the picture of the communal meal disclosed in these passages was the Christian Eucharist.[121] Rather it would seem to me that it may have

---

120. Cf. Acts 20.7; 27.35.

121. Depending heavily on Acts 2.42, J. Jeremias, (*The Eucharistic Words of Jesus* [London: SCM Press, 1966]) makes a point that since it presents the description of the liturgical course of an early Christian service, i.e. 'first the teaching of the apostles and the (table) fellowship, then the breaking of bread and prayers' (p. 119), the κλάσις τοῦ ἄρτου is a technical term for the Eucharist. Insisting that the meal proper preceded the Eucharist, he also contends that κοινωνία in 2.42 should be rendered as the Agape, '(table) fellowship'. This argument of Jeremias has been refuted by other scholars, such as Conzelmann and Haenchen. Here the issue concentrates on the interpretation of the clause κλάσις τοῦ ἄρτου which Jeremias argues is a technical term for the Last Supper. Meanwhile, I.H. Marshall, *Acts*, p. 83, puts it as 'an early Palestinian name for the Lord's Supper in the proper name of the word'.

Against Jeremias, Conzelmann, *Acts*, p. 23, holds that the breaking of bread denotes 'the ordinary daily meal' to the author, although he does not distinguish clearly the daily meal from the Eucharist. Haenchen, *Acts*, p. 191, appears to follow Conzelmann in the same direction, but goes slightly further to argue that 'the κλάσις τοῦ ἄρτου is the name for the Christians' communal meal'.

If we want the κλάσις τοῦ ἄρτου to be discussed with balance, attention must also be paid to the clause in 2.46, κλῶντές . . . ἄρτον, a part of the summary passages which depict the whole aspect of the communal life of the Early Church. Here κλῶντές is a present participle, which means that the breaking of bread and the sharing of food occurred simultaneously. Thus the κλάσις τοῦ ἄρτου is not separated from 'the meal proper', but rather indicates a mode of sharing food among the participants of the communal meal (cf. Lk. 24.30, 35; Acts 20.7, 11; 27.35). Consequently, it turns out that the effort made by Jeremias to separate a meal from the Eucharist in the context of 2.42 becomes fruitless. It seems to me that it is not necessary that the κλάσις τοῦ ἄρτου in 2.42 must be the Christian Eucharist. Rather, as Jeremias himself asserts elsewhere (*Words*, p. 66), the common meals practised in the Early Church could have been 'repetitions . . . of the daily table fellowship of the disciples with him'. Cf. K.G. Kuhn, 'The Lord's Supper and the Communal Meal at Qumran', in K. Stendahl (ed.), *The Scrolls and the New Testament* (London: SCM Press, 1957), pp. 77, 86; Hanson, *Acts*, p. 70.

Meanwhile focusing on the formula of institution of the Last Supper depicted in

been just a communal meal shared by all Christians, including rich and poor members, who attended worship and prayer meetings.[122]

In this context, what is to be understood here is that in antiquity a banquet was seen to have a special meaning; it was rare but precious to the poor (cf. Lk. 14). At that time, there were a lot of poor people who had to earn their daily living otherwise all their families would go hungry. For those poor, to attend a banquet where food was given freely was a rare chance to satisfy their hunger. Thus the wealthy in antiquity sometimes provided the poor with such a banquet with a view to earning fame and honour from the masses (compare Lk. 22.25). If we look into the passages in Acts, keeping in mind the rarity of a banquet in ancient times, we would be surprised to see that the early Christians held a sort of banquet *every day* (καθ' ἡμέραν; 2.46, 47),[123] although the scale of the banquet might have been smaller and simpler than the secular one provided by the wealthy among Luke's contemporaries.

Outstanding in the Christian common meal is, however, that all members attending worship and prayer meetings shared food and bread with one another. In this connection, if we take into account that the dole distribution for the widows in Acts 6.1, possibly food distribution, was provided daily (καθημερινῇ), it may be said that the custom of the common meal in the Jerusalem community referred to in the two passages in Acts (2.42, 46; cf. 20.7-11), was also intended to help the poor in the community satisfy their poverty-induced hunger, or at least was understood in that way by Luke and his readers.

From what we have discussed with respect to the custom of the common meal at Qumran, we can now see that it was a means of helping the poor in the community in relieving them of their hunger as shown

Mark, Luke, and 1 Corinthians, Kuhn, 'Communal Meal', makes a point that 'This formula, in its most original form (i.e. the Markan form of the tradition), describes the Last Supper not as a Passover meal but as a communal meal, the forms of which correspond to those of the cult meal of the Essenes' (p. 85). This point finally drives him to conclude that the daily meals of the Jerusalem community are very similar to the communal meals at Qumran (p. 93).

122. Hengel, *Property*, p. 33; Capper, 'Interpretation', p. 123; Haenchen, *Acts*, p. 191.

123. In this sense, it is also distinguished from the *Havurah*, the Jewish meals which were usually held on particular occasions, such as betrothals, weddings, circumcision, and funerals, and available to the members of the association only (Jeremias, *Words*, pp. 29-31; *EncJud* 8, p. 441).

above. In a word, the common meal was intended for almsgiving to the destitute, such as the widows in 6.1. In this sense, the nature of the common meal in both communities is quite different, although according to recent monographs,[124] a communal meal was practised not only in the Qumran sect but also in the Pharisaic sect and in the various Hellenistic associations and communities. Secondly, what is common between the two communities in relation to the common meal is that the members of both communities shared food with each other in the community. According to Josephus, as shown just above, food was distributed and shared equally among the members of the Qumran community, but this element is not clear in the Jerusalem community. However it can be said that it may be implied in ἅπαντα κοινά (2.44; 4.32) and 'with glad and generous hearts' (2.46). At any rate, what matters here is that both communities held the same custom of sharing food among the members.

What is essentially different between the two communities as regards this custom is the motive of the practice. Earlier in this chapter, we have already pointed out the difference in motive of pooling properties and possessions of the members of the communities to create a common fund. The common meal at Qumran was held as a means of maintaining such an isolated and self-supporting community, but as it was practised in the Jerusalem community one aspect of it was a means of helping the poor in the community in relieving them of their hunger as shown above. In a word, the common meal was intended for almsgiving to the destitute, such as the widows in 6.1. In this sense, the nature of the common meal in both communities is quite different, although at first glance the custom looks similar.

To conclude, when we take into account that the custom of a common meal, such as a social banquet, was used in antiquity by the wealthy as a means of relieving the poor, what we can notice in the custom of sharing food among the members of the community is that the communal meal was used in the Early Church as a way of almsgiving for relieving the poor of their hunger in the Jerusalem community.

e. *Conclusion*

In the above, we have discussed the similarities and dissimilarities between the Jerusalem community and the Qumran community focusing on the systems of the common fund and meal, because it is held by

124. Schiffman, *Scrolls*, pp. 59-67; Weinfeld, *Pattern*, pp. 49, 78.

some scholars that the two communities shared the systems in common. However, our discussion shows that although both communities used slightly similar systems to run their communal life, the basic motive of their systems was so different as to make a clear distinction between the two societies. It is without doubt that the basic motive which the Jerusalem community held to keep it going was caring concern towards the poor and needy around the community, while that of the Qumran community was to keep it pure and undefiled from the outside world, for which the systems of the common fund and meal were used for the sake of convenience.

In addition to this point, strictly speaking, there was no system of a common fund in the early Christian community, since not all members of the community participated in pooling their wealth to create a common fund, but only those who had some means actually performed this service. Consequently, it seems appropriate that it is not to be called a common fund but benevolent contributions of the wealthy towards the poor neighbours. These features of the communal life prevalent in the early Christian community are well in keeping with the nature of Jesus' exhortations concerning almsgiving directed towards the rich in the Gospel.

Chapter 8

THE PRACTICE OF BENEFACTION IN THE GRAECO-ROMAN WORLD

In this chapter, noting that there are a fairly large number of passages in Luke–Acts containing exhortations towards the wealthy to give alms to the poor, and warnings not to hoard, waste, or adhere to material possessions, I feel that it would be very helpful to look at the socio-economic situation of the Roman Empire in the first century CE and what happened then in relation to the poor and their needs.

What I am aiming at in this chapter is, first, to explore any kind of benefaction or almsgiving systems which were operated in the interest of the poor in Graeco-Roman society, and, secondly, to compare the results of such an exploration with Luke's idea of almsgiving related to stewardship of wealth in order that we might see whether those systems of benefaction in the Graeco-Roman society can really be deemed as parallels to Luke's notion of almsgiving which we have already defined in the previous chapters. This knowledge, I believe, would help us to appreciate Luke's theology on almsgiving.

1. *The Plight of the Poor: Attitudes to the Poor in the Graeco-Roman World*

It is generally acknowledged that the times of the Graeco-Roman world can be characterized as a period of extreme inequality in terms of its socio-economic conditions. The rich and powerful were likely to become richer and mightier owing to their current advantages, such as political power and social status,[1] while the poor and helpless were vulnerable to forces which could render them poorer and more helpless

---

1.   Esler, *Community*, p. 172; P.A. Brunt, *Social Conflicts in the Roman Republic* (London: Chatto & Windus, 1971), p. 17.

owing to their present disadvantages.[2] Such advantages and disadvantages of the affluent and the poor derived from the contemporary socio-economic structure which was made in favour of the wealthy, so that the inequality in terms of distribution of wealth and political power was a chronic problem which made the poor suffer greatly.[3]

In this context, to have a general view on the stratification of the Graeco-Roman world around 1 CE might be helpful for us to appreciate the inequality of the society that prevailed at that time. The top of the pyramid of the society was occupied by the aristocracy of the Empire, such as senators,[4] equestrians,[5] and decurions: the former two classes constitute the upper strata of the Roman nobility, while the latter, the lower strata.[6] The ancient literature shows us that these central and local levels of aristocracy constituted less than one per cent of the whole population of the Roman Empire,[7] but this tiny fraction of society is known to have possessed a vast proportion of its total wealth, both in land[8] and in other resources available at that time.[9] In this sense, it may not be an exaggeration to say that the ancient society of the

2.   S. Dill, *Roman Society from Nero to Marcus Aurelius* (London: Macmillan, 1904), pp. 94-95.

3.   In this regard, Finley, *Ancient Economy*, p. 87, remarks that 'it is no objection to say that the reality of equality before the law has always fallen short of the ideal'. Cf. A.H.M. Jones, *The Roman Economy* (Oxford: Basil Blackwell, 1974), pp. 136-37.

4.   Dill, *Roman Society*, pp. 213-14.

5.   Dill, *Roman Society*, pp. 215-16.

6.   R. MacMullen, *Roman Social Relations* (New Haven: Yale University Press, 1974), pp. 93-94; Finley, *Ancient Economy*, pp. 46-47.

7.   W.A. Meeks, *The Moral World of the First Christians* (London: SPCK, 1987), p. 33. Cf. MacMullen, *Relations*, pp. 88-89; G. Sjoberg, *The Preindustrial City* (Glencoe: Free Press, 1960), p. 110.

8.   In antiquity land was the most popular source of income as well as the safest means of wealth for the wealthy and those in power (Finley, *Ancient Economy*, p. 102; Brunt, *Conflicts*, p. 21). 'Since land produced food, which was the one indispensable commodity in antiquity, it was always a rewarding investment, especially for one who was rich enough to ride out a few lean years. Hence the wealth of the elite was based on land, whether inherited or acquired from insolvent neighbors or debtors or as the spoils of war' (Stambaugh and Balch, *Social World*, p. 65).

Besides, the affluent in the Empire also expanded their wealth through rent which came from leasing their lands to the peasants, the vast majority of the population of the Roman Empire, who in turn became impoverished because of high rents and heavy taxes (Jones, *Roman Economy*, pp. 30-31, 38, 42, 122, 125-26, 130, 136).

9.   Dill, *Roman Society*, pp. 94-95. Cf. MacMullen, *Relations*, pp. 94-98.

Graeco-Roman world is to be considered as one which was designed particularly for the elite group of the society, while the rest of the society just existed for helping those privileged to enjoy their lives conveniently.[10] Brunt puts this idea as follows:

> By modern standards the ancient world was always poor and 'under-developed'. If any progress was to be made, it was inevitable that the majority should hew and carry in order that a very few might have the means and leisure to cultivate the arts and sciences.[11]

Below this ruling elite, the merchants and traders took next place in terms of economic affluence, because they could become rich out of the profits that came from their business.[12] Along with these merchants and traders, the skilled workers and the artisans also earned reasonable wages, and, in ordinary conditions, do not seem to have had difficulty with their living.[13]

Apart from these top and middle classes[14] of the society, there remain two lower classes: one is the tenant farmers and the unskilled workers who had to find their daily living through various menial jobs, which might be available on the open market, such as 'burden-bearers, messengers, animal-drivers, and ditch-diggers',[15] and the other is the slaves who were owned by wealthy individuals or the state.[16] Although in view of their social status, the slaves were the lowest class of the contemporary society, yet since they were provided with food and shelter by their owners,[17] they might have been better off than the unskilled

10. Cf. Dill, *Roman Society*, pp. 95-96.

11. Brunt, *Conflicts*, p. 40.

12. Stambaugh and Balch, *Social World*, p. 70-71; cf. Acts 9.36-43; 10.14-15.

13. Jones, *Roman Economy*, pp. 43-44; Dill, *Roman Society*, p. 253.

14. Here I use the term 'middle class' for the merchants and artisans because they had enough wealth not to worry about their living, but H. Hill, *The Roman Middle Class in the Republican Class* (Oxford: Basil Blackwell, 1952), pp. 45-86, reserves the term for equestrians because they were in between two major classes: the senatorial class and the mass of the people. He goes on to assert that the merchants and artisans were not allowed to be included in the middle class (p. 84). Cf. MacMullen, *Relations*, pp. 89-90.

15. Sjoberg, *Preindustrial City*, p. 122.

16. Finley, *Ancient Economy*, pp. 73-74, pointed out that in antiquity there was no clear distinction between slaves and unskilled workers, on the grounds that once anyone was hired, he was nothing more than a slave, servile to his employers. Cf. MacMullen, *Relations*, pp. 114-15.

17. MacMullen, *Relations*, p. 92.

workers who had to depend upon employment which was not always available. Moreover, there was a great range of social conditions in which slaves might live. It is likely that these two low classes were regarded as the poor from the point of view of the upper class.[18]

Especially vulnerable were the unskilled workers who had no jobs to do for getting their daily livelihood. However, they were still given the chance to find employment to earn their living. In a more absolute sense, the term, πτωχός, applies to those who were not able to work at all, such as the blind, the crippled, the lame, the lepers, the deaf, and the mentally handicapped,[19] whose only resort was begging for their survival in the hard-pressed life of ancient times.[20]

Apart from the extremely unbalanced social structure, natural phenomena also made the suffering of the poor more serious. That is, not infrequent famines or droughts in all parts of the Roman world at various times which might cause a desperate shortage of grain caused the poor to suffer greatly,[21] because they did not have any provision to escape it or to protect themselves from such natural disasters. It is known that in such hardships the ancient states and societies had their own ways of coping in order that their citizens would be protected from them, but the ancient literature and documents available to us reveal that there was no system or provision which any state or society of that time had to help the non-citizen poor (see below) escape from hunger and starvation.

Accordingly, it is true that the poor in antiquity were left helplessly abandoned, and for this reason, the rich and mighty always looked down on these poor people.[22] Therefore, unless the wealthy took action to help them survive, they might have perished. Thus in what follows, I will examine this aspect in more detail to see what, if any, parallels there are to the sort of 'wealth stewardship' advocated by Luke, for it is quite relevant to our theme.

18. Cf. Jones, *Roman Economy*, p. 38.
19. Cf. Lk. 4.18; 7.22; 14.13, 21.
20. Cf. Lk. 16.20-21; 18.35; Acts 3.2. See Dill, *Roman Society*, 96. Citing Aristophanes's *Plutus*, Finley, *Ancient Economy*, p. 41, defines a πτωχός as 'the man who was altogether without resources', which he draws from the contrast of πτωχός with πένης.
21. Brunt, *Conflicts*, p. 20.
22. MacMullen, *Relations*, pp. 116-17; Esler, *Community*, pp. 172-73.

2. *State Benefaction and its Limitations*

a. *Greece*

In the Graeco-Roman world, as far as mechanisms of distribution are concerned, city and state governments, on the whole, distributed food to their citizens from time to time, but did not distribute cheap or free grain to their citizenry on a regular basis.

Among ancient states, the case of Crete was so unique and famous that it earned the praise of Plato and Aristotle, the latter who introduced it as the model for his supply and distribution system.[23] The major idea of the Cretan system of distribution is that 'the polis was its citizens, and that whatever resources came its way in the form of booty, fines, dues or produce belonged to the citizens and should be shared out among them'.[24] But such a unique system as that of Crete among Greek cities went through significant modifications by the late fourth century, so that the whole income of the state was not divided among its members, and eventually faded away, so that by the second century CE, distributions in Crete, which were now only biennial, were paid for by the wealthy.

The case of Samos is also fairly unique in the sense that only one continual and annual distribution was carried out there in the Greek world from about the turn of the third century BCE.[25] But here what

---

23. According to the Cretan system of distribution, the whole produce of the soil, i.e. crops and cattle, must be divided by all into twelve parts. The first share shall be for the free-born citizen, the second one for their servants, and the third for craftsmen and foreigners generally, which also shall be the only one liable to compulsory sale (Plato, *Leg.* 847).

Aristotle put it slightly differently: 'out of the whole produce from the public land, one part is assigned for the worship and the maintenance of the public services, and the other for the public mess-tables, so that all the citizens are maintained from the common funds, women and children as well as men' (*Pol.* 1272a).

What is common between these two interpretations as regards the Cretan system of distribution is that they lived a form of communal life, sharing all products of the public lands in common.

24. P. Garnsey, *Famine and Food Supply in the Graeco-Roman World* (Cambridge: Cambridge University Press, 1988), p. 79.

25. We are told from an inscription that more than 100 Samians, probably wealthy citizens who were always expected to subscribe *epidoseis*, contributed modest sums of money to a grain fund. The interest on the investment was put to the purchase of grain from the district of Anaia for the distribution to 'the citizens in residence

is to be carefully noted is that the main purpose of that system in Samos was to establish a permanent fund producing an annual revenue sufficient to provide in advance against emergencies relating to the food supply. In other words, the distribution system of Samos should be understood as a means of providing 'an unfailing supply of food in perpetuity',[26] which had to meet the chronic economic problems of the state.[27] Other cities in Greece, such as Samothrace, Iasos, Thouria of Messenia, Delos, and Thespiae, are also known to have followed the same pattern as the Samian mechanism, in the sense that the main aim of the distribution mechanism of Greek cities in general was to establish a permanent fund for the supply of food.[28]

Here one point should be clarified. With respect to establishing a perpetual fund relating to food shortage, all Greek cities, in general, appear to have been faced with the same difficulty. But with respect to handling the problem, discrepancies are found. Samothrace (early or mid-second century BCE) and Iasos (c. 150 BCE) are seen by some to have followed the same pattern as that of Samos, which means that they established the public funds in the interests of all their citizens, which are known to be distributed freely by the principle of equal rations (*sitometria*).[29] However, in the cases of Thouria of Messenia (2 BCE), Delos, and Thespiae, the city authorities had grain funds, but these were not for free distribution, but for profitable business. This means that those grain funds were not given away gratis, but sold to

individually by their sub-divisions, measuring out to each two measures a month free' (A.R. Hands, *Charities and Social Aid in Greece and Rome* [London: Thames & Hudson, 1968], p. 179). In this inscription, however, we are not told how long such a distribution was maintained.

In addition to this, Garnsey, *Famine*, expresses his doubt about its effectiveness because 'the amount of cash was insufficient to purchase more than a small proportion of the grain requirement of the citizen population' (p. 81). For detailed information about the Samian distribution, see Hands, *Charities*, p. 178, D6.

26. Hands, *Charities*, p. 95.

27. G. Rickman, *The Corn Supply of Ancient Rome* (Oxford: Clarendon Press, 1980), p. 156. The reason for the problem is because a series of contingencies, not least a failure of the corn supply, occurred for every state, and so people had to live with a succession of financial crises (Hands, *Charities*, p. 39). Hence, *epidoseis* by the wealthy originated from this stringent situation to cope with the chronic problem.

28. Hands, *Charities*, pp. 96-97.

29. Hands, *Charities*, pp. 96-97.

individuals who needed them, probably farmers, on condition that they returned their value with interest in the subsequent year.[30]

However, if we follow Garnsey's argument that the case of distribution of Samothrace, and also perhaps that of Iasos, was not 'Samian-style regular distribution', it would not be plausible for us to identify the cases of these two cities with that of Samos. Thus, Garnsey's point seems correct, that is, 'No other city can be shown to have possessed comparable institutions to those of Samos'.[31]

As for the case of Athens, there is no evidence of a permanent public fund for free distribution.[32] In line with this, we find that corn was sold at the normal price during a period of severe shortage of food (329–324 BCE), but not handed out freely. Only when an unexpected gift of corn was given to the Athenians by Psammetichos of Egypt in the mid-fifth century, was it distributed to the citizenry, for which there was an investigation of the citizen list to remove non-citizens in order to reduce the number of recipients. Consequently, it is evident that 'there was no attempt to allocate the gift to those most in need'.[33]

To conclude, as regards the distribution system in Greek society, including the two exceptional cases, Crete and Samos, what should be noted is that the distribution systems were intended for the body of the citizens. Non-citizens, including slaves and foreigners, would have been excluded. Thus, frankly speaking, they were not charity systems, that is, the funds were not intended for the poor in society.[34] The systems were intended for the citizenry who were generally people of moderate means, at least not the destitute. And even in this case, apart from the cases of Crete and Samos, since distribution of free grain was not regular and recurrent (Samothrace and Iasos), and grain was not handed out gratis but with a certain charge (Thouria, Delos, and Thespiae), strictly speaking, it is in doubt whether the ordinary poor citizens benefited much from these systems.

30. Garnsey, *Famine*, p. 81.
31. Garnsey, *Famine*, p. 81.
32. Hands, *Charities*, p. 97.
33. Hands, *Charities*; cf. Garnsey, *Famine*, p. 81.
34. In this connection, Hands, *Charities*, argues that even in the Samian case, since 'there was no suggestion of more generous provision being made for the fathers of large families', it was not intended for the poor (p. 96).

b. *Rome*

The case of Rome is quite different from that of the Greek cities. The foremost difference between the two is that the major problem of the Greeks was not Rome's because the Romans did not need to worry about a permanent fund, since money would have been available from the revenues and profits of Rome's overseas possessions in one way or another.[35] The second reason for the difference lies in the fact that unlike Greek administrations, the Roman state intervened not infrequently in the grain supply of the capital.[36] This practice stretched back to the earliest days of the Republic, and there had been ad hoc distributions by the aediles in various periods. But like the Greek system, grain was not distributed free of charge to the citizens but at a fixed and moderate price,[37] presumably throughout the year. But this changed dramatically in 58 BCE. By instituting the *lex frumentaria*, Clodius abolished the charge for the rations issued in the distributions, and established a free public ration of corn.[38] But from then onwards there were unceasing movements to prune the number of recipients. By 46 BCE, the number of recipients was supposed to have risen to 320,000. Hence, Julius Caesar, during his dictatorship (49–44 BCE), reduced from 320,000 to 150,000 the number of householders who might draw

35. Rickman, *Corn*, p. 156.

36. The import of food is known to have been one of the most important tasks of the emperors of Rome, so in this context 'it may be noted that Roman "capitalism"... tended to develop in contexts associated with the State-tax farming and plantation of corn for export to Rome' (P.W. Pleket, 'Economic History of the Ancient World and Epigraphy: Some Introductory Remarks', *Akten des vi internationalen Kongresses für griechische und lateinische Epigraphik* [Munich: Beck, 1972], p. 249).

37. The fixed price for a ration of a corn at monthly distributions was $6\frac{1}{3}$ asses per modius which was established by the *lex Sempronia* in the period of Gaius Gracchus (123 BCE) (Rickman, *Corn*, pp. 158-59). Thus before the introduction of free grain, for 65 years (123–158 BCE), the grain provided by the state was sold cheaply rather than given away. Hands, *Charities*, p. 102.

Contrary to Rickman (*Corn*, p. 154), in distinguishing a 'normal' price from an 'average' price, de Neeve insists that what was important is not a fixed or 'average' price of grain, but stability of price (P.W. De Neeve, 'Review of "The Corn Supply of Ancient Rome" by G. Rickman', *Mnemosoyne* 38 [1985], pp. 443-48 [447]).

38. According to Cicero's claim, abolition of the charge took one fifth of Rome's revenues, which Clodius compensated for by selling the royal property at Cyprus annexed in 58 BCE (Rickman, *Corn*, p. 172).

free grain.[39] But by 5 BCE, the number of beneficiaries continued to grow and reached 320,000 again, so Augustus, when he found that the list of citizens had been swelled by a considerable number of recently freed slaves, reduced the number to 200,000 by instituting a *recensus* throughout Rome.[40] The number seems finally to have been fixed at 150,000 by 37 CE during the reign of Tiberius.[41] In the scheme of Roman distribution, however, it should also be clearly recognized that this grain was available only to the reduced number of citizens, and that there was no evidence of the poor being singled out for particular relief and dole.[42]

Therefore, in the Roman scheme of distribution of grain to her citizens, it is generally acknowledged that it was also not a charity scheme which the Romans employed to save the poor from hunger and starvation, but a scheme designed for the body of citizens, just as was the case with the Greeks.[43] Along with this, if the facts are considered that at the time of Augustus 'the citizen population of Rome may not have amounted to much more than a fifth of the total resident population of the city',[44] which accords with the general impression of the populace of Rome, and that around the early second century CE there was a distinction between the *plebs Romana* and *plebs frumentaria*, the latter

39. Suetonius, *Caes.* 41.3.

40. Suetonius, *Aug.* 42.3; *R. Gest.* 15.21.

41. Suetonius, *Aug.* 101; Tacitus, *Ann.* 1; Suetonius, *Tib.* 76.

42. 'Whatever else they (distributions of free grain) may have been, they were not a dole for the poor. Even if and when there were limitations set in eligibility, the criterion does not seem to have involved poverty or special need' (Rickman, *Corn*, p. 172).

43. It is known that when a law was passed in 73 BCE, which restricted the number of citizens who could benefit under it, or, the amount of corn which each could buy, there was public protest against the law. What attracts our attention in this protest is the emphasis which the protests placed on 'the *rights* of free men *qua* citizen rather than on the special *needs* of the destitute *qua* men' (Hands, *Charities*, p. 103). This is clear evidence to show how citizenship was appreciated in ancient Roman society.

44. Hands, *Charities*, p. 106. In *R. Gest.* 15.16 it is recorded that Augustus, in 5 BCE, during his eighteenth term as tribune and his twelfth as consul, made a gift of 60 denarii to 320,000 members of the urban plebeians. Adding to this the numbers of their wives, their children, and slaves, though guessed, Rickman came to conclude that the size of the population of Rome at that time would be near to 1,000,000 (F.W. Danker, *Benefactor: Epigraphic Study of a Graeco-Roman and New Testament Semantic Field* [St Louis: Clayton Publishing House, 1982], p. 263; Rickman, *Corn*, pp. 9-10; cf. pp. 179-85).

being regarded as the genuine body of citizens which was to be protected at all costs,[45] more than the majority of the city of Rome itself, which would have been exposed to the threat of hunger and starvation. In this context, we can understand that the concept of *pietas* for the Romans usually had a practical rather than sentimental mode of expression, that is, '*pietas* was essentially connected with a belief in and a self-dedication to the idea of the eternity of Rome, which took precedence over all other considerations'.[46] Therefore, to conclude, in the government scheme of distribution in Rome nothing can be said clearly about charity and benefaction, and apart from the city of Rome, we do not have evidence that there were such similar distribution systems as Rome's elsewhere in the Roman Empire, particularly in the first century CE.

If we take together what has been discussed so far, we can see that state-funded distribution schemes in the ancient Graeco-Roman world were very narrow in scope, which means that they were only available to the citizenry, and were infrequent in the case of ancient Greece. Historical evidence shows us that there was not a fixed and regular system of benefaction in the society of the Roman Empire,[47] in which Luke's community lived in 1 CE.[48] Therefore, since the corn supply was an essential issue throughout the Roman Empire in antiquity, it is no surprise to find that it was 'a regular and highly important item on the agenda of the *ekklesia*'.[49]

Along with the above discussion, an illustration would help us assess the degree of poverty of the poor in the ancient Graeco-Roman world. This is related to a distribution for all, which a donor would afford for

45. Rickman, *Corn*, p. 185. See also n. 43.

46. Hands, *Charities*, pp. 112-13. In relation to this element, Laum, *Stiftungen*, p. 252, regarded the government scheme of distribution of food as 'mehr ein Akt der Politik als der reinen Menschenliebe', which could be seen to be a proper, if cynical, assessment of the Roman mechanism of distribution.

47. Finley, *Ancient Economy*, p. 39; Stambaugh and Balch, *Social World*, p. 64.

48. Esler, *Community*, p. 175. There were a very large number of private gifts, which were given sometimes during a person's lifetime or sometimes at death, and recurrently or non-recurrently. According to the argument by Hands, however, in this giving, 'the poorest class of society was never singled out for specially favourable treatment' (*Charities*, p. 89). Thus, it can be said that the problem of poverty in the poorest class was largely unaddressed in antiquity.

49. Pleket, 'Economic History', p. 247.

a funeral. Hands's explanation about this incident is very helpful to appreciate how bitter the degree of poverty of the poor was in antiquity:

> How far can we suppose that in fact only the poorest class would turn up for a gift which was bound to be comparatively small because of the large number of those eligible to receive it? There is good reason to be cautious of such an assumption. As we have seen, in most city-states the large majority of the population, though not penniless, could not afford to disregard even small material benefits, particularly if the occasion happened to be a public holiday offering no opportunity for material gain by work. On such occasions the 'poor' will have been glad to rub shoulders with the poorest.[50]

3. *Private Benefaction*

b. *Euergetism to the City*
In almost every aspect of socio-economic and political life in antiquity the role of wealthy citizens was immense, so that their influence was to be found everywhere in the Graeco-Roman world. In keeping with this, the wealthy were expected to assume the costs of various public services.[51] Among them, as a conspicuous example, we can mention taking offices in government. This almost directly meant undertaking a burden of expenditure which was usually expected to be spent for public affairs, such as sponsoring games and feasts,[52] among which a typical case was to provide people with food, particularly in times of food shortages resulting from crop failure.[53] In consequence, members of civic governments consisted of the wealthy in communities,[54] and it was natural that officials of civic governments were interested in increasing their benefit as far as possible rather than that of the public. Hence, 'building up the public treasury at their own expense

---

50. Hands, *Charities*, pp. 93-94.

51. Danker, *Benefactor*, D.12, 17, 19, 20.

52. Dill, *Roman Society*, pp. 228-29.

53. 'In case of necessity the city recurred also to the ancient practice of liturgies, that is, of compulsory contributions by rich citizens to aid in the execution of some important public work' (M. Rostovtzeff, *The Social and Economic History of the Roman Empire* [2 vols.; Oxford: Clarendon Press, 1957], II, p. 148). In this sense, Countryman's view appears right, that is, 'Wealth, being associated with the upper orders, implied certain social rights and obligations' (Countryman, *Rich Christian*, p. 25).

54. Dill, *Roman Society*, pp. 211, 220.

by some kind of taxation system' was not to be expected.[55] But when a time of urgent and serious need resulted from such emergencies as famine,[56] bad harvest, epidemic and war,[57] and since state funds were not sufficient to cover it, the wealthy were expected or persuaded to do something on behalf of the poor whose situation was worse off than ever. The honorary public office of curator of the grain supply, *curator annonae*, was one of the major posts taken by the wealthy citizens during times of food shortages or famines.[58] Thus it seems natural that public authorities in communities came to be dependent upon the benefactions of private rich individuals, that is, members of the local elite,[59] because state funds were few, and on the whole most of the wealth in antiquity belonged to a small number of private individuals.[60]

In this context, Garnsey defines the benefaction of the wealthy in antiquity as 'euergetism', and explains it as follows:

55. Garnsey, *Famine*, p. 82.

56. Famine was a constant threat to the people in antiquity which was caused not only by natural adversities, such as excessive rains, drought, severe winter, but also by war which interrupted farming and transport.

In such hardships, the wealthy took all grains from the lands and left the mass of people 'the other leguminous crops', so that owing to this poor diet, the poor easily got all sorts of diseases, and were still facing starvation (R. MacMullen, *Enemies of the Roman Order* [Cambridge, MA: Harvard University Press, 1967], pp. 249-54). Cf. Esler, *Community*, pp. 177-78.

57. As an example, when the people of Callantia were besieged by Lysimachus and were hard pressed by lack of food (313 BCE), Eumelus took under his care a thousand who had left their homes because of famine (Diodorus Siculus, *Bib. Hist.* 20.25.1; cf. Dionysius Halicarnassus, *Ant. Rom.* 4.48.3).

58. For epigraphic evidence which records benefactors acting as *curator annonae* which in the East was called *sitones* or ἀγοράνομοι, see Hands, *Charities*, pp. 175-209, particularly document nos. 2 (330–325 BCE), 6 (second century BCE), 7 (c. 150 BCE), 12 (c. 42 CE), 14 (early first century CE), 15 (1 CE), 23 (not earlier than 50 CE), and 29 (100–150 CE). All of these documents come from Greece or Asia Minor.

According to B.W. Winter ('Secular and Christian Responses to Corinthian Famines', *TynBul* 40 [1989], pp. 86-106), during 51–54 CE when a series of intermittent food shortages happened in Corinth, Tiberius Claudius Dinippus held the high public office, i.e. *curator annonae*, three times in the community, for which 11 inscriptions were erected in order to honour the benefactor. For more documentary evidence, see Rostovtzeff, *Economic History*, pp. 598-600.

59. Except for critical occasions, Roman officials in the provinces seldom intervened in the civic affairs (Winter, 'Responses', p. 95; cf. Garnsey, *Famine*, p. 69).

60. Garnsey, *Famine*, p. 82; Dill, *Roman Society*, p. 219; cf. p. 223.

> Euergetism, the public generosity of the rich, is the hallmark of the standard Mediterranean city throughout our period. After the virtual disappearance of democracy by the end of the fourth century BC, euergetism was the main safeguard of the common people of the town against hunger and starvation in a subsistence crisis.[61]

In a word, it can be said that the Mediterranean world under Roman rule depended heavily upon euergetism rather than other particular mechanisms to provide for cities and ward off food shortages. This aspect in turn evidently reflects the outstanding contrast between 'public poverty and private affluence'.[62] With respect to this point, we find considerable evidence from Greek and Latin epigraphs that euergetism did occur widely throughout Greece and Rome from the fifth century BCE to the second century CE in the form of benefaction.[63] This epigraphic evidence shows that since benefactors did good in various

---

61. Garnsey, *Famine*, p. 82. In addition to this, Garnsey, *Famine*, summarizes and assesses euergetism under the following four headings:

   (i) Euergetism was not motivated by altruism.
   (ii) The class that produced euergetists also produced speculators.
   (iii) Euergetism had definite limits.
   (iv) Euergetism was essentially an ad hoc response, not a lasting solution (p. 82).

In general his assessment of euergetism does not seem positive, but this, I think, reflects reality. This idea of Garnsey regarding euergetism is greatly influenced by those of P. Veyne (*Le Pain et le cirque* [Paris: Seuil, 1976]) and P. Gauthier (*Les Cités grecques et leurs bienfaiteurs* [Paris: Diffusia De Boccard, 1985]).

62. Garnsey, *Famine*, p. 84.

63. W. Larfeld, *Griechische Epigraphik* (Munich: Beck, 1914), pp. 377-81, 422-23. In antiquity, since Homeric times, it appeared obligatory for deities and rulers to ensure the safety and the welfare of those who relied on their benefits. If such commissions were carried out well, then they, i.e. the deities and kings, were recognized as benefactors or saviours. As time went on, those who benefitted were prone to record such recognition in formal civic decrees which were ordinarily incised in stone. According to inscriptions excavated so far, it is noted that as time went on, the category of benefactors was not limited to deities and rulers, but stretched to wealthy citizens, whatever their social status, whose role in antiquity was known to be so important that cities and states counted heavily upon them, particularly in times of crises, such as famine, war, and other calamities.

In relation to this, Danker, *Benefactor*, introduces 53 inscriptions and documents which span approximately six centuries and intends to illuminate the terminology relating to the cultural phenomenon of the interplay between people of excellence and affluence and those on whom they make their impact, in order to determine their meaning in the New Testament corpus (pp. 56-316).

ways[64] to the populace of certain cities who were faced with adversities, the peoples of certain cities resolved to honour them, erecting inscriptions and then holding public ceremonies at which the benefactors were proclaimed, in order that their good conduct of benefaction should be recognized and honoured publicly, by way of recompense for their benevolence.[65]

Along with this epigraphic evidence, Rom. 13.3 and 1 Pet. 2.14 can be pointed out as the New Testament evidence which approves of benefaction and encourages the congregations to do good works and to be public benefactors (compare Rom. 2.10).[66] The picture described in these passages is related to 'a positive role being taken by rich Christians to contribute to the well-being of the community at large and the appropriateness and importance of due recognition by ruling authorities

---

64. Benefactions included bearing the expenses of public services (Danker, *Benefactor*, D.17, 19), furnishing expenditures of enormous sums for relief from the effects of a disastrous earthquake (D.19), providing material for war (D.15), and the supply of grain in times of necessity by diverting the grain-carrying ships to the city or forcing down the price by selling it in the market below the asking rate (D.11).

The erection of public buildings and the adorning of old buildings were also regarded as benefactions in Ephesus and Corinth, along with refurbishing the theatre, widening roads, helping in the construction of public utilities, going on embassies to gain privileges for a city, helping the city in times of civil upheaval (D.8, 11, 20; B.W. Winter, 'The Public Honouring of Christian Benefactors: Romans 13.3-4 and 1 Peter 2.14-15', *JSNT* 34 [1988], pp. 87-103 [101]). Cf. J. Triantaphyllopoulos, 'PARAPRASIS', *Acta of the Fifth International Congress of Greek and Latin Epigraphy, Cambridge, 1967* (Oxford: Basil Blackwell, 1971), pp. 65-66.

65. According to Dionysius of Halicarnassus, in ancient Rome, in the intervals between contests, such as boxing and wrestling, Romans observed these ceremonies, as did Greeks (Dionysius of Halicarnassus, *Ant. Rom.* 7.73.4). In Greece, the Lacedaemonians proclaimed Antigonus to be their saviour and benefactor at public festivals (Polybius, *Hist.* 9.36.5; cf. 5.9.10), and the Syracusans, Dion (Diodorus Siculus, *Bib. Hist.* 16.20.6). See also Winter, 'Honouring', p. 92.

66. Winter dealt with these two passages in his article, 'The Public Honouring of Christian Benefactors', cited in n. 63. There he argued by the help of epigraphic evidence that 'New Testament writers merely reflected a long-established social custom of appropriate recognition of public benefactors' (p. 90). Unfortunately, however, in other passages in the New Testament, such as Gal. 6.10; Eph. 4.28; 1 Tim. 6.18; Tit. 3.8; 2.14, and Heb. 13.16, where New Testament writers also encouraged Christians to do good works, we cannot find any remarks on appropriate recognition of public benefactors. Thus Winter's argument may be valid when it is confined to apply to only those two passages, i.e. Rom. 13.3 and 1 Pet. 2.14.

for their contribution'.[67] Hence these passages, outside of Luke–Acts, which might be regarded as a reflection of the real situation of the Early Church, including Pauline and Petrine congregations, seem to have a significant bearing on Luke's congregation and the texts in Luke–Acts referring to exhortations to almsgiving.

Therefore, we may draw from this observation that Luke's exhortations towards the wealthy in his community to give alms to the poor and destitute in the community out of their wealth are in line with 'a long-established social custom' in the ancient Graeco-Roman world. In other words, it can be said that in the ancient Graeco-Roman world, particularly during the first century CE, wealthy citizens on the whole as part of the community to which they belonged contributed financially and the Early Church, possibly including Luke's church, exhorted them to act as public benefactors.

b. *Euergetism to Clients*
Euergetism is not only to be discovered in such public sectors as contribution by the wealthy to the local government or the citizenry which were faced with harsh economic difficulties, but also in private sectors. Here 'private' denotes some personal relationship between the persons involved, and in terms of euergetism, this kind of private relationship can be found in the system of patronage, a widespread social custom in antiquity, which functioned as a pillar on which ancient society relied. Thus Garnsey properly asserts that 'patronage was an important factor in local politics in all periods'.[68]

What is patronage? Saller offers us a very balanced definition of this kind which is worth quoting here:

> First, it involves the *reciprocal* exchange of goods and services. Secondly, to distinguish it from a commercial transaction in the marketplace, the relationship must be a personal one of some duration. Thirdly, it must be asymmetrical, in the sense that the two parties are of unequal status and offer different kinds of goods and services in the exchange—a quality which sets patronage off from friendship between equals.[69]

67. Winter, 'Honouring', p. 95.
68. Garnsey, *Social Status and Legal Privilege in the Roman Empire* (Oxford: Clarendon Press, 1970), p. 273. Cf. Moxnes, *Economy*, pp. 42-47; S.N. Eisenstad and L. Roniger, *Patrons, Clients and Friends* (Cambridge: Cambridge University Press, 1984), p. 55.
69. R.P. Saller, *Personal Patronage under the Early Empire* (Cambridge:

Eisenstadt and Roniger provide us with three different groups which they distinguish in the relationship of patron–client: the first is the relationship between master and freedman; the second is the relationship between an individual patrician and (1) a plebian, usually a soldier, (2) the local community (*municipia*, *colonia*) and clubs, and (3) the members of the community, such as the class of knight; and the third is the relationship of *amicitia* which was made between the ruling class and other powerful sub-elites.[70] Among these three tiers of patronage, the first category will be discussed here, because the third tier does not appear in fact to involve the poor in the relationship, and the second tier which is not personal will be dealt with later when I discuss the clubs, associations and burial societies.

The master–freedman link is known to be the oldest personal relationship of this kind,[71] set up between a former master and his former slave. A slave in ancient society often had opportunities to obtain freedom because of his faithful service towards his master, or to be released from the bondage of slavery because his master did not want to take any economic burden on behalf of his slaves when he was confronted with economic hardships.[72] This manumission is observed to have been once popular after the Roman authorities allowed freedmen to have free grain distribution.[73] Or a slave who was engaged in industry and trade on behalf of his master more often bought his freedom out of his *peculium*, but after his emancipation he still maintained a relationship with his former master now as his personal patron.[74]

This co-relationship between patron and freedman, now a client, was known to benefit both sides: a patron offered all kinds of protection to his client[75] in order to help him pursue their joint business, because it was normally a sort of joint venture involving both sides. In other words, since the senatorial class was forbidden by law to be involved in trade and industry, they made use of their former slaves who had

Cambridge University Press, 1982), p. 1. Another definition of patronage is to be found in Moxnes, *Economy*, p. 42.

70. Eisenstadt and Roniger, *Patrons*, pp. 52-64; Stambaugh and Balch, *Social World*, pp. 63-64.

71. Cf. G. Hamel, *Poverty and Charity in Roman Palestine, First Three Centuries CE* (Berkeley: University of California Press, 1990), p. 160.

72. Eisenstadt and Roniger, *Patrons*, p. 54.

73. Hands, *Charities*, p. 94.

74. Dill, *Roman Society*, pp. 118-19, 267.

75. Dill, *Roman Society*, p. 119; Garnsey, *Social Status*, pp. 189, 218.

much experience in managing business, and made them work independently for both, ensuring that the former slaves also would get their own share of the profits. Thus in a sense, this tie between patron and client looks like a partnership in a business: the patron provided capital to invest and all sorts of legal and financial protection, whereas the client provided his skill and labour for their business.

Having examined basic features of patronage rather prevalent in various forms and roles in antiquity, we may raise the question as to whether it was a system which really served the poor in the ancient community. To answer this question, notice should be taken of the fact that patronage was also based on the principle of reciprocity—the typical social ethics of the Graeco-Roman world in antiquity.[76] This means that it was not unilateral goodness towards the other, but the exchange of something, such as legal and financial provision on one side and service out of gratitude on the other. Therefore, we are invited to conclude that patronage was not the kind of benefaction which we might expect for the destitute who did not have anything to return for the provision offered by the rich.[77]

c. *The Motives and the Limits of Euergetism*
Here what should be borne in mind is that, according to the historical evidence, such benefaction by wealthy citizens occurred on an irregular basis in the cities of the Roman Empire. One reason for this is that, as pointed out above, benefaction did not originate from altruism or a municipal spirit, but from the interests of the wealthy.[78] Even in

76. Stambaugh and Balch, *Social World*, p. 64; Garnsey, *Social Status*, pp. 189, 218. Cf. Eisenstadt and Roniger, *Patrons*, pp. 252-56.

77. Thus Stambaugh and Balch, *Social World*, p. 64, comment on this point as follows: 'Charity for the poor and destitute, who could not offer anything in exchange, was virtually unknown'.

78. With regard to these interests of the wealthy, we ought to bear one thing in mind, which is that 'fear of famine rather than famine itself was enough to set people on the rampage, as in 57 BC or AD 51' (Garnsey, *Famine*, p. 31). This aspect being considered, we may suppose that at times of famine and food shortage, people would easily have made an appeal to rioting and plundering the properties and goods of the rich. So in order to avoid such incidents, in other words, to secure their properties and even their lives, the wealthy citizens would have been forced to contribute for the benefit of the poor and indigent (cf. Winter, 'Responses', pp. 91-92). For an instance, we can refer to an incident when the mob assaulted the Emperor Claudius in the Forum in 51 CE at a time of food shortage (Suetonius, *Claud.* 18).

the case of food crises, some wealthy people are known to have attempted to profit by hoarding grain in their barns and selling it later at a higher price than usual, or exporting it abroad with a high premium, and even preventing grain from being imported from other areas to force up the price of grain.[79] A principal reason for refuting the idea that benefaction resulted purely from altruism is because on most occasions, when benefactions were made by wealthy citizens or kings, benefactors would have been given honours[80] as well as material rewards. It was not only a cultural convention, but 'a law',[81] that the benefactor

From a Marxist perspective, G.E.M. De Ste. Croix (*The Class Struggle in the Ancient Greek World, from the Archaic Age to the Arab Conquests* [London: Duckworth, 1981]), also asserts this point, in saying that 'the Roman political system facilitated a most intense and ultimately destructive economic exploitation of the great mass of the people, whether slave or free, and it made radical reform impossible. The result was that the propertied class, the men of real wealth, who had deliberately created this system for their own benefit, drained the life-blood from their world and thus destroyed Greco-Roman civilisation over a large part of the empire' (p. 502).

79. Thus, in order to prevent this incident, city authorities frequently made decrees by which they could execute those speculators (Garnsey, *Famine*, pp. 76-78; 32-33).

80. One of the powerful and essential motives of benefaction was *philotimia* or *philodoxia* (love of honour or glory), that is, love of public recognition, which was expressed in forms of titles, inscriptions, statues, and other privileges (Hands, *Charities*, pp. 43, 48; Dill, *Roman Society*, pp. 210, 214, 231).

In this context, what should not be disregarded is that there are some passages in Greek literature where motives of benefaction are revealed not always to be self-centred. Both Aristotle and Pliny the Younger stated an altruistic aspect of benefaction: 'One who gives to the wrong people, or not for the nobility of giving but from some other motive, will not be called liberal, but by some different title; nor will he who gives with pain, for he would prefer the money to the noble deed, which is not the mark of a liberal man' (Aristotle, *Eth. Nic.* 1120a). 'I am also well aware that a nobler spirit will seek the reward of virtue in the consciousness of it, rather than in popular opinion . . . at the time, I was considering the general interest rather than my own self-glorification when I wished the purpose and effect of my benefaction to be known' (Pliny the Younger, *Epp.* 1.8.13).

Thus it should not be said absolutely that on every occasion of benefaction, all of the wealthy tried to obtain honours and material rewards; there were also good motives for benefaction (cf. Dill, *Roman Society*, p. 232). Although this altruistic aspect of benefaction should get attention, weightier emphasis should be laid on the fact that the majority of the material dealing with benefaction in Graeco-Roman literature illustrates the self-centredness of benefaction, as has been argued above.

81. Winter, 'Honouring', p. 90.

expected repayment,[82] and his benefaction could be viewed as a loan.[83] Seneca endeavoured to correct such a view, which meant that benefactors should not necessarily expect recompense.[84] This led to an emphasis on the attitude of recipients who, according to Seneca, should have regarded the benefaction as a debt,[85] and could commit a sin if they failed to repay the benefit.[86] Philo also stressed that the beneficiaries were commanded to repay gratitude,[87] and Cicero too placed emphasis on the great importance of returning gratitude.[88] With this practical aspect of benefaction, that is, reciprocity,[89] in view, it seems hardly

82. Seneca, *Ben*. 1.1.4-8; 2.11.6; 2.24.4; Diodorus Siculus, *Bib. Hist.* 1.70.6; 1.90.2-3; 11.58.4; 5.4.3; cf. 38/39.21; 37.6. 'Geschenke spielen bei Naturvölkern eine grosse Rolle, aber sie erfolgen niemals ohne die Erwartung einer Gegengabe' (Bolkestein, *Armenpflege*, p. 156). For 'die Erwartung der Vergeltung' in Greece, see Bolkestein, *Armenpflege*, pp. 156-70, and for that of Rome, see *Armenpflege*, pp. 317-18.

83. Seneca, *Ben*. 4.12.1; 1.1.3.

84. Seneca, *Ben*. 1.1.9-10; 4.12.1-2; cf. Philo, *Dec*. 167. When Seneca was asked what the recompense for giving was, he stated that it was 'bona conscientia' (*Ben*. 4.12.4).

85. Seneca, *Ben*. 1.4.3-5; cf. Dionysius of Halicarnassus, *Ant. Rom.* 4.9.2-3; 4.10.5; 6.77.2; 8.49.1-2; Diodorus Siculus, *Bib. Hist.* 13.26.3.

86. Seneca, *Ben*. 1.1.13. 'Qui beneficium non reddit, magis peccat; qui non dat citius'.

87. Philo, *Dec*. 165-7.

88. Cicero, *De Off*. 1.47: 'Nullum enim officium referenda gratia magis necessarium est'.

This concern for reciprocity 'affected almost every relationship in the life of the upper class, including the relationship to the gods' (S.C. Mott, 'Power', p. 72). On this ground, Mott considers reciprocity 'an important factor binding Graeco-Roman society together, especially vertically between units possessing different degrees of power' (p. 67). Hence, in this context, it would be rather easily understood that 'Hellenistic benevolence was voluntary, paternalistic, and made little penetration into the lower classes' (p. 72). For more detail about reciprocity of giving, which was pervasive in the Graeco-Roman World, see Hands, *Charities*, Ch. 3.

89. In ancient literature we find that various sorts of reciprocity prevailed throughout different classes of societies:

(1) Between gods and believers: Diodorus Siculus, *Bib. Hist.* 1.29.2; 5.4.3.; 5.67.5; 5.71.1; 5.77.4.

(2) Between kings and subjects: Strabo, *Geog.* 17.2.3; Diodorus Siculus, *Bib. Hist.* 5.83.3; 6.1.8; 11.26.6; 11.58.4; 19.9.6; 37.6; Dionysius of Halicarnassus, *Ant. Rom.* 2.10.1-2.

(3) Between cities or states: Diodorus Siculus, *Bib. Hist.* 13.26.3; 17.14.2; 17.81.1-2; cf. 27.18.2.

possible to believe that benefaction originated from concern about realistic need of the poor and destitute.[90] Underlying this evidence, there would be the Graeco-Roman concept of pity (Greek: ἐλεημοσύνη; Latin: *misericordia*), which can be summarized as follows: 'Pity is appropriately given on an exchange basis to men of like character, and not to those who are not going to show pity in return'.[91] Thus in relation to this, Hands argues that 'in general, therefore, the conditions of the poor were little ameliorated by the rich',[92] although the poor were benefitted by the rich to a limited extent by way of benefaction.

4. *Clubs, Associations and Burial Colleges*

When we are dealing with the system of benefaction in the Graeco-Roman world which played a crucial role in keeping the ancient societies running, it should not be forgotten that it is also found in the life of clubs or associations. Thus there occurs a need to discuss this side of benefaction in antiquity.

As we have seen earlier in the chapter, the ancient world seems to have existed mainly for the nobility, because all the socio-politico-economic systems of the ancient communities appear to have been run for the benefit of the rich and those in power, while the rest of the people existed to keep those systems going smoothly and conveniently. But as time went on, this polarized situation gradually changed, because there appeared professional merchants and artisans whose economic power grew gradually,[93] so that their existence could not be ignored by the nobility. Although they had some degree of wealth and were to some extent in control of financial markets, yet they were still totally isolated from any political power, and were not allowed to entertain themselves in a social atmosphere like the nobility. Thus initially from the purpose of social intercourse,[94] those who were engaged in the same professions began to gather in certain places in order to have social

---

90. Among those most in need, Winter argues that 'real' widows would have been included ('*Providentia* for the Widows of 1 Timothy 5.3-16', *TynBul* 39 [1988], pp. 83-89 [86-87]).

91. Hands, *Charities*, p. 80.

92. Hands, *Charities*, p. 76.

93. Their position was occupied by slaves beforehand.

94. MacMullen, *Relations*, p. 77, puts this notion as 'pure comradeship'.

events such as the common meals for their entertainment,[95] because 'individually weak and despised, they might, by union, gain a sense of collective dignity and strength'.[96]

Therefore, different kinds of occupations throughout the Graeco-Roman world, such as shippers, porters, bakers, carpenters, and so on,[97] begot a variety of clubs of which we can see evidence from the extant inscriptions. Although one of the main goals of those clubs or associations was social conviviality among the members,[98] it is another object that attracts our attention in particular, that is, clubs existed to ensure proper and decent burial after death.[99] In antiquity 'a place for burial was a coveted possession', so that it was available only to the affluent and mighty in the communities.[100] It seems common to all human beings to desire a decent burial, and this concern more keenly affected the poorer people because they did not want to be abandoned disgracefully after death. Thus alongside the social clubs we mentioned earlier, in most urban parts of the Graeco-Roman Empire this kind of a burial club, *collegia tenuiorum*, was very popular amongst the poor, irrespective of their occupation.[101] These burial clubs were more readily tolerated by the Roman authorities who from time to time suppressed professional clubs because of 'the potential of even the most social group to take on a political coloring'.[102]

95. For this reason, these clubs in the Graeco-Roman world should not be considered as identical to guilds in the mediaeval ages or trade unions in our days whose main object is to protect their professional interest from outsiders. Cf. MacMullen, *Relations*, p. 75; Meeks, *Urban Christians*, p. 31; Finley, *Ancient Economy*, pp. 81, 138, 194 n. 57.

96. Dill, *Roman Society*, p. 256; cf. p. 253.

97. These are just a fraction of the whole range of occupations which were present in the ancient societies. MacMullen, *Relations*, p. 73, shows us more lists of the variety of professions in the ancient economy.

98. Dill, *Roman Society*, p. 268; Meeks, *Urban Christians*, p. 79; *The Moral World of the First Christians* (London: SPCK, 1987), p. 113.

99. Dill, *Roman Society*, pp. 259-60; MacMullen, *Relations*, p. 79; Meeks, *Urban Christians*, pp. 32, 78, 162.

100. Dill, *Roman Society*, p. 259. Dill also states, 'It is clear that many of the purely industrial colleges, composed as they were of poor people who found it impossible to purchase a separate burial-place, and not easy, unaided, to bear the expense of the last rites, at once consulted their convenience, and gratified the sentiment of fraternity, by arranging for a common place of interment' (*Roman Society*, p. 263).

101. Hands, *Charities*, p. 60; Meeks, *Moral World*, p. 113.

102. Stambaugh and Balch, *Social World*, p. 125; cf. p. 127; Dill, *Roman Society*,

In the matter of the clubs' management, the professional associations including the burial clubs were run by means of certain rules and regulations fixed by the needs of individual groups. It was known, however, as a common rule that they imposed an entry fee and a monthly membership fee on their members, and gained also extra income, such as fines from those who breached the rules. In the case of the burial clubs, however, these fees and fines were known to be minimal in order to give access to the poor people who were placed at the very bottom of society. In relation to this point, Stambaugh and Balch make a note regarding beggars, the poorest who could not afford to pay even such small membership fees: 'Individuals who were too poor to be able to afford even that were simply carted to a common paupers' grave and dumped into it without any proper ceremony.'[103]

Although these clubs and associations in general relied upon their resources of fees, they also rather heavily counted on the generosity of the wealthy whose contributions would be vital to the welfare of the clubs, for it was not always easy for them to manage to attain one of their aims, that is, social entertainment among the members, especially in the poor clubs, such as the burial clubs.[104] Thus the clubs elected wealthy or influential persons in the communities where they lived who worked as their patrons along with patron gods as well, and expected them to present food and money to the clubs liberally and to provide them with certain places where the members were able to meet together for monthly assembly or the common meals[105] on the festive days.[106] There is much inscriptional evidence for this benevolence of the patrons towards their client clubs and associations, because it became a rule, as we have examined earlier, that in response to the benefaction made by their patrons those clubs involved almost always

p. 254; Meeks, *Moral World*, p. 113.

103. Stambaugh and Balch, *Social World*, p. 125. Cf. Esler, *Community*, p. 177.

104. Stambaugh and Balch, *Social World*, p. 126; Meeks, *Urban Christians*, p. 78.

105. Dill, *Roman Society*, p. 267.

106. The following are typical occasions for club gatherings: 'the anniversary of the foundation, the birthday of founders or benefactors, the feast of the patron deity, the birthday of the emperor, these and the like occasions furnished legal pretexts for meetings of the society, when the members might have a meal together, and when the conversation would not always be confined to the funerary business of the college' (Dill, *Roman Society*, p. 259).

erected inscriptions to give honour and gratitude to their patrons or benefactors.[107]

Having examined the aspects of the clubs' life in the Graeco-Roman world on the whole, we may now raise a question as to whether those benefactions made available to the poor associations by the wealthy patrons are really to be considered as charitable in nature and in terms of purpose. The answer to this question appears to lie in the fact that the money or food which patrons gave away to the client clubs was unequally distributed among the members according to their rank which was intended to be kept, even among the club members. Dill makes a pertinent comment on this point:

> In the humblest of these colleges, the distribution of good fare and money is not according to the needs of the members, but regulated by their social and official rank.[108]

In addition to this inequality of distribution, we should also take notice of the motives of benevolence made by wealthy patrons, also succinctly summarized by Dill:

> The donations or bequests of rich patrons seem to have had chiefly two objects in view, the commemoration of the dead and the provision for social and convivial enjoyment.[109]

By and large the donations were made by wealthy patrons, not primarily out of their pure and sincere sympathy towards the poor but for their own interest and purposes, such as the commemoration of the dead who were possibly husbands or wives of the patrons,[110] or the birthdays of the founders or their relatives, as I have pointed out above.[111]

107. Hands, *Charities*, p. 36: 'Indeed, the very title of *benefactor/euergetes* was itself *philanthropon*, since it did not simply state a fact but conferred a status, indicating that the person on whom it was conferred was in credit, as it were, in respect of the balance of friendly acts. In this sense it was true that the classical benefactor, by virtue of his very title, had his reward' (cf. *Charities*, pp. 52, 79). Meeks, *Urban Christians*, p. 78; Stambaugh and Balch, *Social World*, p. 125.

108. Dill, *Roman Society*, p. 282; cf. pp. 278-79; Meeks, *Urban Christians*, p. 68; G. Theissen, 'Soziale Integration und sakramentales Handeln', in *Studien zur Soziologie des Urchristentums* (Tübingen: J.C.B. Mohr, 1979), pp. 290-317 (291-92).

109. Dill, *Roman Society*, p. 282.

110. Dill, *Roman Society*, p. 262.

111. Dill, *Roman Society*, pp. 268, 277. Esler, *Community*, p. 176, also draws the same conclusion relying on the thesis of Waltzing that 'from a careful survey of the

Nonetheless, it should not be neglected that although selfish motives induced wealthy people to distribute their wealth, yet this support was not in the least insignificant to the poor, however small it might have been. To those who did not know where the next meal would come from, there is no doubt that even a sprinkling of food and money bestowed by the rich must have been very greatly appreciated.

5. *Communal Living*

In this section, I shall discuss another system of financial support intended for the poor, which was also available at times contemporary to Luke. This is the community of goods or communal living exercised by the Qumran community and the communities of the Essenes in Palestine. Previous exploration of this aspect has showed us that the Qumran community kept a sort of community of goods, creating a common fund and practising a common meal among the members.[112]

Here my concern is about whether or not the community of goods kept at Qumran had a charitable purpose towards the poor. We may answer this question by pointing out one of the differences between the Qumran community and the Jerusalem community, which we noticed earlier while dealing with the systems of the common fund and the common meal. That is the motive for creating such systems: while at Qumran it was a means of maintaining its communal life in an isolated place in order to protect the community from the outside world which they believed was corrupt and immoral, it was loving care on behalf of the poor in the Jerusalem community.

It may be true that among the members of the Qumran sect there would not have been the poor, because they are known to have shared everything in common with each other after being admitted into full membership of the community. It means that the poor may have been well taken care of if they were allowed to get into it. Nonetheless, no explicit motivation of almsgiving is revealed in relation to the Qumran

evidence Waltzing has shown, moreover, that neither the professional nor the burial *collegia* had a charitable purpose; it was not their practice to come to the aid of sick or indigent members'.

112. Here we may also include the Therapeutae, the Egyptian contemplative sect. For a link between Therapeutae, Essenes and Qumran, see G. Vermes, 'Essenes-Therapeutae-Qumran', *Durham University Journal* 21 (1960), pp. 97-115; Schürer, *History*, II, pp. 593-97.

sect. Rather, the motif of almsgiving is to be found in the communities of the Essenes as recorded in the Damascus Rule (CD), XIV, 12-16:

> They shall place the earnings of at least two days out of every month into the hands of the Guardian and the Judges, and from it they shall give to the fatherless, and from it they shall succour the poor and the needy, the aged sick and the homeless, the captive taken by a foreign people, the virgin with no near kin, and the maid for whom no man cares . . . [113]

Thus it is believed that instead of the communal living which its brethren community kept with determination for the sake of purity, the town sects appear to have kept faithfully the traditional practice of almsgiving towards the poor and needy which was dictated in the law by God and handed down to the generations to come through history.

In this context, there is a point of significance to which we need to turn our attention. In Acts there occurs just one single incident of almsgiving which the Jerusalem Christian community put into practice: the distribution of the dole to the poor widows (Acts 6.1-2). However, among many exhortations to almsgiving made by Jesus in Luke's Gospel, there is no explicit reference to the widow, whereas the blind, crippled, and lepers are singled out as beneficiaries to be given alms. What this fact reveals is that in the matter of almsgiving, the Early Church at Jerusalem seems to have followed the tradition of Judaism, just as they did in other areas, such as prayer and worship in the temple or synagogues (Acts 3.1-2; 13.13-14; 14.1-2).

6. *Almsgiving in Judaism*

Now bearing in mind what has just been said, we should take into account the practice of almsgiving in Judaism, for there is no doubt that the Christian system of almsgiving was originally derived from its predecessor, and to a great extent affected by it, although there were some substantial differences between them. Thus, in what follows, we will discuss briefly the essence and practice of almsgiving in Judaism, and then we will compare the benefaction system of the Graeco-Roman world described at length previously.

The origin of almsgiving in Judaism is theologically founded on the Exodus of the Israelites from Egypt. In the Scriptures, God is represented as frequently reminding the Israelites of this unique event, when

---

113. Vermes, *The Dead Sea Scrolls in English*, p. 98; cf. p. 15.

He gave them the divine commandments on behalf of the widows, orphans, and strangers[114] who represented the lower orders of society throughout the history of Israel (Deut. 14.28-29; 26.12).[115]

We can enumerate several organized systems of relief or almsgiving directed specifically to the well-being of the poor and destitute both in the Torah and in the Mishnah.[116] To begin with, there is the prescription of the second tithe for the poor in the third and sixth year of every sabbatical cycle.[117] A second edict is related to the Sabbath law on cultivation of crops, by which God commanded the Israelite to let the land lie unploughed and unused during the seventh year, so that the poor might get food from it (Exod. 23.10-11). A third edict concerns the regulations about the harvest which enabled the poor to claim 'the three customary rights' which served to relieve them from hunger and starvation.[118] A fourth edict is found in the decrees of the Year of Jubilee.[119] If anyone who was impoverished had been forced to part with his inheritance, he could reclaim it in the Year of Jubilee (Lev. 25.25-28). Also, among Israelites usury was forbidden for the sake of the poor, so that the poor were to borrow money at no cost, when needed (Lev. 25.35-38; cf. Deut. 15.7-8). A fifth edict concerns slavery among Israelites (Lev. 25.39-55): if an impoverished Israelite should sell himself into slavery, he might have expected more favourable terms than the non-Israelite, and he was also entitled by the law to go free at the Jubilee. This is another exemplary case of a divine

114. Deut. 24.17-18; 10.18-20; 27.19; Exod. 22.21-27.

115. Cf. L.J. Hoppe, *Being Poor* (Wilmington: Michael Glazier, 1987), pp. 5-13.

116. J. Jeremias (*Jerusalem in the Time of Jesus* [London: SCM Press, 1969], p. 132), calls this relief 'public charities', which he distinguishes from private charities made occasionally by individuals.

117. Deut. 14.28-29; 26.12-15. *M. Peʾah* 8.2-9; *M. Šeb.* 5.6, 9, 10. For a further explanation of this, see R. Brooks, *Support for the Poor in the Mishnaic Law of Agriculture: Tractate Peʾah* (Chico, CA: Scholars Press, 1983), pp. 139-56. Cf. E.P. Sanders, *Jewish Law from Jesus to the Mishnah* (London: SCM Press, 1990), pp. 236-37.

118. The regulations are as follows: '(1) the harvesters were not to pick individual heads of grain or grapes fallen to the ground; (2) they were not to go back and harvest the field or the tree again, picking the forgotten sheaf or branch; (3) they were not to harvest the field completely, but to leave a corner' (Hamel, *Poverty*, p. 217). A full commentary on these regulations is preserved in *M. Peʾah*. For exposition of *M. Peah*, see Brooks, *Tractate Peʾah*. Cf. Jeremias, *Jerusalem*, p. 132.

119. For more detail, see Jeremias, *Jerusalem*, pp. 110-11; p. 314.

commandment for the benefit of the poor. All these edicts referred to above can be described as forms of benevolence for the poor in one way or another.[120]

Apart from these biblical regulations made in favour of the poor, there was also a tradition of public charity available to the poor in the Jewish community. In fact there were 'two community-wide charitable institutions' which were particularly intended for the poor and indigent in the Jewish community:[121] one is תמחוי, plate or soup-kitchens, and the other is קופה, the communal fund.[122] As the titles show, the goals of the two institutions were different. תמחוי is a prescription for short-term needs, and was collected to help the poor 'in immediate need of sustenance', providing them with a single daily meal.[123] In this sense it was normally made available especially for the poor travellers. On the contrary, קופה is a prescription for long-term needs, and was created to support the local poor only on a weekly basis. So there were certain rules to determine who was eligible to claim this benefit.[124] It is clear that behind these detailed regulations lies the caring concern of the community for the poor who could not provide for themselves.[125]

Thus, if we take these edicts and traditions into consideration together, it is clear that almsgiving is rooted deeply in Judaism from its beginning. In other words, poor people in the Judaic society were not wholly despised and neglected, but remembered throughout its history (Deut. 15.11). Accordingly, almsgiving was regarded later in Judaism as one of the three pillars of the world, along with the Torah and the Temple service,[126] and the concern for the poor was still maintained in

---

120. Besides the above edicts, we can note many other passages in the Old Testament referring to explicit concern about the poor (Pss. 94.6; 112.9; Isa. 1.17, 23; 10.2; Ezek. 22.7; Zech. 7.10; Jer. 5.28; Prov. 11.24; 19.17; 22.9; 28.27; Eccl. 11.1).

121. Brooks, *Tractate Pe'ah*, p. 147.

122. *M. Pe'ah*, 8.7. Jeremias' rendering of קופה as 'poor-basket' might be misleading (Jeremias, *Jerusalem*, p. 131). Cf. Schürer, *History*, II, p. 437.

123. Brooks, *Tractate Pe'ah*, p. 147.

124. See *t. Pe'ah*, 4.9 (Brooks, *Tractate Pe'ah*, p. 148).

125. Jeremias's comparison of these charity institutions of the Jewish community which, he regards, provided food and clothing with the common meal held by the Early Church at Jerusalem attracts our attention: 'there can be no doubt therefore that these arrangements served as a model for the primitive Church . . . the fellowship meal that was held daily by the Christian community, entailed of itself a daily distribution of aid for its poor members' (*Jerusalem*, p. 131).

126. *Ab.* 1.2.

later Judaism, of which evidence we may recall the Tractate Pe'ah, and the Tractate Maaserot.[127]

There is one further point which needs to be discussed in this connection. Throughout their history, the Jewish people seem to have been faithful in keeping those rules, but their ardent enthusiasm to keep those regulations in a meticulous manner seems to lead to the notion that almsgiving could be identified with 'righteousness' itself: 'Charity and righteous deeds outweigh all other commandments in the Torah'.[128] Thus in this sense we might reckon that Jewish almsgiving was an integral part of law-obedience in Judaism.[129]

Now it is time to compare the system of almsgiving of Judaism with that of Graeco-Roman society, in disclosing noticeable differences between them.

First of all, the object to which alms were given is different. In the case of Judaism, alms are supposed to be bestowed on the real poor and needy, whereas in Graeco-Roman society financial support was directed not to the poor as such, but to one's friends and fellow-citizens, whatever their economic status, who would be able to repay in return, as described previously. Thus, as the concept of pity in that society shows, the poor were not singled out in distributing alms, so in this sense it would be no exaggeration to claim that almsgiving in the proper sense of the word did not exist in Graeco-Roman society.

---

127. For a commentary on this tractate, see Martin S. Jaffee's *Mishnah's Theology of Tithing: A Study of Tractate Maaserot* (Chico, CA: Scholars Press, 1981).

128. *T. Pe'ah*, 4.19. For a comment on this subject, see Brooks, *Tractate Pe'ah*, p. 155. Cf. Sanders, *Jewish Law*, p. 71. With regard to this aspect, D.S. Russell (*From Early Judaism to Early Church* [London: SCM Press, 1986]), pp. 61-62, also makes an interesting note: 'It is of interest to observe that as early as Ben Sira (c. 180 BC), the Greek word ἐλεημοσύνη, which is used seventeen times in the Septuagint to translate the Hebrew word *ṣedaqah* meaning "righteousness" is used with the meaning, "almsgiving".'

129. There are several passages in the Apocrypha which imply this:

> Tob. 4.11: 'for all who practise it charity is an excellent offering in the presence of the Most High',
> Tob. 12.8: 'Prayer is good when accompanied by fasting, almsgiving, and righteousness'.
> Tob. 12.9: 'For almsgiving delivers from death, and it will purge away every sin'.
> Sir. 3.30: 'Water extinguishes a blazing fire: so almsgiving atones for sin'.
> Sir. 29.12: 'Store up almsgiving in your treasury, and it will rescue you from all affliction'.

A second discrepancy that can be observed is related to compensation. Remuneration of almsgiving in Judaism is expected to come from God in this world or in the world to come, but not from recipients. The general import of the recompense for almsgiving in Judaism which can be drawn from Prov. 19.17 is that the giver should expect his reward from God rather than from his beneficiaries, because there was little that the poor could do in return for the alms bestowed on them. But in Graeco-Roman society, the reward for almsgiving is supposed to come directly from beneficiaries in a tangible and immediate form, which constituted the principle of reciprocity, the principle which underlay all transactions and relations among citizens.

From this comparison, we can observe clearly that the scheme of almsgiving in Judaism differed strikingly from that of Graeco-Roman society. It paved the way for the Christian scheme of almsgiving, for the latter is seen to have owed the quintessence of its practice to the former.

7. Conclusion: Lukan Almsgiving in its Social Context

Thus far I have dealt with various types of benefaction systems which were to be found in the Graeco-Roman society around 1 CE, such as state schemes of benefaction, private benefaction to city or community, and the roles of club and burial societies in particular. I have also looked into the motives of such benefactions as well as their limitations.

From this examination, I have found that in the social and historical context of Luke's community, that is, the Graeco-Roman Empire in the first century CE, although famine itself did not occur so often, food shortages resulting from crop failure, war and epidemics, were known to be frequent. In cases of real necessity, the poor in the community were helpless and starved to death unless the rich helped them in contributing grain and money. But such help from wealthy citizens could hardly be expected to happen frequently, because they pursued their own benefits and interests, and the Roman officials in the provinces intervened only on rare occasions. Meanwhile, during normal situations in which no natural calamity occurred, wealthy individuals offered financial support to clubs or associations in which they were involved as patron, but the motives of such financial contribution are also more or less the same as those of other benefactions to be noticed in Graeco-Roman society. To put it simply, we can state that the very subsistence of a community in that time depended heavily upon the wealthy, for without their help and cooperation a vast majority of the populace were threatened with death. Thus the problem was on the part of the rich, which means that the roles which they would have played in ancient society seem to have been more significant than ever.

Apart from these systems of benefaction, the practice that was exercised by the communities of the Essenes arrests our attention, because the members of those communities who were able to earn their living were supposed to help orphans, widows, the elderly and the homeless with their means of a small amount which they had to set aside every month. This practice made by the communities of the Essenes reminds us of the Jewish concept of almsgiving for which God was seen as declaring himself the father of such indigent people.

Now that we have noticed these findings, it is time to point out differences between Luke's prescription of helping the poor and various kinds of benefaction or almsgiving systems found in the Graeco-Roman society contemporary with Luke. In general, benefaction systems that existed in the Graeco-Roman society were based on reciprocity, so that it can be said that in an absolute sense, there was no benefaction designed especially for the poor that came out of pure altruism. Meanwhile, it would seem that Jewish society including the communities of the Essenes can be referred to as one which practised almsgiving without the spirit of reciprocity.

The point we have discovered here may be sharpened when we are reminded of the radical nature of Luke's idea of almsgiving. In many places in Luke–Acts,[130] those who have means are urged to part with their material possessions, to sell them and to distribute their proceeds to the poor, but unlike other benefactors of the Graeco-Roman society, they are discouraged from anticipating any reward from their recipients on earth.[131]

Thus this Lukan notion of almsgiving which is unparalleled in his Gentile environment even if it has partial parallels and precedence in Judaism, enables us to claim that Luke's exhortation of almsgiving towards the wealthy was so radical as to surprise the rich members of his community. However, it seems reasonable for Luke to have given the rich such alarming advice when it was the case that Luke realized

130. For instance, Lk. 11.41; 12.33; 18.22. Cf. Lk. 3.11; 6.38; 14.33; 16.9; Acts 20.35.
131. Lk. 6.35; 12.33-34; 14.13-14; 18.22.

there was an enormous gap between the rich and the poor in terms of socio-economic conditions, and found the poor suffering from hunger and facing starvation as their daily routine. Hence, Luke's particular concern about the rich attached to his sympathy towards the poor appears very reasonable, and along with this we are able to state that Luke wanted to remind the rich members of his community of *their identity as steward* before God, the Master who entrusted them with wealth and property.

In this context, there is one thing that should be remembered: against the ethics of reciprocity prevalent in the society contemporaneous with Luke, Luke appears to have advised his congregation that the boundary of their almsgiving should not be restricted within the community, but extend beyond it, regardless of their membership of the Christian community, out of genuine Christian love towards the poor and needy (cf. Lk. 6.27-38; 14.13, 21-23; Acts 9.41).

Chapter 9

CONCLUSION

This book started with questions concerning Luke's idea of the relationship between wealth and discipleship. I began this book in the light of
several previous studies in the area of the theme of wealth and poverty
in Luke's theology over the last three decades. I found them unsatisfactory in solving the problems we have in Luke–Acts, which are derived
from an attempt to relate wealth to discipleship in Luke's theology:

   (1)   Does Luke have in mind two types of disciples?

   (2)   Is a total surrender of possessions required of all, or just the
          Twelve? What might Luke mean by such a total surrender?

   (3)   In describing the relationship between wealth and disciple-
          ship, is the 'discipleship' motif sufficient, or are there other
          terms or motifs to help us understand Luke?

   (4)   Does Luke have any specific emphasis in the practical consid-
          erations of how wealth is to be employed?

   Previous attempts are found to have failed to reconcile the matter of
wealth and poverty with the theme of discipleship in Luke's theology.
This failure motivates me to investigate a new paradigm, that is, stewardship. The following are the conclusions of my exploration.
   With regard to the *Sitz im Leben* of Luke–Acts, it emerges that
Luke's community would have been located in an urban setting steeped
in the Hellenistic culture somewhere in the Roman East around the
end of the first century CE. Its members would have been Gentiles in
terms of their ethnic background, and in terms of their socio-economic
status, both the rich and the poor, representing the extremes of the
spectrum of contemporary society.

In the second chapter, I investigated the theme of discipleship in Mark's Gospel. Since Mark was a main source for Luke, Mark's view of the disciples and discipleship needs to be compared with that of Luke. My conclusions are that, facing a lingering threat of persecution in his community, Mark urged the Christian friends in his community to follow Jesus their Lord even to the point of death. Jesus is portrayed as a prime example of faithful discipleship, while the failure of the disciples is treated as an example to avoid. In accordance with this idea of discipleship, the disciples in Mark are seen as a limited number of followers of Jesus, who have failed to comprehend Jesus' teaching and instruction in spite of his preferential treatment of them. In line with this concept of discipleship, in Mark the disciples were required literally to leave their wealth (Mk 1.18, 20; 2.14; 10.28).

This notion of discipleship perceived by Mark is compared with that of Luke in Chapter 3, in order to reveal Luke's distinctive concept of it. Luke's community was not confronted with persecution such as threatened Mark's community, and the *parousia* is also seen to be delayed in Luke's Gospel so as to highlight a concern with the daily life of Christians. Thus, Luke's concept of discipleship is different from that of Mark: the disciples in the Gospel are identified with those who appear in Acts, who are represented as a large number of people. Luke appears to tend to portray the disciples in a favourable manner, and to have developed the notion of two types of disciples, such as the itinerant who might be identical to the Apostles, and the sedentary who were seen to accept and to follow Jesus' teaching where they were, even though they did not literally follow after Jesus in his journey to Jerusalem.

In this context, what is particularly noteworthy is that, despite the strict nature of his commands to renounce *all* to follow him, Jesus does not reproach the sedentary disciples who are shown not to have left their possessions and property, but rather appears to accept them as they are, enjoying their entertainment as they invite him and his wandering disciples to meals in their houses. This is a very significant point: Luke's idea of discipleship in view of Jesus' injunction of a total renunciation of wealth is that a small number of the itinerant disciples were required to forsake literally everything, while the sedentary disciples who for Luke were identified with his congregation were asked to forsake the *ownership* of all they possessed.

Having discerned Luke's concept of discipleship, I cannot avoid wondering if the idea of discipleship is after all appropriate to embrace fully his re-oriented concept of wealth. Accordingly, I look at another aspect of Luke's Gospel, distinct from the teacher–pupil relation which constitutes discipleship. On the basis of detailed observation we trace a new motif in Luke which appears to be more pervasive than the teacher–pupil relation, that is, the master–slave relation. In the light of this new dominant motif in the Gospel it is shown that Luke intended to define the proper relation between God, or Jesus, and Christians as the master–slave relation, rather than simply the teacher–pupil relation that constitutes a basic element of Markan discipleship.

Now that a new concept of wealth and the master–slave relation have emerged as conspicuous features distinctive in Luke's theology which have not previously been given appropriate attention, we combine these two features peculiar to Luke, and as a result, suggest a new paradigm for Christians, that is, *stewardship*. After discussing the three stewardship parables, that is, the Parable of the Faithful and Wise Steward (Lk. 12.42-48), the Parable of the Unjust Steward (Lk. 16.1-13) and the Parable of the Ten Minas (Lk. 19.11-27), we identify the requirements of stewardship Luke had in mind as follows:

(1)   What a steward owns does not belong to him but to his master;

(2)   his stewardship is provisional so he may be summoned to account anytime, hence he must be alert all the time;

(3)   there will be judgment of his work: if he turns out to be faithful in his duty, there will be a reward, otherwise punishment.

From this identification of Luke's particular interest in stewardship, we go on to find out how and in what area Luke intended to apply stewardship to the Christian life. This is not very difficult, because it is now commonly acknowledged that there is a strong concern with the theme of the poor and the rich in Luke's writings. Thus in light of the theme of stewardship we examine the wide range of material relating to wealth and poverty in Luke–Acts, and conclude that for Luke a proper way for a Christian as steward to use his possessions is almsgiving in the interest of the poor and needy inside and outside the community.

In addition, I note that this motif of almsgiving continues to be found in Acts, the sequel to the Gospel, so that Luke's special concern with almsgiving is confirmed in this continuity of the theme in Acts.

Also, the communal living practised by the Early Christians at Jerusalem whose main purpose is to help the poor is not so much analogous to that of the Qumran community, as to that of the town-based Essene communities.

Furthermore, in order to find out if there is any contemporary parallel to Luke's concept of almsgiving based on stewardship at his time, I compare Luke's notion with benefaction systems prevalent in Graeco-Roman society at the time. It becomes clear that his concept of almsgiving can be labelled as radical, confronting the contemporary ethic of reciprocity. Its origin can be traced back to Judaism, the matrix of Christianity.

In the final analysis, having noticed that Luke's concept of almsgiving based on stewardship was unique and radical, with no parallel in the circumstances where his community was situated, I conclude this book with the following statement: out of genuine sympathy towards the poor, Luke intended to urge the rich Christians in his community to remember their identity as stewards, and to distribute their wealth to the poor as alms, giving up the ownership of all they possessed.

BIBLIOGRAPHY

The Greek Bible used in this book is *Novum Testamentum Graece* (eds. B. and K. Aland, J. Karavidopoulos, C.M. Martini, B.M. Metzger; Stuttgart: Deutsche Bibelgesellschaft, 1995).

Alexander, L., 'Luke's Preface in the Context of Greek Preface-Writing', *NovT* 28 (1986), pp. 48-74.
—*The Preface to Luke's Gospel* (SNTSMS, 78; Cambridge: Cambridge University Press, 1993).
Allen, W.C., *The Gospel according to St Mark* (London: Macmillan, 1915).
Allison, D.C., 'Was there a "Lukan Community"?', *IBS* 10 (1988), pp. 62-70.
Anderson, H., *The Gospel of Mark* (NCB; London: Oliphants, 1976).
Bailey, K.E., *Poet and Peasant and Through Peasant Eyes* (Grand Rapids: Eerdmans, 1988).
Baldry, H.C., *The Unity of Mankind in Greek Thought* (Cambridge: Cambridge University Press, 1965).
Barclay, J.M.G., 'Paul, Philemon and the Dilemma of Christian Slave-Ownership', *NTS* 37 (1991), pp. 161-86.
Barr, D.L., and J.L. Wentling, 'The Conventions of Classical Biography and the Genre of Luke–Acts: A Preliminary Study', in C.H. Talbert (ed.), *Luke–Acts: New Perspectives from the Society of Biblical Literature Seminar* (New York: Crossroad, 1984), pp. 63-88.
Barrow, R.H., *Slavery in the Roman Empire* (London: Methuen, 1928).
Baumeister, T., *Die Anfänge der Theologie des Martyriums* (Münster: Aschendorff, 1980).
Beall, T.S., *Josephus's Description of the Essenes Illustrated by the Dead Sea Scrolls* (Cambridge: Cambridge University Press, 1988).
Beare, F.W., *The First Epistle of Peter* (Oxford: Basil Blackwell, 1947).
Beavis, M.A., *Mark's Audience: The Literary and Social Setting of Mark 4.11-12* (JSNTSup, 33; Sheffield: JSOT Press, 1989).
Beck, B.E., *Christian Character in the Gospel of Luke* (London: SPCK, 1989).
Belkin, S., 'The Problem of Paul's Background', *JBL* 54 (1935), pp. 41-60.
Bengel, J.A., *Gnomon of the New Testament* (5 vols.; Edinburgh: T. & T. Clark, 1866).
—*1 Peter* (NCB; London: Oliphants, 1971).
Best, E., *Following Jesus* (JSNTSup, 4; Sheffield: JSOT Press, 1981).
—*Disciples and Discipleship* (Edinburgh: T. & T. Clark, 1986).
—*Mark: The Gospel as Story* (Edinburgh: T. & T. Clark, 1988).
Beyer, H.W., 'διακονία', *TDNT*, II, pp. 81-93.
—'κατηχέω', *TDNT*, III, pp. 638-40.

Bigg, C., *Commentary of St Peter and St Jude* (ICC; Edinburgh: T. & T. Clark, 1969).

Black, C.C., *The Disciples according to Mark* (JSNTSup, 27; Sheffield: JSOT Press, 1989).

Black, M., *The Scrolls and Christian Origins* (Edinburgh: Nelson, 1961).

—*An Aramaic Approach to the Gospels and Acts* (Oxford: Clarendon Press, 1967).

—'The Dead Sea Scrolls and Christian Origins', in M. Black (ed.), *The Scrolls and Christianity* (London: SPCK, 1969).

Blinzler, J., 'Jesus and his Disciples', in H.J. Schultz (ed.), *Jesus in his Time* (London: SPCK, 1971), pp. 84-95.

Bolkestein, H., *Wohltätigkeit und Armenpflege im vorchristlichen Altertum* (Utrecht: A. Oosthoek, 1939).

Bornkamm, G., *Jesus of Nazareth* (London: Hodder & Stoughton, 1984).

Bovon, F., *Luke the Theologian: Thirty-Three Years of Research (1950–1983)* (Alison Park, PA: Pickwick Publications, 1987).

—*Das Evangelium nach Lukas (Lk. 1.1-9.50)* (EKKNT, 3.1; Zürich: Benzinger Verlag, 1989).

Bradley, K.R., *Slavery and the Rebellion in the Roman World, 140 BC–70 BC* (London: Indiana Press, 1989).

Brandon, S.G.F., *Jesus and the Zealots* (Manchester: Manchester University Press, 1967).

—'The Date of the Markan Gospel', *NTS* 7 (1960–61), pp. 126-41.

Braun, H., 'The Qumran Community', in H.J. Schultz (ed.), *Jesus in his Time* (London: SPCK, 1971), pp. 66-74.

Brockmeyer, N., *Antike Sklaverei* (Darmstadt: Wissenschaftliche Buchgesellschaft, 1979).

Brooks, R., *Support for the Poor in the Mishnaic Law of Agriculture: Tractate Pe'ah* (Chico, CA: Scholars Press, 1983).

Brown, R.E., 'The Teacher of Righteousness and the Messiah', in M. Black (ed.), *The Scrolls and Christianity* (London: SPCK, 1969).

—'Luke's Method in the Annunciation Narrative of Chapter One', in C.H. Talbert (ed.), *Perspectives on Luke–Acts* (Edinburgh: T. & T. Clark, 1978), pp. 126-38.

Brown, R.E., and J.P. Meier, *Antioch and Rome* (London: Geoffrey Chapman, 1983).

Brown, S., *Apostasy and Perseverance in the Theology of Luke* (Rome: Pontifical Biblical Institute, 1969).

Bruce, F.F., 'Jesus and the Gospels in the Light of the Scrolls', in M. Black (ed.), *The Scrolls and Christianity* (London: SPCK, 1969).

—*The Book of the Acts* (NLCNT; London: Marshall, Morgan & Scott, 1972).

Brunt, P.A., *Social Conflicts in the Roman Republic* (London: Chatto & Windus, 1971).

Bundy, W.E., *Jesus and the First Three Gospels* (Cambridge, MA: Harvard University Press, 1955).

Burney, C.F., *The Aramaic Origin of the Fourth Gospel* (Oxford: Clarendon Press, 1922).

Burrows, M., *More Light on the Dead Sea Scrolls* (London: Secker & Warburg, 1958).

Butler, B.C., *The Originality of St Matthew* (Cambridge: Cambridge University Press, 1951).

Byrne, B., 'Forceful Stewardship and Neglectful Wealth: A Contemporary Reading of Luke 16', *Pacifica* 1 (1988), pp. 1-14.

Cadbury, H.J., *The Style and Literary Method of Luke* (Cambridge, MA: Harvard University Press, 1920).

—*The Making of Luke–Acts* (London: Macmillan, 1927).

—'Erastus of Corinth', *JBL* 50 (1931), pp. 42-58.

Caird, G.B., *The Gospel of St Luke* (The Pelican Gospel Commentaries; London: A. & C. Black, 1968).

Capper, B.J., 'The Interpretation of Acts 5.4', *JSNT* 19 (1983), pp. 117-31.

—' "In der Hand des Ananias…" Erwägungen zu 1 QS 6.20 und der urchristlichen Gütergemeinschaft', *RevQ* 12 (1985), pp. 223-36.

Carson, D.A., D.J. Moo and L. Morris, *An Introduction to the New Testament* (Grand Rapids: Zondervan, 1992).

Cassidy, R.J., *Jesus, Politics and Society* (Maryknoll, NY: Orbis Books, 1978).

Charles, R.H., *Apocrypha and Pseudepigrapha* (Oxford: Clarendon Press, 1977).

Cone, O., *Rich and Poor in the New Testament* (London: A. & C. Black, 1902).

Conzelmann, H., *The Theology of St Luke* (London: Faber & Faber, 1961).

—*Acts of the Apostles* (Philadelphia: Fortress Press, 1987).

Countryman, L.W., *The Rich Christian in the Church of the Early Empire: Contradictions and Accommodations* (New York: Edwin Mellen Press, 1980).

Cranfield, C.E.B., *I and II Peter and Jude* (Torch Bible Commentary; London: SCM Press, 1960).

—*The Gospel according to Saint Mark* (Cambridge: Cambridge University Press, 1963).

Creed, J.M., *The Gospel according to St Luke* (London: Macmillan, 1950).

Crossan, J.D., *In Parables* (New York: Harper & Row, 1973).

—'The Servant Parable of Jesus', *Sem* 1 (1974), pp. 17-62.

Cullmann, O., *The Christology of the New Testament* (London: SCM Press, 1973).

Danker, F.W., *Jesus and the New Age* (St Louis: Clayton Publishing House, 1974).

—*Benefactor: Epigraphic Study of a Graeco-Roman and New Testament Semantic Field* (St Louis: Clayton Publishing House, 1982).

—*Luke* (Proclamation Commentaries; Philadelphia: Fortress Press, 1983).

De Neeve, P.W., 'Review of "The Corn Supply of Ancient Rome" by G. Rickman', *Mnemosoyne* 38 (1985), pp. 443-48.

De Ste. Croix, G.E.M., *The Class Struggle in the Ancient Greek World, from the Archaic Age to the Arab Conquests* (London: Duckworth, 1981).

Degenhardt, H.-J., *Lukas Evangelist der Armen* (Stuttgart: Katholisches Bibelwerk, 1965).

Den Boer, W., *Private Morality in Greece and Rome* (Leiden: E.J. Brill, 1979).

Derrett, J.D.M., *Law in the New Testament* (London: Darton, Longman & Todd, 1974).

—'Ananias, Sapphira, and the Right of Property', in *Studies in the New Testament* (Leiden: E.J. Brill, 1977), pp. 193-201.

Dicharry, W., *Human Authors of the New Testament. I. Mark, Matthew and Luke* (Slough: St Paul Publications, 1990).

Dill, S., *Roman Society from Nero to Marcus Aurelius* (London: Macmillan, 1904).

Dillon, R.J., 'Previewing Luke's Project from his Prologue (Luke 1.1-4)', *CBQ* 43 (1981), pp. 205-27.

Dodd, C.H., *The Parables of the Kingdom* (New York: Charles Scribner's Sons, 1961).

Donahue, J.R., 'Two Decades of Research on the Rich and the Poor in Luke–Acts', in D.A. Knight and P.J. Paris (eds.), *Justice and the Holy* (Atlanta: Scholars Press, 1989), pp. 129-44.

Drury, J., *The Parables in the Gospels* (London: SPCK, 1985).

Dunn, J.D.G., 'The Incident at Antioch (Gal. 2.11-18)', *JSNT* 18 (1983), pp. 3-75.

Dupont J., *Les Béatitudes* (3 vols.; Paris: J. Gabalda, 1973).

Easton, B.S., *The Gospel according to St Luke* (Edinburgh: T. & T. Clark, 1926).

Eisenstast, S.N., and L. Roniger, *Patrons, Clients and Friends* (Cambridge: Cambridge University Press, 1984).

Elliott, J.K. (ed.), *The Principles and Practise of the New Testament Textual Criticism: Collected Essays of G.D. Kilpatrick* (Leuven: Leuven University Press, 1990).

Ellis, E.E., *The Gospel of Luke* (The Century Bible; London: Nelson, 1966).

Ernst, J., *Das Evangelium nach Lukas* (Regensburg: Friedrich Pustet Regensburg, 1976).

Esler, P.F., *Community and Gospel in Luke–Acts* (Cambridge: Cambridge University Press, 1987).

Evans, C.F., *Saint Luke* (TPINTC; London: SCM Press, 1990).

Farmer, W., *The Synoptic Problem* (New York: Macmillan, 1964).

Farrer, A., 'On Dispensing with Q', in *Studies in the Gospels: Essays in Memory of R.H. Lightfoot* (Oxford: Basil Blackwell, 1957), pp. 55-88.

Farrar, F.W., *St Luke* (Cambridge: Cambridge University Press, 1899).

Fearghail, F.Ó., *The Introduction to Luke–Acts: A Study of the Role of Lk. 1.1-4.11 in the Composition of Luke's Two-Volume Work* (Rome: Pontificio Istituto Biblica, 1991).

Findlay, J.A., *The Gospel according to St Luke* (London: SCM Press, 1937).

—*Jesus and His Parables* (London: Epworth, 1951).

Finley, M.I., *The Ancient Economy* (Berkeley: University of California Press, 1973).

—*Ancient Slavery and Modern Ideology* (London: Chatto & Windus, 1980).

—(ed.), *Classical Slavery* (London: Frank Cass, 1987).

Firth, C.B., 'The Parable of the Unrighteous Steward', *ExpTim* 63 (1951–52), pp. 93-95.

Fitzmyer, J.A., 'Jewish Christianity in Acts in Light of the Qumran Scrolls', in L.E. Keck and J.L. Martyn (eds.), *Studies in Luke–Acts* (London: SPCK, 1968).

—*The Gospel according to Luke* (2 vols.; AB; New York: Doubleday, 1981).

—*Luke the Theologian* (London: Geoffrey Chapman, 1989).

Fleddermann, H., 'The Plight of a Naked Young Man (Mk 14.51-52)', *CBQ* 41 (1979), pp. 412-18.

Flender, H., *St Luke: Theologian of Redemptive History* (London: SCM Press, 1967).

Fletcher, D.R., 'The Riddle of the Unjust Steward: Is Irony the Key?', *JBL* 82 (1963), pp. 15-30.

Förster, W., and G. Quell, 'κύριος' *TDNT*, III, pp. 1039-95.

Friedel, L.M., 'The Parable of the Unjust Steward', *CBQ* 3 (1941), pp. 337-48.

Fujita, N.S., *A Crack in the Jar: What Ancient Jewish Documents tell us about the New Testament* (New York: Paulist Press, 1986).

Gächter, P., 'The Parable of the Dishonest Steward after Oriental Conceptions', *CBQ* 12 (1950), pp. 121-31.

Garnsey, P., *Social Status and Legal Privilege in the Roman Empire* (Oxford: Clarendon Press, 1970).

—*Famine and Food Supply in the Graeco-Roman World* (Cambridge: Cambridge University Press, 1988).

Gärtner, B., *The Temple and the Community in Qumran and the New Testament* (Cambridge: Cambridge University Press, 1965).

Gaston, L., *No Stone on Another: Studies in the Significance of the Fall of Jerusalem in the Synoptic Gospels* (NovTSup, 23; Leiden: E.J. Brill, 1970).

Geldenhuys, N., *The Gospel of Luke* (NICNT; Grand Rapids: Eerdmans, 1977).

Gibson, M.D., 'On the Parable of the Unjust Steward', *ExpTim* 14 (1903), p. 334.

Giles, K.N., 'The Church in the Gospel of Luke', *SJT* 34 (1981), pp. 121-46.

Gnilka, J., *Das Evangelium nach Markus* (EKKNT, 2; Zürich: Benzinger Verlag, 1989).

Gooding, D., *According to Luke* (Leicester: IVP, 1988).

Gordon, B., *The Economic Problem in Biblical and Patristic Thought* (Leiden: E.J. Brill, 1989).

Goulder, M.D., *Luke: A New Paradigm* (JSNTSup, 20; 2 vols.; Sheffield: JSOT Press, 1989).

—'A House Built on Sand', in A.E. Harvey (ed.), *Alternative Approaches to New Testament Study* (London: SPCK, 1985), pp. 1-24.

Grant, F.C., *The Gospels: Their Origin and their Growth* (London: Faber & Faber, 1957).

Grant, R.M., *Early Christianity and Society* (London: Collins, 1978).

Grundmann, W., *Das Evangelium nach Lukas* (THKNT, 3; Berlin: Evangelische Verlagsanstalt, 1974).

Gundry, R.H., *A Survey of the New Testament* (Grand Rapids: Zondervan, 1981).

Guthrie, D., *New Testament Introduction* (Leicester: IVP, 1978).

—*New Testament Theology* (Leicester: IVP, 1981).

Haacker, K., 'Verwendung und Vermeidung des Apostelbegriffs im Lukanischen Werk', *NovT* 30 (1988), pp. 9-38.

Haenchen, E., *The Acts of the Apostles: A Commentary* (Oxford: Basil Blackwell, 1971).

Hahn, F., *The Titles of Jesus in Christology* (London: Lutterworth, 1969).

Hahn, F., A. Strobel and E. Schweizer, *The Beginnings of the Church in the New Testament* (Edinburgh: The Saint Andrew Press, 1967).

Hamel, G., *Poverty and Charity in Roman Palestine, First Three Centuries CE* (Berkeley: University of California Press, 1990).

Hamm, D., 'Luke 19.8 Once Again: Does Zacchaeus Defend or Resolve?', *JBL* 107 (1988), pp. 431-37.

Hands, A.R., *Charities and Social Aid in Greece and Rome* (London: Thames & Hudson, 1968).

Hanson, R.P.C., *The Acts* (New Clarendon Bible; Oxford: Clarendon Press, 1967).

Hawkin, D.J., 'The Incomprehension of the Disciples in the Marcan Redaction, *JBL* 91 (1972).

Heil, J.P., 'Mark 14.1-52: Narrative Structure and Reader–Response', *Bib* 71 (1990), pp. 305-32.

Heiligenthal, R., 'Werke der Barmherzigkeit oder Almosen?', *NovT* 25 (1983), pp. 289-301.

Heininger, B., *Metaphorik, Erzählstruktur und szenischdramatische Gestaltung in den Sondergutgleichnissen bei Lukas* (Münster: Aschendorff, 1991).

Hendrickx, H., *The Parables of Jesus: Studies in the Synoptic Gospels* (London: Geoffrey Chapman, 1986).

Hengel, M., *Property and Riches in the Early Church* (London: SCM Press, 1974).

—*The Charismatic Leader and his Followers* (Edinburgh: T. & T. Clark, 1981).

—*Between Jesus and Paul* (London: SCM Press, 1983).

—*Studies in the Gospel of Mark* (London: SCM Press, 1985).

Hill, H., *The Roman Middle Class in the Republican Class* (Oxford: Basil Blackwell, 1952).

Hooker, M.D., *The Message of Mark* (London: Epworth, 1983).

—*The Gospel according to St Mark* (BNTC; London: A. & C. Black, 1991).

Hoppe, L.J., *Being Poor* (Wilmington: Michael Glazier, 1987).

Horn, F.W., *Glaube und Handeln in der Theologie des Lukas* (Göttingen: Vandenhoeck & Ruprecht, 1983).

Houlden, J.L., *Ethics and the New Testament* (London: Mowbray, 1987).

Hunter, A.M., *The Gospel according to Saint Mark* (London: SCM Press, 1959).

—*Interpreting the Parables* (London: SCM Press, 1960).

Ireland, D.J., *Stewardship and the Kingdom of God: An Historical, Exegetical, and Contextual Study of the Parable of the Unjust Steward in Luke 16:1-13* (Leiden: E.J. Brill, 1992).

Jaffee, M.S., *Mishnah's Theology of Tithing: A Study of Tractate Maaserot* (Chico, CA: Scholars Press, 1981).

Jeremias, J., 'Sabbatjahr und neuetestamentliche Chronologie', *ZNW* 27 (1928), pp. 98-103.

—*The Parables of Jesus* (London: SCM Press, 1963).

—*The Eucharistic Words of Jesus* (London: SCM Press, 1966).

—*Jerusalem in the Time of Jesus* (London: SCM Press, 1969).

Johnson, L.T., *The Literary Function of Possessions in Luke–Acts* (Missoula, MT: Scholars Press, 1977).

—*Sharing Possessions: Mandate and Symbol of Faith* (Philadelphia: Fortress Press, 1981).

Johnson, S.E., 'The Dead Sea Manual of Discipline and the Jerusalem Church of Acts', in K. Stendahl (ed.), *The Scrolls and the New Testament* (London: SCM Press, 1958).

Jones, A.H.M., *The Greek City from Alexander to Justinian* (Oxford: Clarendon Press, 1940).

—*The Roman Economy* (Oxford: Basil Blackwell, 1974).

Juel, D., *Luke–Acts* (London: SCM Press, 1984).

Kähler, M., *The So-called Historical Jesus and the Historical Biblical Christ* (Philadelphia: Fortress Press, 1970).

Karris, R.J., 'Poor and Rich: The Lukan *Sitz im Leben*', in C.H. Talbert (ed.), *Perspectives on Luke–Acts* (Edinburgh: T. & T. Clark, 1978), pp. 112-25.

—*Luke: Artist and Theologian* (New York: Paulist Press, 1985).

Keck, L., 'Mark 3:7-12 and Mark's Christology', *JBL* 84 (1965), pp. 341-58.

Kelber, W.H., *The Kingdom of Mark: A New Place and a New Time* (Philadelphia: Westminster Press, 1977).

Kelly, J.N.D., *A Commentary on the Epistles of Peter and Jude* (BNTC; London: A. & C. Black, 1969).

Kilpatrick, G.D., 'ΚΥΡΙΟΣ in the Gospels', in J.K. Elliott (ed.), *The Principles and Practice of N.T. Textual Criticism: Collected Essays of G.D. Kilpatrick* (Leuven: Leuven University Press, 1990), pp. 213-22.

Kingsbury, J.D., 'The Gospel of Mark in Current Research', *RelSRev* 5 (1979), pp. 101-107.

Kistemaker, S.J., *The Parables of Jesus* (Grand Rapids: Baker Book House, 1985).

Klauck, H.J., 'Gütergemeinschaft in der klassischen Antike in Qumran und im neuen Testament', *RevQ* 11 (1982–84), pp. 47-79.

Klein, H., *Barmherzigkeit gegenüber den Elenden und Geächteten* (Zürich: Neukirchener Verlag, 1987).

Kloppenborg, J., 'The Dishonoured Master', *Bib* 70 (1989), pp. 474-95.

Knibb, M.A., *The Qumran Community* (Cambridge: Cambridge University Press, 1987).

Knox, W.L., *The Sources of the Synoptic Gospels* (Cambridge: Cambridge University Press, 1957).

Kodell, J., 'Luke's Use of *Laos*, "People", especially in the Jerusalem Narrative (Lk. 19.28-24.53)', *CBQ* 31 (1969), pp. 327-43.

Kosmala, H., 'The Parable of the Unjust Steward in the Light of Qumran', in *Studies, Essays and Reviews* (Leiden: E.J. Brill, 1978), II, pp. 17-24.

Krämer, M., *Das Rätsel der Parabel vom ungerechten Verwalter* (Zürich: Pas-Verlag, 1972).

Krodel, G.A., *Acts* (Augsburg Commentary on the NT; Minneapolis: Augsburg, 1986).

Kuhn, K.G., 'The Lord's Supper and the Communal Meal at Qumran', in K. Stendahl (ed.), *The Scrolls and the New Testament* (London: SCM Press, 1957).

Kümmel, W.G., *Introduction to the New Testament* (London: SCM Press, 1972).

Lane, W.L., *The Gospel of Mark* (NICNT; Grand Rapids: Eerdmans, 1978).

Larfeld, W., *Griechische Epigraphik* (Munich: Beck, 1914).

Leaney, A.R.C., *The Rule of Qumran and its Meaning* (London: SCM Press, 1966).

—*The Letters of Peter and Jude* (Cambridge Bible Commentary; Cambridge: Cambridge University Press, 1967).

Linnemann, E., *Parables of Jesus: Introduction and Exposition* (London: SPCK, 1982).

Loader, W., 'Jesus and the Rogue in Luke 16.1-8a: The Parable of the Unjust Steward', *RB* 96 (1989), pp. 518-32.

Lohfink, G., *Jesus and Community* (London: SCM Press, 1985).

Loisy, A., *Les évangiles synoptiques I et II* (Ceffonds: Chez L'auteur, 1807–1908).

Lüdemann, G., *Early Christianity according to the Traditions in Acts: A Commentary* (London: SCM Press, 1989).

MacMullen, R., *Enemies of the Roman Order* (Cambridge, MA: Harvard University Press, 1967).

—*Roman Social Relations* (New Haven: Yale University Press, 1974).

Maddox, R., *The Purpose of Luke–Acts* (Göttingen: Vandenhoeck & Ruprecht, 1982).

Manson, T.W., *The Sayings of Jesus* (London: SCM Press, 1957).

Manson, W., *The Gospel of Luke* (MNTC; London: Hodder & Stoughton, 1930).

Marshall, C.D., *Faith as a Theme in Mark's Narrative* (Cambridge: Cambridge University Press, 1989).

Marshall, I.H., *The Origins of New Testament Christology* (Leicester: IVP, 1985).

—*Acts* (TNTC; Leicester: IVP, 1986).

—'Review of "Community and Gospel in Luke–Acts" (written by P.F. Esler)', *JTS* 39 (1988), pp. 564-66.

—*Commentary on Luke* (NIGTC; Exeter: Paternoster Press, 1989).

Martin, R.P., *Mark: Evangelist and Theologian* (Exeter: Paternoster Press, 1972).

Marxsen, W., *Introduction to the New Testament* (Oxford: Basil Blackwell, 1968).

—*Mark the Evangelist* (London: SCM Press, 1969).

Matera, F.J., *What Are they Saying about Mark?* (New York: Paulist Press, 1987).

—'The Incomprehension of the Disciples and Peter's Confession (Mark 6,14-8,30)', *Bib* 70 (1989), pp. 153-72.

McCormick, B.E., 'The Social and Economic Background of Luke' (PhD dissertation, Oxford University, 1960).

McNeille, A.M., *An Introduction to the Study of the New Testament* (Oxford: Clarendon Press, 1927).

Mealand, D.L., 'Community of Goods at Qumran', *TZ* 31 (1975), pp. 129-39.

—'Community of Goods and Utopian Allusions in Acts II-IV', *JTS* 28 (1977), pp. 96-99.

—*Poverty and Expectation in the Gospels* (London: SPCK, 1980).

Meeks, W.A., *The First Urban Christians* (New Haven: Yale University Press, 1983).

—*The Moral World of the First Christians* (London: SPCK, 1987).

Melbourne, B.L., *Slow to Understand: The Disciples in Synoptic Perspective* (Lanham, MD: University Press of America, 1988).

Mendels, D., 'Hellenistic Utopia and the Essenes', *HTR* 72 (1979), pp. 207-22.

Metzger, B.M., *A Textual Commentary on the Greek New Testament* (London: United Bible Societies, 1971).

Michel, O., 'οἰκονόμος', *TDNT*, V, pp. 149-52.

Milik, J.T., *Ten Years of Discovery in the Wilderness of Judea* (London: SCM Press, 1959).

Miller, W.D., 'The Unjust Steward', *ExpTim* 15 (1903), pp. 332-34.

Morris, L., *The Gospel according to St Luke* (TNTC, 3; Leicester: IVP, 1986).

Mosley, A.W., 'Jesus' Audiences in the Gospels of St Mark and St Luke', *NTS* 10 (1963–64), pp. 139-49.

Mott, S.C., 'The Power of Giving and Receiving: Reciprocity in Hellenistic Benevolence', in G.F. Hawthorne (ed.), *Current Issues in Biblical and Patristic Interpretation—Studies in Honor of M.C. Tenney* (Grands Rapids: Eerdmans, 1975), pp. 60-72.

Moule, C.F.D., *An Idiom Book of New Testament Greek* (Cambridge: Cambridge University Press, 1953).

—*The Origin of Christology* (Cambridge: Cambridge University Press, 1980).

Mowry, L., *The Dead Sea Scrolls and the Early Church* (Indiana: University of Notre Dame Press, 1966).

Moxnes, H., *The Economy of the Kingdom: Social Conflict and Economic Relations in Luke's Gospel* (Philadelphia: Fortress Press, 1988).

Mussner, F., 'καθεξῆς im Lukasprolog', in E.E. Ellis and E. Grässer (eds.), *Jesus und Paulus: Festschrift für W.G. Kümmel* (Göttingen: Vandenhoeck & Ruprecht, 1975), pp. 253-55.

Neil, W., *The Acts of the Apostles* (NCB; London: Oliphants, 1973).

Nineham, D.E. (ed.), *Studies in the Gospels* (Oxford: Basil Blackwell, 1955).

—*Saint Mark* (The Pelican Gospel Commentaries; London: A. & C. Black, 1963).

O'Hanlon, J., 'The Story of Zacchaeus and the Lukan Ethic', *JSNT* 12 (1981), pp. 2-26.

O'Toole, R.F., *The Unity of Luke's Theology* (Delaware: Michael Glazier, 1984).

Otto, A., *Die Sprichwörter und sprichwörtlichen Redensarten der Römer* (Leipzig: Teubner, 1890).

Parrott, D.M., 'The Dishonest Steward (Luke 16.1-8a) and Luke's Special Parable Collection', *NTS* 37 (1991), pp. 499-515.

Pilgrim, W.E., *Good News to the Poor: Wealth and Poverty in Luke–Acts* (Minneapolis: Augsburg, 1981).

Pesch, R., *Die Apostelgeschichte (Apg 13–28)* (EKKNT, 5.2; Zürich: Benzinger Verlag, 1986).

Pleket, P.W., 'Economic History of the Ancient World and Epigraphy: Some Introductory Remarks', *Akten des vi internationalen Kongresses für griechische und lateinische Epigraphik* (Munich: Beck, 1972), pp. 253-54.

Plummer, A., *St Luke* (ICC; Edinburgh: T. & T. Clark, 1922).

Pryke, E.J., 'Beliefs and Practices of the Qumran Community', *CQR* 168 (1967), pp. 314-25.

Rabin, C., *Qumran Studies* (Oxford: Oxford University Press, 1957).

Ramsey, W.M., 'On Mark iii 42', *ExpTim* 10 (1898–99), pp. 232, 336.

Rawlinson, A.E.J., *The Gospel according to St Mark* (Westminster Commentary; London: Methuen, 1960).

Reicke, B., 'Instruction and Discussion in the Travel Narrative', *SE*, I, pp. 203-216.

Reumann, J., '"Stewards of God"—Pre-Christian Religious Application of οἰκονόμος in Greek', *JBL* 72 (1958), pp. 339-49.

—'OIKONOMIA-Terms in Paul in Comparison with Lucan *Heilsgeschichte*', *NTS* 13 (1966), pp. 147-67.

Rickman, G., *The Corn Supply of Ancient Rome* (Oxford: Clarendon Press, 1980).

Ross, J.M., 'The Young Man who Fled Naked', *IBS* 13 (1991), pp. 170-74.

Rostovtzeff, M., *The Social and Economic History of the Roman Empire* (2 vols.; Oxford: Clarendon Press, 1957).

Russell, D.S., *From Early Judaism to Early Church* (London: SCM Press, 1986).

Saller, R.P., *Personal Patronage under the Early Empire* (Cambridge: Cambridge University Press, 1982).

—'Slavery and the Roman Family', in M.I. Finley (ed.), *Classical Slavery* (London: Frank Cass, 1987), pp. 65-87.

Sanders, E.P., *Jewish Law from Jesus to the Mishnah* (London: SCM Press, 1990).

Sanders, J.T., *Ethics in the New Testament* (London: SCM Press, 1986).

Schiffman, L.H., *The Eschatological Community of the Dead Sea Scrolls* (Atlanta: Scholars Press, 1989).

Schlatter, A., *Das Evangelium des Lukas* (Stuttgart: Calwer, 1960).

Schmidt, T.E., *Hostility to Wealth in the Synoptic Gospels* (JSNTSup, 15; Sheffield: JSOT Press, 1987).

Schmithals, W., *Das Evangelium nach Lukas* (Zürich: Theologischer Verlag, 1980).

Schnackenburg, R., *The Moral Teaching of the New Testament* (London: Burns & Oates, 1982).

Schneider, G., *Das Evangelium nach Lukas* (2 vols.; Würzburg: Echter Verlag, 1977).

—'Die zwölf Apostel als "Zeugen": Wesen, Ursprung und Funktion einer lukanischen Konzeption', in *Lukas, Theologie der Heilsgeschichte* (Könnigstein: Peter Hanstein, 1985).

—'Zur Bedeutung von καθεξῆς im lukanischen Doppelwerk' (1977), in *Lukas, Theologie der Heilsgeschichte* (Könnigstein: Peter Hanstein, 1985).

Schottroff, L., and W. Stegemann, *Jesus and the Hope of the Poor* (New York: Orbis Books, 1986).

Schürer, E., *The History of the Jewish People in the Age of Jesus Christ* (3 vols.; Edinburgh: T. & T. Clark, 1979).

Schürmann, H., *Das Lukasevangelium* (HTKNT, 3; Erster Teil; Freiburg: Herder, 1969).

Schütz, F., *Der leidende Christus: Die angefochtene Gemeinde und das Christuskerygma der lukanischen Schriften* (BWANT, 89; Stuttgart: Kohlhammer, 1969).

Schweizer, E., *Jesus* (London: SCM Press, 1971).

—*The Good News according to Mark* (London: SPCK, 1977).

—*Luke: A Challenge to Present Theology* (London: SPCK, 1982).

—*The Good News according to Luke* (London: SPCK, 1984).

—*Lordship and Discipleship* (London: SCM Press, 1986).

Scott, B.B., 'A Master's Praise: Luke 16.1-8a', *Bib* 64 (1983), pp. 173-88.

Seccombe, D.P., *Possessions and the Poor in Luke–Acts* (SNTU, 6; Linz: Fuchs, 1982).

Segovia, F.F. (ed.), *Discipleship in the New Testament* (Philadelphia: Fortress Press, 1985).

Sjoberg, G., *The Preindustrial City* (Glencoe: Free Press, 1960).

Stählin, G., 'ἴσος/ἰσότης' *TDNT*, III, pp. 343-55.

Stambaugh, J., and D. Balch, *The Social World of the First Christians* (London: SPCK, 1986).

Stanton, G.N., *The Gospels and Jesus* (Oxford: Oxford University Press, 1989).

Stock, A., *Call to Discipleship* (Wilmington: Michael Glazier, 1982).

Strack, H.L., and P. Billerbeck, *Kommentar zum Neuen Testament aus Talmud und Midrasch* (Munich: Becksche, 1926).

Streeter, B.H., *The Four Gospels: A Study of Origins* (London: Macmillan, 1953).

Sweetland, D.M., *Our Journey with Jesus: Discipleship according to Luke–Acts* (Collegeville: The Liturgical Book, 1990).

Swete, H.B., *The Gospel according to St Mark* (London: Macmillan, 1902).

Talbert, C.H. (ed.), *Perspectives on Luke–Acts* (Danville: Association of Baptist Professors of Religion, 1978).

—*Reading Luke: A Literary and Theological Commentary on the Third Gospel* (New York: Crossroad, 1982).

—'Discipleship in Luke–Acts', in F.F. Segovia (ed.), *Discipleship in the New Testament* (Philadelphia: Fortress Press, 1985).

Tannehill, R.C., 'The Disciples in Mark: the Function of a Narrative Role', in W. Telford (ed.), *The Interpretation of Mark* (London: SPCK, 1985), pp. 134-57.

—*The Narrative Unity of Luke–Acts* (2 vols.; Philadelphia: Fortress Press, 1986).

Taylor, V., *Behind the Third Gospel* (Oxford: Clarendon Press, 1926).

—*The Gospel according to St Mark* (London: Macmillan, 1952).

Theissen, G., 'Soziale Integration und sakramentales Handeln', in *Studien zur Soziologie des Urchristentums* (Tübingen: J.C.B. Mohr, 1979), pp. 290-317.

—*The Social Setting of Pauline Christianity* (Philadelphia: Fortress Press, 1982).

Thompson, B.H.P., *The Gospel according to Luke* (New Clarendon Bible; Oxford: Clarendon Press, 1979).

Tooley, W., 'Stewards of God', *SJT* 19 (1966), pp. 74-86.

Topel, L.J., 'On the Injustice of the Unjust Steward', *CBQ* 37 (1975), pp. 216-27.

Triantaphyllopoulos, J., 'PARAPRASIS', *Acta of the Fifth International Congress of Greek and Latin Epigraphy, Cambridge, 1967* (Oxford: Basil Blackwell, 1971), pp. 65-69.

Turner, N., 'The Minor Verbal Agreements of Mt. and Lk. against Mk', in *SE*, I, pp. 223-34.

Tyson, J., 'The Blindness of the Disciples', *JBL* 80 (1961), pp. 261-68.

Unnik, W.C. van, 'Die Motivierung der Feindesliebe in Lukas 6.32-35,' *NovT* 8 (1966), pp. 284-300.

Van der Horst, D.W., 'Hellenistic Parallels to Acts', *JSNT* 35 (1989), pp. 37-46.

Verhey, A., *The Great Reversal: Ethics and the New Testament* (Grand Rapids: Eerdmans, 1986).

Vermes, G., 'Essenes-Therapeutae-Qumran', *Durham University Journal* 21 (1960), pp. 97-115.

—'Essenes and History', *JJS* 32 (1981).

—*The Dead Sea Scrolls in English* (London: Penguin Books, 1987).

—*The Dead Sea Scrolls: Qumran in Perspective* (London: SCM Press, 1988).

Vermes, G., and M.D. Goodman, *The Essenes according to the Classical Sources* (Sheffield: JSOT Press, 1989).

Via, D.O., *The Parables* (Philadelphia: Fortress Press, 1967).

Vincent, M.R., *Word Studies in the New Testament* (Wilmington: Associated Publishers and Authors, 1888).

Vögel, M., 'Exegetische Erwägungen zum Verständnis des Begriffs καθεξῆς im lukanischen Prolog', *NTS* 20 (1973–74), pp. 289-99.

Vos, G., *The Self-Disclosure of Jesus* (Phillipsburg: Presbyterian and Reformed Publishing, 1978).

Wansbrough, H., 'St Luke and Christian Ideals in an Affluent Society', *NB* 49 (1968), pp. 582-87.

Warfield, B.B., *The Lord of Glory* (Grand Rapids: Baker Book House, 1976).

Webster, D., 'The Primary Stewardship', *ExpTim* 72 (1960–61), pp. 274-76.

Weeden, T.J., 'The Heresy that necessitated Mark's Gospel', *ZNW* 59 (1969), pp. 145-58.

—*Mark: Traditions in Conflict* (Philadelphia: Fortress Press, 1971).

Weinfeld, M., *The Organizational Pattern and the Penal Code of the Qumran Sect* (Göttingen: Vandenhoeck & Ruprecht, 1986).

Wernberg-Moller, P., *The Manual of Discipline* (Leiden: E.J. Brill, 1957).

Westermann, W.L., *The Slave Systems of Greek and Roman Antiquity* (Philadelphia: The American Philosophical Society, 1955).

Wiedemann, T., *Greek and Roman Slavery* (London: Croom Helm, 1981).

Wiedemann, T.E.J., *Slavery* (Oxford: Clarendon Press, 1987).

White, R.E.O., *Luke's Case for Christianity* (London: The Bible Reading Fellowship, 1987).

Williams, F.E., 'Is Almsgiving the Point of the "Unjust Steward"?', *JBL* 83 (1964), pp. 293-97.

Winter, B.W., '*Providentia* for the Widows of 1 Timothy 5.3-16', *TynBul* 39 (1988), pp. 83-99.

—'The Public Honouring of Christian Benefactors: Romans 13.3-4 and 1 Peter 2.14-15', *JSNT* 34 (1988), pp. 87-103.

—'Secular and Christian Responses to Corinthian Famines', *TynBul* 40 (1989), pp. 86-106.

Witherington, B., 'On the Road with Mary Magdalene, Joanna, Susanna, and Other Disciples—Luke 8.1-3', *ZNW* 70 (1979), pp. 243-48.

—*Women in the Ministry of Jesus* (Cambridge: Cambridge University Press, 1984).

Wood, C.T., 'Luke xvi. 8', *ExpTim* 63 (1951–52), p. 126.

Yamauchi, E., *The Stones and the Scriptures* (London: SCM Press, 1973).

INDEXES

INDEX OF REFERENCES

OLD TESTAMENT

Baruch		2 Maccabees	
11.1-2	58	9.23	97
67.7	58	9.25	97

NEW TESTAMENT

Matthew		8.13	112	19.25	142
3.4	170	9.25	81	19.29	63
3.8	123	10.17-18	64	20.8	112
4.10	113	10.20	118	20.16	112
4.18-22	124	10.24	113	20.20	81
5.1–7.29	117	10.25	112, 113	20.23	74, 118
5.1-12	201, 202	10.29	118	20.25-28	128
5.3-10	188	10.32	118	20.26	113
5.3	19	10.33	118	20.27	113
5.6	19	10.38	51, 72	20.28	128
5.16	118	10.40	97	21	123
5.38-48	197	11.27	118	21.15	112
5.39-42	171	12.18	112	21.18-19	122
5.40	171	12.50	118	21.33-46	127
5.42	169, 171	13.27	112, 113	21.34	113
5.45	118	13.28	113	21.35	113
5.48	118, 172	13.52	112	21.36	113
6.1	118	13.54-58	202	22.1-14	127, 186,
6.4	118	14.2	112		206
6.6	118	15.27	115	22.3	113
6.8	118	16.	62	22.4	113
6.9	118	16.12	62	22.6	113
6.11	108	16.13	118	22.8	113
6.14	118	17.1-4	120	22.10	113, 186,
6.15	118	17.5-6	120		197
6.18	118	17.7-10	120	22.13-14	206
6.19-21	136, 183,	17.18	112	22.13	113
	197	17.19	120	23.11	113
6.19-20	183	17.20	120	23.23	201
6.19	216	18.10	118	23.25-56	197
6.20	24, 31	18.19	118	23.26	31, 180
6.24	112	18.23	113	23.27	201
6.25-34	183	18.26	113	24.45-50	135
6.26	118	18.27	113	24.45	113, 143
6.32	118	18.28	113	24.46	113
6.37-38	180	18.32	113	24.48	113
7.1-2	180	18.35	118	24.49	131, 144
7.11	118	19.11-12	76	24.50	113
7.21	118	19.21	24, 31	24.51	139, 143
8.6	112	19.22	191, 192,	25.1-13	125
8.8	112		207	25.14-30	160, 161
8.9	113	19.23	142, 192	25.14	113

Reference	Pages
11.28-33	103
11.39	103
11.45	170
11.48	61
12.13	170
12.48	97
13.20	97
13.34	222
18.18	170
19.23	169
19.39	170
20.21	170
20.28	170
20.39	170
21.7	170

Acts

Reference	Pages
1.5-6	242
1.7	41, 101
1.8	204, 232
1.11	242
1.14	175
1.15	99, 231
1.16	91
1.17	112, 228
1.19	101
1.20	91
1.22	232
1.25	101, 112
2.1-4	73
2.18	112, 122
2.41-47	50, 228
2.41	99, 231, 245
2.42-47	218, 223
2.42	200, 247, 249, 250
2.43-47	223
2.43	225, 242
2.44-45	227, 236, 238, 242
2.44	229, 242, 251
2.45	183, 216, 224, 231, 240, 243, 246
2.46	51, 240, 244, 247, 249-51
2.47	51, 220, 225, 245, 250
3.1-2	277
3.2	28, 51, 232, 256
3.3	28, 232
3.6	240
3.10	28
3.12	101
3.13	112
3.15	232
3.17	114
4.4	231
4.5	114
4.8	114
4.18	50
4.21	220
4.23	101
4.24	112
4.25	112
4.26	114
4.27	112
4.30	112
4.31-35	50
4.31	242, 245
4.32-37	200, 218, 223, 228
4.32-35	17, 223, 227, 236, 238
4.32	99, 101, 143, 225, 226, 229, 242, 245, 251
4.33	242
4.34-35	183, 224, 240, 243
4.34	28, 216, 224, 240-43, 245
4.35	225, 231, 243, 246
4.36-39	231
4.36-37	229, 230, 242
4.37	225, 243
4.38	42
5.1-16	228
5.1-11	31, 228, 230, 232, 242
5.1	245
5.2	224, 225, 243
5.3	225
5.4	240, 244, 245
5.11	245
5.12-16	223
5.13	96, 220
5.14	99, 245
5.22	114
5.26	114
5.42	240
6.1-6	176, 200, 228
6.1-2	277
6.1	112, 219, 224, 228, 240, 246, 250, 251
6.2	99, 228
6.4	112, 228, 240
6.5	99
6.7	99, 223
6.20-23	50
7.7	113
7.10	113
7.11	52
7.22	50
7.27	114
7.35	114
7.42	113
8.9-10	42
8.26-39	48
9.1	99
9.10	99
9.26	99
9.27	230
9.28-36	42